Marriage, Law, and Gender in Re China, 1940–1960

Xiaoping Cong examines the social and cultural significance of Chinese revolutionary legal practice in the construction of marriage and gender relations. Her book is an empirically rich investigation of the ways in which a 1943 legal dispute over an arranged marriage in a Chinese village became a legal, political, and cultural exemplar on the national stage. This conceptually ground-breaking study revisits the Chinese revolution and its impact on women and society by presenting a Chinese experience that cannot and should not be theorized in the framework of Western discourse. Taking a cultural historical perspective, Cong shows how the Chinese revolution and its legal practices produced new discourses, neologisms, and cultural symbols that contained China's experience in twentieth-century social movements, and how revolutionary practice was sublimated into the concept of "self-determination," an idea that bridged local experiences with the tendency of the twentieth-century world, and a revolutionary legacy for China today.

XIAOPING CONG is Associate Professor of History at the University of Houston, Texas.

Cambridge Studies in the History of the People's Republic of China

Series Editors

Cambridge Studies in the History of the People's Republic of China is a major series of ambitious works in the social, political, and cultural history of socialist China. Aided by a wealth of new sources, recent research pays close attention to regional differences, to perspectives from the social and geographical margins, and to the unintended consequences of Communist Party rule. Books in the series contribute to this historical re-evaluation by presenting the most stimulating and rigorously researched works in the field to a broad audience. The series invites submissions from a variety of disciplines and approaches, based on written, material or oral sources. Particularly welcome are those works that bridge the 1949 and 1978 divides, and those which seek to understand China in an international or global context.

Marriage, Law, and Gender in Revolutionary China, 1940–1960

Xiaoping Cong

CAMBRIDGE
UNIVERSITY PRESS

CAMBRIDGE
UNIVERSITY PRESS

University Printing House, Cambridge CB2 8BS, United Kingdom

One Liberty Plaza, 20th Floor, New York, NY 10006, USA

477 Williamstown Road, Port Melbourne, VIC 3207, Australia

314-321, 3rd Floor, Plot 3, Splendor Forum, Jasola District Centre, New Delhi - 110025, India

79 Anson Road, #06-04/06, Singapore 079906

Cambridge University Press is part of the University of Cambridge.

It furthers the University's mission by disseminating knowledge in the pursuit of education, learning and research at the highest international levels of excellence.

www.cambridge.org
Information on this title: www.cambridge.org/9781316602614

First published 2016
First paperback edition 2018

A catalogue record for this publication is available from the British Library

Library of Congress Cataloging in Publication data
Names: Cong, Xiaoping, author.
Title: Marriage, law and gender in revolutionary China, 1940–1960 / Xiaoping Cong.
Description: New York : Cambridge University Press, 2016. |
Series: Cambridge studies in the history of the People's Republic of China | Includes bibliographical references and index.
Identifiers: LCCN 2016014633| ISBN 9781107148567 (hardback) |
ISBN 9781316602614 (paperback)
Subjects: LCSH: Domestic relations – China – History. | Marriage law – China – History. | China – Politics and government – 1949–1976. |
China – Politics and government – 1937–1945. |
BISAC: HISTORY / Asia / General.
Classification: LCC KNQ540.C66 2016 | DDC 346.5101/609045–dc23
LC record available at http://lccn.loc.gov/2016014633

ISBN 978-1-107-14856-7 Hardback
ISBN 978-1-316-60261-4 Paperback

In memory of Professor Feng Qi 冯契 (1915–95), who taught me how to think intellectually and historically.

Contents

Figures

Maps

Tables

Acknowledgments

Although Chinese society bid farewell to the revolution in the 1990s, its legacy in a new historical moment still needs to be reviewed. In the twentieth century the Chinese revolution has been studied through its ideological sources, its political policies, its party leaders, its relations with intellectuals, and its mass mobilization; however, the most significant part of the revolution was its social and legal practices in localities, which has not received enough academic attention. It was from these practices that the revolution developed an effective way of governance and created a set of discourse to speak its own experience. Studying revolutionary legal practice offers a way of looking into the Chinese experience in a particular locality. As the book shows, communism as well as a large amount of new terminology imported from the West (some via Japan) were prevalent in twentieth-century society and intellectual circles. However, it was local practices that digested these neologies, and then new terms such as *zizhu* (self-determination), which contained local experience described in this book, began to emerge. This eventually became the revolutionary legacy for the rest of the century and contemporary China.

This project can be viewed as the continuation of my last book, which ends in the 1930s when young students in teachers' schools became revolutionaries. While looking for a new book topic that could trace the next stage of these students' activities, I encountered a document on the story of "Liu Qiao'er" and her actual prototype. This story triggered my childhood memory of celebratory parties in which the solo of "Qiao'er" was often very popular. It was a symbol of revolution for women who wanted freedom in selecting their marriage mate. I was surprised to learn that the protagonist, Feng Peng'er (Zhiqin), was still alive. This immediately attracted my attention but also made prompt action imperative, given her age. In 2005 I visited Feng Peng'er's home to interview her. It was also on this trip that I learned about the Revolutionary High Court files in the Shaanxi Provincial Archives, and that they were open to the public. This interview and the discovery of this collection of legal documents thus formed a solid foundation for this research project and eventual book. The story of Feng Peng'er itself presents the changing life of rural women in the Chinese revolution. I thus want to express my great appreciation to Feng Peng'er (Zhiqin), whose life experience became an important part of the history of twentieth-century China. Unfortunately, she passed away on February 12, 2015, and was not able to see the publication of an English-language book about her life. However, this book is a fitting memorial.

My deepest gratitude goes to Professor Benjamin Elman, who continues to offer guidance and support to my research projects, as he has always done over the last twenty years. I would also like to show my great appreciation to Professors Gail Hershatter, Joe Esherick, and Meng Yue. While I was still in the stage of composing a grant proposal for this project, Gail gave me important advice and strong encouragement; she later offered insights on my manuscript revision. Joe's positive and invaluable comments on the drafts of my book proposal and introduction inspired me in my manuscript revision. Meng Yue, a dear friend and a preeminent scholar in her field, patiently listened to my various immature ideas on the project while offering her insights that helped me sharpen my arguments. She read the introduction draft and gave me some constructive suggestions for the improvement of this book.

I owe a great debt in my research to my lifelong best friend, Professor Qin Yan at Northwestern Polytechnical University in Xi'an. Our friendship started in college when we were both classmates and roommates. Her pioneering scholarly works on women and society in northern Shaanxi have helped me understand the people and the environment there. She also introduced me to people she was working with and helped me become familiar with the locality and visit those people I needed to see. From the very beginning of this project, I was able to establish a good local connection and conduct interviews smoothly due to her help. She also shared, without reservation, invaluable archival documents she had previously collected. Without her generous assistance this book would have not been written in this way. I feel so lucky to have a friend like her.

I have gained a good deal of academic inspiration and feedback from my scholarly friends and colleagues. On various occasions each provided insightful comments that stimulated me to refine my research. They are Professors Qian Nanxiu at Rice University, Joan Judge at York University, and Susan Glosser at Lewis and Clark College, with whom I discussed various details of my book chapters during my writing. Professor Qian generously shared documents from her rare collection on late Qing women. Several chapters were presented as conference papers at various conferences and workshops, from which I also received valuable feedback that helped refine my chapters. I would also like to thank the following friends and colleagues: Professors Richard Smith, Toni Barlow, Wang Hui, Tim Weston, Song Shaopeng, Peter Zarrow, Rob Culp, Robert Hegel, Ma Zhao, Madeleine Zelin, Li Chen, Bryna Goodman, Janet Theiss, Maggie Kuo, Jennifer Neighbors, Lisa Tran, Liu Chang, Jiang Jin, Guo Yuhua, Yun-cheng Chiang, You Jianming, Lü Miaw-fen, and Drs. Chaohua Wang and Anne Chao. They have offered their professional opinions, inspiration, and assistance in different ways. In the process of publishing certain parts of my research in an article, Professor Pauline Keating and anonymous reviewers provided comments that pushed me to sharpen my argument in the final work.

Special thanks should also be given to my colleagues in the Department of History at University of Houston, particularly Professors Cathy Patterson, Sarah Fisherman, John Hart, and Nancy Young, who offered valuable opinions on various parts of my drafts. My appreciation also goes to Professor Martin Melosi, Linda Reed, Kairn Kleiman, Natalia Milanesio, and Landon Starrs who helped me in various ways. In addition, thanks to both former and current deans of CLASS, Drs. John Antel and Steven Craig, both of whom provided strong support to my research and manuscript writing. My department staff, Lorena Lopez, Donna Butler, Daphyne Pitre, and Gloria Ned also deserve my appreciation for their assistance with my research, travel, and teaching arrangements, as well as many other chores.

From the early stage of my research this book project received a number of grants from both national societies as well as local institutions that supported my fieldwork and archival research. I would like to thank the Bernadotte E. Schmitt Grants for Research in European, African, or Asian History from the American Historian Association that awarded a summer research grant in 2006 for my travel in China. In 2008–09 I had the great honor of receiving a grant from the American Research of Humanities in China from the American Council of Learned Society sponsored by the National Endowment of Humanities, as well the Research Scholar Grant to China from the Fulbright Foreign Scholarship Program. These two generous awards allowed me to stay in China for fifteen months to complete the major work in archives and fieldwork. I also appreciate the grants I have received from University of Houston. In summer 2005 the then Women Studies Program at UH awarded a Faculty Summer Fellowship that helped me initiate my preliminary work on the project. From 2006 to 2016 I received various research funds and travel grants from the University of Houston, such as GEAR, Small Grant, GIA, and Provost Travel Grants, Completion Grant, and Publication Grant that enabled me to finish the last stage of research, travel to conferences, and complete this book. In particular, the UH Faculty Development Leave

Grant that I received in spring 2012 allowed me to focus on conceptualization and finish drafting of most chapters.

Many thanks are due to the staff of the following archives and libraries for their kindness and assistance in locating many invaluable documents that have enriched my book. They are Shaanxi Provincial Archives, Qingyang City Archives, Huachi County Archives, Mizhi County Archives, Yulin City Archives, Yan'an City Archives, Beijing National Library, Shanghai Municipal Library, Shaanxi Provincial Library, and the library of Academia Sinica and the Archival Office of the Investigation Bureau, Ministry of Justice in Taiwan. Moreover, both the history section managed by UH librarian Alex Simons and the interlibrary department of University of Houston library provided much assistance to my research with their professional service.

I would also like to express my gratitude to governmental workers and local researchers in the localities I have visited. Their hospitality and assistance greatly helped the progress of this project. These people are the then party secretary of Qingyang City Mr. Ma Ping, his assistant Mr. Yao Zhengjie, Director of County Office of Cultural Affairs Mr. She Xingfa, Director of County Office of Tourism Ms. Tan, Director of County Archival Office Mr. Zhu, and staff Mr. Zhao Hua. Mr. Yang Zhengfa in Huachi County also presented me his book on the story of Feng Peng'er (Zhiqin), which provided useful information for the starting point to my project.

Some of my old friends from college who worked in local governments, such as Mr. Liu Hanli in Yulin City and Mr. Yang Xiaohe in Yan'an City, also provided assistance in my fieldwork and archival research. I would also like to express my warmest appreciation to my alma mater, Shaanxi Normal University, which hosted my visit for my archival study in Xi'an from 2008 to 2009. During this period my old college friends in Xi'an, such as Professors Jia Erqiang, Zhang Jiancheng, Hou Yongjian, and Han Xuhui at Shaanxi Normal University offered much support in utilizing the school facilities and getting staff assistance for my research. I would like to thank Mr. Wang Bentao, a graduate student then at Beijing Normal University in Beijing, Ms. Deng Tongli and Ms. Zhu Cong, students then at universities of Xi'an, for serving as my research assistants during my fieldwork in these cities.

I would like to thank Ms. Cyndy Brown and Dr. Maura Cummingham, whose special editing skills helped me catch the errors in this book. Ms. Brown also compiled the index for the book. Some sections of this book were previously published as articles in the Journal of *Twentieth-Century China* and *The China Journal*. I am very grateful that the two journals granted me the permission to publish them here.

It is my great pleasure to work with the editors of Cambridge University Press, who provided gracious and professional assistance during the publication process. Dr. Lucy Rhymer, the acquisition editor, possesses excellent vision in selecting this manuscript and believed in its value. Publishing Manager Amanda George and copy-editors and script-setters provided their professional skills to make this book possible. I appreciate the comments from two anonymous reviewers, and Professor Michael Schoenhals as third reviewer. It was my pleasure to accept the invitation from the editors of the Cambridge Studies in the History of the People's Republic of China to include this book in this series. The editors of this series also offered constructive suggestions for the final revision.

I also want to acknowledge another group of friends who supported my work in various ways. My best friend, Dr. Xiaohong Wen at UH, always raises my spirits on my low days. I met Professor Jamie Monson, an African historian at Michigan State University, in 2008 when we were both grantees of ACLS in China. There we offered each other spiritual support and spent some joyful times together in Beijing. My old friend and college mate Professor Zhao Junxiu at Beijing Normal University provided various aids while I stayed in Beijing. In addition, I need to mention my lovely neighbors Ms. Teresa Powell and Ms. Linda Lively, as well as other ladies in my residential complex who watched over my house and watered my plants whenever I was away for my research trips. I have learned a lot from them and we have shared some laughter together.

Finally, I want to give my heart to my family, my mother and my sisters, Li Xin, Wanping, Lixin, and Lixin's husband Ye Sen. For many years I have been away from them, unable to offer help when it was needed but instead focusing on my scholarly work. Not only did they assume my share of family duties, but they have provided various means of support for my work. This book also contains a lot of their warm love for me.

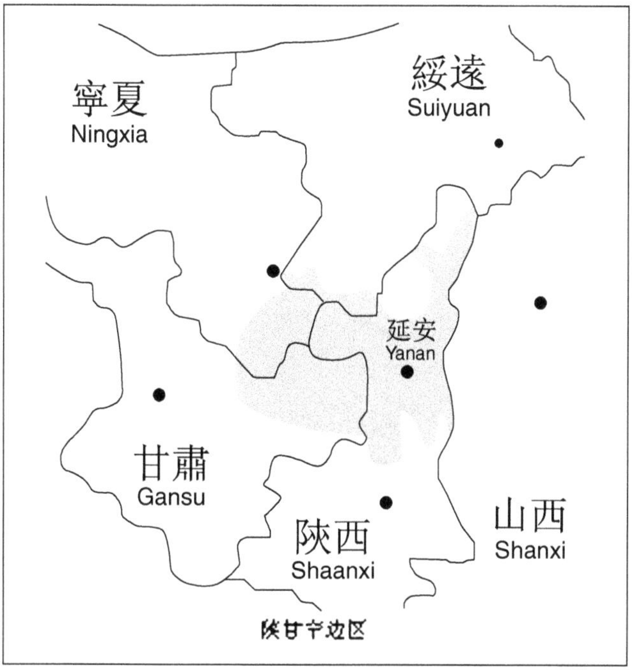

Map 1 The location of the Shaan-Gan-Ning Border Region, 1937–1947

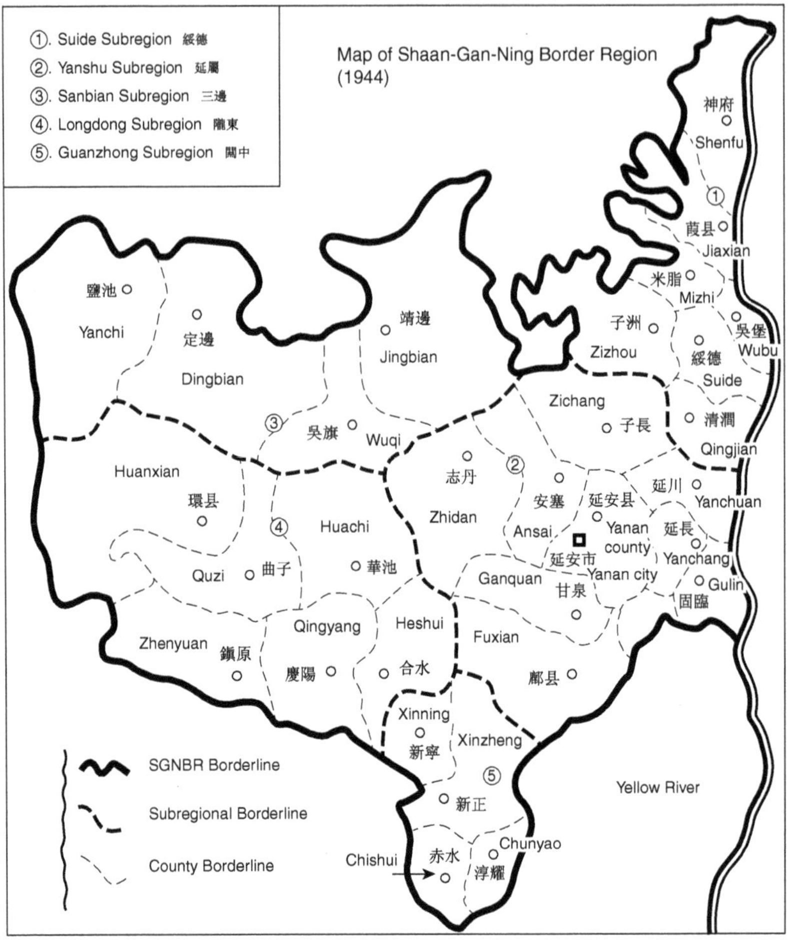

Map 2 Map of Shaan-Gan-Ning Border Region and the division of subregions, 1944
Source: *Jiefang ribao*, July 23, 1944

Introduction

In 1950 a Ping opera (Pingju 评剧) play entitled *Liu Qiao'er* 刘巧儿 was presented on Beijing's stages to accompany the promulgation of the revolutionary new Chinese Marriage Law.[1] It tells the story of a young woman, Liu Qiao'er, who lives in the Chinese revolutionary base area in the 1940s and resists a marriage arranged by her father. As a child Qiao'er was engaged to the son of the Zhao family, but she refuses this engagement because it is not her will and she wants to find her own marriage mate. Liu Qiao'er falls in love with a handsome young man she encounters in a meeting. Later she learns that he is her former fiancé. During this time her father arranges another engagement with an old man, a rich landlord. Her former fiancé's family then comes to the Liu residence and kidnaps Qiao'er for marriage. The county judge punishes the Zhaos for the kidnapping and also annuls Qiao'er's marriage to her lover, her former fiancé. Qiao'er bravely appeals to a higher authority, Prefect Ma, who has a better understanding of the revolutionary principle of marriage and thus reverses the judgment. With the support of the revolutionary government, Qiao'er is able to marry the man of her choice, and the story concludes happily.

This opera was later performed on the national stage and then adapted into a 1956 musical film that was shown throughout China. It is no exaggeration to claim that *Liu Qiao'er* influenced generations of youth from the 1950s to the 1960s. The most famous arioso was on everyone's lips: vocal

> In my childhood, it was arranged that I, Qiao'er,
> Would marry a son of the Zhao family.
> It was my parents' decision, but we two did not know each other.
> How could we be happy together?
> ...
> In a meeting I met this man and liked him very much...
> This time I want to choose my own marriage mate.[2]

[1] A local opera performed in parts of Manchuria and northern China, including Tianjin, Beijing, and Hebei.

[2] *Liu Qiao'er*, directed by Yi Lin, Changchun dianying zhipianchang (Changchun Film Studio), 1956. The implication of this sentence is discussed in Chapter 7.

The arioso's melody and the story's image left a deep impression on my childhood memory because they were frequently presented at many celebratory occasions and workplace parties during the holidays.[3] These artistic works not only created an image of Liu Qiao'er that encouraged women to fight against old marriage practices, but also promoted a new concept of "self-determination" (*zizhu* 自主) that inspired women to choose their own mate in marriage.

The play/film was especially persuasive because it was not fictional but rather based on a 1943 legal case, *Feng v. Zhang*, which involved a dispute between two families over a traditional marriage contract. The case began when a local farmer, Feng Yangui 封彦贵, abandoned the engagement contract of his daughter Peng'er 捧儿 (1924–2015) to the son of another farmer, Zhang Jincai 张金才, and betrothed her to another suitor for a much higher betrothal gift (*caili* 彩礼). A week later, Peng'er ran into her former fiancé, Zhang Bo 张柏 (1922–91), and expressed her wish to be with him. The Zhangs immediately went to Feng's residence and captured Peng'er for marriage to prevent her father from marrying his daughter to the new suitor. Feng Yangui then brought Zhang Jincai to the county court, suing him for kidnapping his daughter.[4]

This dispute occurred in a small village under the jurisdiction of Huachi County. Huachi is located in Eastern Gansu Province, a region traditionally called Longdong (陇东), which became part of the Shaanxi-Gansu-Ningxia Border Region (SGNBR or Border Region, BR, see Map 1) under the rule of the Chinese Communist Party (CCP) in the 1930s. Bordered with the Mongolian prairie, the local culture displayed a mixture of orthodox state ideology and a patriarchal tradition, blended with deeply rooted heterodox steppe customs absorbed from the nomadic people who lived on the vast Mongolian plain. In this region the traditional family, marriage practices, and sexual behavior took various forms, including child-brides-to-be, arranged marriages, marriages by capture, the kidnapping of brides, and marriages through buying and selling, as well as runaway wives, adultery, polygamy, and polyandry. It was a politically insulated area that was not significantly affected by the early twentieth-century events that rocked other parts of China, such as the Qing constitution movement and reform, the Republican Revolution

[3] Many people who lived through the 1950s and 1960s are familiar with this aria from the film and the opera.

[4] Shaanxi Provincial Archives file number 15–842, *Feng v. Zhang*. The collection of the High Court records, titled "The Documents of the Shaan-Gan-Ning Border High Court," is located in Shaanxi Provincial Archives in Xi'an. In the following chapters, all sources from Shaanxi Provincial Archives are abbreviated as SPA plus file number, followed by the document title under or in this file number.

in 1911, the antitraditional New Culture Movement in the 1910s, and anti-imperialism campaigns of the 1920s. The SGN region remained largely isolated from the political upheavals of the late nineteenth and early twentieth centuries until communist forces arrived in the 1930s.

In 1939 the communist government issued a marriage regulation, launching a reform to change the local marriage practices that were considered "backward" by the revolutionary party-state (see Chapter 1). Based on this marriage regulation, the county court punished the Zhangs for kidnapping and invalidated the marriage between Peng'er and Zhang Bo. However, Peng'er refused to accept the result and appealed to the subregional leader, Prefect/Judge Ma Xiwu 马锡五 (1899–1962) (see administrative and legal systems in Chapter 3). After a series of investigations in the village, Prefect Ma overturned the county judgment and pronounced Peng'er's marriage valid. As the principle for judging the marriage case, Prefect Ma highlighted a term – *zizhu* (self-determination) – that had been developed in the legal practice of marriage reform in the SGNBR.

About a year after the legal case was settled, a series of publications, artistic presentations, and performances arose from its social and cultural context and gained political and cultural significance. First, a 1944 article that appeared on the front page of Yan'an's leading communist newspaper *Liberation Daily* 解放日报 (*Jiefang ribao*) presented the case as a model of communist governance and the appropriate judicial method in dealing with unrest in local communities. This article thus brought the story from a remote village on the revolutionary frontier to the political center of Yan'an.[5] Then in 1945 the communist newspaper *Xinhua Daily* 新华日报 (*Xinhua ribao*), located in the Nationalist wartime capital of Chongqing, twice reported the case as a showcase of the SGNBR government's democratic methods. It served as a vehicle for winning women's support in the CCP's competition with the Nationalist government.[6]

Between 1944 and 1956 a group of revolutionary artists and writers reshaped the case of *Feng v. Zhang* into a series of cultural products, taking it from the legal and political realms into the field of artistic and literary creation. In 1944 an artist, Gu Yuan 古元 (1919–96), published a woodcut in *Liberation Daily* to praise the revolutionary way of settling

5 "Ma Xiwu tongzhi de shenpan fangshi" (Comrade Ma Xiwu's Way of Judging), *Jiefang ribao* (Liberation Daily), March 13, 1944.

6 "Bianqu tiaojie hunyin de yige shili" (Marriage Mediation in the BR), *Xinhua ribao* (Xinhua Daily), October 22, 1944; Li Pu, "Yi jian qianghun an" (A Marriage by Kidnapping), *Xinhua ribao*, April 11, 1945 (cited in Liu Fengge *et al.*, *Shaan Gan Ning Bianqu Longdong de qunzhong yundong* (Shaan-Gan-Ning Border Region: Longdong's Mass Campaign) (Qingyang: Zhonggong Qingyang diwei dangshi ziliao zhengji bangongshi, 1994), 90–3).

community disputes that the case exemplified. In 1945 a female amateur playwright, Yuan Jing 袁静 (1914–99), adapted it into a libretto, *Liu Qiao'er Goes to the Law* (*Liu Qiao'er gaozhuang* 刘巧儿告状), and staged it as a local opera in the Yan'an area. In this libretto Yuan not only created an image of a rebellious daughter who dared to resist her father's domination, but also invented the figure of a middle-aged woman who served as a social mother to guide and assist the rebellious daughter. These images of women went beyond the issues of the May Fourth discourse and expressed Yuan's perceptions of gender relations between women and the state during the twentieth-century social transformation and state-building. At the same time, a blind local troubadour, Han Qixiang 韩起祥 (1915–89), recast the story as a ballad, *Liu Qiao's Reunion* (*Liu Qiao tuanyuan* 刘巧团圆), to fit local tastes and gain a broader audience in the SGNBR. From 1946 to 1950 the libretto and the lyrics of the ballad story were published in Yan'an, Manchuria, Hong Kong, and Beijing, along with reports of CCP military and political victories.

The story based on this legal case continued to develop in the 1950s. In early 1950 a new version of the opera *Liu Qiao'er*, derived from Yuan's libretto and Han's ballad, opened in Beijing. It served the purpose of promoting the newly issued Marriage Law. A famous Ping opera actress, Xin Fengxia 新凤霞 (1927–98), played the heroine; her performance contributed to a positive popular reception of the new law and the concept of self-determination. In 1956, based on the well-received opera libretto, the Changchun Film Studio (Changchun dianying zhipianchang 长春电影制片厂) produced a film, *Liu Qiao'er*. Through this film an image of revolutionary womanhood, epitomized by the character Liu Qiao'er, was disseminated to the entire country. Audiences widely accepted this new image of womanhood for a New China.

In the process of these multiple transformations, the focus of the story derived from the 1943 legal case was constantly recast. It shifted from a young woman seeking a favorable ruling to protect her marriage, to the state-promoted way of governance, to showcasing democracy in the BR system, to a new view of marriage and family, and, finally, to new images of womanhood that represented the revolutionary ideal of marriage and gender relations. Since the 1980s the story has been carried on in political campaigns and in even a new wave of contemporary commercialization.

The legal case and the image of Liu Qiao'er derived from this case are critical not only for understanding historical, social, and gender practices in China from the 1940s up to today, but can also shed light on the importance of state-building through legal construction and practice in the Chinese revolution. In this book I first engage with the scholarship on marriage reform in the 1940s' revolutionary region and the study of women's agency, and examine the interplay between the revolutionary state and women's agency in the legal process. I demonstrate how the term *zizhu*, which had its roots in local women's autonomy, was adopted by judicial workers to empower women. Next, from a cultural history perspective, I review the emergence of the term "*zizhu*" and its evolution in the historical and social context of twentieth-century China. By tracing the development of this term, I aim to answer the question of how local agents adopted imported concepts but eventually developed new principles and concepts that contained the social experience of the locality. In doing so, this study brings to the fore a critical difference from postcolonialist theorization of third-world transformation in the twentieth century. Finally, in the analysis of the cultural image of Liu Qiao'er, I decode the complicated process of how the revolutionary party-state, local communities, and the educated elites, in an entangled relationship, recast a local story for its national campaigns for social reform and new gender relations among women, the family, and the state. It also examines how this cultural image and these terms, as a revolutionary legacy, in turn recast the narrative of revolution and legitimated the revolution.

Women's liberation, marriage reform, and women's agency in the Chinese revolution

From the 1960s to the late 1970s, Western scholars had a basically positive assessment of the marriage reform in the revolutionary base area and in the People's Republic of China, but their work focused on the question of the degree to which the CCP and the revolution liberated women from the old patriarchal system.[7] This perspective also dominated the historical study of Chinese women in the 1980s; when scholars examined China's gradual opening since the late 1970s they observed that patriarchal power structures remained in rural society.[8] Through analysis of CCP political documents from the 1940s, these scholars thus concluded that the communist revolution had in fact delayed and even failed

[7] M. J. Meijer, *Marriage Law and Policy in the Chinese People's Republic* (Hong Kong: Hong Kong University Press, 1971); Marilyn B. Young (ed.), *Women in China: Studies in Social Change and Feminism* (Ann Arbor: Center for Chinese Studies, University of Michigan, 1973); Margery Wolf and Roxane Witke (eds.), *Women in Chinese Society* (Stanford, CA: Stanford University Press, 1975); Delia Davin, *Woman-Work: Women and the Party in Revolutionary China* (New York: Oxford University Press, 1980); Patricia Stranahan, *Yan'an Women and the Communist Party* (Berkeley: University of California, Institute of East Asian Studies, 1984).

[8] See Margery Wolf, *Revolution Postponed: Women in Contemporary China* (Stanford, CA: Stanford University Press, 1985).

women's liberation because the CCP compromised with, and even protected, the rural patriarchy, at the price of women's rights, in order to win male peasants' support for wars against the Japanese and the Nationalists (Guomindang or GMD).[9] In the 1980s this assumption regarding marriage reform and the evaluation of its effect was criticized by some scholars for its Western feminist approach,[10] but is still dominant in current Anglophone scholarship on the history of the revolutionary base area.[11]

However, this assumption has difficulty when attempting to explain the case of *Feng v. Zhang* – why would the revolutionary power support Peng'er's appeal and her choice for marriage instead of aligning with the two patriarchs? Second, the liberation discourse makes absolute a progressive value and ignores the possibility that the state's modernization projects could be a double-edged sword that have granted rights and brought opportunities to women while restraining their other rights in other ways.[12] This study demonstrates that the state's policy offered women a chance to escape unhappy marriage through divorce, but also divested a certain autonomy they had previously enjoyed under the patriarchal system, such as running away, practicing polyandry, and marriage by capture. Third, the discourse of liberation sets the CCP as the liberator that views women as victims needing to be saved, thus effacing women's subjectivities. It tells us little about local women: what was their view

[9] See Kay Ann Johnson, *Women, the Family and Peasant Revolution in China* (Chicago, IL: University of Chicago Press, 1983); Judith Stacey, *Patriarchy and Socialist Revolution in China* (Berkeley: University of California Press, 1983); Phyllis Andors, *The Unfinished Liberation of Chinese Women, 1949–1980* (Bloomington: Indiana University Press, 1983). Although some scholars are more positive than others in their evaluation of the marriage reform policy, they admit that the communist revolution did not do enough to change the position of Chinese women in family and in society; see Margery Wolf, *Revolution Postponed: Women in Contemporary China.*

[10] Ann Anagnost, "Transformation of Gender in Modern China," in *Gender and Anthropology: Critical Reviews for Research and Teaching*, Sandra Morgen (ed.) (Washington, DC: American Anthropological Association, 1989), 313–29; Tani E. Barlow, "Asian Perspective," *Gender and History* 1(3) (Autumn 1989): 318–30; Rey Chow, "Violence in the Other Country: China as Crisis, Spectacle, and Women," in *Third World Women and the Politics of Feminism*, Chandra Talpade Mohanty, Ann Russo, and Laurdes Torres (eds.) (Bloomington: Indiana University Press, 1991), 81–100.

[11] For instance, Pauline Keating, *Two Revolutions: Village Reconstruction and the Cooperative Movement in Northern Shaanxi, 1934–1945* (Stanford, CA: Stanford University Press, 1997), 7; Tamara Jacka, *Women's Work in Rural China: Change and Continuity in an Era of Reform* (New York: Cambridge University Press, 1997), 30; Philip Huang, *Chinese Civil Justice, Past and Present* (New York: Rowman & Littlefield, 2010), 109–13.

[12] For example, Kathryn Bernhardt examines women's rights to family property in Republican China, arguing that the Republican law on widow's inheritance granted widows the right to split their husband's property with their children, but at the same time outlawed the traditional practice that a widowed mother had the right to supervise and manage the entire family property of her deceased husband. See her *Women and Property in China, 960–1949* (Stanford, CA: Stanford University Press, 1999).

of marriage, how did they see the reform, and how did they deal with the law and legal system that wanted to change their way of life? Obviously, this top-down perspective based on policy analysis overlooks the actual practice of the reform. A policy-based study is also unable to differentiate the state policy and political campaigns from the actual implementation of the Marriage Law through the judicial system.[13]

Since the 1990s scholarly works have questioned the image of Chinese women in conventional China studies that often portray women as a stereotype of Confucian womanhood – helpless victims secluded in patriarchal families. The new scholars began to search history for the voice and subjectivity of Chinese women. They demonstrated that women were active agents who bravely carved out spaces through their activities and built cultural spheres within the traditional patriarchal system.[14] Although most of these studies focus on elite women who were literate and capable of having their voices be heard, the voices of women from the lower social strata remained silent. With this new direction, some scholars extended their studies on women's agency into the field of law, examining how states from the late imperial time to the twentieth century used law to regulate women and family. Philip Huang, Matthew Sommer, and Janet M. Theiss show that on the one hand the state tried to reinforce ideological control over women's sexual behavior, while on the other hand women were active agents in their marriages and sexuality.[15]

[13] Margaret Kuo's recent book on Republican legal practice in marriage argues that although social movements fell to a low tide in the 1930s, it was the Republican judicial system that concretized and cemented the idea of gender equality (see her *Intolerable Cruelty: Marriage, Law, and Society in Early Twentieth-Century China* (New York: Rowman & Littlefield, 2014), 3–17). In fact, this pattern of development not only existed in the 1940s' revolutionary region but also appeared in the 1950s (see following chapters).

[14] For example, Patricia Ebrey, *The Inner Quarters: Marriage and the Lives of Chinese Women in the Sung Period* (Berkeley: University of California Press, 1993); Dorothy Ko, *Teachers of the Inner Chambers: Women and Culture in Seventeenth-Century China* (Stanford, CA: Stanford University Press, 1994); Christina Gilmartin, *Engendering the Chinese Revolution: Radical Women, Communist Politics, and Mass Movements in the 1920s* (Berkeley: University of California Press, 1995); Susan Mann, *Precious Records: Women in China's Long Eighteenth Century* (Stanford, CA: Stanford University Press, 1997); Susan Mann, *Gender and Sexuality in Modern Chinese History* (New York: Cambridge University Press, 2011); Paul Ropp, Paola Zamperini, and Harriet Zurndorfer (eds.), *Passionate Women: Female Suicide in Late Imperial China* (Leiden: Brill, 2001); Weijing Lu, *True to Her Word: The Faithful Maiden Cult in Late Imperial China* (Stanford, CA: Stanford University Press, 2008); Joan Judge, *The Precious Raft of History: The Past, The West, and The Women Question in China* (Stanford, CA: Stanford University Press, 2008), 188–229; also see her "Talent, Virtue, and the Nation: Chinese Nationalisms and Female Subjectivities in the Early Twentieth Century," *The American Historical Review* 106(3) (June 2001): 765–803.

[15] Philip Huang, "Women's Choices under the Law: Marriage, Divorce, and Illicit Sex in the Qing and the Republic," *Modern China* 27(1) (2001): 3–58; Matthew Sommer, *Sex,*

This new perspective led some scholars to redirect their approach to women's history and reevaluate the effectiveness of the 1950 Marriage Law through field study; their research contradicted conclusions from previous studies.[16]

Meanwhile, some new research has paid more attention to women in lower social groups and has made an effort to discover these women's voices and construct their subjectivities. For example, Hershatter's study of Shanghai prostitutes shows that even subalterns with such low social status could choose their clients carefully and strategically use their bodies to maximize their own interests.[17] In another excellent work, Hershatter addresses gender relations in the tension between state and society and between memories and the reality through interviews with rural women in Shaanxi and by collecting their memories of the political movements in the 1950s.[18] In her work Hershatter sees women as both agents and targets of state reform projects and accurately states that women's concerns centered on marriage and family, though these rural women still seemed to have been "formatted" by the revolutionary narrative in their presentations of their personal stories. A similar problem also existed in the interview with my protagonist, Feng Zhiqin (Peng'er) (see the following). While Hershatter's work made an important contribution in the field of social history, I take the approach of cultural history in the study of rural women to see how this revolutionary rhetoric penetrated into women's narration. On the other hand, through the study of the evolution of a legal case and its cultural presentation, this book also demonstrates the dynamics between rural women and the state, and how these women as active agents created a certain influence on state policy and political campaigns that resulted in the emergence of the term *zizhu*.

Law, and Society in Late Imperial China (Stanford, CA: Stanford University Press, 2000); Janet M. Theiss, *Disgraceful Matters: The Politics of Chastity in Eighteenth-Century China* (Berkeley: University of California Press, 2004).

16 Ellen Judd, "Reconsidering China's Marriage Law Campaign: Toward a DeOrientalized Feminist Perspective," *Asian Journal of Women's Studies* 4(2) (1998): 8–26; Neil Diamant, "Re-examining the Impact of the 1950 Marriage Law: State Improvisation, Local Initiative, and Rural Family Change," *China Quarterly* 161 (2000): 171–98; Neil Diamant, *Revolutionizing the Family: Politics, Love, and Divorce in Urban and Rural China, 1949–1968* (Berkeley: University of California Press, 2000).

17 Gail Hershatter, *Dangerous Pleasures: Prostitution and Modernity in Twentieth-Century Shanghai* (Berkeley: University of California Press, 1997).

18 Gail Hershatter, "The Gender of Memory: Rural Chinese Women and the 1950s," *Signs: Journal of Women in Culture and Society* 28(1) (2002): 43–70; Gail Hershatter, "Virtue at Work: Rural Shaanxi Women Remember the 1950s," in *Gender in Motion: Divisions of Labor and Cultural Change in Late Imperial and Modern China*, Bryna Goodman and Wendy Larson (eds.) (Lanham, MD: Rowman and Littlefield, 2005), 309–28; and Gail Hershatter, *The Gender of Memory: Rural Women and China's Collective Past* (Berkeley: University of California Press, 2011).

From *ziyou* to *zizhu*: a cultural history perspective of neologisms in the 1940s' SGNBR marriage reform

This book builds on the existing scholarship on women's history and gender studies, but questions the prevailing view on the communist marriage reform in the revolutionary base areas through the use of newly available legal documents. Although this study utilizes a legal case and its evolution as the thread for the narrative, this book is an interdisciplinary study that offers multiple angles to the Chinese revolution in the 1940s. Its narration unfolds along with the key story while displaying a synchronic panorama of the revolution that extends to a much broader realm of social history, legal history, cultural history, and gender studies. Most importantly, in this book I seek to understand through a cultural history perspective how the Chinese revolution and its legal practices produced new discourses, neologisms, and cultural symbols that contain China's experience in twentieth-century social movements. Through examining them against historical and social backgrounds, this study presents the Chinese subject and its experience that cannot and should not be theorized in the framework of Western discourse. I also ask to what extent these new discourses and cultural images in turn constructed the revolutionary experience and the state's interpretation of history for the purpose of social mobilization.

According to Clifford Geertz, culture is more of "a semiotic" concept in the webs of significance that human beings have created.[19] Thus, as Lynn Hunt claims, "the accent in cultural history is on close examination – of texts, of pictures, and of actions – and on open-mindedness to what those examinations will reveal."[20] In twentieth-century China the emergence of a large number of neologisms reflected drastic social transformations under the influence of the West that were taking place in the littoral and urban environments. In constructing political discourses and social reform plans, reform-minded Chinese elites largely relied on borrowed neologisms from Western political and social theories, obtained primarily through translations via Japan. However, as Lydia Liu has warned, the translated terms may have simultaneously legitimated Western domination in China since the power relations between Western language and the indigenous language were imbalanced and unequal.[21] Examining

19 Clifford Geertz, *The Interpretation of Cultures: Selected Essays* (New York: Basic Books, 1973), 5.

20 Lynn Hunt, "Introduction," in *The New Cultural History*, Lynn Hunt (ed.) (Berkeley: University of California Press, 1989), 22.

21 Lydia Liu, *Translingual Practice: Literature, National Culture, and Translated Modernity, 1900–1937* (Stanford, CA: Stanford University Press, 1995), 26–9. Unfortunately, she does not discuss the term *zizhu*.

the translation of the traditional term *zi-you* 自由 into *ziyou*[22] not only demonstrates this power relation, but also displays the confusion, conflicts, and divisions in social practices caused by the translation. These translated terms and the social practices based on these translated terms also internalized the relation reflected in the imbalanced development between the littoral and inland areas, between the educated elites and the illiterate population, and between developing urban areas and the vast rural region that was falling behind.

The conventional studies on how the neologies reflect the changing views in twentieth-century China take for granted that in Chinese these translated terms fully signify the connotations of the imported Western terms, while ignoring the implicit meanings of Chinese terms that are deeply embedded in their own history, language, and social context. Chen Jianhua's study of the discourse of "revolution/*geming*" shows that this term has its root in traditional Chinese political discourse, but returned to China from Japan at the turn of the twentieth century with modern connotations of both peaceful reform and violent insurrection. With the radicalism prevalent in the twentieth century and the transformation of the urban communist movement to a rural revolution, it is the term's explicit connotation leaned more toward the traditional Chinese understanding of overturning an old political regime through violent actions.[23] This case points out that uncritically adopting these neologies without scrupulous analysis of their linguistic, etymological sources and social context can lead to cultural incompatibility in practice that would bring social conflict, as my study shows.

In the first three decades of the twentieth century "freedom of marriage" or "free marriage" (*hunyin ziyou* 婚姻自由) was an important agendum in the iconoclastic New Culture and May Fourth discourses that created many images of women in the social and literary fields for the purpose of opposing the Confucian family and patriarchy. This discourse arose at about the same time as the introduction of Marxism, socialism, and communism into China, which strongly influenced the formation of the May Fourth discourse on women and marriage. These doctrines favored liberating women from "feudal" patriarchal oppression

22 The great majority of traditional Chinese words were individual character-based words, particularly in classical writings. In this book I hyphenate or separate the two characters when I discuss its classical connotation and put them together to indicate its modern connotation. This also applies to the use of *zi-zhu*/*zizhu*. However, since the connotation of *zi-zhu* has not changed from its classical connotation, the hyphenation for *zi-zhu* is not strictly made in some cases.

23 Chen Jianhua, *"Geming" de xiandaixing: Zhongguo geming huayu kao lun* (The Modernity of Term "Revolution": An Examination of the Discourse of Chinese Revolution) (Shanghai: Shanghai guji chubanshe, 2000), 1–22.

and loveless marriages, and became an important part of the social transformation of twentieth-century China. However, between the 1910s and 1930s these changes occurred primarily in urban areas among educated women.[24] The broader scale of the twentieth-century social revolution and movement led by the CCP to remold the concept and practice of marriage occurred later in an entirely different social, geographical, and cultural milieu. The marriage reforms in the communist revolutionary base areas of the SGNBR from the 1930s to the 1940s marked an important part of this transformation, and had a profound impact on post-1949 social reform in China. In this reform, however, as displayed in the case *Feng v. Zhang*, adjudication utilized a different principle, *hunyin zizhu* 婚姻自主 (self-determined marriage). Why did the judge use the term *zi-zhu* instead of *ziyou*, which had been widespread since the 1920s in urban areas among educated elites and used in the 1939 marriage regulation? What was the difference between the two terms, and what was the significance of using *zi-zhu* instead of *ziyou*?

Both *ziyou* and *zi-zhu* have traditional roots in Chinese culture and history, and both terms experienced a modern transformation in the twentieth-century social movements. In contemporary dictionaries and in common use, *ziyou* contains dual meanings, one that comes from its classical root meaning "unrestrained volition" or "lawlessness";[25] another meaning of *ziyou* that is more modern and equates to the English "freedom" or "liberty" comes from missionary translation and has been used since the mid-nineteenth century. Through translation the linguistic structure of this term was altered, and thus generated a nuanced connotation differing from its classical root (see Chapter 4). In the traditional term, *zi-you* was a combination of the two words *zi* and *you*, and constructed a combined phrase that means "doing whatever one wants."[26]

[24] In terms of marriage reform, although the Republican legislators created a liberal code on marriage for gender equality, its impact in cities was still limited and it was even less effective in rural areas. See Kathryn Bernhardt, "Women and the Law: Divorce in the Republican Period," in *Civil Law in Qing and Republican China*, Kathryn Bernhardt and Philip Huang (eds.) (Stanford, CA: Stanford University Press, 1994), 187–214.

[25] See *Hanyu da cidian* (Grand Dictionary of Chinese), vol. VIII (Shanghai: Shanghai cishu chubanshe, 2001), 1308. Several decades ago Paul Cohen noticed that in the Chinese language the term *ziyou* "has connotation of license or lawlessness." See Paul A. Cohen, *Discovering History in China: American Historical Writing on the Recent Chinese Past* (New York: Columbia University Press, 1984), 14.

[26] See the example of "ji zong chao zheng, sheng sha zi you" (in control of the dynastic power, [the subject] will kill anyone by his will) in *Hanyu da cidian*, vol. VIII, 1308; also see the example of "Yan zhi Jinwu, xiong di quan gui, wei fu zi you" (Yan held the position of Jinwu and with his brothers became so powerful that they showed this freedom arbitrarily without limits) cited in Liu Zhengtan *et al.*, *Hanyu wailai ci cidian* [A Dictionary of Loan Words and Hybrid Words in Chinese] ([Shanghai: Shanghai cishu chubanshe, 1984]), 410.

After the translation it was transformed into an indissoluble noun that indicated the Western idea of "liberty/freedom."

This imported, new connotation of *ziyou* was widely accepted among urban educated elites from the 1890s to the 1920s, whereas it had no impact on the vast illiterate population in rural areas (see Chapter 4). Thus when the urban-born concept "freedom of marriage" landed on the remote rural soil of the SGNBR, it immediately encountered a cultural incompatibility. First, due to the fact that in this region marriage decisions were in fact the parents' prerogative, this "freedom" became the instrument for fathers to manipulate both daughters and the marriage regulation for their financial gain in a time of economic inflation (see Chapter 1). Second, because the new connotation of *ziyou* had not been made clear to the locals through modern education, local fathers retained its old connotation, believing they were allowed to do whatever they wished in marriage matters. It was in this situation that Peng'er's father abolished her first engagement and betrothed Peng'er to another suitor for greater profit (see Chapter 1). This misunderstanding and incompatibility brought confusion and arguments between local farmers and law executors.

The term *zi-zhu* is neither an alien notion imported from the West through translation, nor an aprioristic concept from theoretical innovation of elite intellectuals. Its rise and formation were closely linked to the legal practice of the Chinese revolution beginning in the 1940s. The term *zi-zhu* appeared in traditional Chinese texts in popular culture during the transitional period of Ming-Qing (*c.* 1600–1700),[27] much later than that of *zi-you*, and was commonly used in marriage-related issues.[28] Etymologically speaking, both *zi-you* and *zi-zhu* express the idea that a person can make his/her own choice or decision; the term *zi-zhu* signifies "to act on one's own, to decide for oneself, or to be one's own master [in doing something]," a meaning very close to "autonomy" in English or, more accurately, autonomously (doing something).[29] Compared to the term *ziyou*/liberty, which as a noun and an abstract concept indicating a condition or a state, both *zi-you* and *zi-zhu* emphasize action and decision making, with strong subjective power and inferred agents/actors. Semantically, *zi-you* allows for open and arbitrary possibilities from the actor's unrestrained mind, while *zi-zhu* hints at a subjective power in

[27] See *Hanyu da cidian (pu ji ben)*, (Grand Chinese Dictionary, Popular Version) (Beijing: Hanyu da cidian chubanshe, 2000), 2185, and *Hanyu da cidian*, 1310.

[28] In one story a fairy tells a man that she has fallen in love with him "but is unable to make her own decision" (*dan bu zi zhu*) to marry him due to her mother's domination. See Pu Songling, "Xihu zhu" (Master of the West Lake), *Liao zai zhi yi* (Strange Tales from a Chinese Studio) (Beijing: Guangming ribao chubanshe, 2009 [reprint]), 255–8.

[29] *Hanyu da cidian*, 1310; *Hanyu da cidian (pu ji ben)*, 2185.

making a decision in regard to a specific issue.[30] At the turn of the twentieth century the term *zi-zhu* was sometimes used when discussing the issue of state sovereignty, but soon retreated from the popular political vocabulary until the 1930s.[31] Unlike *ziyou*, which carries a dual meaning in its modern transformation, *zi-zhu* maintained its original linguistic structure and sole semantic connotation and was easily accepted by the vast rural population as a political term in the 1930s (see Chapter 4).

Because of these linguistic and semantic nuances in modern language, the term *zi-zhu* held much power for the actor to accomplish certain goals. However, it was through legal practice, such as the interplay with rural women and learning local customs that judicial workers developed *zi-zhu* as a principle, one that also was applied to the case of *Feng v. Zhang* as well as many others. Through the adoption of the principle of self-determination, the legal workers of the SGNBR were able to focus on women's choice in marriage. Assisted by newly invented legal strategies and techniques, judicial workers granted women the right to make decisions in their marriages and to have their preferences respected in most marriage disputes. Thus the principle of *hunyin zi-zhu* 婚姻自主 aimed at disentangling women from the old patriarchal system, thereby undermined patriarchal power while empowering women. The legal reform and its practices during the 1940s foregrounded the legitimization of the term *zizhu* in the 1978 Constitution of the People's Republic of China (*Zhonghua renmin gongheguo xianfa* 中华人民共和国宪法). In Article 53, instead of using the term *hunyin ziyou* (freedom of marriage), the legislature announced that "men and women [have the right to] self-determined marriage" (*nan nü hunyin zizhu* 男女婚姻自主).[32] The 1986 Civil Law of the People's Republic of China (*Zhonghua renmin gongheguo minfa tongze* 中华人民共和国民法通则) further defined *zizhu* as an individual's right to marriage (*hunyin zizhu quan* 婚姻自主权), making it a practicable right.[33] The development of

[30] In spite of the fact that both terms indicate the actor's volition, this semantic nuance prevents the two terms/phrases from being interchangeable in constructing a sentence.

[31] According to Hong Kong scholars Jin Guantao and Liu Qingfeng since 1915 this term has rarely appeared in any public written work. See their *Guannian shi yanjiu: Zhongguo xiandai zhongyao zhengzhi shuyu de xingcheng* (A Study on the History of Views: The Formation of Important Political Terminology in Modern China) (Beijing: Falü chubanshe, 2009), 526. In the 1930s most dictionaries of neologisms did not include term *zi-zhu*, meaning that the compilers did not regard this term as important. See Xing Moqing (comp.), *Xin mingci cidian* (A Dictionary of Neologisms) (Shanghai: Xin shengming shuju, 1934).

[32] "Zhonghua renmin gongheguo xianfa, 1978" (The Constitution of the People's Republic of China, 1978), *Renmin ribao* (People's Daily), March 8, 1978.

[33] See "Zhonghua renmin gongheguo minfa tongze, 103 tiao" (The General Civil Law of the People's Republic of China, clause 103, promulgated on April 12, 1986), see

the term *zizhu*, from its birth in the political, social, and legal practices of the 1940s' revolution to the 1986 civil law, entailed China's long journey in the twentieth century, a subject that has not been explored.

Reforming the family for a strong nation-state: *zi-zhu* and national sovereignty

The marriage reform launched by the communist government in the 1940s' SGNBR had a strong continuity with the family-reform movement initiated in the late Qing. Facing Western imperialist powers and a surge of Chinese nationalism, late Qing reformist elites and the intellectuals of the May Fourth generation proposed reforming the family as a way of building a strong nation-state. Although Joan Judge's work shows that in the early twentieth-century social movements some radical feminist activists believed that women were capable of contributing to the cause of China's salvation,[34] the nation-strengthening plan created by the majority male intellectuals still blamed women for China's "backwardness" and "weakness," and thus assumed that women needed to be reformed for the sake of the nation's survival.[35] Meanwhile, as Susan Glosser perceptively points out, when May Fourth radicals vehemently attacked the "traditional" model of the extended family and promoted a new type of conjugal relations characterized by equality,[36] they did not simply adopt the Western view of the nuclear family but "built their rationale for change upon the ancient foundations of Chinese political culture that linked family and state order."[37] This study indicates a strong continuity of the traditional isomorphic relations between family and state order in the anti-traditional movement.

The May Fourth view of family reform did indeed represent the elitist discourse on China's nation-state-building that built on this isomorphic and correlative relation between the state and family originating from Confucian political theory. From this view, state order remained as the extension of family order and then extended to Chinese elites' perception of China's position in international relations.[38] As many scholars have

"Falü tushuguan" (Law Library website), www.law-lib.com/law/law_view.asp?id=3633 (accessed September 8, 2011).

34 Judge, "Talent, Virtue, and the Nation."

35 Liang Qichao, "Bianfa tongyi" (A General Proposal for Reform), in his *Yinbingshi heji: wenji* (Collected Works from Drinking Ice Studio: Article Collections) (Shanghai: Zhonghua shuju, 1932), vol. I, 1–64.

36 Susan L. Glosser, *Chinese Visions of Family and State, 1915–1953* (Berkeley: University of California Press, 2003), 1–26.

37 Glosser, *Chinese Visions of Family and State*, 5–10.

38 In fact, the Chinese term "guojia/state" indicates that the state is the combination of the terms state (*guo*) and family (*jia*), implying that these are in a correlative and coherent

pointed out, in this isomorphic/correlative relation oppressed women in patriarchal families symbolized the fact that the Chinese nation was oppressed by Western imperialism; liberating women from the oppression of the patriarchal family would thus symbolically rid China of the oppression of Western imperialism and colonialism. Family reform was thus an important part of the state-building project since this liberation from oppression would consequently make China a strong nation-state in the world.[39] Meanwhile, for intellectual elites in the urban milieu whose national pride was constantly stung by the humiliation brought by Western powers, the disadvantaged position of Chinese women in patriarchal families was analogous to the position of Chinese urban intellectuals in semicolonial China.[40]

In this mentality, the emergence of the term *zi-zhu* reconnected family and state, and became a practical instrument for both women/family and the Chinese nation-state since they shared this isomorphic structure. The history of the term – originating from marriage-related issues but transforming into a term that stressed national sovereignty during the surge of nationalism in the late Qing and in the 1930s – fitted perfectly into the reform based on this family-state structure. Thus this term became the nexus that interlocked and interwove the isomorphic relations between family and state, and between women's struggle for autonomy and the nation's fight for sovereignty. Thus the emergence of *zi-zhu* from the social movement in the middle of the twentieth century was not a coincidence: from the view of linguistic structure the term *zi-zhu* contains a strong sense of the agent's acting power that could symbolize both women and the nation in action. It is a much more dynamic term than the imported notion of *ziyou*/liberty/freedom, which, after the translation, became a static and indissoluble noun and thus lost the power of action and agency (see Chapter 4).

Although urban-educated youth readily received the May Fourth discourse of "freedom of marriage," their acceptance of the homegrown term *zi-zhu* closely related to the vision of correlative relations of family and state order, especially when they suffered the pain of being in semicolonial cities at the time of national crisis. Thus the term *zi-zhu* brought them a strong sense of acting power and the feeling of being

order because state order is based on family order and the state is an extension of the family. Outside of *guojia* is *tianxia* (under the heaven), which was transformed into a view of China in international relations.

39 Glosser, *Chinese Visions of Family and State*, 5–10; Ko, *Teachers of the Inner Chambers*, 1–5; Gail Hershatter, "The Subaltern Talks Back: Reflections on Subaltern Theory and Chinese History," *Positions* 1(1) (1993): 103–30.

40 Hershatter, "The Subaltern Talks Back."

agents engaging in the reform of society and in saving the nation. Once they were moved to the hinterland from their previous urban residences after the outbreak of the Anti-Japanese War, the majority of petty intellectuals, particularly urban-born educated females, met peasants living at the bottom of Chinese society, from whom they tried to regain strength and autonomy for the sake of the nation's independence. In the wartime milieu, Chinese feminism was heavily imprinted by and interwoven with Chinese nationalism in both the urban and rural environments.[41] The wartime crises created strong nationalistic sentiment in which urban-educated youth, both males and females, willingly submitted themselves to the authority of the revolutionary state. As this study shows, it was also during the war that this group of educated youth achieved personal accomplishments while helping the revolutionary state to victory. They viewed their individual suffering, both material and spiritual, as expressions of their dedication to the nation's independence and autonomy, while also contributing to their own self-fulfillment. From this point of view, we are able to understand the literary and artistic activities of Yuan Jing and Gu Yuan, as well as many others in the 1940s' revolutionary base areas. It was this nationalistic sentiment that trapped them in inseparable and entangled relations with the party-state in the post-1949 era.

The revolutionary state and village communities: the Yan'an Way and "high modernism"

The communist revolution's social reform programs made it the most important historical event in twentieth-century China. It was through this project led by the party-state that new ideas on marriage, such as love-based marriage, monogamy, and state registration of marriage, penetrated into villages through state power and administrative organs. As Chapter 5 relates, the marriage reform, particularly the misunderstanding of the term *ziyou*, encountered local resistance and triggered complaints. How did the revolutionary state of the 1940s manage to survive the trauma of its great loss in the early 1930s and secure its power base in the villages of its revolutionary base area?

The Yan'an period (1935–48) was the decisive phase in paving the way to the CCP's final victory in winning national power in 1949. Mark

[41] Both this young generation of intellectuals who moved to the hinterland and feminist activists in urban areas prioritized national salvation over the feminist agenda, thus interweaving Chinese feminism with nationalism. See Wang Zheng, *Women in the Chinese Enlightenment: Oral and Textual Histories* (Berkeley: University of California Press, 1999), 124–31.

Selden's 1971 work explains that the CCP's "Yan'an Way" was the key to success in that the party's mass-line policy represented the democratic and incorporating nature of the revolutionary state.[42] Although Selden revised his views in 1995 in response to challenges to his theory that emerged in the 1990s,[43] he continues to argue that the CCP's undemocratic nature was still in its inceptive stage during the Yan'an period and only reached full strength after the CCP later won control of the nation.[44] On the other hand, Pauline Keating uses the subregional variety of social and cultural ecology in the SGNBR to explain the CCP's successful and unsuccessful policy implementations.[45] This approach helps explain the CCP's 1949 victory to a certain extent, but leaves some space for questions on how the CCP dealt with village communities and with mobilizing the masses for social reforms, such as the marriage reform, during the Yan'an period.

When James Scott contemplates the reasons for the failure of utopian schemes in the twentieth-century world, he suggests four elements: a state's attempt to make the society and natural environment into a legible order; the "high-modernist ideology" originating from modern science; an authoritarian state; and a prostrate civil society. He points out that states with "high-modernist ideology" often launch reforms intended to improve social conditions and increase the legibility of the society and the natural world. The authoritarian state frequently emerges under the conditions of revolution, war, national struggle for independence, or social and human devastation, during which a weak civil society is unable to resist its high-modernist plans.[46] The communist revolution introduced the most influential social reform projects in twentieth-century China, intended to change both traditional marriage practices and landownership. In the 1940s the CCP brought radical ideas originating from the West and China's urban areas into one of China's most economically undeveloped and socially backwater regions. The CCP not only built a revolutionary party-state, an administrative system, and a modern judicial system on the ruins of the imperial frontier, but also launched a series of social and political reforms, especially marriage reform, to mobilize farmers/peasants for the war. Although these social projects were

[42] Mark Selden, *The Yenan Way in Revolutionary China* (Cambridge, MA: Harvard University Press, 1971).

[43] See Tony Saich and Hans van de Ven (eds.), *New Perspectives on the Chinese Communist Revolution* (London: M. E. Sharpe, 1994).

[44] Mark Selden, *China in Revolution: The Yenan Way Revisited* (London: M. E. Sharpe, 1995), 220–52.

[45] Keating, *Two Revolutions*.

[46] James C. Scott, *Seeing Like a State: How Certain Schemes to Improve the Human Condition Have Failed* (New Haven, CT: Yale University Press, 1998), 1–6.

unquestionably of a high-modernist scheme, the CCP's power gradually stabilized the regional order and even won national victory in 1949.

Did the CCP act as an authoritarian power in ruling the SGNBR in the 1940s? In the SGNBR, the revolutionary state had a workable system to impose its reform policies. The question is: was there a strong civil society that prevented the CCP from turning into an authoritarian state? If we view "civil society" in its Habermasian sense as a phenomenon organized by urban bourgeoisie individuals to resist the domination of an authoritarian state,[47] then in the environment of the SGNBR where over 95 percent of the population was illiterate, the answer is definitely no. However, if we observe the people's resistance to certain state policies in order to protect their own interests and to check the power of the ruling body through articulating their dissatisfaction, while the state also mobilized mass participation of the public in the political and legal processes for this purpose, then the answer may be yes.

The reality was that the CCP built a rather weak state power in the region, especially in its early period, because it was desperately trying to survive through reaching out to local village communities, adopting local culture, and conciliating with the social ecology. After experiencing the devastating Long March and arriving in northern Shaanxi at the end of 1935, the CCP and the Red Army had to fight from 1937 to 1939 to stabilize its territory and redraw its administrative map. Between the late 1930s and the early 1940s, the administrative organs and the party branches at each level (prefecture/*zhuanqu*, ward/*qu*, township/*xiang*, and village/*cun*), as well as social organizations in the villages such as women's associations, peasant associations, and militia were gradually expanding. Meanwhile, the judicial system was also growing from its initial stage of construction to a complete, reconstructed form, as discussed in Chapters 3, 4, and 5.

To implement marriage policies, the revolutionary government as well as the judicial system took serious measures to adjust its incompatible policies and accommodate local knowledge and customs. In fact, the CCP's accommodation to the environment and its adoption of local culture in order to strengthen its force occurred not only in the SGNBR but also in other revolutionary base areas. For example, both David Goodman's research on the Taihang base area in Shanxi and Gregor Benton's study of the New Fourth Army in the Yangtze and the Huai River areas demonstrate the revolutionary government's and army's flexibility and

[47] Jürgen Habermas, *The Structural Transformation of the Public Sphere: An Inquiry into a Category of Bourgeois Society* (trans. Thomas Burger and Frederick Lawrence) (Cambridge, MA: MIT Press, 1989).

adjustment in implementing policies.[48] Elizabeth J. Perry's work on the communist activists in Anyuan also demonstrates this capacity.[49] Facing community protests and resistance to the marriage reform and other issues, the state made efforts to pacify the local opposition through various strategies, including adjusting its legal procedures, sending cadres/judges to villages, and involving villagers in the legal process. In addition, by adopting the strategy of "cultural positioning,"[50] the state was able to borrow local cultural forms such as folk songs, dancing, local fairs, and dramas, and produce new forms of culture for the purpose of persuasion. The 1939 marriage regulation was revised in 1944 and again in 1946 in order to address the concerns of the locals while insisting on the state's revolutionary principles. To minimize litigation and reduce dissatisfaction, the state was willing to compromise with the community by revitalizing the century-old strategies of mediation and community autonomy, encouraging the idea of a harmonious family, and inventing new legal strategies, integrating them into the revolutionary mass-line as a method of fulfilling the revolutionary goals. This flexible strategy and cultural positioning policy enabled the revolutionary state to negotiate with and reshape rural communities while recognizing their traditional autonomy. To a certain extent, these strategies and policies can explain the CCP's gradual growth in the Yan'an period and the fact that the CCP accumulated enough strength to win national power. A combination of the state's flexibility in implementing policies, the persuasion of cultural products, the state's consideration of its survival, and the policy of the mass-line initially restrained its authoritarian impulse. On the other hand, the tactical resistance of local communities also deterred the drive for absolute power.

Legal documents and the voices of women

Prior to the 1980s many scholars of the Chinese revolution and the CCP's history encountered a paramount problem: the lack of concrete

[48] See David S. G. Goodman, *Social and Political Change in Revolutionary China: The Taihang Base Area in the War of Resistance to Japan, 1937–1945* (New York: Rowman & Littlefield, 2000). Gregor Benton, *New Fourth Army: Communist Resistance Along the Yangtze and the Huai, 1938–1941* (Berkeley: University of California Press, 1999).

[49] Elizabeth J. Perry, *Anyuan: Mining China's Revolutionary Tradition* (Berkeley: University of California Press, 2012).

[50] According to Elizabeth Perry, the most effective way for CCP mobilizers to increase the party's influence was its "cultural positioning" policy, which she defines as "the strategic development of a range of symbolic resources (religion, ritual, rhetoric, dress, drama, art, and so on) for purposes of political persuasion." See her *Anyuan: Mining China's Revolutionary Tradition*, 4.

evidence of the implementation of communist policies at the local level and the paucity of views of people from the bottom of society. Most studies had to rely largely on the CCP's official documents and top leaders' writings and speeches. It was obvious that CCP official documents were strongly disposed toward expressing the theoretical objectives and wishes of the top leaders, ignoring the gap between policy-making at the top and the reality that occurred in villages. In many cases scholars had to accept as fact the information garnered from official reports produced by local CCP cadres. Although these reports are valuable for understanding the mentality of local officials, grassroots cadres sometimes exaggerated their work to suggest success, or downgraded conditions to cover up their mistakes.

China's open-door policy of the 1980s offered Western scholars the chance to access documents firsthand in their fieldwork. The gradual opening of Chinese archives to the public in the 1990s also resulted in the discovery of a large number of historical documents in local archives on women in the twentieth century. The publications based on this new research have led to fundamental changes in our understanding of the history of Chinese women and gender.[51] Meanwhile, studies on the 1930s' and 1940s' revolutionary regions have also benefited from this policy of opening archives to the public in that much of the local conditions and details of policy implementation have been revealed.[52]

This research also benefits from the opening of China's public archives and libraries. The basic sources for this study come from various archival documents, local gazetteers, individual memoirs, and personal interviews. It is worth noting that the foremost sources for this book are the documents produced by the SGN High Court (*Shaan-Gan-Ning bianqu gaodeng fayuan* 陕甘宁边区高等法院) from 1937 to 1949. A copy of the whole set of these documents, preserved in the Shaanxi Provincial Archives (SPA),[53] is a rich resource, and contains more than

[51] For example, Wang Zheng, *Women in the Chinese Enlightenment*; Diamant, *Revolutionizing the Family*; Hershatter, *The Gender of Memory*.

[52] For example, Joseph Esherick, "Deconstructing the Construction of the Party-State: Gulin County in the Shaan-Gan-Ning Border Region," *The China Quarterly* 140 (December 1994): 1052–79; Keating, *Two Revolutions*; David S. G. Goodman, "The Licheng Rebellion of 1941: Class, Gender, and Leadership in the Sino-Japanese War," *Modern China* 23(2) (April 1997): 216–45; also Goodman's *Social and Political Change in Revolutionary China*; Lucien Bianco, "Peasant Responses to CCP Mobilization Policies, 1937–1945," in *New Perspectives on the Chinese Communist Revolution*, Tony Saich and Hans van de Ven (eds.) (London: M. E. Sharpe, 1994), 175–91; Benton, *New Fourth Army*.

[53] The original documents of the SGNBR governments and courts were restored in the Shaanxi Provincial Archives from 1950 to the early 1980s, when the Party's Central Archives (PCA) moved this collection to its Beijing location. However, the PCA allowed the SPA to retain a xerox copy of the entire set of original documents. These documents

one thousand volumes that include various types of marriage disputes and other types of lawsuits, both civil and criminal. In addition to court records, legal codes, and memos between judges, these documents also contain complaints, subpoenas, petitions, appeals, verdicts, court orders, and all types of evidence.

Of course, the legal records of the SGNBR High Court have certain problems, including incomplete case files, damaged pages, illegible handwriting, and disorganization. Despite these defects, they hold great value. Unlike those produced by Qing county courts that were often formatted by legal experts (*shiye* 师爷), these documents came from local court secretaries who had limited education and lacked legal training. Their disadvantages at the time have become advantages for us today: the records were written in a plain style based on the original words of the illiterate litigants, both males and females, so that we are able to view these records not through the lens of legal experts but that of ordinary people. The court staff wrote down their complaints and responses by directly recording the dialect and local slang. In some cases the court secretaries also recorded smiles and laughter, as well as expressions of shyness, perplexity, and anger, and even the bodily actions of litigants, all of which increase the vitality and credibility of the material. Due to the special legal strategy and procedure used by the court (see Chapter 4), many women were able to speak for themselves. The records thus provide a credible source for understanding rural women, their minds and their wishes. Moreover, these documents offer a concrete picture of marriage disputes among villagers under communist rule, and the extent and degree of effectiveness to which the marriage reform was carried out. It is these documents that provide a solid basis for this study.

This study also uses personal interviews with various individuals related to SGNBR marriage reform. My most exciting experiences were the two interviews (2005 and 2007) that I conducted with Feng Zhiqin 封芝琴 (Peng'er), the protagonist of the *Feng v. Zhang* legal dispute and the prototype for the image of Liu Qiao'er. After so many visits from various types of people and agencies since the 1980s, she had grown accustomed to telling her own story in a formulaic narration using strong official language. By forming my questions tactically, I was able to learn some interesting things beyond this official narration.

in the SPA were open to the public from the 1990s to 2012, but had never been seen by foreign scholars. Nonetheless, for unknown reasons this SGNBR collection has been sealed since 2012 and become inaccessible to the public.

Figure 0.1 Interview with Feng Zhiqin, July 21, 2005

This study of the case of *Feng v. Zhang*, especially in the early stages at the local level, focuses mostly on the SGNBR, more specifically the Longdong region and later the area of Yan'an. This case and its later transformation into political and cultural domains may not fully translate to other types of revolutionary base areas in localities in which the geographic, social, and cultural ecologies were different from those of the SGNBR. Still, tracing the development of this case from an event in a small village to a cultural symbol for the national campaign offers a particular view of an important dimension of the social revolutionary movements in twentieth-century China.

Overview of the book

The narrative of this book follows the development of the *Feng v. Zhang* case from a local matter in the 1940s to a national artistic presentation in the 1950s, while displaying the legal, political, and cultural agendas surrounding this story in its different phases. Since in each phase the story has a different agent, I link them through the thematic term *zi-zhu*, which I discuss in detail in Chapter 4. The book is divided into three parts, which focus on the three subthemes of marriage, law, and gender construction through sociopolitical, legal, and cultural presentation respectively, in each stage of the unfolding story.

The first part contains Chapters 1 and 2; they describe the local conditions from which women's activities and reform originated. In Chapter 1 I demonstrate that marriage reform was implemented in a geographical, social, and cultural setting different from where the CCP's reform discourse was shaped. The alien concept of marriage and the modernization programs that the revolutionary state imposed resulted in strong conflict between local traditions of marriage and revolutionary reform, of which the case of *Feng v. Zhang* presents one example. Chapter 2 continues the narration of the development of the case, particularly Peng'er's appeal to a higher authority. It first reviews the life of local women, showing how they enjoyed a certain degree of autonomy in love and sexuality under patriarchy and how this autonomy underwent a transformation under the rule of the CCP government when the revolutionary state attempted to regulate marriage based on modern concepts. It demonstrates that these rural women knew how to negotiate new spaces and boundaries between state regulations and their own interests through legal processes and articulate their voices in courts, as the protagonist in this case demonstrated.

Chapters 3 and 4 compose Part II, and focus on the newly established judicial system and its practices, as well as the transformation in practice of the term *ziyou* to *zizhu*. Chapter 3 offers a discussion of the changed verdict in the *Feng v. Zhang* case, and explores the rationale behind the reversal of the adjudication. Through examining the role of the newly constructed judicial system in marriage reform, I display the construction and practice of the judiciary in the 1940s' SGN region that provided the institutional support for women's rights to make their own choices in marriage. Thematically, Chapter 4 first presents a close reading of the new adjudication in the *Feng v. Zhang* case by pointing out its use of the term "self-determination" instead of "freedom" as the grounds for the new adjudication. It then traces the etymologies of the terms *ziyou* and *zi-zhu* in the Chinese intellectual and political contexts, demonstrating that the term *zizhu* concentrates China's experience of synchronistic projects in nation-state-building and family reform since the late nineteenth century and continued in the revolutionary reform projects from the late 1920s to the 1940s.

Part III, comprising Chapters 5, 6, and 7, analyzes the transformation of a local case into a political and cultural symbol. An examination of this legal dispute's conversion into a political issue in the revolutionary center of Yan'an constitutes the main content of Chapter 5. It shows

Figure 0.2 Feng Zhiqin in front of her new house, July 21, 2005

that this case was used as a political and legal model to illuminate the efforts of the CCP party-state in building a relationship with rural communities through the pacification of local protests in the midst of marriage reform.

Chapter 6 recounts how this case was adapted into a local opera and a ballad. It explains how the urban-educated youth of the post-May

Fourth generation, such as Yuan Jing, the author of *Liu Qiao'er Goes to the Law*, helped the CCP to reconceptualize the image of women and recast gender and family relations. It pays particular attention to a new image, in addition to Liu Qiao'er, invented by Yuan Jing: Auntie Li, a social mother who comforts and assists a rebellious daughter such as Liu Qiao'er. I argue that this image in fact redefined the boundaries between family and society and between women and state while representing the perceptions of educated women on continuing the expansion of women's autonomy through generational bonds during this period of social transformation and state-building. Tracing the evolution of the cultural products of the central story of Liu Qiao'er, Chapter 7 focuses on the 1950s, during which the cultural image of Liu Qiao'er was used to promote the newly promulgated Marriage Law and became the national symbol for women's self-determination in marriage. In its transformations into operas and a film, the image of Liu Qiao'er was strongly politicized, which assisted in recasting and spreading the revolutionary narrative. Meanwhile, this cultural image effectively promoted the Marriage Law because the actress who played the heroine, Xin Fengxia, concretized this image through her own life and marriage.

The epilogue concludes with the end of the story and its cultural symbols, as well as its contemporary implications. This brings the question of how the Chinese experience could be theorized in its own historical and social context in twentieth-century social movements and what its revolutionary legacy means to today's development in China.

Part I

Locality, marriage practice, and women

1 The case of *Feng v. Zhang*

Marriage reform in a revolutionary region

basic monetary unit

The legal dispute in question occurred in 1943 in a small village in Eastern Gansu Province. The cause of the dispute can be traced back to 1928, when a farmer in Huachi County, Feng Yangui, betrothed his four-*sui*-old daughter,[1] Peng'er, to Zhang Bo, the five-*sui*-old son of Zhang Jincai, another farmer in a neighboring village.[2] The Zhang family then paid ten silver *yuan* as a betrothal gift.[3] In 1942, when Peng'er reached the legally marriageable age of eighteen years old,[4] Zhang Jincai asked for a formal wedding to marry the young couple. However, Feng Yangui ignored this request and showed no intent to fulfill the engagement agreement. Zhang Jincai then brought Feng to the Huachi County government, suing him for attempting to annul a marriage contract. The county government tried to mediate the dispute but failed because, according to the record, Peng'er herself "strongly objected to the engagement" (*jianjue bu yuanyi* 坚决不愿意). The county government workers had no choice but to invalidate the engagement under the principle of freedom of marriage (see Figure 1.1).[5]

1 The traditional Chinese way of counting people's age uses "sui," which counts a child's age from its conception; so a newborn would be one sui, while passing a New Year adds another "sui." In the SGNBR documents, it is not clear which way was used to record local people's age. If not indicated, I assume that in most cases the locals used the "sui" system. It also happens that local officials converted the "sui" into the common calendar in formal legal documents, so I sometimes still use the word "year-old."

2 Regarding the ages of engagement for two children, the record of the civil case document (see Figure 1.1) is different from the formal legal documents and the newspaper report. Here I adopt the way stated in the legal documents.

3 SPA 15-842, *Feng v. Zhang*. According to another document, this engagement occurred in 1925 when Peng'er was one year old and Zhang Bo was two. See SPA 4-1-65, "Shaan-Gan-Ning bianqu hunyin wenti huiji, 1943" (Collected Documents on Marriage Issues, 1943).

4 This marriageable age was established by the BR Government in the 1939 marriage regulation, but most marriages in the SGN region did not follow this rule. In the following discussion, I present the social and economic changes in the region that made Feng Yangui postpone his daughter's formal wedding date.

5 SPA 4-1-65, "Shaan-Gan-Ning bianqu hunyin wenti huiji, 1943."

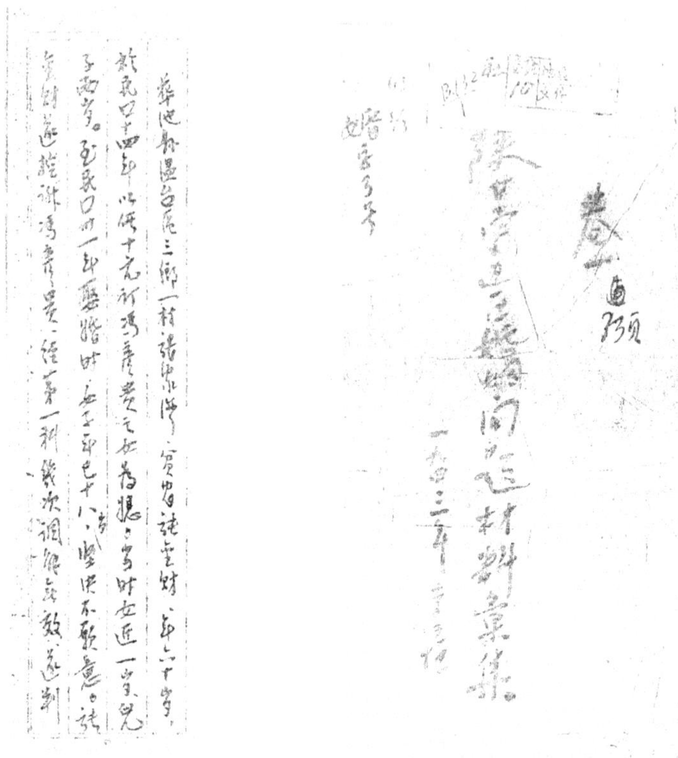

Figure 1.1 The file record for the dismissal of the engagement between Feng and Zhang, SPA 4-1-65

After abolishing this engagement, Feng Yangui attempted to betroth his daughter to a son of another Zhang family for 2,400 Republican *yuan* (*fabi* 法币) plus 48 silver *yuan*[6] as a betrothal gift. However, this move was detected by Zhang Jincai, who had been closely monitoring his former daughter-in-law-to-be even though the government had already annulled the engagement. Zhang Jincai reported Feng to the government for "selling a marriage" (*mai mai hunyin* 买卖婚姻),[7] a violation of the 1939 SGN

[6] *Fabi* is the paper currency issued by the Nationalist government in 1935. One silver dollar supposedly equaled one *fabi yuan*, but beginning in 1940 it was rapidly devalued. In the early 1940s, the BR concurrently circulated three types of currency: old silver *yuan* issued by the Yuan Shikai government in the 1910s, *fabi* issued by the Nationalist government in 1935, and the *bianbi* (Border Currency) issued by the SGNBR government. See the later section on currency rates.

[7] The term "*mai mai hunyin*" used during this period in fact refers to both buying and selling actions. The common translation of this term into "purchased marriages" does

marriage regulation; it was therefore invalidated by the Huachi County government.[8] In 1943, Peng'er's father received another offer from Zhu Shouchang (朱寿昌), who promised Feng 8,000 *yuan fabi* plus four bolts of machine-made fabric and 20 silver *yuan* in exchange for his daughter. On March 10, 1943, Zhu Shouchang came to Feng's home for the engagement ceremony. Zhu delivered 7,000 *yuan fabi*, four bolts of thick blue machine-made fabric, probably valued at 1,120,000 *yuan fabi*,[9] and about three pounds of cotton. The marriage contract was thus settled.[10]

On the thirteenth day of the second month in the lunar calendar,[11] Peng'er followed her mother to a local event in a neighboring village where she ran into her former fiancé, Zhang Bo, a handsome young man.[12] Although the two may have met when they were little, as the Fengs and the Zhangs had a history of exchanging women,[13] this was the first time they had met as adults.[14] On this occasion the two young people exchanged words, which no one knows exactly. The legal document claims that Peng'er expressed her wish to marry Zhang Bo but felt

not fully convey its meaning. In its original meaning, it was an action of two parties, indicating violation on both sides. The translation of "purchased marriage" seems to be placing the blame only on the male party, which is not only a biased term but a total misconception. I therefore translate this term into "buying/selling marriages," which covers both sides of the action. However, in a specific situation I will use either "buying" for those who paid for a marriage, or "selling" for those who gained money from a marriage/engagement.

8 SPA 15–842, *Feng v. Zhang*. Also see "Ma Xiwu tonzhi shenpan fangshi" (Comrade Ma Xiwu's Way of Judging, abbr. Ma's Way), *Jiefang ribao* (Liberation Daily), March 13, 1944.

9 According to *Huachi xian zhi* (*Huachi County gazetteer* [Lanzhou: Gansu renmin chubanshe, 2004], 289), a bolt of plain fabric produced in Xi'an cost 280,000 yuan fabi in 1943. Due to inflation in the 1940s (see the following for the cause and the rate of inflation) and the underdeveloped market system of this region, trade largely depended on barter.

10 SPA 15–842, *Feng v. Zhang*.

11 Although the SGN Border governments all adopted the common calendar in their official documents, villagers continued using the lunar calendar in daily life, especially for family and community events. See the analysis of the exact time in Chapter 3.

12 SPA 15–842, *Feng v. Zhang*; Feng Zhiqin (Peng'er), "Huiyi Ma Xiwu tongzhi" (In Memory of Comrade Ma Xiwu) in *Gansu wenshi ziliao xuanji, di 12 ji* (Selected Documents of Gansu History and Culture, vol. XII) (Lanzhou: Gansu sheng zhengxie [print], 1982), 145–53.

13 Interview with She Xingfa, July 21, 2005. She Xingfa was the director of the Huachi County Bureau for Cultural Development at the time. He accompanied me to Feng Zhiqin's village and introduced me to Feng. According to the contemporary literature and She Xingfa, the most recent marital connection between the two families was that Peng'er's patrilineal aunt married Zhang Jincai's patrilineal cousin. See Yang Zhengfa, *Feng Zhiqin, Liu Qiao'er* (Feng Zhiqin, Liu Qiao'er) (Beijing: Zhongguo guangbo dianshi chubanshe, 2004), 21.

14 The interview with Feng Zhiqin (July 21, 2005) confirmed that they did talk to each other, but some later versions state that they never talked to each other and never even met. See, for example, reports from *Liberation Daily* and *Xinhua Daily* (see Chapter 5).

bad about her recently arranged marriage and her inability to escape from "the execrable family environment." Meanwhile, "Zhang Bo also expressed his adoration of Peng'er. It was at this time that the two decided to be a couple."[15] In 2005, when I interviewed Feng Zhiqin (Peng'er)[16] and asked her what they had discussed, she recalled that they did not talk much but did remember one sentence she had said: "We should not let our thing drop."[17] Given the time and the local context, this sentence does sound like the promise of a commitment.

Zhang Bo returned home and told his father about his meeting with Peng'er. Zhang Jincai had heard about Feng Yangui's new arrangement for Peng'er, to which Zhang Bo now confirmed. On March 18, he gathered about twenty people from his clan, including Zhang Bo, to go to Feng's village. After walking about 30 *li* (about nine miles), this group arrived at the gate of the Feng residence at midnight. Startled in the darkness, the Feng family gave up any attempt at resisting and let the Zhangs take Peng'er away. Once the Zhangs brought Peng'er to their home, a wedding was held immediately.[18] After this frightening night, Feng Yangui sued the Zhangs at the Office of Justice in Huachi County (*Huachi xian sifa chu* 华池县司法处) for kidnapping his daughter. On May 3, 1943, the County Office (court) delivered its verdict, sentencing Zhang Jincai to six months of labor and also arresting and imprisoning Zhang Bo for kidnapping, while invalidating the marriage between Peng'er and Zhang Bo.[19]

Beginning in 1939, when the CCP stabilized its control of the SGN Border Region, the government launched a series of social reform programs that included campaigns against footbinding, gambling, opium-smoking, and many other habits and customs the revolutionary government viewed as backward. The BR government promulgated a marriage regulation (referred to as "the 1939 regulation" in the following discussion), and intended to revolutionize marriage and the family. The 1939 regulation (see below) brought a modern concept of marriage, one that had been shaped in previous decades in the milieu of urban areas under the strong influence of the West, into a rural area largely left behind in the drastic changes of the early twentieth century. Unlike southern China and the coastal regions, this area had experienced no

15 SPA 15–842, *Feng v. Zhang*.
16 In 1957, Feng Peng'er received her official name of Feng Zhiqin that, according to her, was for the purpose of organizational registration. Also see Chapter 7.
17 Interview with Feng Zhiqin, July 21, 2005.
18 Feng Zhiqin, "Huiyi Ma Xiwu tongzhi."
19 SPA 15–842, *Feng v. Zhang*. Also see Feng Zhiqin, "Huiyi Ma Xiwu tongzhi"; "Ma Xiwu tonzhi shenpan fangshi."

transitional stage from the imperial system, through gradual opening up, to the "modernizing" projects of the late nineteenth to early twentieth century. Thus, the political insulation, socioeconomic conditions, cultural atmosphere, and geographic ecology of this locality presented a strong challenge to the CCP's revolutionary projects. The case of *Feng v. Zhang* involved many local practices that the revolutionary government had tried to eradicate, only to be blocked by local resistance. In the conflict between the revolutionary state and the BR communities, the geographical, social, and cultural settings of the case, as in many other cases in the SGNBR, played important roles.

I. From the imperial frontier to the revolutionary base: state-building in Longdong and Shaanbei in the 1930s

Huachi County is located in the eastern part of Gansu Province (see Map 2), a region traditionally called Longdong (literally, the east region of Gansu – "Long" is the abbreviation for Gansu Province; the area is today's Qingyang City).[20] It was one of the most poverty-stricken areas in northern China during most of the twentieth century.[21] While drastic social, cultural, and political changes spread across the coastal regions and cities in eastern and southern China, this area in China's heartland remained basically intact.[22]

It was the communists who entered this political and administrative backwater and launched state-building projects. In 1934, the communist Liu Zhidan 刘志丹 (1903–36), a native of Bao'an County (today's Zhidan County) in northern Shaanxi (Shaanbei) who received training at the famous Huangpu Military Academy in Guangzhou, created a small revolutionary base in Nanliang Township (*xiang* 乡) of Huachi County. In the next year, the Red Army and the Central Committee of the CCP from the Jiangxi Soviet revolutionary base arrived in the region after the Long March. The two forces merged and expanded the revolutionary

[20] The administrative name of this region had been changed several times but "Longdong" indicates its geographical location, which has not changed. In order to accord with the historical records, I use the name Qingyang Prefecture for the Ming and Qing periods, Longdong for the revolutionary period, and Qingyang District/City for the period after 1949.

[21] Qingyang is still one of the most poverty-stricken regions in today's China. Among eight counties in its jurisdiction, six are under the poverty line by the Chinese national standard at least in 2007.

[22] This region, as with the neighboring Shaanbei area, had fallen far behind in the social and economic development of the country since the late Qing. See Keating, *Two Revolutions*, 22–5.

base to Shaanbei and southern Ningxia. The SGNBR thus began to take shape.[23] After the Red Army marched to northern Shaanxi at the end of 1935 and then moved to Yan'an in January 1937, Shaanbei became the center of the communist revolutionary base, where the CCP Central Committee and military headquarters were located. Compared to other revolutionary bases in Shanxi, Hebei, and Shandong that bore the brunt of the Japanese invasion,[24] the Longdong area was remote, and the war against the Japanese had less impact on people's daily lives, especially after 1939.[25] It was in this comparably peaceful environment that the BR government launched its state-building and social reform projects.

Geography, history, and population of the Longdong subregion

As Pauline Keating points out, the Border Region was never an economically or socially homogeneous area.[26] Geographically and socially speaking, Longdong 陇东, of all the subregions (*fen qu* 分区) such as Yanshu 延属 (main/western part of Shaanbei), Guanzhong 关中 (covering small parts of both central Shaanxi and southern Gansu), Sanbian 三边 (southern Ningxia), and Suide 绥德 (northeastern part of Shaanbei), was closest to the Yanshu and Sanbian subregions that composed the majority of the Border Region's territory (see the SGNBR, Map 2). As a geographic region, Longdong is located in the east end of the long horizontal tract of Gansu Province, which shapes an enclave bounded by north Shaanxi and southeast Ningxia. It had been under the jurisdiction of Shaanxi Province up to 1669, when it was incorporated into Gansu Province by the Qing court.[27] Topographically, both Longdong and northern Shaanxi are situated on the same terrain of loess highland in northern China, some of which was favorable for agricultural production. Unfortunately, in the 1940s the revolutionary government controlled the most impoverished areas stretching from the center to the north

[23] For the local revolutionary activities in Shaanbei and Longdong in the 1930s and the relations between the CCP Central Committee from the south and the local revolutionaries such as Liu Zhidan, Xie Zichang, and Xi Zhongxun, see Wen Xiang's well-documented work, *Gaoceng en yuan yu Xi Zhongxun – cong Xibei dao Beijing* (Xi Zhongxun's Grudges with Other Senior Communists) (Hong Kong: Mirror Books, 2008).

[24] Goodman, *Social and Political Change in Revolutionary China*, 13–19.

[25] From 1938 to 1941 Japanese airplanes bombed Yan'an City many times but its army was never able to cross the Yellow River. As a natural barrier, the river goes along the eastern border of the SGNBR and becomes the divider between Shaanbei and Shanxi. There were some conflicts between the CCP army and the Nationalist army along the borderline, but the SGNBR was able to stabilize after 1939.

[26] Keating, *Two Revolutions*, 1–13.

[27] Qingyang diqu zhi bianzuan weiyuan hui, *Qingyang diqu zhi* (Qingyang District Records) (Lanzhou: Lanzhou daxue chubanshe, 1993), 222.

and northeast, where the landforms included the rugged hills and steep ravines of Longdong and Shaanbei.[28] Thus the SGNBR took shape by integrating border areas from three provinces on a similar geographical, social, and ecological foundation, especially in the central to the western part of the SGNBR (see Map 2). It also explains why Liu Zhidan, after his initial revolt failed in northern Shaanxi, moved to Huachi for his reemergence in the 1930s, and why this region became an inseparable part of the SGNBR.

Due to constant wars and its barren lands, the huge northern part of Longdong, as well as its contiguous Shaanbei areas, were places described as a "vast land with sparse population" (*di guang ren xi* 地广人稀) in historical records.[29] The majority of residents were mixed progenies of ancient indigenous minorities and Han military soldiers or immigrants.[30] In the mid-sixteenth century, the population of Qingyang Prefecture was about 213,000, making the average population density eight to nine persons per square kilometer.[31] However, this population was distributed unevenly; the areas of flat tableland in the south abutting central Shaanxi were much more densely populated, while the northern region abutting northern Shaanxi and southern Ningxia had fewer residents. After the reigns of Kangxi, Yongzheng, and Qianlong (1662–1795), the population of Qingyang Prefecture reached its peak at 986,000 in 1820, making the population density up to 66 persons per square kilometer. In the late nineteenth century, the Muslim Rebellion (1861–73) and the Nian Rebellion (1853–68) caused a great drop in the population, plummeting to about 241,000 in 1908, back to the numbers of the Ming period. The population growth remained slow from the beginning of the twentieth century, reaching 318,000 in 1928 or 11.7 persons per square kilometer. From 1928 to 1929 a severe famine hit Longdong, but the effect of the famine on the change in local population remains unknown.[32] The population was unevenly distributed, with a much denser population in the south, while northern counties such as Huanxian had only 13,000 people, or 1.5 persons per square kilometer.

[28] Longdong had been known under the name Qingyang but the Republican government reinstated its historical name, Longdong. To distinguish the name of the geographical area from its administrative name, I use "Longdong region" to refer to the geographical area and "Longdong subregion" to indicate the part occupied by the BR government.

[29] *Qingyang diqu* zhi, 468–9.

[30] Even today in this region the many unique surnames remind people of their remote nomadic ancestors. See *Huachi xian zhi*, 156.

[31] *Qingyang diqu zhi*, 498–500.

[32] Although the local records portray a dreadful picture of the 1928–9 famine, there are no data available for the number of population after 1928. See *Qingyang diqu zhi*, 471–2, 498–500

Between 1940 and 1944, Longdong subregion (only the northern part of Longdong controlled by the revolutionary government) had a population of around 266,000, about ten persons per square kilometer.[33] Given that the communists controlled the most barren and hilly region in the north and northeast, this number is evidence of a successful policy of attracting refugees and immigrants from the zones of war and disasters, and providing a stable life for local residents. Meanwhile, with these newcomers also came numerous conflicts with local residents and other immigrants over land occupation and ownership. Such conflicts became one of several sources of community unease in the 1940s (see Chapter 5).

The vast land of this region was previously controlled by a small number of absentee landlords who resided in Qingyang City or Xi'an, the capital of Shaanxi Province; most local peasants were either landless or tenants, thus posing little obstacle when Liu Zhidan's revolutionary force redistributed the land in villages.[34] By 1941, when the marriage reform was proceeding, most of Longdong subregion had completed the "land revolution" (*tudi geming* 土地革命), as the locals called it.[35] Compared to other subregions of the SGNBR, which only began to carry out the policy of reducing peasants' burden of rent and loan interest after the establishment of the Second United Front, this region was more advanced in land reform.[36] Through the land revolution, the majority of farmers in this region became small landowners. As Mark Selden points out, the CCP's land policy did indeed win the hearts of local farmers,[37] which then created a solid foundation for the subsequent marriage reform. In my 2005 interview, I asked Feng Zhiqin whether her father felt resentment when the government penalized him for "selling a marriage." Feng responded that in fact her father liked the CCP because he had received about 30 *mu* of land in the land revolution. Her father even served as the village head after that event.[38] On the other hand, the CCP's reform of marriages and families, which sought to eliminate many local customs, encountered stronger resistance.

[33] *Qingyang diqu zhi*, 498–500.
[34] *Huachi xian zhi*, 1071–2.
[35] Liu Fengge (chief comp.), *Longdong de tudi geming yundong* (Land revolution in Longdong area) (Qingyang: Zhonggong Qingyang diwei dangshi ziliao zhengji bangongshi, 1992), 2–44.
[36] Keating, *Two Revolutions*, 65–75.
[37] Selden, *The Yenan Way in Revolutionary China*, 79–94.
[38] Interview with Feng Zhiqin, July 21, 2005. It is worth noting that in answering my simple question, Feng Zhiqin made a connection between her father's acquisition of land and her marriage case.

Political history, society, and culture of the locality

The geographical location, character, and political administration of the region shaped its unique social customs and cultural traditions and made it difficult for the CCP government to implement its marriage regulation, particularly in the early period. As a frontier, the imperial management of the region prior to the Qing placed much more weight on its military role than on its civil development. Up to the late Qing, the territory of Qingyang Prefecture was divided into six jurisdictions that included the prefectural seat (Qingyang *fu*), one district (Ningzhou), and four counties (Huanxian, Anhua, Heshui, and Zhenning), in which half of today's Huachi territory belonged to Anhua County (later Qingyang County, today's Qingcheng County) and another half to Heshui County. As a small township, Huachi remained insignificant up to 1934, when the revolutionary Shaan-Gan Border Soviet government, established by Liu Zhidan and Xi Zhongxun 习仲勋 (1913–2002), redrew the administrative map of its controlled region by establishing a number of new counties[39] including Huachi, a combination of two sections from the previous Heshui and Qingyang.[40]

Delayed development of political administration brought about a complex cultural condition. Weak civil administration in imperial times made the region much less influenced by Confucian doctrine, since imperial state ideology penetrated the local society through a dynastic school system and civil service examinations. Although these institutions had a presence in the region, it still lagged behind the advanced areas of southern China.[41] In the entire span of the Ming Dynasty (1368–1644), Qingyang Prefecture, under the jurisdiction of the Shaanxi governor (*buzhengshi* 布政使), produced a total of forty-two *jinshi*, the highest degree-holders in the civil service examinations.[42] Given the fact that the

[39] For example, the new counties of Quzi, Chishui, Chiqing, Xinzheng, and Xinning. See *Huachi xian zhi*, 59–60.

[40] *Huachi xian zhi*, 59–60.

[41] For the numbers of *jinshi* from the southern provinces, see P'ingti Ho, *The Ladder of Success in Imperial China: Aspects of Social Mobility, 1368–1911* (New York: Columbia University Press, 1962), 227–9.

[42] This number comes from *Qingyang fu zhi* (Qingyang Prefecture Gazetteer, compiled by Yang Zaofeng [Gansu renmin chubanshe, 2001 print], 681–83) in early Qing. However, recent study indicates that there were a total of forty-nine *jinshi* during the Ming era. See Ma Xiao, "Ming dai xibei keyu yu shehui huanjing – yi Qingyang fu jinshi yu juren de shi kong fenbu, tedian yiji chengyin wei xiansuo" (The Civil Service Examinations in the Northwestern Region during the Ming Time – In the Cases of *Jinshi* and *Juren* of Qingyang Prefecture and Their Historical and Geographical Distribution), *Ningxia daxue xuebao* (Ren wen shehui kexue ban) (*The Journal of Ningxia University* [Humanities and Social Sciences Edition]) 32(4) (July 2010): 118–30. I assume that the different numbers are caused by the jurisdictional remapping in the Qing, the Republican, and the People's Republic periods.

residents of this region were mostly descendants of Ming military households and agricultural immigrants, this marked a considerable achievement, even if other parts of China produced many more degree-holders.[43] However, due to the fact that the political importance of this region had been largely reduced during the Qing period (see below), its cultural and educational development was also neglected. Thus the number of *jinshi* degree-holders of Qingyang Prefecture went down to only thirteen for the 267 years of the entire Qing period.[44] Given its increased population in the High Qing (*c*. 1662–1795), this was a serious setback.

This cultural lag can be generally attributed to the quality decline in dynastic schools empire-wide and the small number of academies in the region, which failed to popularize education and nurture advanced scholars. Before the 1870s, Qingyang Prefecture had a total of five academies, but the most important ones, such as Fengcheng Academy and Ningjiang Academy, had been ransacked during the Muslim Rebellion. After the 1880s, when both traditional and reformed academies mushroomed in Jiangnan and the coastal areas, only two new academies were established in Qingyang's territory, both located in today's Qingcheng County.[45] From 1912 to 1939 when most of the nation had been transformed into the modern/Western educational system, not a single modern-style secondary school was built in the entire Longdong region.[46] Although eighteen *sishu* (private schools of traditional style) were built during the Republican period (1912–34) and recruited a total of 260 students, the region's modern-style elementary schools were all founded by the communist government in the 1930s and 1940s. In the entire jurisdiction of Huachi, there were only three (modern) elementary schoolteachers and about twenty *sishu* teachers by 1934. It was not until 1956 that Huachi County set up its first junior middle school.[47] The county, as well as its surrounding regions, had such a high illiteracy rate in the 1930s that, as the local gazetteer described it, farmers could not find one literate person in a hundred *li* around a village to read letters from outside or to write spring festival scrolls for them at the Chinese New Year.[48] The undeveloped educational sphere set preconditions for the way the CCP government managed this region and exercised its administrative and legal

[43] Ma Xiao, "Ming dai xibei keyu yu shehui huanjing," 120.

[44] Chen Shangmin, "Qingdai Gansu jinshi de dili fenbu" (The Geographical Distribution of *Jinshi* Degree-holders in Gansu during the Qing), *Zhongguo lishi dili luncong* (Chinese Historic-Geography Journal) 24(4) (October 2009): 71–80.

[45] *Qingyang diqu zhi*, 367–68; *Qingyang xian zhi* (Qingyang County Gazetteer) (Lanzhou: Gansu renmin chubanshe, 1993), 389–90.

[46] *Qingyang xian zhi*, 406.

[47] *Huachi xian zhi*, 651, 684, 673.

[48] *Huachi xian zhi*, 677.

power, given that the party lacked educated manpower. As Chapters 3 and 5 show, the real extension of the CCP administration and the effectiveness of its legal system became possible when a large number of educated people arrived in the BR in the late 1930s and early 1940s (see Chapters 3, 5, and 6).

The local culture rested on an indigenous belief system that was a combination of animistic belief, ancestor worship, Daoism, and Buddhism. This region was once dominated by Buddhism; however, due to frequent wars, flows of population, the low number of residents, and the influence of Mongolian steppe culture, in the twentieth century Buddhism was fully localized and mixed with regional beliefs. The most influential cultural symbols to ordinary villagers were local deities such as the Land-god (*tudi ye* 土地爷), the Jade Emperor (*yu di* 玉帝), the Child-giving goddess (*song zi niangniang* 送子娘娘), and the spirits of natural items surrounding them, as well as past local worthies. In addition to this historical and religious influence, most people of the region shaped their cultural values from local folk songs and traditional dramas performed at local fairs.[49] As Chapter 2 shows, women's views on marriage and love were largely built on this cultural mixture. It was this political and cultural lag that created a gap for the locals to accept the new ideas introduced by the CCP.

The underdevelopment of this region was related not only to its geographical and historical inheritance but also to its changing jurisdiction and declining political and military position during the Qing. First, due to the fact that the Qing imperial territory had reached the vast Mongolian steppe and northwestern frontier, Qingyang became an inland region, less important militarily, no longer needed for imperial defense.[50] Second, before the Qing controlled Ningxia, Qinghai, and Xinjiang, Qingyang occupied an intermediary position in which the Shaanxi governor, who acted as a representative of the imperial court, managed the vast region of western China. Nonetheless, when the imperial frontier expanded to today's Xinjiang and Qinghai, Lanzhou, the new capital of Gansu, became the political center of the new frontier and helped the Qing court manage the western region.[51] Qingyang Prefecture thus lost its role as intermediary and was less important on the Qing political map. Third, placing the Qingyang region under the jurisdiction of Gansu Province distanced Qingyang from the provincial political center and social and cultural network in Lanzhou. In addition,

49 *Huachi xian zhi*, 873–5, 879; *Qingyang diqu zhi*, 934–6; *Chong xiu Zhenyuan zhi* (Zhenyuan County Gazetteer, recompiled) (Lanzhou: Chengwen Publisher, 1935), 648.
50 *Qingyang diqu zhi*, 38.
51 *Qingyang diqu zhi*, 222.

splitting Qingyang away from Shaanxi Province cut off its previous political and social ties with Xi'an. Qingyang thus became a corner forgotten by both the Gansu and Shaanxi governors, making it an insulated region hardly touched by either the imperial court's official policies of state-building or the social and political movements emanating from the coastal region in the early twentieth century.[52] This tendency continued in the Republican period because this region was excluded from the national developing blueprint of the GMD government. In the 1930s and 1940s the most important railway, the Long-Hai Railway, which was intended to link western China to the more advanced coastal region, also left Qingyang behind in its section from central Shaanxi to Gansu. As discussed in Chapters 3 and 5, this century-long underdevelopment created a political vacuum that attracted communist revolutionaries such as Liu Zhidan and Xi Zhongxun, who came to build up their revolutionary base in this area.

Comparably speaking, the southern area of Longdong, contiguous to central Shaanxi, was a more populous and richer place, and also politically and culturally influenced by the orthodox ideology of central Shaanxi and the urbanism of Xi'an. The northern area was under the influence of a more heterodox steppe culture and felt much less control by the Republican Gansu government in Lanzhou and little influence from Xi'an's cultural and economic sphere. In the mid-1930s, the Shaanxi-Gansu soviet government, established by Liu Zhidan and Xi Zhongxun, occupied the much richer southern part of Longdong, but in the 1939 conflict with the Nationalist army, supported by local merchants and big landlords, the SGNBR lost the southern part and had to withdraw to the poorer northern part of Longdong, which had been abandoned by both the Qing and Republican states for a long time.

In the first quarter of the twentieth century, national political changes had little impact on the locality. In contrast to southern provinces and coastal areas where the local gentry were actively involved in the late Qing constitutional movement, the gentry in the Qingyang Prefecture took no action until the revolution knocked on the door. In January 1912, when the Republican polity was established, the Shaan-Gan imperial governor unwillingly released the news of the Qing emperor's abdication to the public, but only recognized the revolutionary regime several months later. As a gesture to catch up with national trends, the prefect mobilized

[52] During my visits to this region in 2005 and 2007, local officials constantly expressed their resentment over being split from Shaanxi and ignored by Lanzhou, and excitedly discussed how to get back Shaanxi through redrawing the administrative map. Part of the reason is the central government's oil policy in the past decade, which favors Shaanbei but leaves Qingyang out.

the local gentries of five counties to set up county assemblies. However, six months later all the assemblies were dismissed by Yuan Shikai's government, an action that raised no complaints from the local gentry. When Yuan Shikai announced the restoration of the imperial system, the Longdong administration supported it.[53]

Although the local elites took a strongly conservative stance toward the social reform and revolutions of coastal areas and big cities in southern China, the regional turmoil in the late Qing and early Republican periods nevertheless devastated the area, especially when the centralized authority collapsed in 1911. Since the late Ming, the Qingyang region had been a site for peasant rebellions, secret societies, and banditry. Li Zicheng's 李自成 (1606–45) uprising in the late Ming, the Muslim Rebellion, and the Nian peasant army in the late Qing ravaged the region. From the 1910s, the Society of the Elder Brothers (*ge lao hui* 哥老会) and the Red Spear Society (*hong qiang hui* 红枪会) had a strong presence in this region that spread to many rural villages up to the 1940s. During the first two decades of the Republic, various warlords coexisted in this region, along with countless bandits and small secret societies.[54]

In contrast, though Westerners gradually entered the Longdong/Shaanbei area, their influence was very superficial. Although Western missionaries arrived in the region, they received little success in converting the locals.[55] Meanwhile, the radical movements of the 1920s in the big cities and the coastal areas caused only a couple of light ripples in this backwater region. The local elite responded to the New Culture Movement and the May Fourth Movement by organizing an anti-footbinding society, which had no influence beyond the county seat of Qingyang. In 1928, a small communist-led guerrilla team fled to Huachi from central Shaanxi after a failed uprising that was quickly smashed by local warlords. In 1930, Liu Zhidan, Xi Zhongxun, Gao Gang 高岗 (1905–54), and Ma Xiwu arrived in the region to organize the underground communist movement; they eventually established a revolutionary base in Nanliang Township of today's Huachi in 1934.[56]

II. Marriage reform and local society

In 1939, when the SGN Border government eventually stabilized the territory, it embarked on intertwined projects of state-building and social reform. The BR government worked on state-building through

[53] *Qingyang diqu zhi*, 47–8, 50.
[54] *Qingyang diqu zhi*, 47–55; *Huachi xian zhi*, 20–1.
[55] *Qingyang diqu zhi*, 589–91.
[56] *Huachi xian zhi*, 20–4.

establishing an effective administrative system at the village level and a sketchy judicial system down to county level (see Chapter 3). Social reform involved the promulgation of the 1939 marriage regulation, which marked the communist ideal of family reform put into practice. The legal system served as a powerful instrument for carrying out this project. However, the communists quickly found that social reality was totally different from the theories on which the 1939 regulation was shaped. They had to reconcile their reform ideals with the situation on the ground.

The 1939 regulation and marriage reform

As leaders of an urban intellectual movement beginning in the 1920s, the early communists organized female urban factory workers in a struggle for better working conditions and higher wages. Nonetheless, the efforts of female leaders in changing women's position in general were not highly appreciated by the top communist leadership, which was dominated by male intellectuals.[57] The early communist leaders also paid little attention to the practical issues of marriage, family reform, and rural women's conditions until a soviet government was established at the Jiangxi rural revolutionary base.[58] In response to demands from rural women who suffered from poverty and unhappy family lives, the Jiangxi Soviet government issued a marriage regulation in 1931, influenced by the 1926 USSR code, which granted women freedom in marriage, particularly in divorce.[59] However, previous studies on marriage reform in the Jiangxi revolutionary base have observed that the real conditions of the implementation and effectiveness of this regulation are difficult to discern due to lack of concrete sources.[60] This regulation was revised into a Marriage Law in 1934 that added a clause to restrain the matrimonial status of Red Army soldiers upon their wives' demands for divorce, an issue discussed in Chapters 2 and 4.[61] Given that the Long March began soon after, this law was apparently never put into practice.

57 Gilmartin, *Engendering the Chinese Revolution*.
58 Stranahan, *Yan'an Women and the Communist Party*, 9–24; Davin, *Woman-work*, 21–3.
59 "Zhonghua Suweiai Gongheguo hunyin tiaoli" (The Marriage Regulation of the Chinese Soviet Republic) in *Jiangxi Su qu funü yundong shiliao xuanbian* (Selected Documents of the Women's Movement in the Jiangxi Soviet Region) (Nanchang: Jiangxi renmin chubanshe, 1982), 33–5; also see Meijer, *Marriage Law and Policy*, 49–53.
60 Meijer, *Marriage Law and Policy*, 42–3; Davin, *Woman-work*, 28–9; Stranahan, *Yan'an Women and the Communist Party*, 9–24.
61 "Zhonghua Suweiai gongheguo hunyin fa, 1934" (Marriage Law of the Chinese Soviet Republic, 1934), *Jiangxi Su qu funü yundong shiliao xuanbian*, 176–8.

After the SGN Border government was established, it issued an improved version of the 1934 Marriage Law in 1939.[62] In a brief text, the 1939 regulation expressed a general principle that epitomized the CCP's ideal model of marriage. It not only reinforced monogamy as the only form of marriage, but also set the basis of marriage as an individual's free will (*zhao benren zhi ziyou yizhi* 照本人之自由意志). The principle of the regulation, simplified into the slogan "freedom of marriage" (*hunyin ziyou*), was broadcast to a wide audience of local villagers. The regulation also showed the state reformative determination, which voiced a strong stand in banning many malpractices in the locality, such as concubinage (*na qie* 纳妾), bigamy (*chong hun* 重婚), the foster child as prospective daughter-in-law (*tongyangxi* 童养媳)[63] or working boy/man as prospective son-in-law (*zhannianhan* 站年汉),[64] buying/selling marriages (*mai mai hunyin* 买卖婚姻), arranged marriages (*baoban hunyin* 包办婚姻), and marriages by any type of force (*qiang po* 强迫). To ameliorate the "bad" custom of underage marriage (*zao hun* 早婚) prevalent in the locality, it set up an eligible age for marriage: women at eighteen and men at twenty. As a modern state, the BR government required the entire course of a marriage to fall under the state's supervision: all marriages and divorces should be registered at the local government office,[65] a requirement intended to overwrite the local custom that legitimated a marriage through social ceremony. The most important content of the 1939 regulation was setting up a series of conditions, such as bigamy, incompatible relations, adultery, family abuse, abandonment, and incurable disease, as eligible grounds for ex parte divorce (see the discussion of specific conditions below and in other chapters).[66] The 1939 regulation embodied the revolutionary state's intent to modernize traditional marriage and family.

[62] "Shaan-Gan-Ning bianqu hunyin tiao li, 1939" (Marriage Regulation of the SGN Border Government, April 4, 1939), in *Shaan-Gan-Ning bianqu funü yundong wenxian ziliao xuan bian* (A Documentary Collection on the SGN Women's Movement) (Xi'an: Shaanxi Provincial Women's Federation [compiled and printed], 1982), 54–6. For the full translation of the 1934 Marriage Law and the 1939 marriage regulation in English, see Meijer, *Marriage Law and Policy*, Appendices, 283–4, 285–7.

[63] Philip Huang argues that the current English terms for *tongyangxi* ("child bride" or "adopted daughter-in-law") do not accurately convey the meaning of the term and suggests using the Chinese term directly (see *Chinese Civil Justice*, 12n). I agree and also adopt the term *tongyangxi* in the following discussion.

[64] This type of prospective son-in-law could be a teenage boy or an adult. I use the Chinese term *zhannianhan* in the following.

[65] As mentioned in Chapter 5, this marriage registration had little success in its implementation.

[66] "Shaan-Gan-Ning bianqu hunyin tiao li, 1939."

However, the implementation of the regulation resulted in strong protest from local villagers, especially the families of young males. This included the protest from Zhang Jincai and his son Zhang Bo, whose previous engagement was invalidated by the county government, resulting in the loss of their *caili*. Their discontent with the reform merged with many others' and became a source of local pressure on the government. Facing this criticism, the BR government revised the regulation in 1944 and then again in 1946 (see Chapter 4 for details).

From the 1970s to 1980s, evaluations of the revisions of the marriage regulations polarized scholars. Meijer's pioneering study on the policy of marriage reforms offers a positive appraisal of its revolutionary nature.[67] Davin is convinced that though the revisions of the marriage regulations compromised the revolutionary principle of marriage, this compromise came about due to "the military and political situation" faced by the Border Region in 1942.[68] It was Davin's sympathetic defense that opened the door for later scholars to question the motive of the revision of the marriage regulations.

In the early 1980s, some Western scholars who visited China were apparently disappointed that socialism had not liberated Chinese women and had not brought dramatic improvements to their lives. These scholars believed that this unchanged condition originated from the revolution's failed promise to women, which could be traced back to the marriage regulations revised in the 1940s. Western observers assumed that the revision was the result of the CCP backing off from its previous idealism and radicalism in the cause of women's liberation in order to gain male farmers' support for its wars against the Japanese and the Nationalists.[69] By attributing the revised policy on women and marriage to the result of a negotiation between rural males as an entity and the all-male leaders of the CCP, this view ignores the dynamics between local farmers' activities (including women) and communist state power. It also overlooks the incompatibility of a radical urban-originated and foreign-imported idea with the social and cultural reality of rural regions. The case of Feng Yangui abolishing his daughter's engagement and the Zhangs' kidnapping of Peng'er exemplified this point.

[67] Meijer, *Marriage Law and Policy*, 42–5.

[68] See Davin, *Woman-work*, 35–40. Unfortunately, she does not provide a solid case in her study and also assumes that the 1939 regulation and its revised terms were not carried out in the area (p. 38). This statement seems to contradict the legal records I have discovered.

[69] See Johnson, *Women, the Family and Peasant Revolution*; Stacey, *Patriarchy and Socialist Revolution*; Andors, *Unfinished Liberation*.

Social structure of the locality and the family revolution

Many of the scholars mentioned above work from the perspective of a totalistic China and on a general assumption that all of Chinese society was dominated by the "Confucian patriarchal family."[70] In reality, the Longdong region formed a strong contrast to the previous CCP revolutionary bases in the south, and the family structure and marriage traditions also departed from the stereotype of "Confucian patriarchy" attacked by the May Fourth discourse and described by some Western scholars.[71] In the 1930s, anthropologist Fei Xiaotong (Hsiao-tong Fei), through examining village life in the Yangzi Delta, pointed out that most Chinese families in the area were small in size, while the large families described in the May Fourth discourse existed only in small numbers in the urban and town areas. Fei demonstrated that the majority of Chinese of lower social strata in rural areas followed this same pattern of small families.[72] Recent scholarship on a village in Hunan further confirms this point, and declares that the large patriarchal families denounced by the New Culture Movement were not only few in number but also existed only as a Confucian ideal of the family, rather than a widespread social reality.[73]

Scholarly works on northern China show that this small family situation was even more dominant there. In the case that there has been no specific research on family structure in the Longdong subregion, we can extrapolate from scholarly works on families and clans of a neighboring region that shared a geographical, social, and cultural resemblance to the Longdong area. Qin Yan and Hu Hong'an's research on clans in northern Shaanxi indicates that most families of middle- to lower-class farmers had only two or three generations living together. Large clans, many of which arrived in the wave of early Ming immigration, did indeed exist, but never in the conditions described in the May Fourth discourse. Due to the slanting land, the low productivity of the soil, and the availability of vast virgin lands in the region, large clans had been continuously breaking down into smaller branches and spreading

70 Johnson, *Women, the Family and Peasant Revolution*, 7–26; Stacey, *Patriarchy and Socialist Revolution*, 15–65; Davin, *Woman-work*, 35–7.

71 See Stacey, *Patriarchy and Socialist Revolution*, 15–65. Although Stacey realized that most peasants had small family size, she still makes an undifferentiated definition of the Confucian patriarchal family by equating elite families and peasant families. See her pp. 21–6.

72 Hsiao-tong Fei, *Peasant Life in China: A Field Study of Country Life in the Yangtze Valley* (London: Kegan Paul, Trench, Trubner & Co., 1939), 27–9.

73 See Tan Tongxue, *Qiao cun you dao: zhuanxing xiangcun de diode, quanli yu shehui jiegou* (The Way of Qiao Village: Morality, Power and Social Structure in a Transitional Village) (Beijing: Sanlian shudian, 2010), 1–14.

out into different hamlets or moving to other regions.[74] Their research also points out that even though the residents of one locale might originate from the same ancestor or belong to one clan, people lived in their own individual households with independent landownership, which led to various disparities in each family's economic condition. Assorted forms of families, constantly in transition, have existed in this region since the early Ming. For instance, the majority were nuclear families of a couple with their unmarried child(ren). When the children grew up, this nuclear family might temporarily develop into a trunk family or a united family, composed of parents with one or more married sons as well as other unmarried child(ren).[75] The region's tradition of dividing the household contributed to the smaller size of families, since it mainly occurred when brothers were married. Once a house was divided, this trunk family or united family would break down, and a number of new nuclear families came into being. This model continued until another circle was complete.[76]

The local gazetteers of Qingyang and Huachi seem to confirm that this region has never had large families. The population of the average household was four to six persons per household from the Han (206 BCE–220 CE) time up to the Ming and the Qing.[77] In the twentieth century, the average household in Longdong region, including Huachi, contained about four people in 1934 and increased to six in 1947.[78] The archival documents of the SGN High Court also prove this point: most litigants had small families, ranging from two to eight persons, with only a few over ten. Furthermore, the fluidity of the population in this region and other factors also contributed to the smaller family size. For instance, seasonal migrant workers, trade caravan stevedores, runaway wives, and drifters looking for food resulted in the instability of families, while a short life expectancy and high infant mortality rate also prevented families from growing in size (see Chapter 2). It was thus very rare to see a large household with extended families in which "five generations (of males) under one roof" lived together, as described in

[74] Qin Yan and Hu Hong'an, *Qing dai yi lai de Shaanbei zongzu yu shehui bianqian* (Changes in Clans and Society in Northern Shaanxi since the Qing) (Xi'an: Xibei gongye daxue chubanshe, 2004), 24–49.

[75] Some research on European family structure in the sixteenth century also shows a similar pattern. See Stephanie Coontz, *The Social Origins of Private Life: A History of American Families, 1600–1900* (New York: Verso, 1988), 18–19.

[76] Qin and Hu, *Qing dai yi lai de Shaanbei zongzu yu shehui bianqian*, 66. Fei's research shows that in the Jiangnan area, dividing the household sometimes even began with one son's marriage (see Fei, *Peasant Life in China*, 56–79).

[77] *Huachi xian zhi*, 157.

[78] *Qingyang diqu zhi*, 550; *Huachi xian zhi*, 144.

Johnson's and Davin's books[79] or the situation in Ba Jin's novel *Family* (*Jia*), in which all brothers and their wives and children lived in the same household.

From the late Qing to the May Fourth period, urban intellectual elites enthusiastically called for rebellion against the large patriarchal family while promoting the nuclear family and conjugal family.[80] However, in Longdong the small-size, many of them nuclear, family had been the dominant form for thousands of years.[81] Thus, this condition sheds light on the limits of the May Fourth discourse and the communist reform ideas guiding the so-called "family revolution," because the May Fourth discourse that aimed to destroy the large patriarchal family was ignorant of social reality. This social reality in fact challenged the legitimacy of the reform theory and made it like "high-modernist ideology."[82]

Meanwhile, the marriage practices that the May Fourth discourse attacked so strongly were also largely absent from Longdong, as well as Shaanbei. In this poverty-stricken region, the forms of marriage and family varied based on the economic conditions of each family.[83] Although monogamy was practiced by the great majority of people, other forms also existed. Contrary to the May Fourth writers who lamented restraints on widows' remarriage, it was common for a widow to remarry in this region, often decided on either by the widow herself or negotiated among the widow, her natal family, and her deceased husband's family (see Figure 1.2).

[79] Johnson, *Women, the Family and Peasant Revolution*, 9; Davin, *Woman-work*, 37.

[80] For May Fourth intellectuals' discussion of family reform and the nuclear family, see Glosser, *Chinese Visions of Family and State*, passim.

[81] *Huachi xian zhi*, 157.

[82] See Scott, *Seeing Like a State*, 2–5.

[83] The information about the social customs described in this section comes from the following documents and scholarly works if not specifically noted: SPA 15–57, "Ge xian youguan de fengsu xiguan" (The Relevant Customs in Local Counties); "Qingjian de hunsu" (Marriage Customs in Qingjian County) in *Jiefang ribao* (Liberation Daily), November 3 and 4, 1942; The Ministry of Justice, Republican Government (compilation), *Minshi xiguan diaocha baogao* (Surveys on the Customs of Civil Affairs) (Beijing: Zhongguo zhengfa daxue chubanshe, 2005, reprint), 799–833; Ding Shiliang and Zhao Fang (comp.), *Zhongguo difang zhi minsu ziliao huibian: Xibei juan* (A Collective Selection of Local Gazettes on Social Customs: Northwestern Region) (Beijing: Beijing tushuguan chubanshe, 1989), 109–26, 184–90; Yan'an Lu Xun Yishu xueyuan (Yan'an Lu Xun Artist Academy), collected and compiled, *Shaanbei minge xuan* (Selected Folk Songs from the North Shaanxi Region), (unknown place of publication: Xinhua shudian, 1949), 1–120; *Huachi xian zhi*, 155–6; *Qingyang diqu zhi*, 919–24. Also see Qin Yan and Yue Long, *Zou chu fengbi: Shaanbei funü de hunyin yu shengyu (1900–1949)* (Getting Out of Confinement: Women's Marriage and Childbearing in Northern Shaanxi, 1900–1949) (Xi'an: Shaanxi renmin chubanshe, 1997), 21–162; and Qin Yan, *Qing mo Min chu de Shaanbei shehui* (The Society of Northern Shaanxi in the Late Qing and Early Republic) (Xi'an: Shaanxi renmin chubanshe, 2000), 87–128.

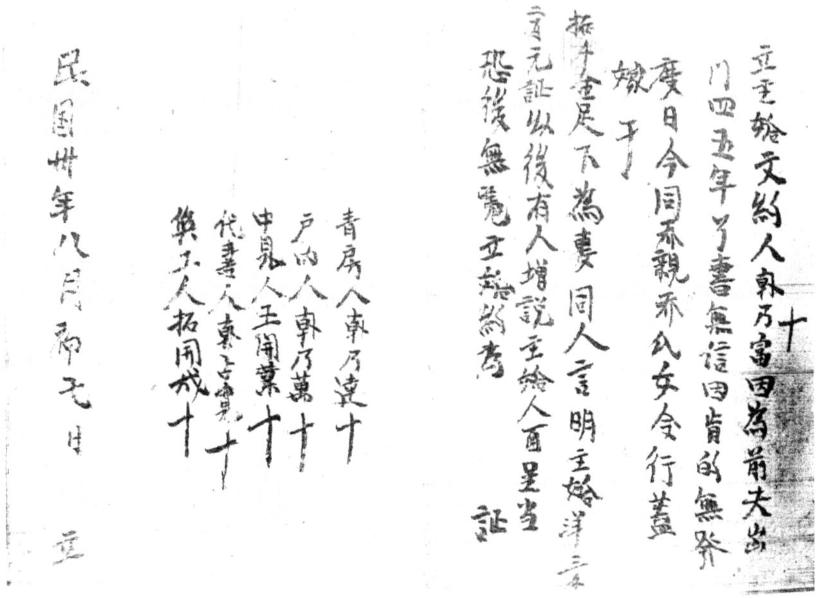

Figure 1.2 The contract for a woman's remarriage, 1941, SPA 15–156

A popular local saying, "a woman's first marriage is decided by her parents, but the second marriage by herself" (*xian jia you die niang, hou jia you benshen* 先嫁由爹娘, 再嫁由本身), reflected the condition that women had certain autonomy in their own remarriage.[84] In fact, in certain places a widow was welcomed into a marriage more readily than an unmarried girl because she already had housework experience, thus saving the husband's family from having to train a newlywed bride. If the deceased husband's family or the widow herself insisted that she stay in that family, the widow could select a husband (*zuo tang zhao fu*, 坐堂招夫, lit., staying home and inviting a husband in), and their common children would be divided as the heirs of the two families.

The practice of renting out a wife (*dian qi* 典妻), a miserable practice described in Rou Shi's short story "A Mother as a Slave,"[85] was indeed present in local custom, but a similar situation also existed for males, though in a different form. If a man was too poor to find a permanent

[84] SPA 15–81, "Bianqu tuishi, shenpanyuan lianxi huiyi fayan jilu, 6" (Collection of Presentations on the Legal Conference, Volume 6), 42.

[85] Rou Shi, *Wei nuli de muqin* (A Mother as a Slave) (Shanghai: Shijie yingyu bianyishe, 1947).

wife, he could accept the option of being a temporary/substitute husband for a woman (*zhao fu*, 招夫, lit., inviting a [substitute] husband in) if her husband were absent from the family for a period of time or had left the family without further contact. He provided full support for his temporary wife until the original husband returned. Under the influence of steppe culture, both sororate and levirate marriages (*zhuan cuo/zhuan fang* 转搓/转房), though rare, existed equally in this region; widowers and/or widows chose their new spouses from the same family in which they had previously been married.[86]

May Fourth writings deplored the miserable conditions of women who began to serve as *tongyangxi* at a young age. As in many other areas of China, this custom was practiced in the SGN region. On the other hand, a similar practice of *zhannianhan* (站年汉) for males, though seen less often than *tongyangxi*, was also not uncommon in Longdong and Shaanbei. A *zhannianhan* was a boy or a young man, mainly those from extremely poor families, who lived with and worked for his betrothed's family while waiting for his future bride to grow up. In this way, the girl's family, which was comparatively better off and needed a male laborer, would take the years of the boy/man's work as payment for the bride price and waive the *caili* from his family. Concubinage (*na/xu qie* 纳/蓄妾) occurred among rich people who could afford more than one spouse, while polyandry was practiced among poor people.[87] This type of marriage occurred when a husband was incompetent, either in physical labor or procreating ability; his wife could invite another man into the family to play the role of husband in order to support the family (*zhao fu yang fu* 招夫养夫), provide regular intimate relations, and produce heirs for both sides of the male line.

[86] Scholarship on premodern times also observes a strong influence of this type of steppe culture on marriage customs among the Han Chinese in northern China. See Jennifer Holmgren, "The Economic Foundation of Virtue: Widow Remarrying in Early and Modern China," *The Australian Journal of Chinese Affairs* 13 (1985): 1–27; and Bettine Birge, "Levirate Marriage and the Revival of Widow Chastity in Yuan China," *Asia Major* 8(2) (1995): 107–46.

[87] In addition to the documents I have discovered from this region, Matthew Sommer also comes to the same conclusion in his study of Qing legal cases in other parts of China ("Making Sex Work: Polyandry as a Survival Strategy in Qing Dynasty China," in *Gender in Motion: Divisions of Labor and Cultural Change in Late Imperial and Modern China*, Bryna Goodman and Wendy Larson (eds.) (New York: Rowman & Littlefield, 2005), 29–54). Also see Zhang Zhiyong's study of the northern China revolutionary base area during the 1940s, "Huabei kang Ri genjudi funü yundong yu hun wai xing guanxi" (Sexual Affairs and Women's Movement in Northern China Revolutionary Base Areas), *Kang Ri zhanzheng yanjiu* (Studies on the Anti-Japanese War) 1 (January 2009): 77–86.

In this region as well as Shaanbei, the major form of marriage was virilocal, which was seen as the embodiment of patriarchal domination by the May Fourth discourse and by some contemporary scholars.[88] However, the uxorilocal marriage (*zhui xu/zhao xu/er nüxu* 赘婿/招婿/儿女婿) was also frequently seen in Longdong and Shaanbei. Unlike in other parts of China, where a uxorilocal husband sometimes experienced strong discrimination from villagers and was mistreated by the wife's family, in this region uxorilocal marriage was practiced in various forms and commonly accepted, though a husband had to follow the terms of the contract made before the wedding.[89] In contrast to the May Fourth writers' criticism of the Confucian family, the family system and these "heterodox" marriage practices in the region fundamentally functioned as a strategy for survival and propagation rather than gender oppression,[90] because each form of marriage applied to both males and females.

In the marriage practices of the SGN region, patriarchal power was embodied in arranged marriages for minors, both girls and boys. The ages for formal weddings ranged from thirteen to seventeen for girls and fifteen and up for boys/men, but parents frequently arranged engagements for their children beginning at age two.[91] Under this system, not only girls but also boys had to submit to their parents' authority. Such engagements were accompanied by the transfer of a certain amount of *caili* from the boy's family to the girl's as a symbol of the consent of the two families. Wang Yuesheng argues that in traditional society, parents' domination of their children's marriages was based on the same property

[88] For example, Johnson, *Women, the Family and Peasant Revolution*, 12.

[89] The most important issue in the ante-marital contract was whether or not this marriage was one of a "husband selling his surname" (in which a man changed to his wife's surname as did all their future children, thus the husband had full rights as a son in inheritance and in the business of the wife's clan), a "non-selling his surname" (in which a man lived in the wife's home but did not change his surname and all children followed the father's surname; in this condition he had no right to inheritance of any property and no say about the wife's family business) or "a half-selling his surname" (in which a husband did not change his surname but their children would be divided with both surnames equally and that a husband's right in his wife's family affairs was defined in the ante-marital contract).

[90] Unlike Johnson, who sees family as a totally male-dominated domain, Davin objectively observes senior women's privileged position in a patriarchal system (*Woman-work*, 49–50); on the other hand, in order to employ male domination as a target, Johnson presents the division of males and females as the basic form in the Chinese patriarchal system. To emphasize this point, she regards uxorilocal marriage as a "deviation" that was formed out of women's shame rather than male obedience (*Women, the Family and Peasant Revolution*, 12).

[91] *Qingyang diqu zhi*, 919–20; also see Qin and Yue, *Zou chu fengbi*, 45–8.

relation, since marriage is a process of property transformation.[92] This point was well-exemplified in the marriage practice of this region. The engagement was accompanied by a series of ceremonies with various mediators in attendance, and included a written or oral contract. Since the betrothal was conducted when the children were still young, it was obviously a family affair presided over by the parents – mainly fathers but occasionally mothers as well – rather than a decision made by the two engaged individuals.[93]

The implementation of the 1939 marriage regulation required a premise of individual freedom for carrying out one's free will that was lacking in the traditional marriage practices of this region. In the dispute of *Feng v. Zhang*, the title of the legal case in Chinese indicates that it was a conflict between the two engaged families, not between Peng'er and Zhang Bo as individuals. Although both were eighteen years old, the modern age of majority, in the local tradition only a formal wedding granted both persons adulthood. Thus, a couple's marriage business had to be conducted by their parents.[94] The revolutionary government was still unable to separate individual men and women from the family; this separation was the target of the legal practice discussed in Chapters 3 and 4.

As Scott points out, any high-modernist scheme for social changes has to rely on the existing society for its operation, but incorporating old systems may result in the failure of the reform plan.[95] When the communist state launched a social revolution of marriages and families, it not only had to deal with "backwardness" in marriage practices, but also tackle the property relations hidden behind marriage disputes. These "informal relations" defined by modern marriage, such as engagements, were either practiced before the coming of the CCP government or conducted in private after the promulgation of the 1939 regulation. Unfortunately, these issues were not addressed by the 1939 regulation, indicating that the revolutionary leaders failed to anticipate the challenges of carrying out their reform projects in a location much different than where they had previously worked.

92 Wang Yuesheng, *Qingdai zhongqi hunyin chongtu toushi* (An Analysis of Marriage Conflicts during the Mid-Qing Period) (Beijing: Shehui kexue wenxian chubanshe, 2003), 15.

93 See *Qingyang diqu zhi*, 921–2; *Huachi xian zhi*, 881–2; Qin and Yue, *Zou chu fengbi*, 67–74.

94 The documents of the SGN Border courts disputes on engagements and divorces indicate that, as under Qing rule, these disputes were mainly between two or three families instead of two or three individuals.

95 Scott, *Seeing Like a State*, 6.

III. Social conflicts: the economic motive behind marriage disputes

After the 1939 marriage regulation was promulgated, the divorce rate increased, as did cases of abolishing engagements.[96] The 1939 record shows 48 marriage-related disputes (*hunyin jiufen* 婚姻纠纷) among 273 total legal cases in all counties. In only the first six months of 1941, however, marriage disputes increased to 71 out of a total of 271 of all kinds of case.[97] Another source indicates that the number of marriage disputes was 225 cases in 1943.[98] In the great majority, it was the woman's side (*nü fang* 女方), mostly their families, who proposed the divorce or the ending of the engagement (see the discussion of "woman's side" in Chapter 2).[99] At the same time, a strong expression of discontent from some male farmers was also escalating.[100] Superficially, these phenomena are easily read as a sign of the realization of women's liberation through "freedom of marriage," or as an indication that conservative male farmers were upset about the erosion of male domination. However, if we carefully scrutinize concrete cases of marriage disputes, we find a totally different picture.

In the 1940s, many marriage disputes, including divorces and broken engagements, were related to the widespread local custom of betrothal gifts (*caili*). The payment of *caili* varied in terms of time and amount, although the first *caili* was paid at the time that the engagement was settled. When the formal wedding date approached, some grooms' families provided additional gifts to fill out the bride's dowry; others did not. In some locales, the groom-to-be's family had an obligation to maintain the bride-to-be's family by constantly offering material and manual help. The first *caili* was likely to be grain or silver dollars for the bride's family, while the additional gifts given to the bride before the wedding (*er cheng li* 二成礼, i.e. the second gift) mainly consisted of clothes, fabrics,

96 I am using the term "marriage dispute" here instead of classifying them into "divorce" and "engagement dismissals" because the original document does not separate the two. Please see the following discussion.

97 SPA 15–175, "Lei Jingtian Bianqu sifa gongzuo baogao, 1941.10" (Lei Jingtian: The Report on the Border Legal Works, October 1941).

98 Zhang Shibin, Feng Yingchun, and Hui Xingwen, *Shaan-Gan-Ning bianqu gaodeng fayuan shi ji* (The Historical Records of the SGNBR High Court) (Xian: Shaanxi renmin chubanshe, 2006), 76. The number of legal cases may not be accurate because of different sources for reports made at the time. It must be noted that in the context of the SGNBR, the term "marriage dispute" (*hunyin jiufen*) did not simply mean divorce, as I clarify in the following section.

99 As discussed in Chapter 2, in the context of the SGNBR the term "woman's side" (*nü fang*) did not mean the woman in a marriage dispute or a divorce case.

100 SPA 4–65, "Guanyu lihun de zhiyi" (Questioning the Issue of Divorce).

cosmetics, jewelry, or some personal goods such as quilts, bedding, washbasins, mirrors, and the like. Although brides in the region were expected to bring a dowry of a certain amount of goods from their natal families to their husband's families, the dowry was always much smaller than the original *caili*. In the late Qing and the early Republican periods, *caili* was rather small, since it was only a token signifying a promise of marriage or a deposit for a bride. However, with the deterioration of the rural economy, natural disasters, famines, and bankruptcy of farmers in the region in the 1920s, the price for *caili* gradually increased in the 1930s. To the SGN government, this practice blurred into what the marriage regulation called "buying/selling marriage," causing serious problems for legal practices in the 1940s.

For multiple reasons, the price of *caili* was stimulated to an unprecedented level in the 1940s. First, this region had always had an unbalanced ratio of the sexes: in 1909, the rate between the sexes in Anhua (part of which became the current Huachi) and Dongzhi (today's Qingcheng) counties were about 100 females to 117 males. In 1925, the male population in Heshui County (part of current Huachi) was 53.67 percent, while the female was only 46.33 percent. This imbalance continued; in 1947, four counties (Qingyang, Ningxian, Zhenyuan, and Zhengning) maintained the rate of 100 females to over 115 males.[101] Shaanbei area faced a similar condition.

Second, the arrival of communist power in the region brought in a large male population, including army soldiers, government workers, and war refugees, which enlarged the gap between males and females. This imbalance in Yan'an area reached thirty males to one female prior to 1938 and eighteen to one in 1941. With more female students arriving from cities after 1938, the gap gradually narrowed, but it still stood at eight to one in 1944.[102] The condition in the peripheral region outside of Yan'an City was not as bad, but the discrepancy still existed. According to Zhu Hongzhao's investigation, the alleged policy of "twenty-five-eight-regiment" (*erwu ba tuan* 二五八团), which was supposed to limit the number of cadres and military officers getting

[101] See *Qingyang diqu zhi*, 519. As there was no record on the practice of female infanticide in this region, the reason for such an imbalanced sex ratio must be related to the lifestyle and poverty (see Chapter 2), especially high rate of deaths of young females in childbirth. By the 1960s, the gap between females and males in this region started to decline to about 100:106, a rather natural ratio that lasted until the 1990s.

[102] Zhu Hongzhao, *Yan'an: Ri chang shenghuo zhong de lishi, 1937–1947* (Yan'an: Daily Life in History, 1937–1947) (Guilin: Guangxi shifan daxue chubanshe, 2007), 283. Xie Juezai also confirmed that in 1942, the ratio between males and females in Yan'an was about twelve to one. See Huan Nan [Xie Juezai], "Lu bian xian hua" (A Small Talk at the Side of Stove), *Jiefang ribao* (Liberation Daily), March 16, 1942.

married,[103] was in fact not seriously implemented, especially outside of Yan'an.[104] Legal documents prove that there were certain lower-ranking officers and soldiers marrying local women.[105] This new group of males, especially those who worked in government offices or lower-ranking military officers stationed locally whose livelihoods were guaranteed by government supplies, now entered the local marriage market. Between the existing male–female imbalance and the arrival of even more men seeking wives in an area where women were in short supply, families with marriage-age sons found that they had to pay higher amounts of *caili* to attract a bride.

This rapid increase of the population in a region that was geographically small, economically underdeveloped, and lacking in natural resources caused widespread inflation and the devaluation of currencies, which also contributed significantly to the rising price of *caili*. In the early 1930s, the price of a *caili* could range from two to fifty silver *yuan* depending on the area, but was mostly around ten to twenty *yuan*. However, by the middle of the 1940s, the price of the *caili* had risen to as high as one million to one and a half million Republican *yuan* (*fabi* 法币)[106] in Yan'an and Eastern Gansu, where inflation was more intense, while the lowest price was 3,000 *yuan fabi* in Fuxian, or 200,000 *yuan* Border Currency (*bianbi* 边币) in places less affected by currency devaluation.[107] This high price

103 The rumored policy alleged that those cadres and military officers who were over the age of twenty-five with more than eight years of service and holding the rank of regiment officers enjoyed priority in getting married. According to Zhu, this was only a rumor and no official document has ever proven its existence (Zhu Hongzhao, *Yan'an: Ri chang shenghuo zhong de lishi*, 243).

104 Zhu Hongzhao, *Yan'an: Ri chang shenghuo zhong de lishi*, 243.

105 For example, the Zhu Jinhua case (SPA 15–1471) and the Cheng Taohua case (SPA 15–1335).

106 Beginning in 1940, *fabi* had devalued rapidly. In some Nationalist-controlled regions, it devalued into one silver dollar for 1,000 in the mid-1940s and 2,000–3,000 *fabi* in the late 1940s. In the Communist-controlled region, the devaluation rate of *fabi* seemed comparatively slower. On the other hand, the SGN government also issued its own currency, *bianbi* (Border currency) in 1941, attempting to reduce the impact of *fabi* devaluation while developing its own currency. *Bianbi* circulated concurrently with *fabi* and silver *yuan* for some years in most of the SGN region, but *bianbi* gradually replaced *fabi* and silver yuan beginning in the mid-1940s. The SGN government originally designated one *bianbi* as equal to one *fabi*. However, inflation in the SGN region eventually stabilized the exchange rate of one *fabi* to nine *bianbi* in the mid-1940s. This situation lasted until 1949. See *Huachi xian zhi*, 528–30; Huang Zhenglin, *Shaan-Gan-Ning bianqu xiangcun de jingji yu shehui* (Rural Economy and Society in the Shaan-Gan-Ning Border Region) (Beijing: Renmin chubanshe, 2006), 104–19; Selden, *The Yenan Way in Revolutionary China*, 180–1; and Zhu Hongzhao, *Yan'an: Ri chang shenghuo zhong de lishi*, 3–24.

107 SPA 15–72, "Hunyin wenti yu hunyin tiaoli, 1945" (The Issue of Marriage and the Marriage Regulation, 1945).

of *caili* astounded Xie Juezai 谢觉哉 (1884–1971), a former director of the BR High Court who was then in charge of the legal system in the government. He recorded a report on a marriage case from the *Liberation Daily* in his diary on March 16, 1943: "He [Meng Qingcheng] said that his family paid three *dan* grains,[108] two oxen, seven *shang* [plots][109] of fertilized land, a half *shang* of rice field, plus 5,000 *yuan fabi* to engage a wife for his brother." Xie Juezai exclaimed, "How could a woman be so expensive?!"[110] It should be noted that this was about the same time that the case of *Feng v. Zhang* occurred. The ten *yuan caili* Feng Yangui received in 1928 was considered a good price at that time, but by 1943 it was a negligible amount.

Facing such inflation, Feng Yangui felt that his daughter's *caili* was set too low, as did most families that had engaged their daughters in the 1920s and 1930s. Like many families, Feng Yangui demanded that the groom-to-be's family pay a second *caili* just before the wedding,[111] since the previously optional wedding gifts had now become mandatory.[112] Moreover, in most cases the amount of the second *caili*, in contrast to its previously symbolic nature, was now substantial and included currency, grain, and special gifts for the bride. If the groom's family refused or could not afford to pay, the wedding was postponed indefinitely or even cancelled. For the majority of girls' families, the most convenient method was to pretend that the first betrothal at the girl's young age had never existed, and then find another family willing to pay the current price for the girl when she reached marriageable age.[113] The wedding would then be promptly held. By the time the family of the first fiancé discovered this cheating, the girl would already have been married for some time and the money from the second family was already spent. The family of the first fiancé would file a lawsuit against the girl's family, while the second groom's family also sued the girl's family for

[108] *Dan* is a weight unit in the region; one *dan* is about 15 kilograms or 400 pounds.

[109] *Shang* was a land unit in this region; one *shang* is about three *mu* or a half acre.

[110] Xie Juezai, *Xie Juezai riji* (Xie Juezai's Diary) (Beijing: Renmin chubanshe, 1984), 428.

[111] According to contemporary literature, Feng demanded this several times but Zhang refused to pay (Yang Zhengfa, *Feng Zhiqin, Liu Qiao'er*, 26).

[112] Second betrothal gifts did not exist until the 1940s in many areas. It was a recently formed practice during the time of inflation. See SPA 15–39, "Wei cheng qing mai mai hunyin ruhe chuli" (Request Instruction from the High Court on How to Deal with Purchased Marriages).

[113] In English, "girls" and "women" have a clearly distinct age difference. In the cases of this region, the distinction between a girl and a woman was decided by her marital status. Although the legal marriageable age of eighteen years was set up by the 1939 regulation, many local families still followed traditional customs by marrying their daughters off in their early teens. Therefore in the following discussion, I use both "girls" and "women" mostly in their local sense.

cheating.[114] In the records of the SGN courts, a legal category was titled "*yi nü liang/duo xu*" 一女两/多许 (one girl betrothed to two or more families or two men fighting for one woman); this was the exact situation in the case of *Feng v. Zhang*.

There are many other cases similar to *Feng v. Zhang*. For example, in 1941 the SGN High Court took a case from the local court of Ansai County. Two men, Xu Zhiting and Cao Jingui, had sued Jing Furong and his stepdaughter, Feng Run'er, in a dispute over which man would have Run'er as his wife. In 1929, Run'er's biological father, Mr. Feng, had engaged his three-year-old girl to a boy, Xu Zhiting, receiving 24 silver *yuan* as a *caili* from the Xu family. However, when Mr. Feng passed away (unclear when), his wife, Woman Feng-Liu, married Jing Furong, which brought Run'er into the Jing family. They then moved from Anding County to Ansai County in 1936. It was here that Jing Furong found another match, Cao Jingui, for his stepdaughter and received 40 *yuan* for this betrothal. In 1937, when the family finances were declining, Jing Furong sent thirteen-year-old Run'er to the Cao family as a *tongyangxi*. Two years later, a formal wedding was held for Run'er and Jingui. When the news of this marriage traveled back to Run'er's former residence in 1940, the Xu family came to Jing's family to ask for Run'er. When Woman Feng-Liu acknowledged the original betrothal, this dispute had the basis for a court case. The Xu family sued Jing and Cao in Ansai County, asking for Run'er to be returned to the Xu family to marry Zhiting. The local court voided both the marriage and engagement based on the fact that Run'er was not at a legal marriageable age. It ruled that once Run'er reached the age of eighteen, she would have the right to choose her spouse.[115]

Some disputes were even more complicated and involved multiple parties. For example, in 1942 Sun Changyou of Huanxian County betrothed his widowed daughter-in-law to Liu Tuzi for 1,400 *yuan fabi*, while his daughter-in-law's natal family promised her to Chen Zijie for 400 *yuan fabi*. At the same time, the widow herself chose to become engaged to a certain Mr. Ma for 600 *yuan fabi*. These multiple engagements eventually developed into a criminal case when Liu Tuzi and his villagers kidnapped the widow. Luckily, with the intervention of the local government, the widow was granted the right to make her own decision.[116]

[114] According to some studies, this type of cheating motivated by requesting more caili also occurred in some parts of southern China during the mid-Qing period. See Wang, *Qingdai zhongqi hunyin chongtu toushi*, 6–13.

[115] SPA 15-1293, *Cao Jingui v. Jing Furong*.

[116] SPA 4-1-65, "Shaan-Gan-Ning bianqu hunyin wenti huiji, 1943" (The Collection on the Issue of Marriage in the Shaan-Gan-Ning Border Region, 1943).

Table 1.1. *Data from various counties on the dismissal of engagements, 1944*[117]

	Reasons for requesting the dismissal	Number of cases	Requested by men's side	Requested by women's side
1	Instigation of natal family (*niang jia tiao suo* 娘家挑唆)	3		3
2	One girl betrothed to two families (*yi nü liang xu* 一女两许)	4		4
3	[Girl] demanding self-determination (*yao qiu zi zhu* 要求自主)	4		4
4	[Fiancé has] mental problems (*shen jing bing* 神经病)	2		2
5	[Fiancé] sexually impotent (*bu neng ren dao* 不能人道)	1		1
6	[Fiancé] lied about [his] age (*yin man nianling* 隐瞒年龄)	2		2
7	[Girl's] aversion to a poor fiancé (*xian pen* 嫌贫)	2		2
8	Absent soldier in the Anti-Japanese War without contact (*kang Ri junren wu xin* 抗日军人无信)	3		3
9	Absent fiancé without contact (*wai chu wu xin* 外出无信)	1		1
10	Fiancé deceased (*wei hun fu si* 未婚夫死)	1		1
	Total	23		23

One 1945 statistic has a detailed category that separates engagement disputes from divorces.[118] It shows that in 1944, various county courts dealt with a total of twenty-three cases demanding the dismissal of engagements, but in the first six months of 1945 this number increased to fifty-six. All of these cases were brought to the government by the women's side (*nü fang* 女方).[119]

Among the reasons listed, physical causes (mentally ill, sexually impotent, and deceased) made engagements easy to dismiss because they were legitimate reasons in both local tradition and the revolutionary regulations. Categories eight and nine also followed the rule that if the fiancé's absence without contact (including military soldiers) lasted

[117] SPA 15–72, "Shaan-Gan-Ning bianqu hunyin wenti yu tiaoli."
[118] The 1944 marriage regulation eventually set up a term to control the practice of engagements (see Chapter 4), therefore the data in 1945 separated engagement disputes from divorces.
[119] SPA 15–72, "Shaan-Gan-Ning bianqu hunyin wenti yu tiaoli."

for a certain number of years (usually three to five years), the engagement could be dismissed, as discussed in Chapters 3 and 4. Economic motives dominated the remaining reasons for requesting the dismissal of an engagement. The explanations of "one girl betrothed to two families" and "aversion to poor fiancé" were directly linked to economic motives, while "instigation of natal family" involved the natal family demanding more *caili* or a suitor with a higher bid. The category "demanding self-determination" was much more complicated, because it had to be examined on a case-by-case basis. Many cases proved that girls' families used this legal rhetoric to conceal their economic motives, which will be discussed in Chapters 2 and 3.

Certain divorce cases were also related to *caili*, since for the most part, divorce through the government did not deal with property division prior to marriage. (In Chapters 2 and 4, there is a detailed discussion of divorce cases.) For example, in 1943 Zhidan County received a lawsuit concerning Chen Yu (or Chen Lü), the wife of Li Yucheng's grandson (no mention of the name), who was betrothed by her father to Liu Zhenhai's son. Chen Yu's father, Chen Dengyun, an opium addict, despised the poor family his daughter had married into. When Liu Zhenhai paid him handsomely for his daughter, Chen persuaded her to divorce her husband. The father brought Chen Yu to the local government for a divorce, and she then married Liu Zhenhai's son. Li Yucheng thus sued Liu Zhenhai and Chen Dengyun, and the divorce later was overturned by the High Court.[120]

Given this background, Feng Yangui's motives for abolishing his daughter's early engagement can be fully explained. Feng's action was not only that of the head of a family responding to the economic and political changes in the SGNBR during the 1940s, but also a person utilizing revolutionary policy for his own profit. In terms of their attitude toward the marriage reform, male farmers can be roughly divided into several groups: those who had sons and those who had daughters, leaving those who had both daughters and sons in an ambivalent middle ground. It is thus too absolute to say that male farmers as a conservative entity strongly resisted the marriage reform. We can assume that Feng must have welcomed the marriage reform for his own gain, but major complaints and protests came from those men who had sons and had made engagements a decade previously, like Zhang Jincai.

[120] SPA 15-842, *Li Yucheng v. Liu Zhenhai and Chen Yu*; SPA 15-27, "Bianqu gaoyuan: pan an shili kuolu" (The BR High Court: A Summary of Selected Cases).

IV. Law and social practice: dealing with cultural and legal incompatibility

The incompatibility of communist policy with local practices was also rooted in different views on marriage. In the modern concept, a formal marriage starts from the moment of either the state's or church's validation of the union between a man and a woman; but in the traditions of SGN Border society, a marriage began with the engagement which equated to a marriage in local custom. The term "marriage disputes" (*hunyin jiufen* 婚姻纠纷), often used in official documents, did not simply mean divorces but also meant disputes over broken engagements.[121] An engagement contract also initiated a process of property transformation through *caili*-giving that could last for more than a decade while the engaged couple was growing up. Also, the engagement was seen as an indissoluble part of a full-fledged marriage, which was confirmed by the future wedding. This is also why the wedding was called "*guo men*" 过门 (moving to [husband's] house) in many regions in China, only indicating the completion of the entire marriage process.[122] In the modern legal reform, the 1932 GMD Civil Code gave certain considerations to the status of engagement and its related property issues, but it placed betrothal gifts in a special category of "donations" in exchange for the bride's trousseau.[123] The 1939 regulation, which promoted a radical concept of marriage, did not consider engagement to have any legal status and therefore did not set up any terms for engagements, nor for related issues such as property disputes.

For this reason, although the 1939 regulation banned the practice of "buying/selling marriages" in principle, that proved difficult to enforce in reality. While the regulation did include certain terms on dividing connubial property that favored women, it set up those terms on the postulation that the property was held only by an existing marital couple, without considering the situations of property transfer between engaged families prior to a "modern" marriage. This created a huge loophole

[121] Kathryn Bernhardt also notices this phenomenon that the late imperial court treated an engaged daughter as a wife in certain cases, thus making the engagement contract more formal in Qing society. See her, "A Ming-Qing Transition in Chinese Women's History? The Perspective from Law" in *Remapping China: Fissures in Historical Terrain*, Gail Hershatter, Emily Honig, Jonathan N. Lipman, and Randall Stross (eds.) (Stanford, CA: Stanford University Press, 1996), 42–58.

[122] This was not only a social custom in SGN society but also a traditional marriage practice for most of China. See Guo Songyi, *Lunli yu shenghuo: Qing dai de hunyin guanxi* (Ethics and Life: Marriage Relations in the Qing) (Beijing: Shangwu yin shu guan, 2000), 121–3.

[123] Meijer, *Marriage Law and Policy*, 26–7.

for implementing the ban against buying/selling marriages. Even if the definition of buying/selling marriages could be extended to the process of a wedding, it still did not have practicable significance. In the great majority of cases, the transfer of *caili* occurred long before the formal wedding – sometimes more than a decade earlier, especially when the *caili* contained consumable and immeasurable elements such as labor service and long-term financial aid. The 1939 regulation thus put the issue of engagement and its related "gift" transfer in the hands of local government officials and legal workers without giving it any legal basis or detailed definition. In the early 1940s, when the implementation of the regulation caused so many conflicts, we see that local courts constantly wrote to the High Court asking for a definition of buying/selling marriage and its distinction from local *caili* practice.[124] In Chapter 4, we will see that the revised 1944 regulation, which though it still failed, at least tried to remedy this loophole.

Theoretically, the 1939 regulation that promoted freedom of marriage and prohibited buying/selling marriage benefited both men and women. Ideally, it allowed men and women to choose each other on the basis of mutual love while eliminating the connection between material gain and marriage. The communists expected that young men and women, especially young males from poverty-stricken families, would embrace this policy that was in accord with the CCP's revolutionary principle on class line. As the previous section showed, young women and their fathers welcomed this policy for a reason totally different from its original intention. It was young poverty-stricken males who vigorously opposed the policy[125] because breaking an engagement without repayment equal to the original value was not simply a dispute concerning marriage but a financial dispute, and a problem of fairness in the eyes of the locals.

Under the 1939 marriage practice, male peasants who had paid for their engagements and marriages had no way to succeed, especially in a time of economic inflation. A family would spend all of its assets (*qing jia dang chan* 倾家荡产) to engage a wife for its son, expecting that the contract would be honored. However, inflation often caused destitution, and the original contract was also lost. This group of farmers described their situation with the phrase "losing both woman and property" (*ren cai liang kong/shi* 人财两空/失). Due to the widespread inflation of the 1940s, the value of returned *caili*, even with compensation, was far below its original value and not enough for a payment for a new wife. Moreover, most girls'

[124] SPA 15–33, "Chishui xian sifachu qingshi guanyu zaohun ji maimai hunyin wenti, 1942" (Chishui County Office of Justice Requesting Instruction on Minor Marriages and Buying/Selling Marriages, 1942).

[125] SPA 15–40, "Zenyang jinzhi mai mai hunyin?" (How to Stop Purchased Marriages?).

families had already spent the money and could offer no way to pay it back. In some cases, the original gift included land; this land had been cultivated by the girls' families for years and it was impossible to return it to the boys' families.[126] This situation of "lost both" threatened the survival of this group of poor male peasants.

A 1942 divorce case in Yan'an demonstrates this problem. Chen Zhifang (wife) married Li Hancheng (husband) at the age of fourteen, but the two did not get along. Two years later, Chen filed for divorce, but Li strongly opposed it. In court, Li explained the reason: in order to marry Chen, he had sold the only plot of land he owned for *caili* and had become penniless. He could not accept that Chen wanted a divorce without repaying the money. Li used the exact words prevalent in the region to describe his situation, saying that he would "lose both the woman (wife) and the money." When the court delivered a divorce verdict and asked Chen to return the money from her betrothal to Li, Chen replied, "Only if the government law stipulates the return of the money at divorce will I do it."[127] Of course, there was no law for a return of *caili* in 1942, and so the court could not do anything about it.

In this system, canceling a marriage/betrothal contract fell into a loophole in the 1939 regulation. It created a huge rift in a society where people depended on social contracts. Like many other types of contracts in the region, the marriage engagement had been highly respected and deemed a formal legal document in any dispute; one local gazetteer described it as "one promise that will never change."[128] Any party who abandoned the contract had to offer compensation to the other party or it was brought to legal authorities as a marriage dispute.[129] If negotiation failed, the party who felt unfairly treated could take action against the other party. Local gazetteers record that "kidnapping" the bride, a practice that originated from the ancient custom of "marriage by capture" (*qiang hun* 抢婚), a tradition from the steppe culture, was not uncommon in the region up to the 1940s and even lingered into the 1950s.[130]

[126] These problems were discussed at the 1945 legal conference. See SPA 15–80, "Bianqu tuishi shenpan yuan lianxi huiyi fayan jilu, 5" (Collection of Presentations from the Legal Conference, Volume 5), and SPA 15–81, "Bianqu tuishi shenpan yuan lianxi huiyi fayan jilu, 7" (Collection of Presentations from the Legal Conference, Volume 7).

[127] SPA 15–1340, *Chen v. Li.*

[128] *Chong xiu Zhenyuan zhi*, 478. Also see Wang, *Qingdai zhongqi hunyin chongtu toushi*, 48.

[129] Facing this reality, local government cadres and legal workers did not separate broken engagements from divorce cases in their reports and treated the two with the same principle and in the same category as divorce until the 1944 regulation began to distinguish between them. So the number of divorce cases adopted in previous scholarship that cite these reports may not be accurate.

[130] SPA 15–57, "Ge xian fengsu xiguan"; *Qingyang diqu zhi*, 924; *Chong xiu Zhenyuan zhi*, 478; also see Qin and Yue, *Zou chu fengbi*, 33–4.

Due to the failure of the law in delivering justice in the eyes of the locals, villagers created a solution by devising their own rules, as occurred in the case of *Feng v. Zhang*. Both the Bureau of Civil Affairs of BR (*Bianqu Min zheng ting* 边区民政厅) and the High Court admitted that the practice of kidnapping had been revived in the SGNBR during the 1940s. They confessed that it was the government's mishandling of cases of marriage disputes that resulted in an increasing number of kidnapping cases (*qiang hun*).[131] For example, the case of Jia Yingui was caused by "one girl betrothed to two men" and then developed into a kidnapping. Before the land revolution, Jia Yingui's parents paid Zhang Fengliang a certain amount to engage Zhang's daughter, Zhang Hainüzi, to Jia Yingui. In 1939, when Zhang Hainüzi reached the age of fourteen (a marriageable age in local custom), the Jia family paid a second betrothal gift, asking the Zhang family for a formal wedding. However, Zhang accepted the second *caili* but hid his daughter on the wedding day so that the Jias were unable to take the bride home. In 1941, Zhang Fengliang betrothed his daughter to another man, Li Yongchang from Anding County (today's Zichang County), for another amount. The Jia family immediately filed a lawsuit in Yan'an County court, which ruled the marriage contract to be a buying/selling marriage and therefore annulled it. The government also reasoned that the girl, Zhang Hainüzi, was only sixteen years old and thus not eligible for marriage. However, Jia's family, which had already paid a good deal for the marriage, felt the ruling was unfair and appealed to the High Court in 1942. The High Court supported the decision of the county court, but required Zhang Fengliang to return the *caili* to the Jia family. Before the final sentence was formally delivered to him, Zhang Fengliang disappeared without repaying his debt.[132] In early 1943, when Li Yongchang, the second fiancé that Zhang Fengliang had selected for his daughter, was to bring Zhang Hainüzi to his home for their wedding, Jia Yingui kidnapped the bride on the way. Jia then brought Zhang Hainüzi to his home to marry her. Li Yongchang filed a lawsuit with the local government, suing Jia for kidnapping his wife.[133]

Even more upheavals were brought by those soldiers whose wives or fiancées left them during their time in the service. Those women followed a local custom that when an absent husband lost contact with their home, the wife could remarry but needed to return to her original

[131] SPA 4-1-66, "Hunyin wenti cailiao, 1944" (Documents on the Issue of Carriage, 1944); 4-1-65, "Hunyin wenti huiyi, 1–4" (Collected Documents on the Marriage Issue); and SPA 15–72, SGN High Court: "Shaan-Gan-Ning bianqu hunyin wenti yu tiaoli" (The Issue of Marriage and the Marriage Regulation in the SGN Border Region, 1945).

[132] SPA 15–1333, *Jia Yingui v. Zhang Fengliang*.

[133] SPA 15–847, *Li v. Jia*; and SPA 15–1332, *Zhang Weijin v. Bai Fenglin*.

husband once he came home. This also became a situation of two men fighting for one woman, discussed in Chapter 2. Since these remarriages were conducted in private and beyond governmental supervision, local governments following the modern law could not help the soldiers in bringing their wives/fiancées back. The most frequent situation was that a visiting or discharged soldier kidnapped his previous wife or fiancée. In the case of a discharged soldier named Lei Shangzhi, Lei organized his family to kidnap his ex-wife, Woman Cui, from her second husband.[134] Liu Lian, an active soldier, brought his fellow soldiers to kidnap his ex-fiancée.[135] In Qingjian County, a soldier, Shi Youcai, threatened his ex-fiancée with a bomb, forcing her to return to him regardless of the fact that she had been married to another man for years and already had three children. In Yanchuan County, a discharged soldier led the village self-defense team in kidnapping his remarried ex-wife.[136] These kidnappings were often accompanied by brutality such as illegal detainment, beating, and rape. The army sometimes became involved in these activities as well, creating conflicts between civilian offices and military units, as in a case discussed in Chapter 4.

Although the local government tried to prevent violence in marriage disputes, events sometimes spun out of control and local government officials were involuntarily involved in violent actions. A 1945 report from Jiaxian County describes a case of kidnapping. When a township government of Mizhi County approved the request from a family in its jurisdiction to dismiss their daughter's early engagement, her fiancé from Jiaxian County kidnapped the girl. The township head of Mizhi tried to implement the verdict by bringing about twenty armed men from the local militia to the former fiancé's village and attempting to take the girl back. This action developed into a huge fight between the Jiaxian villagers and the Mizhi militiamen, and both sides suffered casualties in the fighting. When this official mission failed, the girl's natal family organized another action that eventually snatched the girl back. Settlement of the case was delayed for years and still had not been closed by the time the report was written in 1945.[137] From this perspective, we can understand the verdict of Huachi County on kidnapping because it was part of local governments' efforts to suppress violence in legal disputes.

[134] SPA 15–26, *Li Rongchun v. Lei Shangzhi* in "Bianqu panli huibian, 1944" (A Collection of Case Files in the BR, 1944).

[135] SPA 15–27, "The Case of Liu Lian Kidnapping Shi Xiuying."

[136] SPA 15–72, SGN High Court: "Shaan-Gan-Ning bianqu hunyin wenti yu tiaoli."

[137] SPA 15–294, "Jiaxian hunyin faling zhixing zongjie, 1945" (A Report on the Implementation of the Marriage Regulation in Jiaxian County, 1945).

However, we cannot jump to the conclusion that kidnapping was invariably a violent act against the woman's will; some women also used this as a means to marry the man they preferred rather than follow their family's arrangements. This may also apply to the case of Peng'er; in the following chapter, I will discuss the hidden role Peng'er played in the so-called "kidnapping." Although marriage by capture or kidnapping as a local practice was not specified in the cursory 1939 regulation, it could be categorized under "marriage by force." It was under this consideration that Huachi County invalidated the marriage between Peng'er and Zhang Bo. To the Office of Justice in Huachi County, this verdict was a "by-the-book" case, but it offended all parties. An appeal would soon follow.

2 The appeal

Women, love, marriage, and the revolutionary state

Not surprisingly, the verdict of Huachi County upset everyone, but it was Peng'er who responded most impetuously. In both her 1982 memoir and my 2005 interview with her, Feng Zhiqin (aka Feng Peng'er; for her name change, see Chapter 7) confirmed that in spite of her bound feet, she walked about eighty *li* (about twenty-four miles) in two days to Qingyang, where the prefectural civic center was located, and met with Prefect Ma Xiwu.[1] Ma listened to her petition and showed great sympathy. Ma defined Peng'er's case as an example of "feudal marriage" that should be eradicated. Ma then promised Peng'er that he would look at her case carefully and indeed visited Peng'er's village several days later. They met again when Peng'er was working under a mulberry tree, where Ma encountered her on his way into the village.[2]

Superficially, Peng'er's story looks like a typical communist textbook case, in which a brave woman, guided by the communist idea of freedom of marriage, dared to challenge the old patriarchal authority and fight against an arranged marriage. As in the "Gold Flower Story," in which a woman was liberated from an unhappy marriage and an abusive husband with the help of the CCP government,[3] Peng'er's case was used by many communist authors as a persuasive example of how the CCP liberated women from traditional family and patriarchal oppression.[4] It seems also to be a case that confirmed the May Fourth discourse about women resisting the oppression of the patriarchal family. On the other hand,

[1] Interview, July 21, 2005; and Feng Zhiqin, "Huiyi Ma Xiwu tongzhi." This article was written in memory of Ma Xiwu, based on Feng's oral narration and a local secretary's notes (Feng was illiterate and remained semi-illiterate).

[2] See Yang Zhengfa, *Feng Zhiqin, Liu Qiao'er*, 51–2 and Qingyang shi zhengxie and Huachi xian zhengxie, *"Liu Qiao'er" chuanqi rensheng* (The Legendary Life of "Liu Qiao'er") (Lanzhou: Gansu renmin chubanshe, 2005), 44–5.

[3] Jack Belden, *China Shakes the World* (New York: Harper & Brothers, 1949), 275–307.

[4] Different accounts of this story have been published since the early 2000s by local government officials for the purpose of the "Red Tourism." For example, Yang Zhengfa's *Feng Zhiqin, Liu Qiao'er*, and Qingyang shi zhengxie and Huachi xian zhengxie, *"Liu Qiao'er" chuanqi rensheng.*

although some American scholars since the 1980s have challenged the CCP's official version of its role in fighting for women's rights, this case also does not seem to support their hypothesis that the CCP sacrificed women's rights in exchange for male peasants' support, as argued in the Introduction and Chapter 1.

In her 1982 memoir, Feng Zhiqin revealed the motive behind her appeal: she felt dreadful about the situation because as a result of the county's verdict, "my family members (*qin ren* 亲人) were put in jail and my good marriage was destroyed."[5] She never mentioned any resentment toward her father. Obviously, when she talked about "family members," she was referring to the Zhangs, including Zhang Bo, since the county verdict did not punish her father. After many years her memory may have declined, but it still appears likely that protesting Huachi County's unfair ruling and saving her good marriage were the motives behind her appeal. The rationale for her appeal could have come from a long tradition in Chinese culture that regarded "saving family members" (*jiu ren* 救人) and "protesting against an unfair ruling" (*su yuan* 诉冤) as markers of good virtue for a responsible woman in both Confucian legend and popular culture. These have consistently served as major themes in traditional dramas.[6] As we shall see in Chapter 6, however, when her story was later developed into librettos, Peng'er's action was transformed into a scenario in which a brave daughter protests against her father.

In this chapter, I see women of the broad SGNBR as active agents and highlight the consistency behind their resistance to and cooperation with both the old patriarchy and the new revolutionary force. In this approach, I try to understand the seeming contradiction of Peng'er's early rejection of her first engagement and her later fight to marry her former fiancé. I place this action within a broader social and cultural background – not only by examining the local women's culture and their lives, their views of love and marriage, and survival skills under the traditional patriarchal system, but also by looking into the transformation of their lives and views on marriage under the revolutionary state. From this perspective, I see modern state policies concerning women's rights and the programs of changing women's position, including those of the communist state in the SGNBR, as a double-edged sword. When these policies tried to destroy old patriarchal power and granted women rights

[5] Feng Zhiqin, "Huiyi Ma Xiwu tongzhi," 146.

[6] R. David Arkush, "Love and Marriage in North Chinese Peasant Operas," in *Unofficial China: Popular Culture and Thought in the People's Republic*, Perry Link, Richard Madsen, and Paul G. Pickowicz (eds.) (Boulder, CO: Westview Press, 1990), 72–87.

in marriage, they also deprived women of some of the traditional autonomy they had previously exercised under patriarchal power. Meanwhile, like their male counterparts, rural women also experienced an adjustment under the rule of the new revolutionary state by developing new strategies and tactics to carve out new space through their interactions with the CCP government and its legal system. From this perspective, we may gain a better understanding of Peng'er's appeal rather than seeing rural women as victims of old tradition, or this case as a new revolutionary myth.

I. The revolutionary discourse of "freedom of marriage"

The reform programs in the SGNBR of the 1940s were based on a modern discourse that had been gradually developed since the late Qing in the coastal areas of China. This discourse revealed the intellectual elite's views of both a changing relationship between family and state in twentieth-century China and an unchanging Confucian view of family and state order.[7] It provided a thrust and guide for changing the social reality, but due to the broad range of social, geographical, and cultural varieties in China, the effects of its practice need to be examined.

The communist ideology concerning marriage reform had two sources: one was based on the strongly anti-traditional and anti-patriarchal May Fourth discourse, and the other was the Marxist-communist theory of women's emanicipation. In the May Fourth discourse, women were seen simply as victims of the patriarchal family; many May Fourth writers focused on what they considered the miserable condition of women, which caused many young females to wither away within traditional patriarchal families due to loveless arranged marriages.[8] Some authors included the Confucian doctrine regarding women's chastity and restrictions against widows' remarriage as further examples of Confucian oppression of women.[9]

[7] See Glosser, *Chinese Visions of Family and State*, 4–10.

[8] See, for example, Pa Chin (Ba Jin), *Family* (translated by Sidney Shapiro) (Prospect Heights, IL: Waveland Press, 1989 [1972]). Also see Mao Zedong's comments on the suicide case of Ms. Zhao, "Duiyu Zhao nüshi zisha de piping" (On the Criticism of the Suicide of Ms. Zhao), "Zhao nüshi de renge wenti" (The Character of Ms. Zhao), and "Shehui wan'e yu Zhao nüshi" (The Evil Society and Ms. Zhao), in Zhonggong zhongyang wenxian yanjiushi and Zhonggong Hunan shengwei *Mao Zedong zaoqi wengao* bianjizu (comp.), *Mao Zedong zaoqi wengao* (An Article Collection ofYoung Mao Zedong) (Changsha: Hunan chubanshe, 1990), 413–14; 416–17; and 424–7.

[9] Lu Xun, "Wo zhi jie lie guan" (My View of Chastity), and Hu Shi, "Zhencao wenti" (The Issue of Women's Chastity), in *Wu si shiqi funü wenti wenxuan* (Collections on Women's Issues Published in the May Fourth Period) (Beijing: Sanlian shudian, 1981), 106–14 and 115–23.

Within the May Fourth/Marxist-communist ideology that the Chinese communist revolution drew on, women were seen as victims of the patriarchal family and Western imperialism, but also as agents of social revolution. This theoretical duality could create a theoretical dilemma. On the one hand, the revolution recognized women's agency, based on which women could be mobilized for the social revolution and the productive work. It was also possible that women's emancipation could be postponed or even sacrificed for a better good, dictated by the imperatives of national crises and world revolution. This theoritical duality led to some CCP leaders swinging between requiring that women make sacrifices for the cause of human liberation and supporting women's demands for improving their living conditions and social status.[10] It was also based on this duality that some Western scholars in the early 1980s assumed that the former had taken place in China, where women's emancipation seemed an unfulfilled promise. In reality, however, this book shows that Chinese women were seen as both victims and agents because the party-state demanded women make sacrifices for the national war and their struggle for human emancipation, while it also promoted women's agency in self-determined marriage.

Based on this theory, early communist cadres in rural areas believed that free divorce was the best solution for women's emanicipation and would bring women from their previously confined family life to a much broader social domain. Through divorce, a woman would be able to gain independence from patriarchal oppression and break away from family ties in order to plunge into the social revolution. To overturn rural patriarchal power and the family system, the revolutionary governments in Jiangxi as well as other revolutionary base areas issued marriage regulations that granted women freedom in marriage, especially in divorce (see Chapter 4). Thus, the degree of accessibility to free divorce became the yardstick for women's liberation, and any restraint on divorce was seen as "a concession" to male conservatism, as Meijer believed.[11] As this chapter and Chapters 3 and 4 demonstrate, this view may simplify the issues of marriage and the source of women's unhappiness.

[10] Wu Yuzhang, "Zhongguo funü zai Wu Si yundong zhong zou shang le ziji jiefang de daolu" (Chinese Women on the Road of Self-liberation in the May Fourth Movement, 1939?), *Shaan-Gan-Ning bianqu funü yundong wenxian ziliao xuan bian*, 84–91; Deng Yingchao, "Kang Ri minzu tongyi zhanxian zhong de funü yundong" (The Women's Movement in the United Front of the Anti-Japanese War, 1939), *Shaan-Gan-Ning bianqu funü yundong wenxian ziliao xuan bian*, 61–73.

[11] Meijer, *Marriage Law and Policy*, 42–5; also see Fernando Galbiati, *P'eng P'ai and the Hai-Lu-Feng Soviet* (Stanford, CA: Stanford University Press, 1985), 198. Criticism of the revisions of the 1944 and 1946 regulations was also based on the same principle (see Introduction and Chapter 1).

By launching a marriage reform with a radical idea, the CCP expected that its policy on freedom of marriage would save women from suffering in unhappy families and loveless marriages. The 1939 regulation gave the right to file for divorce to either side. In the case of a divorce through agreement, the couple only went through the registration in government but the complication came from ex parte divorce. An ex parte divorce would be granted by the court after the couple had exhausted negotiations if any of the following ten conditions had occurred, prioritized by order: (1) bigamy (*chong hun* 重婚), (2) total incompatibility in (the couple's) emotional relations and intolerable cohabitation (*ganqing yizhi genben bu he, wufa jixu tongju* 感情意志根本不合，无法继续同居), (3) adultery (*tong jian* 通奸), (4) spousal abuse (*nuedai ta fang* 虐待他方), (5) abandonment in bad faith (*eyi yi qi* 恶意遗弃), (6) criminal framing of spouse (*tumou xianhai ta fang* 图谋陷害他方), (7) impotence (*buneng rendao* 不能人道), (8) incurable disease (*huan buzhi zhi eji* 患不治之恶疾), (9) couple had lost contact for one year or more (*sheng si buming guo yi nian* 生死不明过一年), or (10) other important reasons (*qita zhongda shi you* 其他重大事由).[12] The liberal spirit of this regulation is highlighted by the second condition (emotional relations) of term 11 (divorce conditions), which situated the basis of a marriage in loving feelings between the couple and one's willingness to enter into the union.

Due to how the communist concept of marriage differed from that of the locals, the direct consequence of this reform was an increase in marriage disputes as well as villagers' complaints and protests (the scale and extent of these protests will be discussed in Chapter 5). This phenomenon has been seen by some Western scholars as a sign of women's liberation from patriarchal oppression as well as conservative male peasants' reactionary response, as discussed in Chapter 1. What are missing here, however, are women's views, activities, and voices under the traditional patriarchal system, as well as their interactions with and transformation under the revolutionary state. Moreover, from the perspective of women as victims longing for salvation, the contradiction between Peng'er's annulment of her early engagement and her later fight to marry her former fiancé would not fit into the revolutionary narrative of women's liberation. By understanding local culture and women's activities, we can see that Peng'er's story was never a simple duplication of "Gold Flower" or similar communist textbook heroine.

[12] "Shaan-Gan-Ning Bianqu hunyin tiao li, 1939," term 11, in *Shaan-Gan-Ning bianqu funü yundong wenxian ziliao xuan bian*, 54–6.

II. Women in the local patriarchal system: love, sexuality, and marriage

As in many other agricultural societies, in China patriarchal power formed the main force of the local power structure, in which a senior male member, usually the father, held control over other members of the family. However, this is an abstract definition that only describes a static system of patriarchal order; in practice, this power might be compromised, intervened in, and even limited by other members participating in specific activities and operations. In reality, patriarchal power never operated in the absolute form described in the works of May Fourth authors or some scholars, as Dorothy Ko has pointed out.[13] At the same time, the traditional definition of patriarchy also overlooked a mother's active role in her daughter's marriage and love life. As I continue to discuss the case of *Feng v. Zhang* in Chapter 6, Peng'er's mother played a very important role in making arrangements for Peng'er to meet Zhang Bo and in passing messages to the Zhangs. Thus the current work suggests that it was in the dynamics of the system that rural women were able to carve out some space for themselves through their actions and support of each other.

Women's living conditions in the region: a society in distress

Women's position in the patriarchal family varied due to local custom. In the general history of Chinese women, the practice of female infanticide has been described as evidence of women's suffering.[14] However, female infanticide does not appear in any local records of this region, although it was widespread in some areas of southern China and sometimes occurred in central Shaanxi.[15] Scholarly research shows that in Shaanbei/Longdong, when a woman worshipped the Child-giving Goddess, she begged for a boy, but was always willing to settle for a girl (*zhong nan bu xian nü* 重男不嫌女).[16] Although in other parts of China

[13] Ko, *Teachers of the Inner Chambers*, 10–11.

[14] Ono Kazuko, *Chinese Women in a Century of Revolution, 1850–1950*, Joshua Fogel (ed.), Kathryn Bernhardt, Timothy Brook, Joshua Fogel, Jonathan Lipman, Susan Mann, and Laurel Rhodes (trans.) (Stanford, CA: Stanford University Press, 1978), 140–2; Stacey, *Patriarchy and Socialist Revolution*, 44–5.

[15] There is no record of this social practice in the region in any of the compilations of the local gazetteers by the imperial elites of Ming and Qing, the governments of the Republic, or the People's Republic. See Fu Xueli, *Qingyang fu zhi* (1557, reprint 2001); Yang Zaofeng (comp.), *Qingyang fu zhi* (1660, reprint 1993); *Chong xiu Zhenyuan zhi* (1935); *Qingyang diqu zhi* (1993); *Huachi xian zhi* (2004); *Huanxian zhi* (1993); *Qingyang xian zhi* (1993). Of course, it does not mean that there was absolutely no such practice. It is possible that this practice was so rare that it was felt not worth recording.

[16] Qin and Yue, *Zou chu fengbi*, 170–1.

where poor families could not afford expensive dowries, this resulted in the practice of drowning girls at birth,[17] in this region baby girls were not considered a burden. Instead, they were valued as a family asset because the imbalanced ratio of the sexes resulted in a high demand for girls, as discussed in Chapter 1. The SGN High Court recorded several cases in which two or three families fought for the custody or residential rights of a young girl.[18] Upon a widow's remarriage, if a girl was too young to leave her mother's care, the deceased father's clan tried to negotiate an agreement with the widow to be sure that the girl would be returned to her patrilineal family in the future.[19] Although the motivation for these custody disputes was the girls' future value for *caili*, there were also cases involving a stepfather's emotional connection with a girl, or a desire to improve a girl's living condition. This practice at least guaranteed girls' lives and their care.

In the conventional narrative of Chinese women's history, marriage for a woman meant entering a miserable stage in which she suffered endlessly under her tyrannical in-laws and husband. This did happen to many women in the SGNBR region. But at the same time, a wedding marked adulthood for a female in this region, meaning that she could escape her parents' authority as early as her teens. In addition to the different hairstyles that single and married women wore, the terms for women also reflected the distinction of adult from minor. For example, an unmarried female was called "*nüzi*" 女子 (girl), while a married female was called "*poyi*" 婆姨 (woman). A *poyi*, even if under the age of eighteen, still enjoyed adult privileges, while a *nüzi* of the same age was considered a minor who had to follow her parents' instructions.[20] If a girl was lucky, she married into a parentless household; if she was not, a married woman would try every means possible to benefit from the system. For instance, the tradition of dividing a household among brothers after marriage allowed some young women to be in charge of their own households instead of suffering their in-laws' abuse (see Chapter 1).

Due to the harsh weather, particular geographic environment, and difficult working conditions, the local records state that the majority

[17] Guo Songyi, *Lunli yu shenghuo*, 126–33.

[18] SPA 15–29, "Panjueshu cunben, 1946" (Preserved Copy of Adjudications for 1946); SPA 15–1574, "Cao Huaihou Liang Wenlin an" (*Cao Huaihou v. Liang Wenlin*).

[19] SPA 15–806, "Bi Shenghua shangsu an" (The Case of Bi Shenghua's Appeal).

[20] In this region, the distinction between a "girl" and a "woman" was not based on a female's age, as in contemporary Western society, but on her marriage status. Therefore, to avoid confusion with the English definition, I will use "women/woman" to indicate those who were involved in marriage disputes in the following discussion, regardless of their ages, and sometimes "girls/girl" in most disputes over engagement.

of women in this region followed a gender division that women hardly worked outside the family domain.[21] Although women were skillful at traditional women's work such as making clothes, embroidery, and other types of handicrafts, the isolation of the region and its low-level market economy limited the value of their work. These products were primarily for family use or gifts, and thus brought little economic profit to women. Women were largely dependent on the support of men for food, cash, and labor. In the 1930s, the regions of Shaanbei and Longdong were involved in a gradually opening market of modern goods that further devalued local women's handicrafts. Archival documents show that many *caili* during the 1930s and the 1940s included some machine-made fabrics from cities. In addition to the traditional currency, grains, and handicrafts, many modern industrial products as well as urban-style cosmetics and enamel washbasins became a regular part of *caili*.

In the 1930s and 1940s, women generally lived lives of great misery from extreme poverty and dreadful living conditions. Besides the pain of footbinding and abuse at the hands of husbands and in-laws, women of this region also suffered from many other problems that made them heavily dependent on men. With no knowledge of or technology for birth control and no sanitary facilities, a married woman was usually in a constant cycle of pregnancy, childbirth, and childrearing, which also made it impossible for her to work outside the home. Scholarly research observes that in the 1940s, one woman in Qingjian County was pregnant twenty times, from age sixteen to forty-six, with seventeen births and three miscarriages; another Qingjian woman gave birth twelve times.[22] Women suffered from unsanitary conditions in childbirth that could take their lives easily or leave them with endless gynecological maladies. Even if they escaped that, the great majority of mothers still suffered emotionally because of the extremely high rate of infant mortality. A 1942 survey in Ansai County, near Yan'an, showed an infant mortality rate as high as 81 percent.[23] Suide County, in a comparably economically and culturally developed subregion, seemed to be doing better by having a 58 percent

[21] Gail Hershatter's work makes a significant contribution by arguing that women frequently worked outside but were systematically forgotten and undervalued (see *The Gender of Memory*, pp. 129–53). It might be true for the region of Central Shaanxi where Hershatter did her investigation, but due to Shaanbei and Longdong's geographical and ecological conditions, it was rare for women to work outside in the hills before the CCP's mobilization of women to work in the fields during the Grand Production Campaign of the 1940s.

[22] Qin and Yue, *Zou chu fengbi*, 5.

[23] Jiang Ping, "Si de dao bi sheng de duo: Ansai weisheng shiyan qu diaocha" (Deaths Exceed Births: A Survey in Ansai Public Health District), *Jiefang ribao*, March 4, 1942.

child mortality rate.[24] The Huachi County gazetteer records that in 1948 the rate of infant mortality was close to 80 percent,[25] much higher than the national average of 25 percent during the same period.[26] These constant physical and emotional traumas also prevented women from working in the fields and having independence. In the 1930s, CCP workers discovered that this high degree of dependence led women to rely on marriage to better their lives; demanding a second *caili* thus became one strategy for survival.[27]

Women's life under patriarchy: love, sexuality, and marriage

Like many places in traditional China, the girls and young women, as well as the boys and young men of SGNBR, could not escape the fate of arranged marriages and remarriages. Many mismatched unions caused great physical and emotional pain for women. In the vast regions of Longdong and Shaanbei, as well as parts of Shanxi and other western areas of northern China, a long tradition of oral history exists in which ordinary people, including women, sing about their lives and express their feelings. These popular folk songs tell us a great deal about women's feelings of love and hate, sorrow and happiness, as well as about their sexual experiences. Many of these folk songs were recorded by the artists of Yan'an in the 1940s and published in a collection, though it is possible that some original views on sexuality were filtered out by the collectors (see Chapter 6).[28]

Some songs bravely express the tender feelings of women toward their lovers. The song "Shepherd Boy" (*Wu ge fang yang* 五哥放羊) relates that a girl enjoyed her time with her fiancé. When he leaves for shepherding somewhere else, the girl sings about how much she misses him and her hopes that he will come back soon to marry her.[29] In a happy marriage, the wife could articulate her strong feelings of love for her husband, telling him how much she misses him:

[24] "Yan shi beiqu weisheng jiancha, Suide ertong siwang lü jing ren" (A Public Health Investigation in the North Region of Yan'an; The Death Rate of Suide Children is Surprisingly High), *Jiefang ribao*, April 2, 1942.

[25] *Huachi xianzhi*, 142. Also see Qin and Yue, *Zou chu fengbi*, 190–202.

[26] Cited in Qin and Yue, *Zou chu fengbi*, 190.

[27] SPA 15-57, "Ge xian fengsu xiguan."

[28] Lu Xun yishu xueyuan, *Shaanbei minge xuan*. According to the preface, though named "Shaanbei Folk Songs," the songs published in this collection also included all areas of the SGN region. The remaining songs, besides those in this collection, were published in the 1950s, and some were republished in the 1980s.

[29] "Wuge fangyang" (Shepherd Boy), *Longdong geming geyao* (Revolutionary Lyrics in Longdong) (Lanzhou: Gansu renmin chubanshe, 1982), 14–16.

While hills and streams are still here,
I am home but you are not.

I miss you every time I have a meal,
And my tears drop into my bowl.

Even with no wind, the treetops swing,
Yet you have not appeared even in my dreams.

[Opening up] a green watermelon that shows red flesh,
But I [am too shy to] open up to anyone that I miss you to death.

One moment it is a gust and one moment a shower,
[Likewise, my mood swings so wildly that] I cannot tell where I am.[30]

In songs about unhappy marriages, women lament mismatched unions arranged by their money-loving parents, and curse the matchmakers who malevolently concealed the bad character of their prospective fiancés and the poverty of the fiancé's family. They claim that these are the reasons that they suffer from unhappy marriages.[31]

When marriage did not include love, women would look for some alternative relationship for emotional support and sexual satisfaction.[32] Certain widespread local customs, such as "making a friend" (*jiao pengyou* 交朋友), "taking a partner" (*da huoji* 搭伙计), or "having a sworn-brother" (*zhao gan gege* 找干哥哥), provided outlets for these women to deal with unhappy marriages.[33] Some folk songs declare that it is natural for everyone to have a sworn-brother or a sworn-sister; life was not considered worthwhile if a person had no such "friend."[34] The most popular folk song across a large part of western Shanxi, northern Shaanxi, and Eastern Gansu is the ballad "Lan Huahua" (兰花花). It tells the story of a girl, Lan Huahua, who was "the most beautiful girl of all thirteen provinces,"[35] and who had a sworn-brother (lover), but was forced to marry into a rich family with an ugly child groom. She could not wait to see her lover after the wedding:

Fetching a piece of lamb meat and holding a bowl of millet cake,
I am rushing forcefully to my sworn-brother's home.

It is not something else I love about him,
I simply love him at the age of twenty.

[30] See Xie Juezai, *Xie Juezai riji*, 880–1.
[31] "Xin tian you" (Songs Wandering on the Sky), *Shaanbei minge xuan*, 33–6.
[32] Also see Wang Yuesheng, *Qingdai zhongqi hunyin chongtu toushi*, 55–9.
[33] A sworn-brother/sister in this region could be one's fiancé/fiancée or lover, or a casual relation; in some cases the term was used to describe two acquaintances.
[34] "Xin tian you," *Shaanbei minge xuan*, 29.
[35] The Ming Empire was once divided into thirteen provinces. It is likely this song originated in the late Ming or early Qing.

Once together we two have endless things to say,
We really want to be together, whether in life or death.[36]

Through the singing of songs, women reveal their taste in men: they prefer those who have a "bright complexion with double eyelids,"[37] who are handsome, strong, and young.

Young women would love to meet young men,
Those old men with grey beards thus become losers.
...
Riding on a donkey and holding an umbrella,
I am circumspectly looking for a handsome man.[38]

I do not care whether you have money or silver,
I simply love you for your tight and straight body and double eyelids.[39]

Since the seventeenth century, under the various influences of Neo-Confucian doctrine, family pressure, state ideology, and psychological reason, women in Jiangnan elite families competed in chastity.[40] Matthew Sommer suggests that the Qing state reformed and reinforced the law in order to control the sexual behaviors of both men and women in lower social strata,[41] but as with Qing state-building projects, this control over women's sexual behavior seemed unable to reach this region until the 1940s. Although the local gazetteers record some women, mostly from upper-class families, who pursued chastity, and although the state rewarded chaste behavior,[42] ordinary women of the SGNBR region in the lower social strata had a very active sexual life. The folk song "Taking a Partner" (*Da huoji* 搭伙计), widespread in Shanxi, Shaanbei, and Longdong, tells the story of Li Guijie, a girl married at the age of fourteen who did not get along with her husband. He left home for business and never returned. From the age of fifteen to twenty-three, Guijie took three men as life partners who supported her physically and emotionally.

36 "Lan Huahua," *Longdong geming geyao*, 26–7.
37 "Qiong si qiong huo bu bianxin" (Never Change My Heart Regardless), *Longdong geming geyao*, 32–5.
38 "Xin tian you," *Shaanbei minge xuan*, 29–30.
39 Dang Yinzhi (comp.), *Xintianyou wu bai shou* (A Collection of 500 Songs-of-wandering-in-the-sky) (Xi'an: Shaanxi renmin chubanshe, 1993), 63.
40 For female chastity during the Ming and Qing times, see Janet Theiss, "Managing Martyrdom: Female Suicide and Statecraft in Mid-Qing China," *Nan Nü: Men, Women and Gender in China* 3(1)(2005): 47–76; T'ien Ju-k'ang, *Male Anxiety and Female Chastity: A Comparative Study of Chinese Ethical Values in Ming-Ch'ing Times* (Leiden: Brill, 1988); Weijing Lu, *True to Her Word*.
41 Sommer, *Sex, Law, and Society in Late Imperial China*, 1–17.
42 Fu Xueli and Yang Zaofeng, *Qingyang fu zhi*, 349–53, 767–71.

Her relationships with these men and their departures to pursue their own married lives brought great pain to her.[43]

Many folk songs boldly spoke about sexual activities and played a role in awakening young girls' sexual consciousness. But more importantly, the living conditions of the region contributed to the premature sexuality of girls and boys. Due to widespread poverty, many peasants only owned one cave-room (*yaodong* 窑洞), in which all family members, including parents and growing children, slept on one *kang* 炕, a bed built of mud bricks that normally took up about one-half of the space of a cave-room.[44] In this situation, girls often observed their parents' activities in the night and learned an open attitude toward sex, as one song demonstrates:

> The flowers of buckwheat are spread all over the field,
> Here is a young fellow who is very naughty,
> He pulled me into a small valley,
> And gave me a kiss that is so crispy.
>
> [Thus] a piece of fresh lamb braised with a bowl of white noodles,
> You have no wife and I have no man,
> We two are just like a cluster of garlic,
> Being unripe and becoming ripe together.[45]

In this song, "a piece of fresh lamb braised with a bowl of white noodles" is a sexual metaphor for the clash of two young bodies. The song also hints that it was a pleasant sexual experience and a good match because lamb meat with braised noodles is a luxurious and palatable dish in the local cuisine. The words "unripe" (*sheng* 生) and "ripe" (*shu* 熟) indicate the process of the two turning from unfamiliar to familiar and their sexuality from unskillful to skillful.

The records of the SGNBR High Court confirm this open attitude toward sexuality; in many cases, women had sexual affairs if they were not happy with their husbands.[46] Many divorce cases also related to extramarital sexuality, and it was primarily women who conducted these affairs and initiated the divorce. During the 1940s, the SGNBR had a special popular term for extramarital affairs: "guerrilla warfare" (*da youji* 打游击). This term normally indicated a military strategy that was broadly used by the CCP-led forces during the Anti-Japanese War. In

[43] "Da huoji" (Taking a Partner), *Shaanbei minge xuan*, 69–76.
[44] Qin and Yue, *Zou chu fengbi*, 55.
[45] "Tan jia" (Visiting Home), *Shaanbei minge xuan*, 88.
[46] Adultery was a punishable behavior under GMD law (see Philip Huang, *Code, Custom, and Legal Practice in China: The Qing and the Republic Compared* [Stanford, CA: Stanford University Press, 2001], 182), but in the SGNBR it was only a condition for divorce, not a punishable offense.

guerrilla warfare, military forces and militia teams attacked the Japanese Army irregularly by applying informal military techniques; this military term was borrowed as a metaphor for extramarital sexual affairs because both had similar irregularity and informality.

In some cases, it is clear that a woman having an affair did not mean that she wanted a divorce. The case of Woman Li and Gao Wufeng offers a dramatic and tragic example. In 1943, Gao Wufeng, an aide-de-camp of Nationalist Army Corps Twenty-two, went to Yan'an for a mission but fell sick in a country inn on the way. The wife of the inn's owner, Woman Li, took good care of him, resulting in an affair that lasted for more than half a month. Upon his leaving, Gao tried to bring Woman Li with him, but she had no intention of leaving her husband. Gao first threatened Woman Li and her family with his gun, then forced Woman Li to drink a bowl of opium juice; fortunately, the woman was saved. At this point the situation became the talk of the town, so scandalous that the local revolutionary government had to arrest Gao and send him to his superior officer. On the way back, Gao took his own life by drinking a bowl of opium juice.[47]

Many divorce cases also involved extramarital affairs. However, instead of men wanting to divorce their unfaithful wives, it was quite the opposite. Compared to similar cases in the mid-Qing,[48] women in the 1940s' SGNBR seemed aware of how to use the newly available right to divorce stipulated in the new marriage regulation to solve their troubled marriages. When a woman had an affair and requested a divorce, her husband often refused to accept it in spite of his wife's affair. The High Court documents record many cases of this type.[49] In the 1942 case of *Zhang Ying v. Liang Fucheng*, the court suggested that the husband, Liang Fucheng, settle the case, saying that if he did not accept divorce, his wife would continue to have "guerrilla warfare." The pitiful husband replied that he could tolerate that as long as the affair did not take place in front of his eyes.[50] In the 1942 divorce case of *Wu Guojun (husband) v. Dong Shaolin (wife)*, Dong was a nurse in a Yan'an refugee factory and Wu was a guard in the CCP military committee. They married in 1937 and had a child, but began fighting when the husband accused

[47] SPA 15–842, "Gao Wufeng zisha an" (The Case of Gao Wufeng's Suicide).

[48] Similar situations also occurred during the Qing period. See Wang Yuesheng, *Qingdai zhongqi hunyin chongtu toushi*, 167–81.

[49] Such as the cases of "*Wu Guojun v. Dong Shaolin* in Yan'an, 1942" (SPA 15–1340), "*Zhang Ying v. Liang Fucheng*" (SPA 15–1397), "Dang Xiuying an" (The Case of Dang Xiuying) (SPA 15–946), and "Zhao Pinglan bei bang an" (The Case of Zhao Pinglan's Kidnapping) (SPA 15–948).

[50] SPA 15–1397, *Zhang Ying v. Liang Fucheng.*

Dong of "guerrilla warfare." Dong immediately filed for divorce, but Wu opposed it. In the court investigation, Dong openly admitted the affair and also stated that they did not have a good sex life because Wu's penis was too short. Additionally, Dong confessed the even more fatal fact to her husband in court that their only son was from another man. In this situation, the court had no choice but to grant the divorce in spite of Wu's opposition.[51]

It is clear that the family structure and marriage forms in this region were used as strategies for production, procreation, and survival, all of which had to support the family economic plan, as discussed in Chapter 1. On the other hand, love and sexuality were viewed as more individual affairs that did not necessarily fall within the circle of family and marriage. Although elite women in Jiangnan were able to carve out a space within the Confucian patriarchal family system, their sexual behavior and loving feelings were under much closer scrutiny in the family domain. Wealth and social status allowed these women to have certain freedoms,[52] whereas the women from lower social strata in Shaanbei/Longdong had more autonomy in personal feelings and sexual activities.

Up to the 1940s, neither the state nor patriarchal authority in this region had formulated a strong ideology or legal regulations regarding women's love lives and their sexual behavior outside of marriage.[53] This social reality led us to rethink the definition of patriarchy and its control over women. Patriarchal power had indeed controlled the institutions of family and marriage, and this control was enforced through arranged marriage and strictly restrained use of divorce. On the other hand, the patriarchs of local society had complete awareness of women's unruly activities in love and sexuality, but found this behavior difficult to control and sometimes had to tolerate and accept it. In this sense, women in the lower social strata had more control over their bodies and their feelings, which represented a higher degree of autonomy. It was the CCP revolution that brought modern concepts and attempted to compress family, marriage, sexuality, and love into a homocentric circle, with love as the axis. This attempt to transform social life as a state-building project resulted in a conflict between the SGN revolutionary state and local women.

[51] SPA 15-1340, *Wu Guojun v. Dong Shaolin*.

[52] Mann suggests that many elite women in Jiangnan also were able to learn about sexuality and expressed their desire for sexuality in their literary or other works (see her *Precious Records*, 60–3). However, women's sexuality in elite families was inevitably under close surveillance. Also see Ko, *Teachers of the Inner Chambers*.

[53] For the Qing state's control over ordinary women's sexual behaviors, see Sommer, *Sex, Law, and Society in Late Imperial China*; and Theiss, *Disgraceful Matters*.

Resistance to the patriarchy: women running away and "being kidnapped"

Although violent acts such as kidnapping were used in marriage disputes, as in the case of *Feng v. Zhang* and many others discussed in Chapter 1, kidnapping could also be a method employed by women to resist patriarchal domination. Due to the remaining influence of matrilineal family practices in the steppe culture, as well as the fluidity of the population, young women of the SGN region had some autonomy that often manifested itself in certain "abnormal" behaviors when seen through the eyes of the state. When the patriarchal family structure imposed unhappy marriages on women, or the abuse of in-laws and/or husbands became unbearable, some local women used any means possible to escape.

Running away from the husband's home was one option for a desperate wife. For centuries, the BR had been a place with a high degree of migration. Population control or restrictions on movement basically did not exist during the social chaos of the late Qing and the early Republican periods. Because of the geographical conditions and the fact that transportation and communication systems were undeveloped in the region, a husband's family would have to spend a great deal of time, money, and human resources to track down and retrieve a runaway wife. In contrast, once a woman arrived in a new location she could find a man to start a new life with and pay for her costs on the road. Running away offered women a second chance – if the action were successful. For example, the High Court recorded a 1943 case in which Gao Ruifu and his wife, Woman Gao, lived in Jiaxian County, but she ran away from her husband in 1941 and was married to another man, Gao Yingcai, for over two years before her husband found her.[54] In a 1943 divorce case, Du Guirong could not bear the abuse from her mother-in-law and husband and ran away with her sister-in-law (her husband's brother's wife) to Suide County, where the two women found jobs in a refugee factory. When her husband eventually located her, she immediately filed for divorce and married one of her fellow workers (see Figure 2.1).[55] In 1945, a woman, Gao Lanying, escaped from her husband's abuse by running away from Yan'an to Ansai County, where she sold herself (*zi mai ben shen* 自卖本身) into a marriage and used the money (*caili*) to pay off all the debts incurred during her escape. In possession of her own money, she bought some pretty clothes for

[54] SPA 15–845, "Gao Yingcai shangsu an" (Gao Yingcai's Appeal).
[55] SPA 15–1470, *Zhang Huaibao v. Du Guirong.*

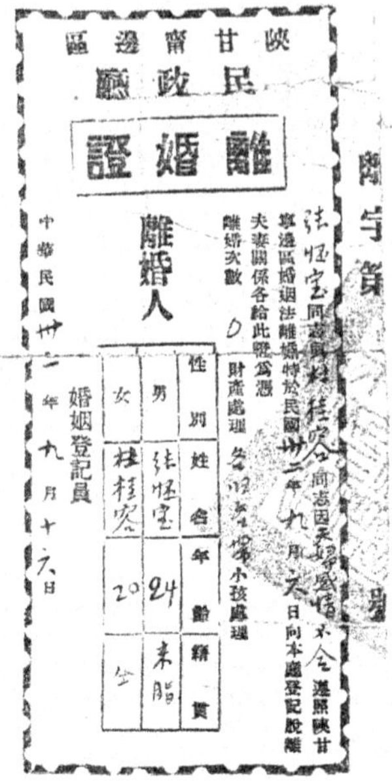
陝甘寧邊區
民政廳
離婚證
張懷寶同志與杜桂容同志因夫婦感情不合遵照陝甘寧邊區婚姻法離婚特於民國卅二年九月六日向本處登記脫離夫妻關係各給此證為憑
離婚次數 0
財產處理
小孩處理
離婚人

性別	姓名	年齡	籍貫
男	張懷寶	24	米脂
女	杜桂容	20	仝

婚姻登記員
中華民國卅二年九月十六日

Figure 2.1 SGNBR-issued divorce certificate, SPA 15–1470 (*Zhang Huaibao v. Du Guirong*)

herself and offered a treat in a local restaurant to those who had helped her on the road.[56] As these women were found by their husbands and their cases brought before the government, they have left traces in the historical record.

There may be many other cases in which the women were not found, enabling them to start over somewhere new. For example, in 1941 a Qingyang girl, Cheng Taohua, who did not like the marriage her father and brother had arranged for her, eloped with a man and married him on the way. After they were caught, the case was brought to the county court as a marriage dispute. During the trial, when Taohua was temporarily staying at the home of a woman cadre whose husband was the commander-in-chief of local military forces, she married herself to a soldier and the two ran away, escaping without a trace. Runaway women

[56] SPA 15–1576, "Shi Yude qi bei guai mai an" (The Case of Shi Yude's Wife Being Abducted and Sold).

like Cheng Taohua took the risk that they could be violated, killed, or sold into even worse conditions. It was thus up to the woman to decide whether or not running away was worth it.

Due to the dangers that a runaway woman might face, most women chose to run away with other men. Philip Huang's research points out that Qing law categorized running away into various terms, including consenting to seduction (*he you* 和诱), abduction (*lue you* 略诱), consenting to abduction (*he lue* 和略), or desertion of husband (*bei fu zai tao* 背夫在逃). The Qing law made a distinction between *he you*/*he lue* and *bei fu zai tao*, in which the term "*he*" designated a woman's consent. Huang believes that these terms indicated that the man was the active agent, while the woman was a passive agent with no choice. These terms reveal the Qing concept of women in marriage that women were subjected to male domination to various degrees. Huang suggests that Republican law rejected the specific terms that had indicated hierarchical relations in the Qing law in favor of equal status of all citizens before the law.[57] In fact, the Qing court might have underestimated the active role of women in making the decision to run away.

In theory, the 1939 marriage regulation did not have terms that addressed runaway wives; instead, it followed Republican law by setting up terms such as "abandonment in bad faith" (*e yi yi qi* 恶意遗弃) as grounds for divorce that applied to both men and women. It also established "absence without contact for over a year" as a condition for divorce that could be claimed by either side. On the other hand, in regard to selling a woman through abduction or kidnapping/capture, the 1939 regulation did not offer detailed instructions, but instead summarized them as either buying/selling marriage or marriage by force. In practice, the High Court sometimes used the Qing legal terms, for a number of judges had been trained in late imperial schools and inherited the early Republican tradition in legal terminology (see Chapter 3). By using certain traditional terms, the High Court may have implied that men were still viewed as the dominant party – a view that to a certain extent also fitted with the communist ideology that viewed women as victims of patriarchy. For example, in 1946 Li Huaishu, a farmer in Yan'an County, reported to the Yan'an Court that his wife had run away with Li Fucai, a resident of Yanchang County. The two runaways were captured by a local self-defense team and brought to the township government. After a brief investigation, they were set free on bail for further investigation. However, they once again eloped without a trace. The document on their case used a term indicating it was an act of seduction

[57] Huang, *Code, Custom, and Legal Practice in China*, 161–5.

and abduction (*you guai* 诱拐),[58] which did not convey the fact that the woman likely exercised her own volition in going away with the man.

In fact, the term "seduction and abduction" concealed women's true intentions. A woman might run away with her lover, a neighbor, or a relative, but it was sometimes for reasons of security and sometimes to disguise her true identity to avoid unnecessary suspicion. The local residents used various terms, all peaceful in nature, to describe a woman running away with a man: *gua zou* 挂走 (hooking away), *kua zou* 挎走 (bringing away), or sometimes *kua zou* 跨走 ([two] stepping away) or *yin zou* 引走 (guiding away). Although the term *gua zou* still carried a slight hint that a man lured a woman away, the other terms were more neutral, suggesting that the woman was willingly running away with the man without any coercive intention. Local folk songs convey villagers' views of this behavior: in a song in which the daughter of an inn-owner runs away with a man hired to care for the animals, the parents use the term *kua zou* 挎走 (bringing away) to narrate the story.[59] While these words imply that men were the more active party, in fact it was often women who were seeking such opportunities to escape their situations.

These endemic terms sometimes appear in court testimony from villagers or lower cadres that reveal local views of this issue. For example, in 1946, Yan'an County reported the case of Li Zengzhi's lost wife; the document written by a village cadre used the term *kua zou* (bringing away). When the same report was sent to the High Court, the title on the cover page was changed to *guai zou* 拐走 (seduced abduction),[60] indicating the changed nature of the case. Another case occurred in Yan'an in 1943, in which Zhang Dehou's wife was brought away by the Hu brothers to Fuxian County. Although this case also used the nonviolent term *kua zou* instead of *guai zou*, it still used a passive sentence construction, indicating that the woman had played a relatively passive part.[61] In the case of Gao Lanying mentioned above, Gao's husband also stated that his wife was "guided away" (*yin zou*) by someone.[62] The local culture recognized the volition of a runaway woman to an extent, even though her actions were conducted with a man's help. Similarly, in the aforementioned case of Cheng Taohua, it was very likely that Taohua used those two men for her own escape, rather than being abducted by them.

58 SPA 15–1133, "Li Fucai you guai ren qi an" (Li Fucai Abducted Someone's Wife).
59 "Dianjia shi nü" (Inn's Owner Lost His Daughter), *Shaanbei minge xuan*, 94–5.
60 SPA 15–1076, "Li Zengzhi qi bei Li Zhongxun guaizou" (The Case of Li Zengzhi's Wife Being Seduced and Abducted by Li Zhongxun).
61 SPA 15–842, "Zhang Dehou qi bei Hu Haiqing kuazou an" (The Case of Zhang Dehou's Wife Stepping Away with Hu Haiqing).
62 SPA 15–1576, "Shi Yude qi bei guai mai an."

A case in a legal dispute categorized as kidnapping for marriage (*qiang hun* 抢婚) might in fact be a runaway or a consented act, as happened in the case *Feng v. Zhang*. Occasionally, when family surveillance prevented a girl from leaving her home, she sent a message to her lover revealing her whereabouts, hinting at or urging an action. For example, a 1940–3 case in Yanchang County involved similar elements to *Feng v. Zhang*. In 1940, Zhang Qin, a native of Yan'an and a revolutionary cadre of the Communications Department of the Northwestern Bureau (*Xi bei ju tongxun chu* 西北局通讯处) in Yan'an, sued her own elder brother for selling her fourteen-year-old younger sister, Zhang Lawa, to Liu Baoqing, a farmer in Yanchang County, for marriage. Yanchang County invalidated the engagement and confiscated the *caili*, then penalized Zhang's brother with three months of labor service. About a year later, Zhang Qin arranged for her sister to go Yan'an for education, but on the way Zhang Lawa was "kidnapped" by Liu Baoqing and the two got married. Zhang Qin was very angry and sued Liu for "kidnapping" her little sister. When the Yan'an court issued a subpoena, neither Zhang Lawa nor Liu Baoqing appeared in court. Instead, Zhang Lawa sent a letter to her elder sister informing her that she wanted to be with Liu and did not want her sister to intervene in her life. Not believing that this was her sister's free choice, Zhang Qin urged the court to speed up the trial. Eventually, in 1943 the court brought both Liu and Lawa to face the charges. During the court investigation, Zhang Lawa was placed alone in a room and separated from both her sister and her husband; she then told the judge that it was she who informed Liu when she was going to Yan'an and asked him to come pick her up along the way. She also reaffirmed her statement in her letter to her sister that she wanted to marry Liu Baoqing. In addition, Zhang Lawa joyfully told the judge that she was already pregnant.[63] In this case, Zhang Qin believed that she was helping her sister escape from an arranged marriage and a kidnapping, but this charge was overturned by her sister's words.

In this context, we need to reexamine Peng'er's kidnapping. The court recorded that Peng'er's father held the engagement ceremony with Zhu on March 10 (common calendar) at Feng's home, and that Peng'er met Zhang Bo on the thirteenth day of the second month of the lunar calendar (*gu er yue shisan ri* 古二月十三日),[64] while the kidnapping took place

[63] SPA 15–891, "Zhang Lawa heLiu Baoqing hunyin an" (The Marriage Case of Zhang Lawa and Liu Baoqing). The court secretary described the shy and joyful look on Zhang Lawa's face in her conversation with the judge during the investigation.

[64] The SGNBR governments adopted the calendar of the common era in their official records. In some cases, the government workers converted lunar calendar dates to the

on the night of March 18 (common calendar).[65] If the date of Peng'er's meeting with Zhang Bo is converted to the common calendar, we find that the thirteenth of the second lunar month of 1943 was exactly March 18,[66] a week after the engagement with Zhu Shouchang and the same day the two met! This is not a coincidence. Considering the timing of the meeting and her words as described in the writ, it was obvious that Peng'er urged Zhang Bo to take action because she alone could not leave her father's supervision (see Chapter 1). Peng'er's words made Zhang Jincai's decision to bring his future daughter-in-law home much easier. Thus the so-called "kidnapping" occurred that night.

III. Local women and the revolutionary state

When revolutionary power gradually extended and penetrated into the lives of ordinary villagers in the 1940s, local women had to adjust to the new government. Although the new state provided women with some support in political policies, social programs, and legal codes, it also restrained women's behavior and ate away at the space they had previously carved out in the patriarchal system. The state intended to use its visions of the ideal marriage and family life to reshape local women's lives and their views of marriage. Correspondingly, women's autonomy underwent a transformation in response to the changes and projects of the new state. They sometimes collaborated with, sometimes resisted, and sometimes manipulated the state's ideological rhetoric and policies in legal processes. Local women's reconfiguration of their subjectivity was clearly embodied in their presentations in legal cases, in which they fearlessly defended or explained their behavior and motives. Since in any society or at any time women are not a united entity, their responses to state policy and state power varied based on their social position and interests.

The revolutionary state: mobilization of women for sacrifice

Since the mid-1930s, when the revolutionary movement led by Liu Zhidan began to mobilize women in this region, its leaders promoted

official calendar in local residents' reports or testimony if necessary. If officials were unable to do the conversion, a common practice was to mark the lunar calendar date with the character(s) of "ancient/traditional calendar" (*gu li* 古历) or "outdated/abolished calendar" (*jiu/fei li* 旧/废历) in front of the dates villagers provided. This was how it was marked in Ma's writ.

65 Feng Yangui sued the Zhangs for the kidnapping immediately after it occurred. The date in the local court record should be from the common calendar.

66 Li Wei (comp.), *Wannianli* (A Calendar for Ten Thousand Years) (Beijing: Zhongyi guji chubanshe, 2008), 93.

a social reform agenda that included advocating freedom of marriage and an end to footbinding, and prohibited other social customs such as violence against women, gambling, and opium smoking.[67] Nonetheless, from a Marxist-nationalist perspective, Chinese women as a whole were also considered the victims of capitalism, imperialism, and militarism, represented at the time by Japanese invaders. Working from this assumption, and by adopting their previous experience from urban social movements, the early communist "woman-work"[68] emphasized political campaigns, public speeches, establishing various political assemblies, and promoting membership in communist-led organizations.[69] In other words, woman-work was not just about revolutionizing the family, but also liberating the nation.

In practice, this policy ignored social realities and women's basic needs, and thus the communist women's movements from 1936 to 1942 encountered some difficulties. Many women leaders complained that rural women were not responding to revolutionary campaigns and that pushing woman-work forward had proven more difficult than anticipated. Meanwhile, grassroots women workers constantly urged the top leaders to give some consideration to women's particular needs and their special interests, especially issues concerning family and marriage and improvement of women's living conditions. Community women workers also organized activities such as struggling against abusive mothers-in-law and husbands, forcing the unbinding of feet, and liberating *tongyangxi*.[70] These activities were often used as a local strategy to mobilize women's support for the communist movement, though they did not require a long-term commitment. It was not until 1939 that the conditions of the Border Region were stabilized enough to pursue a social revolution. Moreover, before the communist government trained

[67] Xi Zhongxun zai Shaan-Gan-Ning bianqu compiling committee, *Xi Zhongxun zai Shaan-Gan-Ning bianqu* (Xi Zhongxun in Shaan-Gan-Ning Border Region) (Beijing: Zhongguo wenshi chubanshe, 2009), 160.

[68] "Woman-work" was a term used by the CCP to describe their method of mobilizing women to engage in social movements. By using it as her book's title, Davin takes on the CCP official view of women's activities. See Davin, *Woman-Work*.

[69] "Bianqu dangwei guanyu bianqu funv qunzhong zuzhi de jueding, 1937" (The Decision of the BR Party Committee on Women's Mass Organizations in the BR, 1937), *Shaan-Gan-Ning bianqu funü yundong wenxian ziliao xuan bian*, 3–6.

[70] Shi Xiuyun, "Bianqu funü diyici daibiao dahui taolun zongjie jianghua, 1938" (Concluding Remarks at the First Conference of Women Representatives in the BR, 1938), *Shaan-Gan-Ning bianqu funü yundong wenxian ziliao xuan bian*, 17–19 and 25–8; also see Li Youyi, "Hongjun jiaodao shi zai Qingyang pianduan" (Some Memory Pieces on the Red Army in Qingyang), in *Gansu wenshi ziliao xuanji*, 12 (A Series of Collections of Documents on Gansu's Culture and History, ser. 12) (Lanzhou: Gansu sheng zhengxie, 1981), 6–10.

a group of local women workers, the social reform programs remained basically on paper because the early communist women workers who came from the south had a language barrier that prevented effective communication with northern women in villages.[71] Beginning in 1939, the social reform movement was not limited to the promulgation of the marriage regulation, but operated as a systematic program in which the revolutionary state also reaffirmed its resolution to ban other social ills as well.[72]

However, this modern state power, though revolutionary in principle, still possessed a certain conservative character in its pursuit of "legibility," as Scott puts it.[73] The SGNBR state took the radical measure of liberating women, but it also sometimes turned to restraining women and cutting back some of the space they had previously enjoyed. For example, in the 1939 regulation the state set bigamy as a first condition for divorce. The reason for this was not only to promote monogamy, but also to protect women from abuse by men who practiced concubinage. In the practice of the 1940s, this rich/urban-region-originated clause was actually more frequently applied to women than to men in this area. In a poverty-stricken region like the SGNBR, the situation of a man having more than one woman was limited to an extremely small number of wealthy people (see Chapter 1). Most of them had fled the revolutionary area, especially in a region like Longdong, where the land revolution from 1934 to 1937 had already thoroughly destroyed the landlord class. "Bigamy" was basically an empty term, because in over one hundred marriage disputes recorded by the High Court, there were only a few cases related to this situation, most of which dealt with women from the Nationalist region who had taken refuge in the SGNBR.

Although an unintended consequence, some poor women were penalized because of the bigamy ban. First, the local custom of polyandry (*zhao fu yang fu*), practiced by women from families desperate for survival, was banned. Normally, the government required that the

[71] Qingyang xian fulian (Qingyang County Women's Federation Association), "Cai Chang tongzhi zai Qingyang" (Comrade Cai Chang in Qingyang), in *Qingyang wenshi ziliao*, 1 (A Documentary Collection of Qingyang's History and Culture, vol. I) (Qingyang: Qingyan xian zhengxie *et al.* print, 1999), 69–79. This situation gradually improved after the CCP trained a group of local women to work as grassroots leaders.

[72] Gansu sheng funü lianhehui Qingyang diqu bianshichu fuyunshi xiaozu (comp.), "Longdong gedi fulian gongzuo jielue" (A Briefing on the Works of the Women's Federation in the Longdong Region), in *Longdong funü yundong shi ziliao huibian* (A Collection of Historical Documents on the Women's Movement in the Longdong Region) (Qingyang: Gansu sheng funv lianhehui Qingyang diqu bianshichu fuyunshi xiaozu print, 1982), 69–70.

[73] See Scott, *Seeing Like a State*, 2–5.

wife divorce one of her two husbands.[74] This would add to the desperation of a woman whose original husband might be physically disabled or chronically ill, preventing her from leaving him alone. By divorcing her second husband, she would lose all sources of support for herself, her first husband, and their children. Second, although both the imperial legal code and the patriarchal system strongly constrained women's right to divorce, some legal basis and community traditions did exist that allowed women to remarry under certain conditions, such as a husband's absence for a certain period.[75] This remarriage often took the form of a woman either marrying out (*li jia* 离家 or *zou ren* 走人) or inviting a husband in (*zhao fu*), as discussed in Chapter 1. However, the modern state's control over marriage often deemed such illicit practice bigamy, though the state offered the option of divorce.

Third, the penalty for bigamy was also applied to those women who ran away from their original husbands and married another one. In the local tradition, if a runaway woman was found but unwilling to return to her former husband, the second husband could settle the case by paying compensation so that the former husband could find a new wife.[76] In the worst case scenario, the former husband could conduct a kidnapping to get her back, which would lead to a legal dispute between the woman's two husbands. The documents of the High Court show that the government did not recognize remarriages of runaway women, since they had not officially divorced their first husbands. The process of settling a divorce case through the government could last from six months to two years, during which time the wife would need financial support that the husband often refused to provide. As long as a husband was filing appeals, the case remained an open one; according to the law, neither the husband nor the wife was allowed to remarry during this period. Sometimes it happened that a woman remarried after the first divorce verdict by the county court, while her husband was still appealing the case to the High Court, and thus her new marriage was then ruled bigamous.[77] This

[74] SPA 15–1498, "Guo Jungao zhao fu yang fu an" (The Case of Guo Jungao Having One Husband to Support Another).

[75] According to Huang, the Qing legal code allowed women to remarry if the husband had been absent for more than three years, but it would consider an absent husband to be an outlaw (Huang, *Chinese Civil Justice*, 27 and *Code, Custom, and Legal Practice*, 162). Also see Wang Yuesheng's *Qingdai zhongqi hunyin chongtu toushi* (27–9), which records the imperial practice in some regions that a wife could remarry if her husband was absent for three years.

[76] This type of solution was even suggested in some mediating cases in the SGN courts.

[77] For instance, *Zhao Zhixiang v. Liu Fenglan/Wen Yi* in "Gaoyuan panjueshu huiji zhi er" (Collected Documents on the High Court Adjudications, vol. II) (SPA 15–30), and previously mentioned runaway wife cases such as "Gao Yingcai shangsu an" (SPA 15–845).

situation had nothing to do with political idealism or conservatism, but simply an adherence to legal formalities carried out by the modern state.

When a state puts forth its own terms for marriage and family, it must also act to maintain those terms. As such, the revolutionary state tightened population control and restricted movement. First, after the Nationalists blocked off the SGNBR in the early 1940s, a person needed a travel pass to go beyond his/her village, which made running away more difficult for women. In the aforementioned case of Du Guirong, it was the village head who sympathized with her situation and gave her a travel pass so that she could escape.[78] Second, with the gradual completion of the administrative system down to the village level, the state sometimes assisted in locating a runaway wife upon a husband's request, even if it was only to urge her to deal with their divorce case. In 1946, a farmer from Yan'an, Zhang Zhijin, wrote to Ma Xiwu and asked Prefect Ma to help him find his wife, forty-one-year-old Shi Xiuying, who had taken his daughter and run away with Yang Zhizhong, a barber in Zaoyuan Complex in Yan'an.[79] Zhang had recently heard that his wife was spotted in the Qingyang County seat. In the letter, he added that his wife and her sister had left together, thus his brother-in-law, Xu Zhi'er, was also looking for his own wife. Qingyang County officials did find Shi Xiuying and persuaded her to return to her hometown to deal with Zhang Zhijin.[80] In most cases, when a runaway woman was brought to the government, she was advised by the local authority that if she wanted to file for divorce, she had to do so in her home jurisdiction.

On the other hand, the state also sought to ensure that a returned runaway wife would not be mistreated by her husband, to avoid a situation of Woman Wang described in Jonathan Spence's book *The Death of Woman Wang*.[81] In Chapter 4, I will discuss the procedure of divorce and government measures to secure women's safety after their return home. It displays the importance of confirmed abuse by a husband (and/or his family) in the courts' consideration of a wife's divorce request.

Soldiers' wives and fiancées: women who did not want to wait

If Shaanbei and Longdong women had managed to carve out their own spaces under the patriarchal system, it is logical to assume that they would also work to create new niches under the revolutionary state. In fact, the

[78] SPA 15–1470, *Zhang Huaibao v. Du Guirong*.
[79] Zaoyuan Complex was the headquarters of the Communist Central Committee.
[80] SPA 15–1076, "Liu Youfu Zhang Guihua an" (The Case of Liu Youfu and Zhang Guihua).
[81] Jonathan Spence, *The Death of Woman Wang* (New York: Viking Press, 1978), 99–132.

legal documents of the SGN High Court in the 1940s show that they did. In studying women and the Chinese revolution, some scholars tend to view the communist state as an all-encompassing and omnipresent power over women's lives, a simple substitution for the oppression of the old patriarchal family and state. Under the new regime, these scholars argue, women were still powerless victims who either surrendered to a new patriarchal state or were passively reformed, recast, and schooled in state ideology, then mobilized as a state instrument for social movements.[82] In the process of state-building, the modern state needed to destroy the traditional patriarchal structure, untethering women from it by making them individually subject to state power. For its own sake, as well as ideology, the revolutionary state was thus willing to support women's fight against local patriarchal power. But those scholars overlook how women themselves learned how to deal with the new power within the changing society of the SGNBR. The legal cases in the SGN courts show that local women applied a range of cultural resources, both old local traditions and new revolutionary rhetoric, to legitimize their actions.

In the SGNBR, there was a group of women whose marriages and family lives were strongly affected by the communist revolution and the marriage regulations. This group of women had a special name, *kangshu* 抗属, or family members of soldiers in the anti-Japanese army. Broadly defined, this term could indicate any family member of a soldier in the anti-Japanese army; however, in the context of marriage, it was used specifically for soldiers' wives and fiancées. Facing the harsh circumstances of the 1940s, the Border government was under siege from the Nationalist army and frequent attacks by local warlords and bandits around the borderlines. This was also a vital moment for state-building and solidifying the revolutionary base that ongoing social reform had helped establish as a more effective government for the war against Japan. This situation required the government to maintain a strong army for survival and protection. However, the "problem of soldiers' marriages" (*kangshu hunyin wenti* 抗属婚姻问题), as official documents termed it, became a major headache for the government, including cadres and legal workers at the township, county, and district levels as well as the higher authorities in Yan'an. It was this pressure that led the BR government to modify the regulation for the marriages of soldiers.

82 For instant, Guo Yuhua, "Xinling de jitihua: Shaanbei Ji cun nongye hezuohua de nvxing jiyi" (Collectivization of the Soul: Women's Memories of Agricultural Collectivization in Ji Village, Shaanbei), *Zhongguo shehui kexue* (Social Sciences in China) 4 (2003): 79–92; Wu Xueshan, "Forging Marriage" (trans. Hui Xiao), *Inter-Asia Cultural Studies* 7(3) (2006): 504–12.

The central problem was that the 1939 regulation did not contain a special clause concerning soldiers' marriages. The 1934 Jiangxi Revolutionary Marriage Law had already stipulated a waiting period for a divorce request from a Red Army soldier's wife,[83] but the 1939 regulation, despite the precedent of the 1934 law, abolished this point for unknown reasons. Two possible explanations for the absence of such a clause are either that this reflected a view that soldiers' wives or fiancées should wait indefinitely for their men to return, or a view that soldiers' women should be granted the same rights as civilian women, and soldiers should not have any special privileges in marital disputes. At a time of national crisis, the CCP might have presumed that local women, along with the rest of society, would unconditionally support its policies regarding women's liberation from feudal patriarchy as well as the nation's liberation from imperialism. This expectation was expressed in the dictum of a 1942 case, *Zuo Run v. Wang Yinsuo* (see below), by the Trial Committee of the Border Government (TCBG, *Bianqu zhengfu shenpan weiyuanhui* 边区政府审判委员会):[84]

> The Border region is now facing the most intensive phase of resisting Japan. If soldiers are thwarted by marriage troubles, [they will be defeated by Japan and] the enemy will invade our region. If this occurs, the women in the border region would be brutally violated. Therefore, men are strong so they should carry guns to the front line. Comparably, women are rather effeminate (*rou ruo* 柔弱) so they should stay at home to do their duties (of course, with the exception of certain women) so that their husbands will have no cause to worry on the front line.[85]

Nonetheless, this expectation was challenged in legal practice by women's activities. The marriage regulation often became a resource for these women to achieve their own goals.

Between 1943 and 1945, the Qingjian County government conducted a survey in two townships from two separate wards (*qu* 区), township number three in Xinshe ward (XSQ) and township number five in Dianzigou ward (DZGQ). The survey showed that 50 percent of a total of thirty-eight soldiers' wives or fiancées were "having problems" with their marriages or engagements (see Table 2.1).[86] According to the survey, most of these absent soldiers had joined the Red Army between

[83] See "Zhonghua Suweiai gongheguo hunyin fa" (April 8, 1934).
[84] See Chapter 3 for discussion of the SGNBR legal system.
[85] SPA 15–1336, *Zuo Run v. Wang Yinsuo*.
[86] SPA 15–220, "Qingjian liang xiang kangshu hunyin" (The Marriage Problems of Soldiers' Wives/Fiancées in Two Townships in Qingjian County). In the Border Region, an engagement was accorded semi-marriage status, according to local customs; therefore in certain circumstances the cancellation of an engagement was considered a divorce case.

Table 2.1. *Statistics on soldiers' marriages in two townships of Qingjian County (1943–5)*[87]

Conditions of soldiers' wives	Number of persons: XSQ Township No. 3	Number of persons: DZGQ Township No. 5	Subtotal	Notes
Remarried with the permission of in-laws and wife's natal family	3	2	5	Includes two cases of engagements
Remarried on the woman's own decision		1	1	
Remarried, but local gov't ordered wife to return to previous husband's family		1	1	Engaged, but fiancé sent a letter allowing the girl to leave
Remarried, but returned to previous husband when he came back; when previous husband refused to accept her she left again	1		1	
In-laws allowed wife to invite a live-in substitute husband	1	1	2	
Wife had invited a substitute husband; when previous husband returned, wife made the substitute husband leave	1		1	
Misconduct (including demand to remarry and committing adultery)	5	1	6	One had no contact for six yrs; one was engaged
Developed a mental problem		1	1	Husband disliked wife; he passed by the county in 1941 but did not go home
Misconduct led to suicide		1	1	
No problems living with husband's family	4	15	19	
Total	15	23	38	

[87] SPA 15–220, "Qingjian liang xiang kangshu hunyin." Although the date of the document is missing, it can be determined from context that the survey was conducted between 1943 and 1945.

1934 and 1937. By the time of the survey in the mid-1940s, the majority of the soldiers had been away from home for almost a decade, and some had even lost contact with their families. This condition created huge pressure on local governments, which had to constantly alleviate the anxiety of soldiers' wives and fiancées.

In these cases, the local customs that granted a woman the right to remarry or invite in a substitute husband during her husband's absence had been used by some women as a strong argument for remarrying or leaving their husband's families (see Figure 1.2 in Chapter 1). According to the records of the SGN courts, these types of cases were not limited to the two townships where the survey was conducted.

The local culture offered women a particular vision of family life and marriage, in which a husband stayed at home and provided material and emotional support. Local folk songs spelled out the miseries of women without men at home.[88] Legal workers in the Longdong region admitted that local woman preferred to marry ordinary farmers, rather than soldiers.[89] In many cases, the wives/fiancées of absent solders fell into a long-term depression and threw tantrums. Soldiers' wives/fiancées frequently cried at local government offices, "tearing up like rainfall," and refused to do any productive work unless their husbands returned. They begged their in-laws and local government officials for pity, comparing their short young lives to flowers: "how long can a flower maintain blooming?" "[It cannot wait until] green leaves turn to red then red leaves to dried yellow." "We may not lack food or clothing, but we have no men."[90] These complaints indicate that women's expectations of marriage included food, labor, and a husband who could stay at home. These women's activities brought a large number of marriage disputes to local governments that involved runaway wives, kidnapping, bigamy (polyandry), adultery, and cases of two or even three men fighting for one wife/fiancée.

Some in-laws, half in an attempt at attaining family peace and half for material gain, followed local customs and allowed these women to leave for another marriage. For example, a case in Yan'an County shows that Lei married Woman Cui in 1934 and Cui gave birth to a girl the next year. In 1935, Lei joined the Red Army and left the village. In 1940, Woman Cui married Li Rongchun by paying the Lei family a large amount of *caili* to obtain her freedom.[91] In Zichang County, the Liu family engaged

88 Lu Xun Yishu xueyuan, *Shanbei minge xuan*, 18–21 and 40–2.
89 SPA 15-1495, "Sun Shanwen shangshu an" (Sun Shangwei's Appeal).
90 SPA 15-72, "Shaan-Gan-Ning bianqu hunyin wenti yu tiaoli."
91 SPA 15-26, *Li Rongchun v. Lei Shangzhi.*

their son, Liu Lian, to the daughter of the Shi family, Shi Xiuying (different one from previously mentioned case), at a young age. Liu Lian joined the Red Army in 1935 and then went to the front line. In 1936, Shi Xiuying's father passed away; Xiuying was sent to the Liu family as a *tongyangxi*. Unable to bear her mother-in-law's abuse, Xiuying left the family by paying for her freedom in order to marry a man named Li.[92] A similar situation occurred in Mizhi County. Zhang Piyou was engaged to Wu Meixiang, but Zhang became a soldier and did not contact the family for years. With the agreement of the Zhang family, the engagement was abolished so that Wu Meixiang could marry someone else.[93] In all these cases, the woman's new husband had to pay a substantial amount of *caili* to the family of the woman's previous husband or fiancé. Nonetheless, in the eyes of the state these new marriages were illegal and could be ruled bigamous because most remarriages were informal, following local custom, and had not involved an official divorce.

For those families that did not want to lose their daughters-in-law, the alternative was to invite in substitute husbands. In the aforementioned survey in Qingjian County, three of the thirty-eight soldiers' wives had substitute husbands. Similar cases can be found in other places; for example, in Yanchang County, after Liu Fu's son joined the army in 1936, his daughter-in-law became very angry and frequently threw tantrums, demanding her husband's return. In order to comfort his daughter-in-law, Liu had no other choice but to invite a man in as her substitute husband. In this case, Liu Fu warned the man that once his son returned he would have to leave immediately.[94]

Some women decided to divorce their soldier husbands by using various excuses, including those that adopted revolutionary rhetoric. Due to the omission of a specific clause for soldiers' marriages in the 1939 regulation, if a soldier's wife wanted to file for divorce, she had to meet the condition of "total incompatibility in emotional relations." However, as we will see, this condition was hard to prove. For example, in 1930 Li Lian (wife) married Zhao Huaizhen (husband) in their hometown in Zhengning County. According to later court records, both admitted that their married life was good for the first decade. Zhao then joined the army stationed in Yan'an, and also helped Li Lian get a job in the Yan'an Medicine Factory in 1940. After Li Lian came to Yan'an, their relationship seemed to take a downward turn and the two grew distant. In 1945,

92 SPA 15–27, "Zichang xian qiang hun an" (Kidnapping Cases in Zichang County), in "Bianqu Gaoyuan: Pan'an shilu kuolu, 1945."
93 SPA 15–29, *Zhang Piyou v. Wu Meixiang*, in "Panjueshu cunben, 1946."
94 SPA 15–72, "Hunyin wenti yu hunyin tiaoli"; and SPA 15–1498, "Guo Jungao zhaofu yangfu an."

Li filed her first divorce request in Yan'an City Court, but the court believed that her request was baseless. After this dispute, the couple's relationship rapidly deteriorated, and domestic violence occurred. Li used this to file a second and ultimately successful divorce request. However, Zhao appealed to the High Court, swearing that their relationship had been fine until Li became a worker in the medicine factory, after which she had disparaged him as a soldier and scorned his poor family background. Li rebutted that their marriage was arranged and she felt no affection for him (*mei ganqing* 没感情).[95] It seems odd that Li stated "arranged marriage" (*baoban hunyin* 包办婚姻) as the grounds for divorce, given that she had admitted in the local court investigation that their marriage had been good for ten years; it seems this was simply a legal tactic. She also filed on the grounds of "total incompatibility in emotional relations," but when the court requested concrete examples, Li could only complain that Zhao's family was so poor that they had no quilts. After another court investigation, the High Court concluded that Li's demand for divorce was based on her aversion to Zhao's soldier status and his poor family background, which could not be considered valid conditions for divorce.[96]

Revolution regulations and rhetoric, on the other hand, offered local women certain options and resources in seeking new lives. Similar to the above case, many other women used various official terms that they learned from the revolution as their grounds for divorce. For example, in the case of *Wang Yingde* (husband) *v. Cao Xiuying* (wife), Cao asked for a divorce from her farmer husband in order to marry a cadre, giving the reason of "want[ing] to be revolutionary" (*yao geming* 要革命).[97] In the case of *Han Wenguang* (husband) *v. Li Guihua* (wife)/*Sun Guilin* (man), Li, a peasant woman who worked as a nanny in a government kindergarten, wanted to divorce her husband, Han Wenguang. In addition to claiming "incompatibility in emotional relations" and "arranged marriage" during the court investigation, Li also used the highly political term "family oppression" (*jiating yapo* 家庭压迫) in her divorce request.[98] In the previously mentioned case of *Zhang Huaibao* (husband) *v. Du Guirong* (wife), Du filed a paper

[95] Here it seems inadequate to translate *gan qing* as "emotional relations," as discussed before. It is definitely inaccurate to say that they had no "relations" or no "emotional relations." I therefore translate *mei gan qing* as "no affection."

[96] SPA 15–26, "Li Lian lihun an" (Li Lian's Divorce Case), in "Bianqu panli huibian, 1944."

[97] SPA 15–26, *Wang Yingde v. Cao Xiuying*, in "Bianqu panli huibian, 1944."

[98] SPA 15–29, *Han Wenguang v. Li Guihua/Sun Guilin*, in "Sa wu niandu panjueshu cunben, 1946."

asking for divorce, stating that she was "oppressed by the patriarchal system" (*jiazhang zhidu de yapo* 家长制度压迫) and her divorce was the beginning of being more "progressive" (*jinbu* 进步).[99] The list of such examples could be very long.

Regarding soldiers' marriages, the Border Government tried to respond to the situation by issuing a temporary document in January 1943, the "Instructions on the Divorce of Soldiers' Wives/Fiancées."[100] It stipulated that a soldier's wife would be granted a divorce if the soldier had not had contact with the family for five years, while a fiancée of a soldier had to wait for three years. This term was soon inserted into the formal revised marriage regulation in 1944 and 1946, which attempted to correct the 1939 omission of a specific regulation for soldiers' wives and fiancées. In the revised 1944 regulation, a three-year waiting period applied to both civilians' and soldiers' fiancées, while a five-year period applied to soldiers' wives (see Chapter 4). In the end, there was no fundamental difference from the previous Qing and Nationalist laws.[101]

In the same "Instructions," the government also ordered the establishment of a furlough system that would enable soldiers stationed in the BR to return to their homes every eighteen months.[102] We can see that without women's activities in demanding the return of their soldier husbands/fiancés, there would be no compromise on a required waiting period in marriage and the furlough system. The legal documents confirm that this furlough system was implemented, since some cases were brought to the government during soldiers' visits home. In addition to the furlough system, I speculate that the widespread practice from the mid-1940s up to the 1960s in which each company of the communist army installed a literate secretary (*wenshu* 文书), may relate to the issue of stabilizing soldiers' marriages. In this system, the secretary of a company would assist illiterate company commanders in bookkeeping and reading instructions from and writing reports to superior officers. One important duty of the secretary was to teach soldiers basic literacy, as well as to write and read letters for illiterate soldiers in order for them to keep up communication with their families and wives/fiancées. However, this topic goes beyond this book's range and must be explored in future work.

[99] SPA 15–1470, *Zhang Huaibao v. Du Guirong.*

[100] "Shaan-Gan-Ning bianqu kangshu lihun chuli banfa" (Measures Dealing with Soldiers' Divorces), *Shaan-Gan-Ning bianqu funü yundong wenxian ziliao xuan bian*, 155–6.

[101] See Huang, *Code, Custom, and Legal Practice in China*, 162 and 185.

[102] "Shaan-Gan-Ning bianqu kangshu lihun chuli banfa."

"Freedom of marriage" in practice: fortification of the family agent

The argument that promoting "freedom of marriage" would benefit women was only partially true in the SGNBR. It did indeed benefit women in some ways, but not how the policymakers originally intended. The legal documents indicate that the great majority of engagement dismissals and divorce cases were proposed by the woman's side (*nü fang*, see Table 1.1 in Chapter 1), a phenomenon that could be easily read as a triumph of women's demand for free marriage and women's resistance to arranged marriages. In fact, in Chinese the term *nü fang* is fully contextualized. In the reality of the SGN region of the 1940s, most families and parents of women represented *nü fang*, especially in the case of a broken engagement. Even though in some rare cases women represented themselves on paper, they could also be influenced by their families and/or third parties. Due to the fact that engagements were family matters involving transfer of family property, the representatives in a dispute were often not the man and woman in question, but the two fathers. This was the situation in the case of *Feng v. Zhang*. Since in local culture marriage marked adulthood for both men and women, neither Peng'er, nor Zhang Bo could represent themselves. Thus, the full title of this case is "Feng Yangui and Zhang Jincai in dispute over the marriage of [Feng's] daughter and [Zhang's] son." The wording indicates that Feng Yangui represented the woman's side, while Zhang Jincai represented the man's side (*nan fang* 男方). In this situation, the will of the woman's side definitely did not represent Peng'er's intent.

When a male, especially a father, represented the woman's side, as the head of a family he would put the family's survival strategy ahead of the woman's happiness. In the best case scenario, women's families hoped to gain more income to either improve family conditions or pay off debts. This was the situation in the 1946 case of *Xu Shengyou v. Ma Fugui*, in which Xu's recently widowed daughter was sold by her father for more than one million *bianbi yuan* in order to pay family debts.[103] In the worst case scenario, a father, brother, or an influential third party would try to sell a woman to support his bad habits. From the late Qing up to the 1950s, some males in Chinese rural communities had taken up bad habits such as smoking opium or gambling. In addition, rural communities had groups of idlers who did not want to engage in productive work in the fields.[104] These idlers or rogues were always looking for the

[103] SPA 15–1574.
[104] For instance, the case of *Wang Mingxuan v. Liu Zhiban* (SPA 15–29) and the case of Chen Yu's divorce, mentioned in Chapter 1 (SPA 15–842).

opportunity to make money without working, such as in the case of *Zuo Run v. WangYinsuo* discussed below.[105]

When we consider that this group of males often represented the *nü fang*, a proposed divorce or broken engagement becomes a less accurate indicator of women's liberation. In this situation, the actual beneficiaries were the woman's family, especially the father and/or the third party. Freedom of marriage did not change the structure of patriarchal domination and did not empower women; rather, it allowed property to be moved from grooms' families to brides' families. Even worse, this policy in fact reinforced patriarchal control over women by encouraging them to collaborate with their fathers for material gain, while the father or third party used these gains to manipulate the women. By reinforcing fathers' control over daughters, the policy gave local patriarchal power new momentum and caused new injustices rather than liberating women as intended.

Peng'er's case offers a strong example of this kind of situation, which appears frequently in the documents of the SGNBR High Court. The official policy against arranged marriage and buying/selling marriages, and the state's promotion of "freedom of marriage," provided a legal basis for canceling marriage contracts with minimal cost. Normally a girl, often accompanied by her father, went to the township or ward government to demand a divorce or a dismissal of the original engagement in the name of freedom of marriage and in protest of arranged marriage. Given the continuous inflation of *caili*, most girls' families had a strong motive to do this, as many cases in Chapter 1 demonstrate. Also, a father needed the collaboration of his daughter, since in most cases the government required a clear expression of consent from the girl herself regarding her marriage. Due to the fact that patriarchy was still a dominant force at the time, daughters could not freely reject their fathers' words in front of government officials. This was exactly what Feng Yangui had done in 1942 when he manipulated Peng'er to go with him to the township government where they annulled Peng'er's engagement to Zhang Bo. In 2007, when I interviewed Feng Zhiqin for the second time, I asked if she presented herself on site when her first engagement was abolished. After being used as a model of free marriage for so long, she had become accustomed to repeating an official formulaic version of her own story, but apparently it was an unexpected

[105] Also see Cong Xiaoping, "Zuo Run su WangYinsuo: 20 shiji 40 niandai SGN bianqu de funü, hunyin yu guojia jian gou" (Zuo Run v. WangYinsuo: Women, Marriage and State-building in the 1940s' SGN Border Region), in *Kaifang shidai* (Open Times) 208(10) (October 2009): 62–79.

question. Feng Zhiqin's face had a certain elusive expression, and she then admitted, though she seemed unwilling, that "It was my father who wanted me to go." It was very likely that as a shy young lady, Peng'er did not want to contradict her father's words at the government office when her father spoke for her. Peng'er voiced her father's words when she declared that she "strongly objected to the engagement," but her statement was counted as a request from the woman's side, even the woman herself.

In the documents of the High Court there is an interesting term, *jiaosuo/tiaobo* 教唆/挑拨 (abetting and/or instigating), which appeared in many marriage-related cases. This term indicates that there was a third party involved in marriage disputes. These third parties mostly came from women's natal families. It is understandable that women were easily influenced by their natal families because in traditional Chinese rural areas, when a newlywed woman had not yet established her position in her husband's family or developed her own social network in the village, her natal family was her only support in any family affairs, exactly the situation in Margery Wolf's discussion of uterine families.[106] Initiating a divorce process resulted in a woman's separation from her husband's family, and she became more dependent on her natal family. However, like Peng'er's father, a woman's natal family may also have had its own ulterior motives. A woman's dismissal of her engagement or a divorce could thus become a war between the natal family and the husband's family.[107] Because of the family's involvement, women in this conflict were rarely able to express their own desires and did not escape patriarchal domination. It was often likely that a woman, having left her previous husband through divorce, was soon forced by her natal family or a third party to marry another man she did not know. Divorces in this condition were thus basically patriarchs' means to material gains, not women's weapons against arranged marriages. Realizing the complicated relations and motives behind these marriage disputes, legal workers began to search for a better solution and have more involvement in the cases, as discussed in Chapter 4.

This situation did not mean that a woman was unaware of her own interests and happiness; however, her consent to her parents' dismissal of her engagement or marriage was often related to various situations that had nothing to do with the union. In some cases, daughters willingly collaborated with their fathers for the noble motive of saving

[106] See Margery Wolf, *Women and the Family in Rural Taiwan* (Stanford, CA: Stanford University Press, 1972), 32–41.
[107] For example, in the case of *Cao Cuncheng v. Fu Jincai* (SPA 15–1334).

their families from desperate financial troubles. Other women did it because they also received some reward from the move. Under the patriarchal system, a woman normally had no right to own property, but the one exception was her dowry. Early engagements benefited fathers and families, since the *caili* was paid with silver *yuan* and grain, and in some cases plots of land, but a considerable amount of the second *caili* before the wedding went directly to the woman herself as her dowry. This was the only chance for a woman to gain property and to enjoy any amount of "luxury" goods. If she did not grasp this chance, she could end up owning nothing and have no power in her future husband's family.

Sometimes the woman herself may not have intended to divorce or end the engagement, but could not resist her parents' requests or the temptation of wealth. For example, in the case of Tian Fanshen, the girl's mother wanted to get more *caili* from another suitor and thus convinced Fanshen to break her engagement, though it was against Fanshen's will.[108] In the case of Li Neng and Hu Shengqing, with the support of the judicial system, a young woman and a young man successfully won their case for a self-determined marriage despite protests from the woman's mother; however, they then filed for divorce shortly after they got married. Prefect Ma Xiwu went to the village to do an investigation and found out that the daughter, Li Neng, could not bear her mother's constant pressure, and she had thus reluctantly filed for divorce.[109] Chapter 4 discusses similar cases of divorce processed in an open court. It is therefore easy to understand that in the deliberations of the SGNBR courts when dismissing an engagement or a divorce, the court also made "instigation of natal family" one of the categories (see Table 1.1 in Chapter 1). This category not only indicated the failure of the 1939 marriage policy, in that it viewed women as victims and deprived them of agency, but also exposed how male farmers were able to manipulate the flawed policy by pressuring their daughters into ending an engagement or marriage when that would result in a beneficial outcome for their natal families. In Chapter 4, I will show that BR courts developed a new principle, certain legal techniques and strategies that would be able to exclude patriarchal influence from a dispute so that the will of a woman could be manifested.

108 SPA 15–294, "Jingbian xian hunyin jiufen cailiao" (The Document on Marriage Disputes in Jingbian County).

109 Gao Haishen and Ai Shaorun (comp.), *Shaanxi sheng zhi: shenpan zhi* (Shaanxi Provincial Gazetteer: Volume on the Judicial System) (Xi'an: Shaanxi renmin chubanshe, 2007), 76–7.

IV. The case of *Zuo Run v. Wang Yinsuo*

The challenges that women presented to the Border Government's idealistic expectations were manifested in the case of *Zuo v. Wang*, as well as in many other cases. From 1940 to 1942, the Yan'an court and the High Court processed a case in which a young woman, Zuo Run, wanted to divorce her soldier husband, Wang Yinsuo.[110] The two were engaged in 1938 and married in fall 1939, when Zuo was fifteen years old. Five months later, in early 1940, Wang Yinsuo was conscripted by the Yan'an Guard Regiment of the Eighth Route Army, which was a military unit stationed locally. Zuo was unhappy with Wang's absence and asked Wang's brother to take Wang's place in the army. When this failed, she threatened to divorce Wang. After her husband discovered that she was having an affair with a local merchant, Zuo returned to her natal family, then filed for divorce at the Yan'an local court in late 1940, claiming that her marriage was an arranged one to which she had never consented.

The case of *Zuo v. Wang* was one of many seeking divorce or the end to an engagement filed by the women's side regarding their absent soldier husbands/fiancés after the 1939 regulation was promulgated but before the 1943 Instruction on Soldiers' Marriage was published. Zuo's case took a winding course through the local mediation, the county court, the High Court, and the highest legal institution, the Trial Committee of the Border Government (TCBG, see Chapter 3). The Yan'an local court also tried to mediate the case by making the two sides work together, but Zuo Run stated that she would rather die if the court did not grant her a divorce. In court, Zuo Run boldly argued that "marriage in the Border Region is on the principle of self-determination (*bianqu de hunyin shi zizhi de* 边区的婚姻是自主的). When I am oppressed (*shou yapo* 受压迫) horribly, how can I survive [if it continues]?" On the other hand, Wang Yinsuo insisted that he would rather die than divorce. Yan'an Court indeed gave some consideration to Wang Yinsuo's soldier status because of the tradition in the Jiangxi Soviet period (for example, the term in the 1934 Marriage Law) and military opinion, but that was not a decisive element. Since Zuo stated that it had been an arranged marriage, in 1941 the Yan'an City Court invalidated it as a marriage contract on the basis of the fact that Zuo Run was only seventeen years old and thus too young for marriage. By the same token, the court penalized Zuo Run's parents with three and six months of labor service, respectively, for selling their daughter into marriage. The court also issued a

[110] SPA 15–1336, *Zuo v. Wang*. All the following information came from this case unless specified.

restraining order preventing Zuo from remarrying until she reached the statutory age.

Dissatisfied with this result, Wang appealed the case to the High Court in 1942, but the High Court supported the local court's verdict and dismissed Wang's appeal. Wang then filed another appeal, this time with the then-highest legal institution of the BR, the TCBG (see Chapter 3 on the BR judicial system). In this appeal, Wang challenged the finding of arranged marriage, saying that they had met before the engagement, and that after he gave Zuo several silver *yuan* in person as a gift, Zuo had agreed to the marriage. He disagreed with the court's depiction of his marriage as an engagement contract and provided a list of guests at the wedding ceremony to prove it was a full-fledged marriage. Wang also claimed that the quality of their marriage was fine until he was recruited. It is very likely that Wang was telling the truth, because the engagement occurred when the Zuo family took refuge in Wang's village during the Japanese bombing of Yan'an City in December 1938. The Zuo family even rented a cave-room in Wang's residence and stayed there for several months, giving Wang and Zuo plenty of opportunities to acquaint themselves with each other.

Under the 1939 regulation, Zuo Run needed to prove her case by demonstrating "total incompatibility in emotional relations and intolerable cohabitation." When the court asked for evidence of this incompatibility, Zuo stated that Wang did not give her the new clothes he had promised, that her parents were penalized for an arranged marriage in the primary trial, that she had been injured from Wang's beating, and that she did not like rustic men (*xiangxia ren* 乡下人). She also claimed that she was angry with Wang because he had forced himself on her in bed, which was the key evidence for "intolerable cohabitation" in a divorce case. At the same time, she also asked the court to grant her freedom to marry, since she had reached the statutory age for marriage in 1942. To prove that Wang Yinsuo had forced sex on her, Zuo Run told of her youth and naiveté, saying that on her wedding day she was carried in a sedan chair to Wang's home. She had no idea what was going on (*huli hutu de* 糊里糊涂地) until that night, when Wang tried to rip off her clothes; she then realized that "Wang was going to wreck (*pohuai* 破坏) my body." According to her, she resisted to the point that Wang had to stop, and thus they could not live together. Zuo's statement, especially her naiveté concerning sex, created great sympathy for her in both the Yan'an local court and the High Court. The court officials believed Zuo's story and assumed that Zuo was still too young to have a sexual life. It became the grounds for the local court to grant the dismissal of the marriage contract. However, considering the fact that Zuo Run had an affair with a merchant shortly after her marriage and another one during the process of the TCBG's investigation, Zuo may not have been as sexually naïve as she claimed.

Wang rebutted Zuo's words by presenting his side of the story with many details about their wedding to prove that their marriage was based on mutual consent and that they did not only have a good relationship but had also been living together. It was with her family's intervention that their relationship took a downward turn. Wang described their wedding night, that Zuo had asked him to help her family with more money and more grain, and also wanted Wang to promise her that she would never have to do any work at home. She also asked if it was possible for the two of them to move to the city of Yan'an instead of staying in Wang's village. Wang agreed to all the conditions, and the two then went to sleep peacefully. Wang also claimed that their relations had been good before he was recruited by the army. Since then, Zuo Run's mother had stayed with her all the time, even at night; the couple thus had no chance to be alone together and reconnect. Wang stated that it was Zuo's parents who urged Zuo to file for a divorce so that Zuo's father would be able to sell her into another marriage. At this point, the case became a *Rashomon*-like story,[111] a "she-said-he-said" situation so that judges could not make a decision on the basis of the words from either side.

After deliberations, the TCBG overturned the previous verdicts and ruled that the marriage of Wang and Zuo was valid and the two should carry on their conjugal duties. The TCBG offered a rather detailed explanation for this surprising conclusion, which became the grounds for dealing with *kangshu* marriages (cited in the previous section), requiring that women support their husbands in fighting against the Japanese. Moreover, its concern about women's material motives and demands for more *caili* was also critical of the revised marriage regulation of 1944 (see Chapter 4). After examining previous court testimony and the new evidence of Zuo's second affair, the TCBG members concluded that Zuo's divorce request did not fit the conditions for a finding of "total incompatibility in emotional relations." The TCBG conducted another investigation and discovered that Zuo Run had lied about the injury she claimed had resulted from Wang's beating, which was in fact self-inflicted during her running away from a village cadre during the mediation. In the writ the TCBG also explained that other factors such as promise of material gain, penalty to her parents, and aversion to rural

[111] *Rashomon* (1950) is a Japanese film directed by Akira Kurosawa; it observes that everyone involved in an event would lie for their own interests and that the facts are difficult to determine.

men were not legitimate grounds for divorce. They determined that the motive behind Zuo's request for divorce was that she preferred to marry a merchant rather than a farmer or a soldier. This motive was not based on "incompatibility in emotional relations"; instead, it exposed Zuo's true goal of material gain via marriage. The committee believed that this kind of motive for divorce represented a "backward" proclivity among young women in this region and should be eradicated. Upon further investigation, the committee discovered that Zuo Run's father was a notorious rogue (*liu mang* 流氓) in the community. It was he who had urged his daughter to divorce Wang in order to find a richer husband to support his bad habits. In this case, Zuo Run, regardless of her arranged marriage, was not an innocent victim of patriarchal power but a young woman strongly influenced by and aligned with the patriarchal system. The TCBG also gave certain consideration to Wang Yinsuo's soldier status, but the key for denying the divorce was not this factor; rather, it was Zuo Run's motives behind the divorce request and her parents' bad influence that made the TCBG overrule the previous verdict.

Conclusion

This chapter has demonstrated that women of the region were active agents in search of a way to carve out space for themselves, and that they tried to benefit from both the traditional patriarchal system and the revolutionary government. Women's activities proved that they had ways to assert control over their own bodies in matters of love and sexuality, using both traditional culture and modern revolutionary rhetoric as a legitimating source. Peng'er's decision to marry Zhang Bo and her appeal of the case should be viewed within this social and historical context. It was the existing autonomy of women in love and sexuality that became the foundation for the revolutionary judiciary to develop the legal principle of self-determination in the marriage reform, as shown in Chapter 4.

Part II

Legal practice and new principle

3 The new adjudication

Judicial construction in marriage reform

After receiving Peng'er's appeal, Prefect Ma visited her village. By conducting his own investigation among fellow villagers and cadres, Ma clarified several facts and made a new adjudication. First, his judgment condemned Feng Yangui for "selling" his daughter multiple times for profit as if she were livestock. The profit of seven thousand *yuan* (*fabi*) *caili* that Feng Yangui received from Zhu Shouchang was confiscated by the court; in addition, Feng was penalized with three months of labor service. Second, Ma denounced Zhang Jincai's way of dealing with the marriage dispute. He suggested that Zhang should have either made the utmost effort to persuade Feng or brought Feng to court. The kidnapping was wrong because it violated the law and disturbed the social order. As a result, Zhang Jincai was sentenced to two years and six months of prison time. All other participants in the kidnapping but Zhang Bo received sentences varying from half a year to several months.[1] In the previous adjudication made by Huachi County court, Zhang Bo was also sentenced to some jail time for the kidnapping but the new adjudication changed it. Prefect Ma did not impose any penalty on him though he was the reason for the kidnapping and also actively participated in it; instead, Ma ratified his marriage with Peng'er without any penalty. The writ did not explain the reason why Zhang Bo escaped punishment, but it should be viewed in the context of the government trying to maintain a peaceful relationship with the village communities, as discussed in Chapter 5.

In Ma's adjudication, the most notable issue was his rationale for the approval of Peng'er and Zhang Bo's marriage. He explained that although the "marriage" (technically the engagement) was arranged by their parents in 1928, it was based on a widespread local custom (*dangdi yiban shehui guanli* 当地一般社会惯例). Most importantly and substantively, the adjudication continued, "however, both Peng'er and Zhang Bo have already consented for a long time (*shuang fang zao yi tongyi* 双方早已同意). Therefore this court will make a new judgment. Based on

[1] SPA 15–842, *Feng v. Zhang.*

the principle of self-determination of a man and a woman in a marriage (*nan nü hunyin zi zhu yuanze* 男女婚姻自主原则) that was carried out in the Border Region, their union is valid."[2] Finally, the writ criticized Huachi County's previous adjudication for its superficial and dogmatic application of the law to the case "without being concerned with the substance of the event" (*zhi kan xianxiang bu kan benzhi* 只看现象不看本质). It also berated the county court for its connivance with Feng Yangui in selling his daughter and its neglect of both Peng'er's and Zhang Bo's desire for a self-determined marriage. Based on the above reasons, Ma overturned the county court's previous decision (see Figure 3.1).[3]

Ma's adjudication highlighted certain important aspects of the Border Region's judicial construction. Intentionally or unintentionally, his decision aligned with the BR's judicial construction of the time. It also reflected the key position of the judicial system in marriage reform, and vice versa. First, Ma advised that Feng and Zhang should talk over their issue and also could resort to legal means as a last resort. It implied that the imperial tradition of using mediation as a possible means of solving civil disputes within a community could be applied to the current marriage dispute, but it also reminded villagers to turn to the CCP government if talks failed (see Chapter 5).

Second, Ma's decision admitted that local customs, such as engagements and arranged marriages with *caili*, could be acceptable as long as the revolutionary principle of "self-determination" was not violated. This suggested that a legal adjudication should be made on the basis of a full understanding of the circumstances and had to be attuned to the local customs and practices. Third, Ma's criticism of Huachi County's decision brought in a very important issue: that in legal practice, law workers should not apply the law only based on "legal words," but on the "legal principle" and revolutionary policy.

In fact, the issue of superficially and/or formalistically applying the law to a case without focusing on the substance of the event reflected a dilemma of the BR's judicial construction, as well as in China's legal modernity since the nineteenth century: a struggle between following the letter of the law and adjusting legal practice based on local circumstances, or between legal formalism and historical practice, as Philip Huang puts it.[4] In addition to possible contradictions between legal formalism

2 *Ibid.*
3 *Ibid.*
4 Philip Huang fiercely criticizes the influence of "legal formalism" on the modern Chinese legal system. See his *Chinese Civil Justice*, 1–11, 228. In his book, he defines "legal formalism" as a legal thought that "emphasized especially the universality and scientific nature of law and the use of deductive theory to arrive at absolute truths" (3). He further

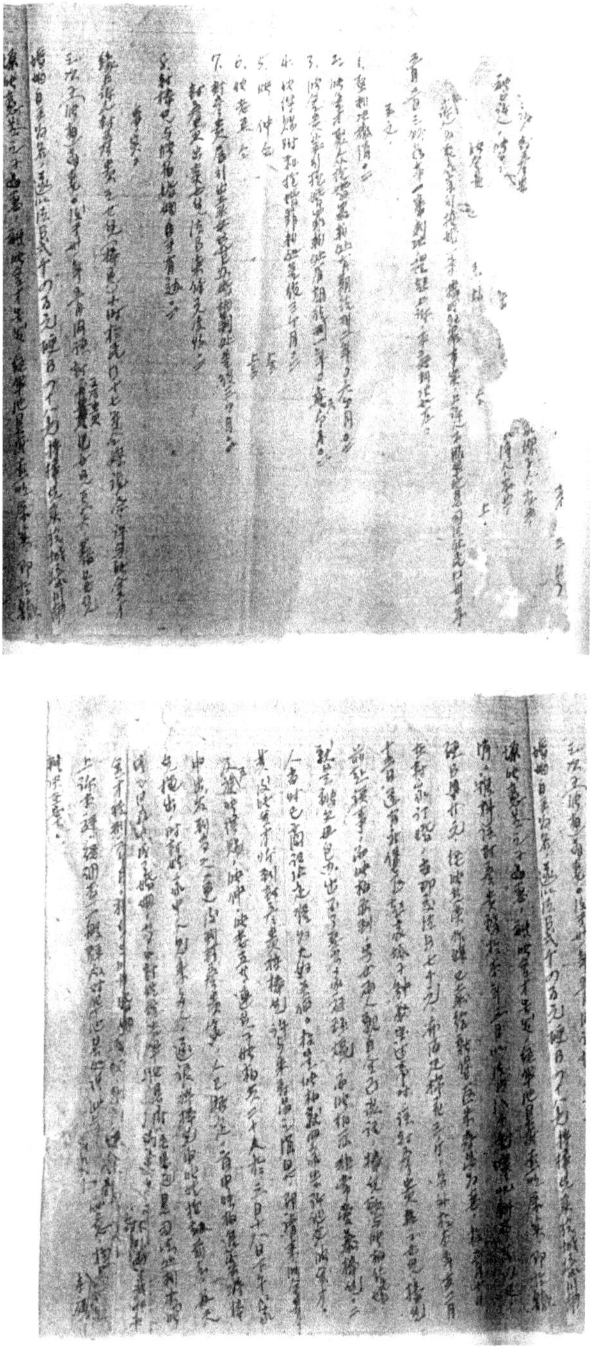

Figure 3.1 The new adjudication of the case *Feng v. Zhang*, 1943, SPA 15–842

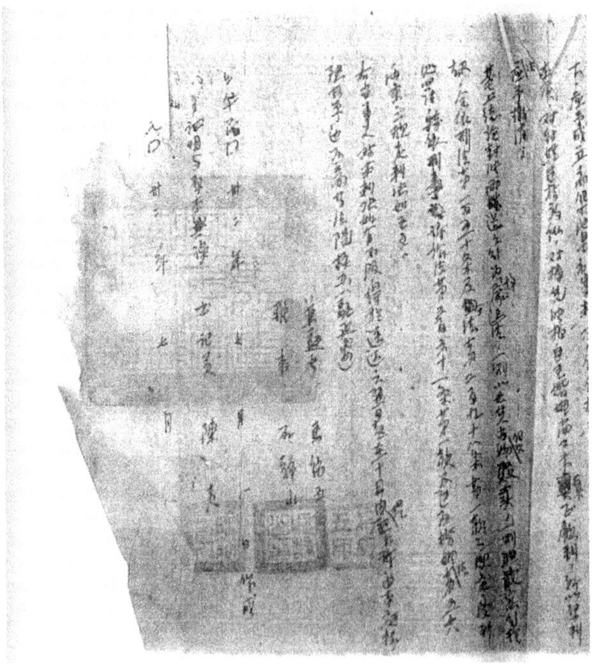

Figure 3.1 (*cont.*)

and local practice, another issue was even more critical: as a revolutionary state that launched a reform program, should the party-state be bound by its legal form and procedure, or should it look toward an idealistic end? What would happen if legal formalities came into conflict with revolutionary goals, as in the case of *Feng v. Zhang*? Third, in an environment in which legal forms were incomplete and unable to provide detailed guidelines for dealing with a broad spectrum of cases, how was a legal practitioner able to reach a justifiable judgment? The verdict of Huachi County provides a good example of this dilemma without giving consideration to the fact that Feng was the party which violated a higher principle of the reform. In light of this contradiction, Ma's new adjudication was of great importance in the construction of the communist judicial system and set an important legal precedent for the 1940s and the post-1949 period. The legal practice of this time played a key role in solidifying the revolutionary view of marriage and gender and in reshaping local marriage practices. On the other hand, these marriage disputes and the local culture involved in them seriously challenged the modern legal system that the CCP had established, and forced legal workers to search for suitable solutions in the process of constructing its legal system.

I. Constructing a new workable judicial system for the SGNBR: 1937–46

The period 1937 to 1946 was the most critical time for the BR judicial system, which went through a tortuous transformation from a primitive structure to one with a de facto three-tiered court system. The construction of the judicial system also shifted from an early desultory practice of mixing imperial tradition with a USSR-inspired style, to attempting to set up a relatively independent judicial system on the Nationalist model, and finally ending up with a less independent system that mingled with the administrative one. The final form that it took was a result of the interaction of different thoughts about developing a revolutionary judicial system.

The judicial system of the SGN in transition: 1937–41

From the time of its birth in the communist movement in the late 1920s and early 1930s, the revolutionary judicial system was imbued with a

clarifies that legal formalism is a doctrine that "jurisprudence … ought to be based on a limited number of axioms and multiple theorems derived therefrom, with are then applied to all fact situations" (228). I accept and use this definition in this book.

strong ideological and partisan rhetoric and marked by influence from the USSR model. In the Jiangxi revolutionary base, the legal construction of the soviet central government mainly focused on certain particular aspects in order to legitimize the newly born revolutionary power, such as a new constitution that granted power to the revolutionary government, organizational regulations that helped reestablish rural order, and statutes on landownership that attracted peasants to the revolutionary force.[5] The judicial system itself, as well as the statutes and penal law, also originated from the urban experience of social movements in the 1920s, in which penal codes were used to punish "class enemies" such as traitors, counterrevolutionaries, corrupt governmental officials, and tyrannical landlords. Not until the CCP secured its rule in the rural revolutionary base areas in the SGNBR did it realize that the revolutionary state would have to deal with community life and civil disputes over minor matters, in addition to those relating to the lofty revolutionary cause. Thus, the civil code came into being much later than its penal regulations.[6]

Still, a sketchy judicial system in the Chinese Soviet Republic in Jiangxi began taking shape in 1933, mainly on paper. In this system, the people's commissariat of justice in the central government and a supreme court composed the highest judicial power. At the local level, a judicial committee and a court were the basic legal institutions. During this period, some cases might be brought to trial, but political interference and the pressure of mass opinion had a great impact on legal procedures, given that the judicial system served political purposes. Moreover, the penal system was often used in service to the party's internal affairs by persecuting political dissenters inside the revolutionary camp, a practice copied from the USSR.[7] Generally speaking, during this period the communist legal system was still in a primitive stage; it is difficult to evaluate its actual operation and implementation due to the lack of historical evidence. On the other hand, revolutionary administration and public

[5] For earlier studies on the legal system of the Chinese Soviet Republic in the Jiangxi period, see W. E. Butler (ed.), *The Legal System of the Chinese Soviet Republic, 1931–1934* (New York: Transnational, 1983). Due to the lack of archival documents, the chapters in this edited volume are all based on the authors' readings and interpretations of the legal codes produced in the revolutionary region at this time, rather than analysis of concrete cases. Also see Zhang Xipo and Han Yanlong (comp.), *Zhongguo geming fazhi shi* (A History of the Chinese Revolutionary Legal System) (Beijing: Zhongguo shehui kexue chubanshe, 2007). For the same reason, we still know little about the actual implementation of the law and the operation of the judicial system during this period.

[6] Zhang Xipo and Han Yanlong (comp.), *Zhongguo geming fazhi shi*, 245–77, 329–33, 516–67, and 676–85.

[7] Trygve Lötveit, *Chinese Communism 1931–1934: Experience in Civil Government* (Lund, Sweden: Studentlitterature, 1973), 106–44; Butler, *The Legal System of the Chinese Soviet Republic*, passim.

violence sometimes substituted for legal practice.[8] In any case, all these systems soon collapsed with the CCP's departure on the Long March in 1934. However, some practices from the previous Jiangxi Soviet system were inherited by the newly established BR court system and comprised the remaining USSR influence. In the 1940s, with the newly established judicial system under the influence of the Nationalist model, the elements of USSR judicial influence were largely reduced, though some practice, such as the public trial which was turned into the practice of open court, continued (on the practice of open court, see Chapter 5).

After the establishment of the Second United Front, the Border government made a critical revision of its previous judicial system, transforming it into a relatively formal one that would be subject to the nominal authority of the Nanjing Nationalist government. In July 1937, when the High Court of the BR (*Bianqu gaodeng fayuan* 边区高等法院) came into being, it was set as a second-tier court in the nation's three-tiered court system. Theoretically, the offices of justice (*xian sifa chu* 县司法处) in each county were designated for primary trials, while the BR High Court acted only as the appellate jurisdiction, subject to final review by the Nationalist Supreme Court in Nanjing. However, in the political reality of China at the time, the BR government operated independently, meaning that the High Court in fact served as both the appellate jurisdiction and the site of final adjudication.[9]

In order to carry out its revolutionary ideals, the High Court attempted to break away from the imperial tradition, previous soviet experience, and existing Nationalist judicial system while building a new system. Lei Jingtian 雷经天 (1903–59), the director of the High Court (*gaoyuan yuan zhang* 高院院长) in 1937, promised that the new judicial system would make legal procedures more convenient for the working classes and that the courts would accept any form of complaint or petition (oral or written) from a litigant. Moreover, the courts would process any type of litigation with no fees, thus guaranteeing that illiterate villagers and poor people could seek justice through the judicial system. In order to serve the people better, he suggested that a new judicial system should eliminate people's fear of an intimidating authority. Thus, he ordered the courts to change their traditional terrifying authoritarian style of courtroom interrogation and replace it with face-to-face conversation with litigants.

Lei also recommended a special form of legal procedure, "the public trial by the people" (*renmin de gong shen* 人民的公审), in which any case

[8] *Ibid.*
[9] SPA 15–175, "Lei Jingtian: Bianqu sifa gongzuo baogao."

closely related to the interests of the public should be held as an open trial in order to educate the people. Court procedures would be followed in selecting the jury and presenting its members with evidence, but an open trial in a public venue would be held to invite discussion among the masses. He believed, however, that the final verdict should be made by judges and jury together rather than simply following the public view of the case.[10] This type of public trial inherited from the previous Jiangxi Soviet experience but mingled with community mediation and open court as part of judicial procedures, is discussed in Chapter 5.

From 1937 to 1941, this system barely operated due to multiple reasons. Facing political, military, and economic pressures from the Nationalist government, local warlords, and bandits, the Border government had to vigorously mobilize its military and civil forces to stabilize its territory, and then remap its administrative institutions and jurisdictions.[11] Due to the lack of manpower in general, and particularly in legal personnel, the High Court prioritized the construction of the judicial system at the top level, but left legal problems at the county level to administrative cadres.[12] During this period, even the leadership of the High Court changed constantly. Xie Juezai was appointed in July 1937 as the first director (*yuan zhang* 院长) for one month, but was soon replaced by Dong Biwu 董必武 (1886–1975) for the next three months. In October 1937, Lei Jingtian, a revolutionary veteran who had worked in the Jiangxi Soviet government and had experienced the Long March, took over the directorship and remained in the position until March 1945. During his long term of service, Lei took an interim leave during which Li Mu'an 李木庵 (1884–1959) was appointed as acting director (*daili yuanzhang* 代理院长) from April 1942 to December 1943. After Lei's term, in March 1945 Wang Ziyi 王子宜 (1908–83) became the director for one year, then Ma Xiwu took over the position in April 1946 and stayed in it until January 1950, when the SGNBR High Court was dissolved.[13]

[10] SPA, 15–175, "Lei Jingtian, Bianqu sifa gongzuo baogao." Also see Wang Shirong, Liu Quan'e, Wang Jide, and Li Juan, *Xin Zhongguo sifa zhidu de jishi – Shaan-Gan-Ning bianqu gaodeng fayuan* (The Foundation of the Judicial System for New China – SGNBR High Court) (Beijing: Shangwu yinshuguan, 2011), 1, 40–1, 48.

[11] Ren Zhonghe, "Shaa-Gan-Ning bianqu xingzheng quhua yanbian gaishu" (The Changes in Administrative Mapping in the SGNBR), *Lishi dang'an* (Historical Archives) 3 (1988): 116–19 and 126.

[12] SPA 15–175, "Lei Jingtian, Bianqu sifa gongzuo baogao."

[13] Zhang Shibin, Feng Yingchun, and Hui Xingwen, *Shaan-Gan-Ning bianqu gaodeng fayuan shiji* (The Historical Records of the SGNBR High Court) (Xi'an: Shaanxi renmin chubanshe, 2006), 36–48. Also see Wang Shirong *et al.*, *Xin Zhongguo sifa zhidu de jishi*, 96–106.

In the local institutions, the High Court designated a judge with various titles (*chengshenyuan*, *shenpanyuan*, *caipanyuan*, 承审员, 审判员, 裁判员or *tuishi* 推事)[14] to lead an office of justice in each county as the primary court. Although the High Court actively established short-term training programs, the number of trained legal personnel could not meet the needs of an expanding judicial system. Therefore, many county-heads (*xian zhang* 县长)[15] in fact played the role of judge, while the county security offices took responsibility for imprisonment as well as prosecuting, investigating, and trying the cases.[16] To a certain extent, this system inherited these practices from both imperial times and the early Republic, in that a county magistrate took responsibility for judicial adjudications with the assistance of his staff. It also reflected the BR's situation of the time, which involved a shorthanded legal system and lack of finances for running independent courts. This practice may also come from a consideration that judicial adjudications could be effectively carried out through the administrative system, since the legal system did not have its own powers of implementation.

Formalizing the revolutionary judicial system: 1941–3

From 1941 to 1943, the High Court experienced another transformation, conducted by a group of well-trained legal experts who were communists but had experience working in the Nationalist judicial system before coming to the Border Region. They participated in building the judicial system and tried to formalize it according to their ideas of legal modernity. Among them, Li Mu'an, Zhu Ying 朱婴 (1889–1970),[17] Lu Fomin 鲁佛民 (1881–1944),[18] and Zhang Shushi 张曙时

[14] In the early period, most legal workers were called by the various titles listed here that reflected the remaining influence of the USSR and Jiangxi practice. After the formalization of the legal system after 1941 that copied the Nationalist system to some extent, judges were called "*tuishi*," a term inherited from the early Republican legal system, while the various early titles were assigned to junior judges.

[15] The normal English translation of the head of a county in the imperial time is magistrate (*zhi xian*). I believe that the translation of "county-head" for "*xianzhang*" is most accurate for reflecting the intent of the revolutionary government.

[16] SPA 15–175, "Lei Jingtian: Bianqu sifa gongzuo baogao."

[17] Zhu Ying graduated from the famous law school at Chaoyang University (Chaoyang daxue) in Beijing in the 1920s and arrived in Yan'an in 1939. See Hu Yongheng, "1943 nian Shaan-Gan-Ning bianqu tingzhi yuanyong *Liu fa quan shu* zhi kaocha – zhengfeng, shengan dui bianqu sifa de yingxiang" (On the Suspension of Invoking the Six Codes in the 1943 SGNBR), *KangRi zhanzheng yanjiu* (Studies on the Anti-Japanese War) 4 (2010): 90–102.

[18] Lu Fomin graduated from Shandong College of Law (*Shandong zhengfa xuetang*) in 1915 and worked as a lawyer before becoming a communist. See Li Juan, "Geming chuantong yu xifang xiandai sifa linian de jiaofeng jiqi shenyuan yingxiang" (A Cross

(1884–1971)[19] were the most important figures, while Wang Huai'an 王怀安 (1915–2015)[20] and Ren Fuzhong 任扶中 (1908–80)[21] were also notable in this formalization process. This legal reform, however, ignited a huge conflict with other legal workers in the Border Region.

Li Mu'an belonged to the first group of Chinese legal experts trained by a Western-style law school established in the late Qing, and was one of the preeminent and most senior legal workers among the Chinese communists in the Yan'an period.[22] He graduated from the Capital College of Law (*Jingshi zhengfa zhuanmen xuetang* 京师政法专门学堂) in 1909 and took the position of the public prosecutor-general (*jianchazhang* 检察长) of the Guangdong provincial government in the early Republic. He then practiced law in the areas of Beijing and Tianjin in the 1910s and became the public prosecutor-general of Fujian Province in the 1920s. During this time, he became involved in some social activities and joined the CCP in 1925. In participating in the Northern Expedition (1926–8), he established a broad connection with people in both the GMD and CCP camps during the First United Front period (1924–7).[23] After 1927, when the GMD and CCP split, Li worked for communist underground organizations in Nationalist-controlled areas before he arrived at the SGNBR in spring 1941.[24]

Fire between the Revolutionary Tradition and Western Legal Thought and its Influence), *Fazhi yu shehui fazhan* (Rule of Law and Social Development) 4 (2009): 38–47.

19 Zhang Shushi graduated from Jiangsu and Zhejiang College of Law and Politics (Liang Jiang Zhengfa Xuetang) in the 1900s and joined the Chinese Revolutionary Alliance (*Tongmenghui*) in 1909. He joined the CCP in 1932. See Hou Xinyi, "Faxue de Zhongguo xuepai: Yuanyin, fangfa ji houguo – yi Yan'an xin faxuehui wei zhongxin de kaocha" (Chinese Legal School: The Origin, Method and Result – Examining the Society of New Law for China in Yan'an), *Zhengfa luntan* (Zhengfa Forum) 6 (2006): 13–16.

20 Wang Huai'an joined the CCP while studying at the Law School of Sichuan University in 1936. He came to Yan'an in 1940 and became a judge in the BR in 1942. See Sun Qi, "Wag Huai'an Xiansheng fangtan lu" (An Interview with Mr. Wang Huai'an), *Huanqiu falü pinglun* (xiaji kan) (Global Law Review, [Summer Issue]) (2003): 173–9.

21 Ren Fuzhong graduated from the Department of Law at Henan University in 1936 and worked in the Nationalist Henan Provincial High Court. He came to Yan'an in 1937 and became the chief clerk of the SGN High Court. In 1942, he became the chief-judge of a county court. See Hu Yongheng, "1943 nian Shaan-Gan-Ning bianqu tingzhi yuanyong Liu fa quan shu zhi kaocha."

22 Perhaps only Dong Biwu, the second director of the High Court and later the vice-president of the PRC, can compete with his credentials and experience in law among the CCP leadership.

23 There are different versions of Li's background, but there is no question that he was one of the earliest legal experts. See Hu Yongheng, "1943 nian Shaan-Gan-Ning bianqu tingzhi yuanyong Liu fa quan shu zhi kaocha"; and Hou Xinyi, "Faxue de Zhongguo xuepai: yuanyin, fangfa ji houguo." Also see Zhang Shibin *et al.*, *Shaan-Gan-Ning bianqu gaodeng fayuan shiji*, 43–4.

24 See Wang Shirong *et al.*, *Xin Zhongguo sifa zhidu de jishi*, 27. Also see Zhang Shibin *et al.*, *Shaan-Gan-Ning bianqu gaodeng fayuan shiji*, 43–4.

Li Mu'an's arrival pushed forward judicial construction in the Border Region. Almost immediately, he was appointed as the public procurator-general from April 1941 to January 1942. Li held a strong view of judicial construction that differed from that of Lei Jingtian, the then-director of the High Court; a conflict began to rise. To prevent the clash, the leaders of the BR Government arranged for Lei to take an official leave, while Li became the acting director of the High Court from April 1942 to December 1943.[25] Li devoted himself to the formalization and professionalization of the sketchy judicial system by proposing the enhancement of the autonomy of public prosecutors, the development of an independent three-tiered court system with a supreme court for handling final decisions inside the BR, adoption of the Nationalist law codes, reform of the prison system, and training of professional legal personnel.[26]

In 1941, Li Mu'an, Zhu Ying, Lu Fomin, and a small group of people who had received legal training or worked in the Nationalist judicial system prior to coming to Yan'an organized a professional association, the Society of New Law for China (*Zhongguo xin fa xue hui*, SNLC 中国新法学会), which became an instrument for promoting their version of judicial construction in the BR.[27] As the public procurator-general in 1942, Li Mu'an tried to expand the role of the Public Prosecutor Office (*jiancha chu* 检察处) by transforming it from an appendage of the High Court to a more independent office. He also ordered the installation of a public procurator at each level of jurisdiction, and encouraged its independent operation. However, when the BR encountered economic difficulties in 1942, this plan became unrealistic. Thus, the public prosecutor office in the High Court was soon disbanded and the plan for a public prosecutor in each jurisdiction also failed.[28] In fact, the true reason for repealing the public prosecutor system was more than the economy: it was also related to the fight between the different legal views discussed below.

The most important reform Li Mu'an promoted was to transform the existing two-tiered court system into a real three-tiered court system, with a BR supreme court handling final judicial reviews. From October 1941 to April 1942, Li launched the project of building "Local Courts" (*difang fayuan* 地方法院) in "the Central Counties"

[25] See Wang Shirong *et al.*, *Xin Zhongguo sifa zhidu de jishi*, 50–1.
[26] Wang Shirong *et al.*, *Xin Zhongguo sifa zhidu de jishi*, passim.
[27] Hu Yongheng, "1943 nian Shaan-Gan-Ning bianqu tingzhi yuanyong Liu fa quan shu zhi kaocha."
[28] Wang Shirong *et al.*, *Xin Zhongguo sifa zhidu de jishi*, 50–1.

(*zhongxin xian* 中心县), a model probably taking after the Nationalist judicial system. This plan required one modern-style court to be set up in the most populous county of each subregion of the BR, where the subregional civic center was located.[29] According to this design, these local courts would serve as the primary trial courts by taking over all legal duties from the county offices and placing them in a much more formalized and modernized local court staffed by well-trained legal personnel. Nominally, a local court in a central county would be subject to the leadership of the subregional administration, but professionally each local court would follow the instruction of the High Court and independently try all legal cases from the counties in its subregional jurisdiction. These local courts were soon abolished in 1943 and replaced with the branch office of the High Court (*gao yuan fen ting* 高院分庭) after the "review of judicial works" (see below).[30] The intention of Li's systematic reform was to make judicial authority more professional and formalized so that people's lawsuits would be handled in correct procedure by authorized courts and a group of well-trained legal workers who would guarantee due process. In Li's view, the current High Court should only have served as an appellate jurisdiction; its role in final reviews thus needed to be assigned to another independent institution, a new supreme court of the SGNBR.

This reform plan was ideal and neat, but also aimed at the muddled condition of the judicial system at the time. Up to 1941, the BR's judicial system was still in an initial stage of chaos, in which many basic issues such as which level of court should handle a particular case had not been decided. There were many more problems: jurisdictional divisions, the status of limitation of lawsuits, appellate procedures, and the limits to appeals were either not clearly defined or totally absent in legal statutes. Due to this uncertainty, some cases were confined to a primary trial for their final decision without possibility for appeal, while other cases went through an endless appeal process. Moreover, because there was no clear rule on the level of trial, the High Court was sometimes busy dealing with primary trials that should have been the responsibility of lower courts.[31] Li believed that a supreme court would end this confusion and prevent endless appeals while still ensuring the people's right to an appeal.[32] Since the BR was eager to improve its judicial system, the three-tiered court structure sounded attractive to leaders at

[29] See Wang Shirong *et al.*, *Xin Zhongguo sifa zhidu de jishi*, 45n.
[30] Wang Shirong *et al.*, *Xin Zhongguo sifa zhidu de jishi*, 45–7.
[31] SPA 15–175, "Lei Jingtian: Bianqu sifa gongzuo baogao."
[32] Wang Shirong *et al.*, *Xin Zhongguo sifa zhidu de jishi*, 65–6.

the top, such as Lin Boqu 林伯渠 (1886–1960)[33] and Li Weihan[34] 李维汉 (1896–1984).[35] Li Mu'an was appointed to the acting directorship.

The SNLC played a key role in advocating the establishment of a supreme court in the Border Region. When the Border Region Council (*Bianqu canyihui* 边区参议会), the highest legislature, rejected the idea of a supreme court, the SNLC came out with a compromise measure. In August 1942, the Border government approved its idea for a top judicial committee, the Trial Committee of the Border Government (TCBG) subject to the Border government, rather than to the Border Region Council. It functioned as a supreme court for the final legal reviews of both civil and criminal appeals. Both the president and vice-president of the Border government then served concurrently as the chair and vice-chair of the TCBG respectively; the members of the committee came from various departments of the Border government. Since the chair, vice-chair, and the members of the TCBG were too busy with the daily routine of their own departments and unable to pay attention to legal issues, the committee's work landed on the shoulders of its secretary-general (*mishuzhang* 秘书长), Zhu Ying. In most cases, Zhu Ying drafted a statute or a final adjudication and sent it to the committee members simply for their signatures.[36]

Li Mu'an and his fellow legal experts also promoted other issues in normalizing the Border Region's legal practices, such as adopting the Nationalist legal code, the *Book of Six Codes* (*Liu fa quan shu* 六法全书), because the BR did not have a codified law for many offenses. Li believed that a revolutionary state like the SGN Border government should allow the use of capitalist legal codes because those laws represented a progressive view and provided certain protections to working people, especially the criminal law that offered very detailed statutes for legal practice.[37] At the same time, Li launched a reform of the prisons by transforming the previous SGN jail system from a place for short detention and labor services into a modern-style prison where offenders would be locked up to serve their sentences. Li, Zhu, and the other SNLC members also pushed tightening up the qualifications for legal workers so that those who had only received limited legal training in short-term programs established by Lei Jingtian would be removed from the system. Zhu and Li demanded

[33] Lin was the president of the Border government at the time.

[34] Li Weihan was a communist veteran and at the time served as the secretary-general of the Border government.

[35] Wang Shirong *et al.*, *Xin Zhongguo sifa zhidu de jishi*, 65–6.

[36] Wang Shirong *et al.*, *Xin Zhongguo sifa zhidu de jishi*, 65–7. Also see Li Juan, "Geming chuantong yu xifang xiandai sifa linian de jiaofeng jiqi shenyuan yingxiang."

[37] SPA 15–96, "Gaodeng fayuan Li Mu'an Lei Jingtian yuanzhang guanyu sifa gongzuo de jiantao huiyi fayan jilu" (Speeches of the Directors Li Mu'an and Lei Jingtian on the Meetings for Legal Review).

that all legal workers should graduate from law schools and pass a rigorous bar examination. For this purpose, the SNLC proposed setting up a law school at the newly established Yan'an University in 1941 to train legal personnel. They also suggested recruiting well-trained legal personnel from the Nationalist region to fill positions in the shorthanded BR judicial system.[38]

The reform program that Li and other legal experts promoted obviously had a strong imprint of the 1930s' Nationalist legal system, which had adopted European and American models wholesale. This reform, though it ignited a strong conflict in 1943, represented the Nationalist element in the hybrid new legal system created after the dispute.

II. Searching for a hybridized model for the revolutionary judicial system

The judicial system and its practice during the Yan'an period are often seen as the "revolutionary legal tradition" in the contemporary legal system, in contrast to a modern/Western legal system. I argue, however, that the so-called revolutionary legal tradition created in the 1940s in fact involved multiple elements integrated into a new judicial system. It included the imperial and early Republican legal traditions, influence from the Soviet Union, and Nationalist legal concepts and models as mentioned above. In particular, as we will see, it was through the continuous reforms in the actual legal practices of the 1940s in marriage and social reform projects, and in the interplay with local communities, that these multiple elements gradually hybridized into the revolutionary judicial system.

The review of judicial works in 1943: an independent or a centralized system?

The reform of Li Mu'an and his fellow legal experts encountered a huge setback in 1943 when Lei Jingtian returned from his leave and realized that the goals, operation, and personnel of the High Court had departed sharply from those under his previous tenure. A conflict between Lei and Li and other legal experts broke out, which led to an important event in SGN legal history, "the review of judicial works" (*sifa gongzuo jiantao* 司法工作检讨).[39]

[38] Li Juan, "Geming chuantong yu xifang xiandai sifa linian de jiaofeng jiqi shenyuan yingxiang."

[39] According to the archival documents I have seen, the "Review of Judicial Works" in 1943 was definitely relevant to the Yan'an rectification campaign. On the other hand, this review was not simply political but also legal in nature, because it covered all important issues in the construction of the Shaan-Gan-Ning judicial system in the 1940s. Since this

This review also involved most members of the High Court, as well as the top leaders of the Border government, such as Lin Boqu, Xie Juezai,[40] and Li Weihan, who eventually concluded it.[41]

The review centered on issues that strongly embodied the differences in perspective that the two sides had concerning legal structures and practices. The foremost issue was whether the court system should be three-tiered or two-tiered. Lei insisted that a two-tiered court system helped to shorten the legal process and reduced the number of appeals. Zhu Ying argued that according to modern legal concepts, a three-tiered court system would secure final justice and the supervision of local courts by a supreme court. To this argument, Lei replied that constitutionally, the Border Council, as the highest legislature in the BR, would be able to guarantee final justice and provide the highest supervision.[42]

The fight was also extended to the second issue, whether or not the judicial system should be independent from the leadership of the party. Lei Jingtian rebuked Li Mu'an for expanding the power of the Public Prosecutor's Office and for his idea of a three-tiered court system. He also attacked Zhu Ying for favoring absolute judicial independence and seeking to build a judicial system only subject to the Border Council, with independent finances, personnel, and other resources. Li Mu'an fought back by accusing the previous legal system of "guerrilla-warfare style" (*youji zuofeng* 游击作风) and stated that he believed in an independent and professional legal system for protecting people's rights. To Li's point, Lei argued that the independence of a public prosecutor and judicial review would lead to a deviation from the party's political leadership and its centralized authority (*yiyuanhua* 一元化), and conflict with the goals of the revolution as a whole. Moreover, it would disperse already limited material resources and manpower and create many inconveniences for ordinary villagers.[43] The difference between Lei and Li was also manifested in their views on recruiting legal personnel. Lei believed that the

book focuses on the relationship between marriage reform and the legal system, as well as gender construction, it would digress to devote much length to the review. Moreover, it requires many more documents than I have now in order to evaluate this issue in a just and proper account. In this situation, I leave the topic of Yan'an politics and legal construction to my next book project.

40 Xie was the vice-chairman of the Border Region Council at the time.

41 SPA 15–96, "Gaodeng fayuan Li Mu'an Lei Jingtian yuanzhang guanyu sifa gongzuo de jiantao huiyi fayan jilu."

42 Li Juan, "Geming chuantong yu xifang xiandai sifa linian de jiaofeng jiqi shenyuan yingxiang."

43 SPA 15–96, "Gaodeng fayuan Li Mu'an Lei Jingtian yuanzhang guanyu sifa gongzuo de jiantao huiyi fayan jilu."

reform Li and Zhu had promoted tried to put judicial work into the hands of a small group of legal elites, thus excluding less-educated people with working-class backgrounds from entering the judicial system.[44] Lei was particularly angered at Zhu's abuse of his power as the TCBG's secretary-general in inserting his personal beliefs into the legal construction and intending to exclude the party's leadership from the judicial system.[45]

In the 1990s, when all of Chinese society bade farewell to the revolution, only a few contemporary scholars revisited the subject of the SGN legal system, and their evaluations were often based on whether they held an overall negative or positive view of the revolution. Some scholars are convinced that the legal reformers of that time, particularly Zhu Ying, were criticized because of the political campaign of 1942, in which they were questioned about their loyalty to the party.[46] Some believe that the conflict between Lei Jingtian and SNLC members reflected the clash between revolutionary tradition and Westernized legal concepts in the BR; Lei represented the so-called "worker-peasant cadres" (*gongnong ganbu* 工农干部), while Li Mu'an and Zhu Ying represented the well-trained legal intellectuals.[47] This view may offer a superficial explanation, but simplifies the issue, as it seems unwise to label Lei Jingtian a "worker-peasant cadre" since he was one of a handful of communist leaders in Yan'an who had a college education. In contrast, some scholars argue that the failure of the SNLC's attempt to search for a new judicial model for China was rooted in the geographical isolation of the Border Region and economic pressures that interrupted their work.[48] A more insightful comment comes from Wang Shirong, who posits that Li, Zhu, and other members of the SNLC were criticized in the 1943 review not only because these legal experts were seeking a Western-style judicial independence from the party, but also because their reform of formalization brought back the imperial *yamen* style of legal practice within a revolutionary judicial system.[49] Unfortunately, Wang does not develop this point, but his observation touches on a very important issue in Chinese legal modernization: whether a legal reform should follow a formalistic line or fit into the Chinese reality and revolutionary goal of

[44] *Ibid.*
[45] *Ibid.*
[46] Hu Yongheng, "1943 nian Shaan-Gan-Ning bianqu tingzhi yuanyong Liu fa quan shu zhi kaocha."
[47] *Ibid.*; Li Juan, "Geming chuantong yu xifang xiandai sifa linian de jiaofeng jiqi shenyuan yingxiang."
[48] Hou Xinyi, "Faxue de Zhongguo xuepai: yuanyin, fangfa ji houguo."
[49] Wang Shirong *et al.*, *Xin Zhongguo sifa zhidu de jishi*, 67.

social reforms. In fact, the system's incompatibility with the social reality of the BR at the time was indeed a problem.

It is true that in the 1940s Li and Zhu advocated a radical reform that proved to be unsuited to conditions in the BR. First, establishing a supreme court in the SGNBR may have had political consequences, because it implied an intention of the CCP to break up with the GMD in the Second United Front. It is assumable that a consideration of avoiding this implication may have been the reason that the SGNBR Council turned down the SNLC proposal. Second, as a substitute supreme court subject to the Border government, the TCBG suffered from a flawed design because a litigant still had the constitutional right to appeal the TCBG's decision to the Border Council.[50] This would bring doubt on the authority of the TCBG.[51]

Third, economically speaking, an independent court system was not practical. In 1942, all the governments in the BR dealt with huge financial pressures imposed by the Nationalist government. At this time, most government workers had to engage in manual labor, working in the fields in order to meet their basic needs and support themselves.[52] An independent judicial system required a set of material resources and manpower that was very scarce in the BR during this time. As discussed in Chapter 1, due to the history of underdevelopment in education, this region could not provide enough educated manpower to fill those positions. Many cadres at local government offices had only a limited education or no education. It was unthinkable and unrealistic to set aside a group of well-educated people specifically to serve as judges, public prosecutors, court officers, secretaries, investigators, wardens, and so on in each jurisdiction and separate them from the regular administrative system.

Fourth, the formalized design of professionalization, such as the establishment of a Local Court system, like many high-sounding and well-intended reforms since the late Qing, proved to be a failure. These local courts were located in the seats of larger counties in each subregion and thus unreachable for most villagers in the residential hamlets scattered among vast hilly terrains. Similar to the traditional *yamen* officials, in that they simply stayed in courtrooms located in regional political

[50] In the 1940s' SGNBR, the BR Council was the highest constitutional authority that had the power to overturn any adjudication.

[51] SPA 15-175, "Lei Jingtian: Bianqu sifa gongzuo baogao"; Wang Shirong *et al.*, *Xin Zhongguo sifa zhidu de jishi*, 62–3.

[52] For the economic condition of the 1940s' BR, see Huang Zhenglin, *Shaan-Gan-Ning bianqu shehui jingji shi, 1937–1945* (Socio-economic History of the SGN Border Region, 1937–1945) (Beijing: Renmin chubanshe, 2006).

and cultural centers, the BR judges waited for litigants to come to them rather than reaching out to communities to solve legal disputes promptly. Moreover, beginning in 1941, the CCP launched a campaign, calling for its cadres to "[go] down to village" (*xia xiang* 下乡) for the purpose of stabilizing and pacifying village communities (see Chapter 5). This practice diverged from the demand from the CCP leadership that required its cadres to reach out to village communities. The design of the Local Court system also had its functional flaw because when all legal powers were concentrated in the hands of local courts, it deprived the county-heads of remote areas of the ability to effectively and promptly tackle disputes and crimes in villages. If not handled well and in a timely manner, many legal disagreements could develop into much more serious conflicts, such as a marriage dispute resulting in a kidnapping and a murder.

Finally, legal formalization and professionalization also required a certain amount of paperwork – written complaints, petitions, and written records as evidence – which became another insurmountable obstacle in a region where over 95 percent of the population was illiterate.[53] People like Lei Jingtian viewed this as elitist domination that deprived illiterate farmers of legal rights. In the 1943 review of judicial works, some critics revealed that Zhu Ying particularly delighted in his ability to use the classical style of imperial judicial jargon in composing writs that were totally incomprehensible to junior legal officers and ordinary people.[54] In this system, any lawsuit would likely result in a consumption of time and money and would be unfavorable to the poor because of geographical distance of the court, as well as the difficult literacy obstacle and procedure complication. Under these circumstances, it became even more difficult for rural women to file a lawsuit and/or utilize the judicial system regarding problems of divorce or family abuse.

It was indeed that the judicial system favored by the legal experts such as Li Mu'an, inclined to a Westernized and abstract rendering of legal principles, would not have either benefited the party's leadership or fitted the best interests of the populace. This professionalized judicial system was not conducive to implementing social reforms, particularly not marriage reform. Even if it is more independent and formalized, when a judicial system is unreachable to ordinary people, promising justice is nothing more than empty talk. Under such conditions, ordinary people developed their own ways to seek their view of justice that sometimes led to lawless actions and violence, such as the kidnappings and

[53] Wang Shirong *et al.*, *Xin Zhongguo sifa zhidu de jishi*, 107–08.
[54] Wang Shirong *et al.*, *Xin Zhongguo sifa zhidu de jishi*, 69.

violence discussed in Chapter 1. The case of *Feng v. Zhang* was one of many reflecting this trend.

Inventing the "revolutionary tradition": a hybrid judicial system in the making, 1943–9

In the end, in the fight between Lei Jingtian and Li Mu'an, neither could claim a full victory. Both lost some battles and won others. After the 1943 review, the TCBG was repealed but the court system did not return to its previous two-tiered form; instead, it became a nominally two-tiered system but operated as a three-tiered one in actuality. First, the revised court system reinstalled the office of justice at the county level for primary trials, with the county-head concurrently serving as the chief-judge. Second, although the High Court in Yan'an was restored to its dual role as appellate jurisdiction and the highest court for final decision, certain organizational modifications were made to provide convenience to appellants from all subregions and supervision over primary and appellate courts. In 1943, after the repeal of the Local Court system, the High Court decided to set up a branch office of the High Court (*gaodeng fayuan fenting* 高等法院分庭) in each subregion. Organizationally, each subregional court served as a branch office of the High Court that held the original authority of the High Court in appeals; operationally, however, its adjudication could be appealed at the High Court in Yan'an. It was also subject to the direction of the High Court's headquarters, which had the right to overturn verdicts made by subregional branch offices.[55] In this way, the High Court retained the final authority on an appealed case, which would reduce possible mistakes in primary trials, and oversaw appeals in subregional branch offices. On the other hand, the adjudications of branch offices could also be final decisions that could not be appealed, particularly in certain cases such as criminal misdemeanors and minor civil disputes. This could reduce the burden of the High Court in Yan'an as an appellate jurisdiction, while preventing the endless appealing of minor cases. Meanwhile, it would also save the High Court's time and energy for major cases. In this revised system, a primary trial became locally available to the majority, while at the same time, appellate jurisdiction was not too distant. It also assigned final review of the most complicated and significant cases to the High Court in Yan'an.

In this 1943 reorganization, the High Court established four branch offices covering the subregions of Suide, Sanbian, Longdong, and

[55] Wang Shirong *et al.*, *Xin Zhongguo sifa zhidu de jishi*, 47, 60–3.

Guanzhong. In addition, the Yan'an Local Court retained its position as a municipal court but also functioned as a branch office for the Yanshu subregion.[56] A subregional prefect (*zhuanyuan* 专员) concurrently served as the chief-judge (*tingzhang* 庭长) of the subregional branch office, and the operation of the court was thus automatically mingled with the subregional administrative system. Such a structure has to be understood on the basis of its historical circumstances, because the communists were regional power-holders dealing with a complicated situation that required a great deal of pragmatism and a high level of flexibility.

Legally speaking, this design of a system operating in three tiers would remedy the problems from the previous system by providing security for people's rights to trials and appeals. Politically, this new design of the court system manifested the centralized leadership of the CCP and the Border government, which mobilized all their strength to realize their revolutionary goals, since the system required county-heads and subregional prefects to concurrently serve as judges in their jurisdictions in order to respond to community problems promptly. Economically, it saved financial resources and manpower by mingling the judicial system into the administrative system, which allowed local leaders to settle cases in a timely manner and implement the court's verdict. This system also served the purposes of the BR government in pacifying communities, as will be discussed in Chapter 5. In terms of form, this system satisfied Lei Jingtian's desire for a two-tiered system for shortening trials, but in function it met Li Mu'an's requirement of a three-tiered court system for due process, judicial review, and supervision.

In this new system, the SGN High Court did not totally reject the ideas that legal experts advocated. In fact, some of their views on judicial reform were actually integrated into the BR judicial system and then brought into the national system after 1949. For example, in addition to the establishment of the branch offices in subregions, in 1946 the BR not only restored the public prosecutor system by establishing the Public Prosecutor Office in the High Court, but also allowed its operation to be relatively independent.[57]

In terms of adopting the *Book of Six Codes*, Wang Ziyi, the director of the High Court in 1945, claimed that the BR did not totally reject the Nationalist legal codes, but it did clarify the extent to which they should be applied. He announced that when legal workers found the BR's legal code too vague and too abstract, they would be allowed to

[56] Wang Shirong *et al.*, *Xin Zhongguo sifa zhidu de jishi*, 61–3.
[57] Wang Shirong *et al.*, *Xin Zhongguo sifa zhidu de jishi*, 51.

invoke clauses and terms from the *Book of Six Codes*, especially its penal codes, as a reference in delivering a verdict. However, Wang also emphasized that legal terms borrowed from the *Book of Six Codes* should not be contradictory to the revolutionary principles of the BR.[58] Moreover, members of the BR Council and the High Court devoted themselves to writing a series of detailed legal codes that fitted the situation of the BR. It was under these circumstances that the marriage regulation was revised twice, which I will discuss in Chapter 4. The archival documents of the High Court also prove that court workers in the BR continued using Nationalist codified law; for example, Ma Xiwu employed the BR's principles for marriage disputes in judging the case of *Feng v. Zhang*, but he relied on the Nationalist legal code in penalizing the kidnapping (see Chapter 4).[59] In determining the qualifications of legal personnel, the High Court used the previous short-term training programs and also followed the suggestion of legal experts to establish a law department at Yan'an University after 1942.[60]

Through this dynamic process, the judicial system of the BR gradually improved into a full-fledged one that contained all elements from its history and encompassed all resources through conflict, compromise, reform, and reconfiguration. It was this hybrid system that thus laid the foundation for the post-1949 legal system. Of course, during this time conflicts and compromise were also involved in implementing the law in a specific location. The revolutionary principles and modern legal concepts interacting with local traditions and customs added another important dimension to this hybrid system, as shown in the below section and in Chapter 5. This dynamic created a new practice and a new legal consensus that became the revolutionary legal tradition for the construction of the PRC legal system.

Moreover, the continuing influence of those legal experts of the Yan'an period in the post-1949 legal system suggests the endurance of this hybrid tradition. Li Mu'an, Zhu Ying, Lu Fomin, and others, though they were criticized in the 1943 review, continued to serve in various important positions in the SGNBR legal system in the remaining years of the 1940s, and became doyens of the new PRC judicial system after 1949.[61] In fact, the so-called clash between "revolutionary tradition" and

[58] Wang Ziyi, "Shenpan yu tiaojie" (Adjudication and Mediation), *Jiefang ribao*, January 17, 1946; also see Wang Shirong *et al.*, *Xin Zhongguo sifa zhidu de jishi*, 105.

[59] For the specific legal code Ma adopted in this case, see Chapter 4.

[60] Li Juan, "Geming chuantong yu xifang xiandai sifa linian de jiaofeng jiqi shenyuan yingxiang."

[61] In the 1950s, Li Mu'an was the vice-minister of the Judicial Ministry of the PRC; Zhu Ying was the secretary-general of the branch office of the Supreme Court in the Grand

"Westernized legal concepts" did not end with one conquering the other; instead, the two were blended into a hybrid system that carried over legal practices from before 1949. Since the revolutionary tradition before 1949 was constantly in the making, when we talk about "the CCP's revolutionary tradition," we need to be clear which period and which form of revolutionary tradition are being discussed.

Of course, those who designed this system did not anticipate its potential future deficits. Wang believes that the BR legal system was not simply an institution for trials and appeals of both criminal and civil cases; rather, it should be seen as part of the CCP's comprehensive social governance over this region, which could not be achieved solely through legal institutions.[62] In Qiang Shigong's view, the legal system only represented a part of the BR government apparatus in the comprehensive governance of the party-state.[63] This view is particularly convincing in regard to implementing marriage and other social reform programs, as well as consolidating the BR for wartime. It is indeed true that mingling the political administration with the judicial system provided a convenient means for political interference in the judicial process, which became a frequent practice in the post-1949 period (and has continued in the reform era). However, this style of judicial system also had theoretical foundations that were deeply rooted in Chinese history and tradition (see below).

On the other hand, the lack of judicial independence was a common historical phenomenon of the 1930s and 1940s, in that both the GMD and the CCP could not help dominating the judicial system. Xu Xiaoqun's research shows that "a partyized judicial system" resulted in only limited independence of the Nationalist judicial system during the Nanjing Decade.[64] In this specific historical time, both GMD and CCP considered themselves to be revolutionary parties and responsible for using revolutionary principles to guide the legal system in state-building and social reform. It was the special nature of this historical period that created a legal tradition that would affect later practice.

Northwest Region. Lu Fomin passed away in 1944 from a serious illness. Other people in this group of the SNLC continued to work in important positions in the legal system of the PRC in the 1950s and beyond.

62 Wang Shirong *et al.*, *Xin Zhongguo sifa zhidu de jishi*, 59.

63 Qiang Shigong, "Quanli de zuzhi wangluo yu falü de zhilihua" (Power in Organized Networks and Law in Administration), *Beida falü pinglun* (Peking University Law Review) 3(2) (2000): 1–61.

64 Xu Xiaoqun, "The Fate of Judicial Independence in Republican China, 1912–37," *The China Quarterly* 149 (March 1997): 1–28.

III. Legal practice: formalism or local flexibility under the revolutionary principle?

One important issue in Ma Xiwu's adjudication was how the law treated local custom. Legal formalism emphasizes "the universality and scientific nature of law and the use of deductive theory to arrive at absolute truths," and that "jurisprudence … ought to be based on a limited number of axioms and multiple theorems derived therefrom, which are then applied to all fact situations."[65] How was a legal system that requires universal law and a limited number of axioms based on deductive theory able to distinguish marriages based on the individual's volition from those that had been arranged, given the variety of marriage practices spread across the BR? In fact, during and after the review of judicial works, the top leaders of the SGNBR legal system pondered how to make the law compatible with the locality and deliver justice that satisfied both the people's expectations and revolutionary interests.[66] Therefore, the 1943 review of judicial works should not be seen as simply a political or purely a legal matter; rather, it touched on much more complicated issues in the construction of the SGNBR judicial system, as well as the entire modern Chinese judicial system.

As one of the important regional leaders of the SGNBR, what was Ma's stance during the judicial review and the reconfiguration of the system that followed? Ma was not a theorist but a pragmatic man who based his response to the question of handling marriage disputes on examples from his own legal experience. His criticism of Huachi County in fact manifested his view of proper judicial construction: the law should be followed in spirit and essence, and its words should not be applied mechanically. The new law needed to find a way to reconcile with local customs in order to reach a decision that would be accepted by the community (see Chapter 5). It was at this time that Ma's way of judging, discussed in Chapter 5, started becoming a political model. The essence of "Ma's Way" lies in its combination of a flexible formality and solid revolutionary principles.

[65] Huang, *Chinese Civil Justice*, 2 and 228.

[66] Zhu Suli argues that judicial independence as an abstract concept and a practice works well in Western society; however, in China's case, the party's interference in the legal process has its historical traditions and political considerations, as the party acts in response to people's expectations. See his "Political Parties in China's Judiciary," *Duke Journal of International and Comparative Law* 17 (2007): 533–60. Although Zhu's view reflects his observations of contemporary China, this practice is indeed rooted much more deeply in the revolutionary tradition of the 1940s.

Modernity and locality: between legal formalism and reality

In the early 1940s, the consequences of the incompatibility of the 1939 marriage regulation were evident from local resistance. The judicial system of the BR often faced problems in its implementation, since an arranged marriage might be consented to by both the man and the woman, as in the case of Zhang Lawa and Liu Baoqing, and was always processed with the concomitant transfer of *caili* (as discussed in Chapters 1 and 2). This type of marriage would be in accord with the revolutionary freedom-of-marriage principle, but also violate it. Moreover, the accompanying material exchange infringed on the law even in a marriage to which both parties consented. In fact, at the core of this dilemma was how the law could reconcile essence and formality while also harmonizing local customs with revolutionary regulations in its implementation. In most cases, marriage practices followed local customs that the revolutionary state regarded as backward, although in essence some marriages were consistent with the revolutionary principle of self-determination. In the case of *Feng v. Zhang*, Ma criticized Huachi County's verdict because it insisted on legalities that banned any type of arranged marriage and marriage by force, but neglected the fact that the two young people consented to the marriage. Furthermore, the Huachi County court failed to conduct a thorough investigation to determine the wishes of Peng'er and Zhang Bo; instead, it solely depended on the testimony of Feng Yangui. In contrast, Ma's adjudication manifested his approach: flexibility in formality, but adherence to revolutionary principles of reform to ensure that the outcome would be acceptable to all parties. From this ruling, we can understand Ma's view of legal modernity that legal practice should bridge local customs and modern law rather than create a dichotomy between the two, thus avoiding antagonism between the state and local communities. The broader significance of Ma's legal practice in communist local politics will be discussed in Chapter 5.

It was an important task for legal workers to give consideration to how revolutionary law could be compatible with local culture. In October 1941, the director of the High Court, Lei Jingtian, proposed that laws should fit the "good" customs of the local communities because "law is the combination of humanity (*ren qing* 人情) and principle (*dao li* 道理). It is necessary for lawmakers to give consideration to both … The law of the BR ought to accord with the BR's humanity and principle" (*he yu Bianqu de ren qing dao li* 合于边区的人情道理).[67] In regard to inquiries from local courts on the *caili* issue, Lei stated,

[67] SPA 15–175, "Lei Jingtian: Bianqu sifa gongzuo baogao." I here temporarily translate *ren qing* as "humanity" and *dao li* as "principle," but offer a detailed discussion of these terms in the following section.

The frequent mistakes of local county courts are: regardless of the privy parties' consent to a marriage and their ages, once gift transfer was involved the marriage was penalized as a buying/selling marriage. This [practice] caused a good deal of discontent and it is wrong. We need to respect the privy parties' wishes and make [the ruling] compatible with the humanity/human sense and social customs (*he yu ren qing shisu* 合于人情世俗).[68]

Since 1942, Xie Juezai, as a former director of the High Court and one of the top leaders in charge of legislation, had begun to think about the relations between law and local custom. He argued that "law comes out of human sense (*ren qing*). Certain customs accordant with human sense are law, which should not only be respected but also be adopted into formal legal code."[69] In May 1943, about the same time as when Ma Xiwu was tackling the case of *Feng v. Zhang* in Huachi County, Xie Juezai once again wrote in his diary about his understanding of a good law. According to him, a good law needed to achieve "balance between the principle and the actual circumstances/human sense" (*he qing he li ji shi hao fa* 合情合理即是好法).[70] Xie's account and other adjudicatory writs reveal that CCP legal workers were seriously considering how best to integrate local culture into legal process. From then on, the discussion of balancing *qing* 情, *li* 理 (principle), and *fa* 法 (law) became more frequent in the BR's judicial adjudications.

The term *qing* is a complex term, containing a wide range of connotations that are used in various conditions. The constellation of this word encompasses both subjective aspects, such as feelings, emotion, and sentiment, and objective aspects, such as conditions, circumstances, and reality.[71] A recent scholarly discussion of *qing* has focused on the presentation of its subjective connotation, examining sentiments and desires expressed in Ming-Qing literature[72] and public sympathy in

[68] SPA 15–175, "Lei Jingtian: Bianqu sifa gongzuo baogao."

[69] Huan Nan (Xie Juezai), "Yi de shu: bu jin ren qing" (A Piece of Thoughts: Things Are Lacking Human Sense), *Jiefang ribao*, August 4, 1942.

[70] Xie Juezai, *Xie Juezai riji*, 469.

[71] Cihai bianji weiyuanhui (comp.), *Cihai* (Ocean of Lexicons) (Shanghai: Shanghai cishu chubanshe, 1980), 870; Hanyu da cidian bianji weiyuanhui (comp.), *Hanyu da cidian* (The Grand Chinese Thesaurus) (Shanghai: Hanyu dacidian chubanshe, 2000), 1161; Gudai Hanyu cidian bianxiezu (comp.), *Gudai hanyu cidian* (A Dictionary to Classical Chinese Language) (Beijing: Shangwu yinshuguan, 2006), 1263.

[72] For the "*qing* cult" of the Ming-Qing periods, see Anthony Yu, *Rereading the Stone: Desire and the Making of Fiction in Dream of the Red Chamber* (Princeton, NJ: Princeton University Press, 1997), 56–66; Martin Huang, *Desire and Fictional Narrative in Late Imperial China* (Cambridge, MA: Harvard University Press, 2001), chapter 2; and Martin Huang, "Sentiments of Desire: Thoughts on the Cult of Qing in Ming-Qing Literature," *Chinese Literature: Essays, Articles, Reviews* (December 20, 1998): 153–84.

Republican society.[73] In fact, there are also aspects of *qing* that relate to its objective aspect, such as *qing kuang* 情况 (situation) and *shi qing* 事情 (real condition), *min qing* 民情 (the people's living condition or people's view), *shi qing* 实情 (things), and so on.[74] The earliest use of the term *qing* in relation to the judicial process is recorded in the *Zuo Zhuan* (Zuo's Commentary, *c*.722–453 BCE), which uses *qing* to refer to situations and circumstances.[75] On the other hand, when *qing* is brought in to justify a legal case by citing its social circumstances such as culture, religion, or custom, it is often expressed as *ren qing* (humanity, human instinct, human relations, protocol, rites, etc.). In imperial state management and legal practice, *qing* became an important element in parallel to the other two elements in legal practice, *li* and *fa*.[76]

Thus in the Chinese language, *ren qing* also refers to a human instinct/sense or the normal attitude of human beings in certain circumstances (*ren zhi chang qing* 人之常情), human mentality, people's emotions or wishes, public conditions, or human relations, as well as a concrete situation such as social relations.[77] Meanwhile, *ren qing* may not be an abstract concept or unseen emotion in constructing a social network; as Yunxiang Yan shows, gift giving, in which gifts are a material embodiment of *ren qing*, is based on social custom but also forges a power structure in a rural community.[78] In the legal process, *qing* also has a sentimental and emotional aspect, especially when the offender uses it to beg for leniency due to his/her involuntary condition (*qing fei de yi* 情非得已).

China does indeed have a long tradition of searching for a balance between *qing*, *li*, and *fa* in making a legal decision. Both Li Qicheng's and Liang Zhiping's works show that the late imperial legal system operated

[73] For the presentation of "*qing*" in the Republican urban society, see Eugenia Lean, *Public Passions: the Trial of Shi Jianqiao and the Rise of Popular Sympathy in Republican China* (Berkeley: University of California Press, 2007), 4–6, 13–16, chapter 3, and 217–18n.

[74] Cihai bianji weiyuanhui (comp.), *Cihai*, 870; Hanyu da cidian bianji weiyuanhui (comp.), *Hanyu da cidian*, 1161.

[75] For example, the sentence "da xiao zhi yu, sui buneng cha, bi yi qing" originated from the *Zuo Zhuan* (*The Zuo's Commentary*), meaning that a ruler must make a judgment on the basis of understanding the real situations/conditions of each case, even if he was unable to conduct a thorough investigation of all the cases in person (cited from *Cihai*, 870, term of *qing*). In this sentence, *qing* as a verb can be translated as "understanding the concrete circumstance."

[76] Huang, *Chinese Civil Justice*, preface, iii; Li Qicheng, *Wan Qing ge ji shenpanting yanjiu* (A Study of the Court System in the Late Qing) (Beijing: Beijing daxue chubanshe, 2004), 15–16.

[77] Cihai bianji weiyuanhui (comp.), *Cihai*, 303; Hanyu da cidian bianji weiyuanhui (comp.), *Hanyu da cidian*, 190.

[78] See Yunxiang Yan, *The Flow of Gifts: Reciprocity and Social Networking* (Stanford, CA: Stanford University Press, 1996).

on the basis of balancing these three elements.[79] Some scholars believe that *ren qing* did not necessarily constitute a challenge to state or legal authority. Li Qicheng defines *ren qing* as "human instinct on justice that reflects the heavenly principle and the state law." On the other hand, he also admits that this human instinct can be uncertain, since it is based on individual experience and social position, and thus sometimes conflicts with the other two elements. He points out that the Qing judicial concept intended to reconcile all three aspects: *tian li* 天理 (heavenly principle), *ren qing* (human instinct/sense), and *guo fa* 国法 (state law) in order to reach authentic justice.[80] According to Huang, both Qing legal codes and newly introduced European legal concepts encountered difficulties when adjudicating civil disputes in rural communities. Most imperial and Republican judges thus took real-life circumstances into account to make a decision on a case. This observation shaped Huang's conception of imperial Chinese legal practice of a triad: theoretical presentation was one aspect, actual practice another, and the two together became a third.[81] This triadic legal process led to a belief that considering the balance of the three elements, *qing*, *li*, and *fa*, would reach the essence of justice.

Due to the fact that *qing* or *ren qing* was often embodied in the social customs that dominated people's lives and behaviors, it became a social reality that legal practitioners could not ignore. In legal petitions, appellants often pleaded for leniency or claimed innocence based on certain objective conditions (extenuating details) or social circumstances (humanity/social relations). By emphasizing these objective circumstances, appellants would attempt to attribute their actions to environmental conditions rather than admitting an intentional violation of the law. This would distinguish the offender's intention: he or she was not challenging state authority by breaking the law, but merely performing an unintended action in response to existing customs or extenuating circumstances. For example, when the BR court workers accused local farmers of violating the law by purchasing marriages, the litigants often defended themselves by claiming that given the existing conditions in the locality, one could not find a wife without paying a high price. In doing so, petitioners appealed to a much broader understanding of humanity and called for common sense under extenuating circumstances. They sought to find common ground with legal workers by representing themselves as

[79] Li Qicheng, *Wan Qing ge ji shenpanting yanjiu*, 15–16; Liang Zhiping, *Qing dai xiguan fa: Shehui yu guojia* (The Common Law of the Qing: Society and State) (Beijing: Zhongguo zhengfa daxue chubanshe, 1996), 17–18.
[80] Li Qicheng, *Wan Qing ge ji shenpanting yanjiu*, 15–16.
[81] Huang, *Chinese Civil Justice*, 5–10.

human beings responding to concrete (and disadvantageous) situations; litigants often pushed the boundaries in negotiating for a favorable legal outcome. In this situation, a judge needed to not only learn the basic facts of the case, but also take into account all of the objective conditions and details of a case relevant to a justified adjudication.

Therefore, *qing* is a dynamic process of circumstances embodied in local culture, rather than simply sentiment, humanity, social relations, or even social protocol. For example, in 1945 Ansai County processed a case in which a woman remarried when her soldier husband was serving the military. When her original husband returned, he brought her home, but she was then kidnapped by her second husband. The judge of the Office of Justice of Ansai County, He Xingwang, ruled that the woman should return to her original husband. In the dictum, He wrote that:

> when Gao Zhangbao [the woman's original husband] was fighting on the front line, his wife did not want to wait but remarried [without a divorce]. Making her return [to her original marriage] was based on the circumstances [that Gao's original husband had returned from the front line] (*an qing zhui hui* 按情追回) that is proper to the local custom [normal human sense] (*he hu ren qing* 合乎人情).[82]

From the view of the law, since the woman did not divorce her first husband, her second marriage was illegal, though acceptable in local custom. At the same time, local custom required the woman to return to her original husband once he came home. In this case, he believed that his adjudication was justifiable based on the revolutionary principles of protecting the soldier's marriage (*li*), the woman's illegal marital status (*fa*), and local custom (*ren qing*).

Legal practice in a locality: understanding local knowledge

Is law a universal rule or a localized concept? From an anthropological approach, Clifford Geertz rejects the universalization or generalization of any cultural models and favors a native approach to a cultural system that includes taking into account law, common sense, religion, and arts.[83] Borrowing insights derived from anthropological studies, Geertz suggests that law may need to translate local facts and concepts and thus understand how local society operates. He stresses the importance of "local knowledge" in law because it contains people's wisdom on the

[82] SPA 15-946, "Gao Zhangbao He Siwen kangshu hunyin an" (The Case of Gao and He Regarding a Soldier's Marriage).

[83] Clifford Geertz, "Introduction," "From the Native's Point of View," "Common Sense as a Cultural System," and "Art as a Cultural System," in *Local Knowledge: Further Essays in Interpretive Anthropology* (New York: Basic Books, 1983), 9–13, 55–120.

"artisan task of seeing broad principles in parochial facts."[84] It is apparent that law must be local, and legal authorities need to learn about and respect local knowledge in order to have a good sense of how to deliver justice under specific circumstances.

With the goal of gaining a better understanding of local communities and their culture, from 1943 to 1944 the High Court launched a broad survey of local customs, which was conducted by various courts throughout most SGNBR counties. In its questionnaire, the High Court explained its motive in conducting the survey: the social customs that were profound, widespread, and deeply rooted in local communities would affect legal implementation. The High Court believed that social customs were relevant to legal practice because laws were made on the basis of general human relationships or human instinct (*yi ban ren qing* 一般人情). Therefore, every case in the courts should be decided based on the principles of "heavenly principle" (*tian li*), "state law" (*guo fa*), and "humanity" (*ren qing*). For this reason, the High Court urged the local courts to collect information on local customs in as much detail as possible, so that this data could be used as the reference for legal practice (*zu zi falü yunyong, tongshi zuowei cankao* 足资法律运用, 同时作为参考).[85] Of course, in the SGNBR the "heavenly principle" differed from the Qing Confucian moral principle; instead, it was based on the revolutionary principles of the CCP's social reform programs (see below).

The county courts responded to the survey request and provided detailed information about marriages, the local clans and their social functions, landownership transfers, social contracts, funeral customs, inheritance, and dress codes, as well as land rental and pawning, family structure, human relations, appellatives in families and communities, and local holidays and fairs. This collection of surveys provides the rich details of the social and cultural background of the SGN region described in Chapters 1 and 2 of this book. Some county courts also reported on certain social vices such as violence, stealing, gambling, and opium-smoking. When they responded to the High Court's questions about the definition of social customs and their relevance to the law, most local court workers replied that social customs were the law of the people, to which people had consented and would willingly obey. The court workers also believed that they could use local customs as references in judging legal cases.[86] The question on the position of local

[84] Clifford Geertz, "Local Knowledge: Fact and Law in Comparative Perspective," in *Local Knowledge: Further Essays in Interpretive Anthropology*, 167–234.
[85] SPA 15–57, "Ge xian fengsu xiguan."
[86] *Ibid.*

customs in the formation of the modern legal system was an extremely important one.[87]

In addition, this survey is significant due to the fact that it preserved a large number of precious historical records about local customs. It indicates the shift in the legal practice of the BR to a more community-oriented approach, along with the CCP's transformation from an urban-oriented intellectual organization to a party embedded with a rural population in a specific locality in the 1930s and 1940s. Meanwhile, as a revolutionary party, the CCP established the goal of reforming society through the practice of a "modern" legal system that operated through rational formality. Adopting local customs in its legal practice added another dimension to the judicial construction that could help achieve the balance between revolutionary principles (*li*), state law (*fa*), and local circumstances (*qing*) to reach legal results acceptable to local communities. On this basis, as discussed in Chapter 5, the party tried to minimize litigation through revitalizing community mediation and autonomy.

Between revolutionary principles and social circumstances: the case of Zhao Fanshen

In imperial times, Confucian ideology and ethics were the state's "heavenly principle" (*li*), under which the legal system did not necessarily have to be separated from the administrative system. Of course, in the Yan'an period, the "principle" was different from the Confucian doctrine followed by the Qing and other imperial powers; instead, it was based on the revolutionary principles of the CCP's social reform programs. As a revolutionary power intending to reform the "backward" and "feudal" society, unconditionally following local custom risked compromising the party's revolutionary nature and resulting in a failed mission.

[87] Liang Zhiping's excellent work on the common law of the Qing period offers a good case regarding the relations between social customs and state laws. See his *Qing dai xiguanfa*. On the other hand, Jerome Bourgon criticizes the conventional view regarding the tenstion between Western legal theories and Chinese customs. He believes that in the making of Republican legal codes, reform-minded Chinese legal experts and bureaucrats invented a thing called "the Chinese custom" as a legal entity to be compatible with Western law. See his "Uncivil Dialogue: Law and Custom did not Merge with Civil Law under the Qing," *Late Imperial China* 23(1) (June 2002): 50–90; and "Rights, Freedoms, and Customs in the Making of Chinese Civil Law, 1900–1936," in *Realms of Freedom in Modern China*, William C. Kirby (ed.) (Stanford, CA: Stanford University Press, 2004), 84–112. I can only agree with him to a limited extent. Bourgon's articles, methodologically speaking, try to deny the possibility of generalization through emphasizing the particularity of concrete existence. Due to limited space here, Bourgon's views and his methodology need to be discussed on some other occasion.

By the same token, a fully independent judicial system may have also sacrificed revolutionary goals and principles for its formality, procedure, or self-consistency. Thus, in the triangular relationship of *qing*, *li*, and *fa*, the state especially emphasized the importance of *li*/principle, a revolutionary principle that provided guidance for legal practice and the legal system.

Following the same logic of the imperial state, the BR's legal system was also seen as an instrument to carry out revolutionary principles. In this triad, revolutionary goals/principles supposedly took priority over the judicial system as an instrument; thus, it had to be under the control and supervision of the party-state, rather than operating independently. In the case of *Feng v. Zhang*, the county verdict followed legal procedures and codes, but failed to accord with revolutionary principles that respected an individual's choice in his/her marriage. In the eyes of the revolutionary party, in an age of reform, an independent legal system might compromise the goal of revolution, or even become a weapon against it. This was the point that Ma criticized in his adjudication.

Many cases in the SGNBR proved that including social protocol and human relations in legal adjudication could complicate the picture and lead to a compromise between legal formality and revolutionary principles; thus it was necessary for the party to supervise the judicial system, making sure it served revolutionary purposes. Documents show that it was not unusual for local cadres or junior judges to prioritize local customs and downplay the tenets of the marriage regulation. In the end, however, at the higher level of court, the principle still held its ground, though with a certain degree of compromise with local customs. For this point, the case of Zhao Fanshen in the following may provide such an example, that a high authority would be able to insist on the principle.

Zhao Fanshen, a young woman from Zizhou County, was raised by her grandfather and paternal uncle after the death of her father and remarriage of her mother. When she reached marriageable age, her grandfather and uncle engaged her to a man, He Shengchang, who paid a considerable amount of *caili* to Zhao's grandfather. However, Zhao immediately opposed the engagement and sued her own family in county court. This is one of a few unusual cases in the collection of the SGNBR court records I have seen in which a woman represented and spoke for herself. The county government followed the local custom that once the Zhao family received the *caili*, the engagement was valid. Zhao Fanshen bravely appealed to the Suide Subregional Court (branch office of the High Court), which ruled that since the woman objected to the engagement, it should be dismissed. The next step was He Shengchang's appeal to the High Court, but the High Court agreed with the adjudication of the Suide Subregional Court, believing that the principle of women's self-determination should not be compromised. However, under the 1944 regulation (see Chapter 4), the High Court ruled that the Zhao family should return the *caili* with compensation.[88] This case showed that in the lower-level government, policy implementation was easily compromised by local customs. It was a higher level of the revolutionary judiciary system that insisted on its principles. This finding accords with Diamant's research on rural areas in the 1950s' marriage reform, in that the upper level of cadres and judges supported rural women in their pursuit of divorce, while local cadres were indifferent and unsupportive.[89] In this case, all three elements worked together for an acceptable verdict.

In Ma's view, tolerating local custom (*ren qing*) did not necessarily have to infringe on revolutionary principles (*li*). It was the bad judgment and dogmatism of Huachi County that brought the two into conflict. Thus, in 1944, when the *Liberation Daily* published the article on Ma's way of judging, it appeared that after top leaders reflected on the legal system, the Border government began to see in which direction the judicial system ought to go. Therefore, when the article commented on Ma's adjudication of the case of *Feng v. Zhang*, it adopted Xie Juezai's legal view on *qing* and *li*, believing that it "fits the social circumstances and principle while very reasonable and fair" (*ru qing ru li, feichang qiadang* 入情入理, 非常恰当).[90] Moreover, the influence of this concern also affected the revisions of the marriage regulations in both 1944 and 1946, which will be discussed in the next chapter.

In constructing a new legal system, the BR legal workers tried to bridge the modern legal system and local customs. In this attempt to understand and negotiate with local customs or, as we may put it, "the social reality," legal workers adopted the historical terms *qing*, *li*, and *fa* to adjust their practice. In this condition, understanding *qing* as objective circumstances that included social customs, protocol, and local culture rather than a subjective emotion and desire, as contemporary scholars have argued, helps us comprehend the effort the BR judiciaries made in constructing a more effective judicial system.

[88] SPA 15–1497, *Zhao Fanshen v. He Shengchang*.
[89] Neil Diamant, "Re-examining the Impact of the 1950 Marriage Law: State Improvisation, Local Initiative and Rural Family Change," *The China Quarterly* 161 (March 2000): 171–98.
[90] "Ma Xiwu tongzhi de shenpan fangshi."

4 A new principle in the making

From "freedom" to "self-determination" of marriage through legal practice

Although the case of *Feng v. Zhang* was closed, we should return to Prefect Ma's writ because it included an important terminological change that contained the legal grounds for adjudication. In the writ, Ma first invoked the Nationalist legal code as the grounds for criminal penalty.[1] Then the marriage adjudication was made on the basis of the 1939 marriage regulation. It is most significant that instead of using the term "freedom of marriage" (*hunyin ziyou*) that had been propagated in the BR or "on the basis of the individual's free will," as the 1939 regulation terms it, Ma announced that "under the principle of self-determined marriage in the Border Region" (*Bianqu hunyin zizhu de yuanze* 边区婚姻自主的原则), the union of Peng'er and Zhang Bo was valid.[2]

In the 1939 regulation, the term "freedom/*ziyou*" was at the heart of the general principle for marriage. Ma's statement of "self-determination" as the principle for marriage in the Border Region seemed legally rootless. This thus raises many questions concerning why Ma used "*zizhu*" instead of "*ziyou*" as the principle on which to judge a marriage and what the effects of this change were. Was it only a rhetorical variation of free marriage, or did it signal a meaningful turning point in the marriage reform? Where did the term "self-determination/*zizhu*" come from, and how was it different from "*ziyou*"? What was the reason for this terminological change? What was the significance of this change of phrase in the context of the 1940s' SGNBR, as well as the broader twentieth-century social movements in China? How important was this neologism in the social and cultural context and in legal practice in the

[1] See SPA 15–842, *Feng v. Zhang*. Ma resorted to the articles 150 and 298 from the Penal Code of the Nationalist law to penalize the forced marriage to a third party and kidnapping, and article 361 from the Criminal Law for appellate procedure. See *Zhonghua minguo xingfa, 1935* (The Penal Code of the Republic of China, 1935) and *Zhonghua minguo xingshi susong fa, 1935* (The Criminal Law of the Republic of China, 1935), *Yuedan jianming liu fa* (Yuedan Collection of the Concised Six Codes) (Taipei: Yuanzhao chubanshe, 2007), 15th version, 6–21, 6–36, and 7-59-60.

[2] SPA 15–842, *Feng v. Zhang*.

1940s' SGNBR? More specifically, why and how did legal workers in the SGNBR invent or adopt the term *zizhu* to substitute *ziyou*? How important were legal practices and the judicial system in recasting the neologism for a more effective implementation of the marriage reform?

This chapter traces the terminological evolution of both *ziyou* and *zizhu* from a historical perspective, as well as the way they acquired legitimacy and modernity through social movements and legal practice. It shows that based on legal practice, the revolution had taken over a vernacular term and invented its own discourse and principles of marriage that were more compatible with local conditions than those brought from the littoral cities. By inventing self-determination through legal practice, the revolutionary state empowered women in the battle against patriarchy. This principle and its practice reversed the urban-born guideline that saw divorce as the pathway for women's liberation and independence, which proved incompatible with local customs in the SGNBR. Instead, the BR law sought to design a better method for improving the position of women and their living conditions in marriage, empowering them rather than simply granting them a divorce.

I. From "freedom" to "self-determination": terminology and statutes

From the days of the New Culture and May Fourth movements to the 1930s, the social movement for the reform of family and marriage initiated in coastal and urban areas under the influence of the West developed the idea of "freedom of marriage" in opposition to arranged marriages, as well as other types of marriage that were considered to oppress women and youth. Under this influence, the CCP in the Jiangxi Soviet base areas also promulgated marriage regulations and a law in the early 1930s that set this term as the basic principle of marriage reform, stating that "marriage ought to be based on the principle of freedom" (*hunyin yi ziyou wei yuanze* 婚姻以自由为原则).[3] This section first examines the terminological evolution of the word "freedom" in Chinese society, and then reviews how the various marriage regulations in the Jiangxi Soviet period prior to the 1939 regulation were built on this principle. It also examines the origin and evolution of the neologism "self-determination," as well as the distinctions between the two terms. Only by understanding those differences can we comprehend the confusion that the term "freedom"

[3] "Zhonghua Suweiai gongheguo hunyin tiaoli, 1931" (Marriage Regulation of the Chinese Soviet Republic, 1931), *Jiangxi Su qu funü yundong shiliao xuanbian*, 33.

brought to actual practice, and appreciate the regulation revisions in 1944 and 1946.

The dual meanings of the term "freedom" in twentieth-century China

In the phrase *hunyin ziyou*, the emphasis is on *ziyou*, which equates to "freedom" or "liberty" in English. However, the Western-originated concept does not cover the full meaning of *ziyou*. The term *ziyou* contains dual connotation in the modern Chinese language that derives from two different origins. One is from its traditional root meaning in Chinese classics, which can be traced back to the historical records and a poem from the fourth century and indicates a free decision arising from one's unrestrained volition.[4] The other can be translated into English as either the noun "freedom/liberty" or the adjective "free" (though not meaning "no charge").[5] Linguistically, the traditional meaning of *zi-you* as a phrase originated from its structure as a "noun-verb/subject-predicate" word that literally means "self [doing things] by following one's unrestrained mind/volition"[6] while the translated term *ziyou*/liberty simply formed an indissoluble noun that changed the structure of the term.

The Western concept of "liberty/freedom" was first introduced to China during the late Qing through the translation of Western texts. According to contemporary studies, the earliest appearance of the term *ziyou* in the translation of the English term "liberty" was in the middle of the nineteenth century in English–Chinese dictionaries composed by European missionaries who had mastered the Chinese language to a degree.[7] In the following decades, from the 1850s to the

4 For example, a narrative poem from the fourth century, *Kongque dong nan fei* (Peacock Flying toward Southeast), has the sentence "ru qi de zi you?" (how could you [make the decision] by your own will?) that may be the earliest appearance of "*zi you.*" See *Hanyu da cidian*, (*pu ji ben*), 2185.

5 *Hanyu da cidian*, 1308. Edmund Fung believes that in contemporary Chinese, *ziyou* connotes six concepts, ranging from personal freedom and social liberation to democracy and human rights. Nevertheless, besides the endemic meaning of *ziyou*, the other connotations all originated from the West. Edmund S. K. Fung, "The Idea of Freedom in Modern China Revisited: Plural Conceptions and Dual Responsibilities," *Modern China* 32(4) (October 2006): 453–82.

6 *Hanyu da cidian*, vol. VIII, 1308.

7 According to Hu, the early missionaries also used "*zizhu*" for "liberty" first, but then changed to use *ziyou* for liberty. Hu Qizhu, "Wan Qing 'ziyou' yuci de shengcheng kao lue" (The Formation of the Term "Ziyou" in the Late Qing, the 1820s–1900s), in *Zhongguo jindai shi shang de ziyou zhuyi* (Liberalism in Modern China), Zheng Dahua and Zou Xiaozhan (eds.) (Beijing: Shehui kexue wenxian chubanshe, 2008), 127–45; Xiong Yuezhi, "Wan Qing ji ge zhengzhi cihui de fanyi he shiyong" (The Translation and Uses of Some Political Terms in the Late Qing), *Shi lin* (History Forest) 1 (1999): 57–62.

1880s, *ziyou*/*zi-you* and *zizhu*/*zi-zhu*[8] casually and randomly appeared in the writings of both missionaries and Chinese officials. It seems that Chinese officials still used the term *zi-you* in its classical meaning, while the missionaries offhandedly switched between *ziyou* and *zizhu* to indicate liberty/freedom.[9] The term *ziyou* or *zizhu* as used by missionaries before the 1890s was never clearly defined and was confined only to their own use, without influence on Chinese elites.[10] In about the 1870s Japanese scholars borrowed the term *ziyou* from the missionaries' dictionaries, without noticing its classical meaning in Chinese, to designate liberty/freedom, but this move attracted very little attention from the Chinese elites. Xiong Yuezhi observes that before the 1890s, the Chinese elites hesitated to adopt *zi-you* to indicate liberty/freedom because they were aware of its negative connotation of lawlessness and arbitrariness.[11] It was Huang Zunxian 黄遵宪 (1848–1905) who adopted *ziyou* as liberty/freedom in the 1880s when he resided in Japan as a Chinese diplomat. Nonetheless his work was not published in China until a decade later,[12] about the same time when the term began to spread. As a result, up to the 1890s most Chinese elites still insisted on the classical meaning of *zi-you*.

The use of *ziyou* to designate liberty/freedom became conspicuous among Chinese elites after the Sino-Japanese War (1894–5) and during the 1898 reforms, thanks to Liang Qichao's and Yan Fu's writings during this time,[13] especially Yan Fu's 严复 (1854–1921) translation of the

[8] As Liang Qichao points out, in the majority of cases in classical Chinese, the unit of the word rests on its individual character, which is able to present the meaning of a word. See Fedrico Masini, *Xiandai hanyu cihui de xingcheng* (The Formation of Modern Chinese Lexicon and its Evolution toward a National Language: The Period from 1840 to 1898) (trans. by Huang Heqing) (Shanghai: Hanyu da cidian chubanshe, 1997), 94. On the other hand, the vernacular language often uses a multi-character (multi-phonetic) term as the unit of a word. Since the classical term was used on the basis of individual characters, in this chapter I will hyphenate or separate the two characters when I discuss its classical connotation and put them together to indicate its modern connotation. This also applies to the use of *zi-zhu*.

[9] Hu Qizhu, "Wan Qing 'ziyou' yuci de shengcheng kao lue"; Xiong Yuezhi, "Wan Qing ji ge zhengzhi cihui de fanyi he shiyong." Also see Masini, *Xiandai hanyu cihui de xingcheng*, 64.

[10] Hu Qizhu, "Wan Qing 'ziyou' yuci de shengcheng kao lue." The study by Jin Guantao and Liu Qingfeng also confirms this point. See their *Guannian shi yanjiu: Zhongguo xiandai zhongyao zhengzhi shuyu de xingcheng*, 525–6 and 611.

[11] See Xiong Yuezhi, "Wan Qing ji ge zhengzhi cihui de fanyi he shiyong"; also see Hu Qizhu, "Wan Qing 'ziyou' yuci de shengcheng kao lue."

[12] Hu Qizhu, "Wan Qing 'ziyou' yuci de shengcheng kao lue." Also see Jin Guantao and Liu Qingfeng, *Guannian shi yanjiu: Zhongguo xiandai zhongyao zhengzhi shuyu de xingcheng*, 611–12.

[13] Hu Qizhu, "Wan Qing 'ziyou' yuci de shengcheng kao lue."

works of Herbert Spencer and John Stuart Mill.[14] As an overseas student who had studied in England and returned to China, Yan Fu unquestionably understood the authentic connotation of liberty/freedom in Mill's work. Instead of literally converting the English title *On Liberty* into *Lun ziyou* – using the term *ziyou*, which had already returned from Japan – Yan translated it into "On the Boundary of the Rights between Society and Individuals" (*Qun ji quan jie lun* 群己权界论).[15] In the text, however, Yan used the term *ziyou* to indicate liberty/freedom, perhaps for the convenience of translation and with an eye to brevity.[16]

Translating *zi-you* into "*ziyou*/freedom/liberty" in the late nineteenth century resulted in the transformation of this term from a word with power of action (noun-verb/subject-predicate structure) into an indissoluble multi-character noun that dismissed the acting power of the subject in order to equate it to its Western connotation. Linguistic transformation also brought about semantic changes that had to be defined carefully and intellectually. However, Yan Fu's translations were all written in classical Chinese and circulated only among top elites at the turn of the twentieth century. As a result, this intellectual and semantic transition somehow occurred only in the urban environment, while the majority of the rural population with no modern education still thought of *ziyou* in terms of its traditional meaning.

Owing to the fact that it derived from a Western theory and that the Chinese elite participated in its creation, the term *ziyou* was widely accepted by reform-minded urban-educated elites under the political and intellectual influence of the West in the early twentieth century.[17] In the urban environment in the late 1910s and 1920s, these terms frequently appeared in newspapers and magazines[18] and were adopted by

[14] Although Yan Fu's translation of both Herbert Spencer's *A Study of Sociology* and John Stuart Mill's *On Liberty* were published in 1903, chapters of these works had been published in newspapers in the late 1890s.

[15] Hu Qizhu believes that Yan Fu was the first to not only define ziyou as liberty/freedom but also make it specify the right of the individual. See Hu Qizhu, "Wan Qing 'ziyou' yuci de shengcheng kao lue."

[16] In the translation of Spencer's *A Study of Sociology*, Yan Fu borrowed the term ziyou to indicate liberty. See Yan Fu (trans.), *Qun xue yi yan* (A Study of Sociology) (Beijing: Commercial Press, 1981 [reprint]), 29–30).

[17] Jerome B. Grieder, *Hu Shih and the Renaissance: Liberalism in the Chinese Revolution, 1917–1937* (Cambridge, MA: Harvard University Press, 1970); Huang Kewu, "Jindai Zhongguo de ziyou zhuyi: yuan qi yu yan bian" (Liberalism in Modern China: Its Origin and Evolution), in *Zhongguo jindai shi shang de ziyou zhuyi*, Zheng Dahua and Zou Xiaozhan (eds.) (Beijing: Shehui kexue wenxian chubanshe, 2008), 27–43.

[18] See Bing Wen, "Hunyin ziyou" (Freedom of Marriage) and Lu Qiuxin, "Hunyin ziyou he de mo ke la xi" (Freedom of Marriage and Democracy), in *Wu si shiqi funü wenti wenxuan*, 233–5 and 242–5.

young educated rebels. They called for "freedom of love" (*ziyou lian ai* 自由恋爱), "freedom in courtship" (*ziyou shejiao* 自由社交), "freedom in making friends" (*ziyou jiao you* 自由交友), "free divorce" (*lihun ziyou* 离婚自由), and so forth.[19] The early communist intellectuals thus brought this term, along with the influence of the USSR's marriage law, into their Jiangxi revolutionary base areas.

"Freedom as principle": the marriage regulations and law in southern revolutionary base areas, 1931–4

In 1931, the newly established soviet government in the Jiangxi revolutionary base area promulgated a marriage regulation that established "freedom as the principle of marriage" (*yi ziyou wei yuanze*). It also regulated that the government abolish all "feudal arranged, forced, and buying/selling marriages" and the system of *tongyangxi*. It promoted monogamy while banning polygamy (*yi fu duo qi* 一夫多妻). Most importantly, it also stipulated a principle for freedom of divorce that would grant an ex parte divorce to either party.[20] In spirit but not in word, this regulation might have been influenced by the Soviet Union's code of 1926, especially in granting women freedom in marriage and divorce. However, the USSR code put more stress on "absolute equality" and "mutual consent" in a marriage registration, rather than spelling out the terms "freedom" and "free will."[21] Therefore, the 1931 regulation seemed to stem more from the May Fourth discourse by taking freedom as its grounding principle. Regarding the divorce term, the regulation of the Jiangxi Soviet Central (JSC) government was very brief and had only two articles in addition to this principle: one allowed ex parte divorce, and the other required divorce registration. Both were clear evidence of copying the USSR code. The 1934 Marriage Law, a revised version of this marriage regulation, added one more article that set some limits on soldiers' wives requesting ex parte divorce.[22]

[19] In the 1930s, these words were collected into a special type of dictionary, the dictionary of neologisms (xin mingci cidian). See Xing Moqing (comp.), *Xin mingci cidian*, 51. Also see Xu Huiqi, *"Nala" zai Zhongguo: Xin nüxing xingxiang de suzao ji qi yanbian, 1900s–1930s* ("Nala" in China: The Image of New Women and Its Evolution, the 1900–1930s) (Taiwan: National Cheng-Chi University, 2003), 189–245.

[20] "Zhonghua Suweiai gongheguo hunyin tiaoli."

[21] See *The Soviet Law on Marriage: Full Text of the Code of Laws on Marriage and Divorce, the Family, and Guardianship* (Moscow: Co-operative Publishing Society of Foreign Workers in the USSR, 1932), 3–13. In the dissolution of a marriage, the 1926 USSR code also granted individuals the right to an ex parte divorce.

[22] "Zhonghua Suweiai gongheguo hunyin fa."

The communist movement was never a unified entity with a uniform policy, but rather an undertaking with strong regional diversity.[23] This was certainly true in the realm of marriage reform. The USSR influence on unconditional ex parte divorce was limited to the area of the Central Soviet base in Jiangxi.[24] In 1931, the Xiang-Gan (Hunan-Jiangxi) Provincial Soviet (HJPS) government issued a much more detailed marriage regulation, which surpassed that of the Central Soviet government. It was the first known revolutionary regulation that detailed banning of specific marriage practices, such as polygyny, buying/selling of marriage, concubinage, *tongyangxi*, and chastity system in addition to its general principle of "freedom."[25] In contrast, the banned list in the JSC regulations was much shorter.[26]

In its ex parte divorce conditions, this regional regulation had some important differences from that of the JSC government. The HJPS regulation set up nine conditions for divorce, which were very similar to the conditions in the 1939 regulation. The HJPS regulation stipulated that when one party filed for divorce but the other party disagreed, the local (most likely county or township) soviet government had to conduct a thorough investigation of his/her objection,[27] meaning that the divorce needed to fit the grounds in the regulation. This is an administrative detail to ex parte divorce that did not exist in the JSC region.

Moreover, one term in this regional regulation is worth noting. In 1931, it had already set up terms to prevent soldiers' wives from seeking an ex parte divorce, three years before a similar restriction was written into the 1934 Central Soviet Marriage Law. This provides additional evidence against the view of some Western feminists that during the Jiangxi period, the CCP supported a radical policy for women's divorce rights that was then pulled back in the SGN period, since the latter constrained

[23] See Saich and van de Ven (eds.), *New Perspectives on the Chinese Communist Movement* (discussed in Chapter 5), which gathered a group of studies on various revolutionary regions regarding the variety in communist policy on social reform and mobilization.

[24] The details of how the USSR marriage law was transmitted to China are still unclear; however, the fact that the CCP issued an independent law on marriage and family separate from the general civil code embodied the USSR influence. See Wang Geya, "Yu wai fa yingxiang xia de Zhongguo hunyin fa gaige" (The Reform of the Marriage Law under the Influence of Foreign Laws), *Bijiao fa yanjiu* (Journal of Comparative Law) 5 (2007): 70–81; Li Xiuqing, "Xin Zhongguo hunyin fa de chengzhang yu Sulian moshi de yingxiang" (The Evolution of the Marriage Laws in PRC and the Influence of USSR Models), *Falü kexue* (Science of Law) 119(4) (2002): 76–89.

[25] It is very likely that the regulation of the HJPS government was under the influence of the Nationalist legal codes, since the regulation of the Central Soviet government had no term prohibiting a marriage between blood relatives, which does not appear in JSC regulation and law.

[26] "Zhonghua Suweiai gongheguo hunyin tiaoli."

[27] *Ibid.*

soldier wives' ex parte divorce. From the very beginning, this was a practical issue, even an issue of survival. Similar to the situation in the JSC region, we still do not have any concrete documents regarding its practice at the local level, so it is not clear how these terms changed and were introduced in the 1934 Law.

It was the establishment of power in the SGNBR that gave the CCP enough time to put into practice its idealistic policies and develop neologisms and concepts based on that practice. However, *hunyin ziyou* led to an unintended result because of local misinterpretation, especially when it was taken out of its previous intellectual and urban context. When it was put into the SGN social and cultural setting, the term *ziyou* resumed its traditional phrase structure, with the strong implication of "(doing anything about) a marriage by following one's unrestrained will" (*zi-you*). Moreover, in 1939, when a location where family agency was still dominant and marriage a family practice, *ziyou* was hijacked by and bundled into family agency, becoming the father's privilege. It was this incompatibility in freedom that caused tremendous problems in legal practice. Farmers, mostly women's fathers, or the women – prompted by their parents – argued with local officials and courts, asking for their *zi-you*.[28] The legal documents indicate that the High Court and local courts frequently tried to clarify the term by stressing that *ziyou* did not mean acting without restraint and that "a freedom out of law is not real freedom" (*chu hu falü zhiwai zhi ziyou, buneng renwei zhenzheng zhi ziyou* 出乎法律之外之自由, 不能认为真正之自由).[29] We can recognize that the dictum referred to the confusion of the term in the locality.

From "freedom" to "self-determination" through social practice

In fact, due to its alien origins and its multiple meanings, *ziyou/zi-you* had become an ambivalent term in twentieth-century China and thus experienced a frustrating fate.[30] Correspondingly, this fate also affected liberalism (*ziyou zhuyi* 自由主义) in playing a role on the Chinese political stage and in intellectual circles, particularly because of its strong negative connotation in the Chinese sematic context as a lawless and anarchistic concept which also affected the Chinese revolution. In 1939, Mao

[28] Cong Xiaoping, "Zuo Run su Wang Yinsuo: 20 shiji 40 niandai SGN bianqu de funü, hunyin yu guojia jian gou."

[29] SPA 15–1495, *Sun Shanwen v. Wang Shenggui*; SPA 15–1407, *Lian Shenghai v. He Xianglin*.

[30] He Xiaoming, "Jindai Zhongguo ziyou zhuyi: Bu jie guoshi de jingshen zhi hua" (Liberalism in Modern China: A Spiritual Flower without Fruit), in *Zhongguo jindai shi shang de ziyou zhuyi*, Zheng Dahua and Zou Xiaozhan (eds.), 14–26.

Zedong wrote a short essay, "Opposing *Zi-you*-ism" (*Fan dui zi-you zhuyi* 反对自由主义),[31] which defined *zi-you zhuyi* in its local/vernacular meaning. In this article, Mao created a long list of the symptoms of "*zi-you*-ism," including irresponsibility, licentiousness, selfishness, carelessness, unprincipled and discretionary behaviors, indulgence, lack of discipline, and opportunism, all of which were destructive to the revolutionary cause.[32] It was this connotation of *zi-you zhuyi* (*zi-you*-ism) that dominated most Chinese people's understanding of Western-originating *ziyou zhuyi* (liberalism) for decades, from the 1940s until Western liberalism was reintroduced into China in the 1990s.[33] Thus Western liberalism, either as a political banner or as pure intellectual thought, only attracted a limited number of followers among Chinese elites in the twentieth century.[34]

On the other hand, the term *zi-zhu*/self-determination traveled a different path in twentieth-century China. In Chinese literature, the emergence of the term *zi-zhu*, much later than that of *zi-you*, occurred mostly in marriage-related situations written by a Ming-Qing litterateur and dramatist, Li Yu (1611–80),[35] and famous Qing novelist, Pu Songling (1640–1715).[36] It signifies "to act on one's own, to decide for oneself, or to be one's own master [in doing something]," a meaning very close to "autonomy" in English or, more accurately, autonomously (doing something).[37] The term *zi-zhu* had a similar linguistic structure of noun-verb/subject-predicate to *zi-you* and both *zi-you* and *zi-zhu* emphasize action and decision-making, with strong subjective power and inferred agents/actors. Semantically, however, *zi-you* allows for open and arbitrary possibilities from the actor's unrestrained mind, while *zi-zhu* hints at a subjective power in making a decision regarding a specific issue.[38]

[31] I translate this type of *zi-you zhuyi* as "*zi-you*-ism" to differentiate it from "liberalism" (*ziyou zhuyi*).

[32] Mao Zedong, "Fan dui zi-you zhuyi," (Opposing Zi-you-ism) *Mao Zedong xuanji* (Selected Works of Mao Zedong), vol. II (Beijing: Renmin chubanshe, 1968), 330–2. It's very likely that Mao had no knowledge of Western liberalism and interpreted the "*ziyou zhuyi*" (liberalism) based on the classical meaning of *zi-you*. Of course, his indigenous understanding also fitted the requirement of building a Leninist party.

[33] See Jin Guantao and Liu Qingfeng, *Guannian shi yanjiu*, 403–20; Geng Yunzhi, Zheng Dahua, and Yu Zuhua, "Lishi weishenme mei you xuanze ziyou zhuyi" (Why History Did Not Select Liberalism) in *Zhongguo jindai shi shang de ziyou zhuyi*, 1–10.

[34] See Fung, "The Idea of Freedom in Modern China Revisited."

[35] Li Yu stated in a story that since the hero was raised by a father-like guardian, he "could not make a decision" on his own marriage (*bu neng zi zhu*). See *Hanyu da cidian*, 1310; *Hanyu da cidian (pu ji ben)*, 2185.

[36] See Chapter 1's citation from Pu Songling, "Xihu zhu".

[37] *Hanyu da cidian*, 1310; *Hanyu da cidian (pu ji ben)*, 2185.

[38] In spite of the fact that both terms indicate the actor's volition, this semantic nuance prevents the two terms/phrases from being interchangeable in constructing a sentence.

The modern transformation of the term *zi-zhu* can also be traced back to the nineteenth century. The term *zi-zhu* was brought into the political realm in the middle of the nineteenth century because the early missionaries could not distinguish the nuances between *zi-you* and *zi-zhu*. They struggled between the two words, but finally designated *ziyou* for "liberty."[39] At least in the late 1890s, a group of women writers still used the term *zi-zhu* to describe marriage-related issues,[40] while male authors gradually extended the notion of this term to issues of state sovereignty. For example, in his writing, Yan Fu tried to make a clear distinction between *ziyou* and *zizhu* by stating that "individuals value *ziyou* while nations/countries value *zizhu*" (*shen gui ziyou, guo gui zizhu* 身贵自由，国贵自主),[41] designated *zizhu* to sovereignty. In the late Qing social and political movements, the use of the term *zizhu* for state sovereignty appeared in Zhang Binglin's 章炳麟 (1869–1936) famous writing for revolution.[42] Thus in the political environment of the late Qing and the early twentieth century, when the existence of the Chinese nation was threatened by Western powers and weak Manchu rulers, *zizhu* was fully extended from a term used only for family affairs (desire for/describing marriage autonomy) to one applied to questions of state autonomy (independence/sovereignty). It was the traditional concept of family state order that proved the key to the transformation of this term as a political lexis when it reappeared in the 1930s.

After the casual appearance in late Qing political and international texts, the term *zi-zhu* dropped out of mainstream social and political terminology in early twentieth-century social movements and only

[39] In an early missionary dictionary of 1844, the Western concept of liberty/freedom was rendered in Chinese as "the gist/principle of self-determination" (*zi-zhu zhi li*). See Xiong Yuezhi, "Wang Qing ji ge zhengzhi cihui de fanyi he shiyong"; Hu Qizhu, "Wan Qing '*ziyou*' yuci de shengcheng kao lue." Jin Guantao and Liu Qingfeng point out that there may have been other uses of this term during this time but they were very rare. See Jin Guantao and Liu Qingfeng, *Guannian shi yanjiu*, 525.

[40] See *Nü xuebao* (Women's Journal) (August 1898): 3b, (September 1898): 2a–2b. I sincerely appreciate Professor Nanxiu Qian at Rice University who points out the use of this term in the writings of *Nü xuebao* and shares her precious source with me. See her *Politics, Poetics, and Gender in Late Qing China* (Stanford, CA: Stanford University Press, 2015), 156–7.

[41] Hu Qizhu, "Wan Qing 'ziyou' yuci de shengcheng kao lue," and Jin Guantao and Liu Qingfeng, *Guannian shi yanjiu: Zhongguo xiandai zhongyao zhengzhi shuyu de xingcheng*, 526–7.

[42] Zhang Binglin, "Bo Kang Youwei lun geming shu" (Letter Opposing Kang Youwei's Views on Revolution), *Zhang Taiyan xuan ji* (Selected Works of Zhang Taiyan [Binglin]) (Shanghai: Shanghai renmin chubanshe, 1981), 155–86. He used the words "*Han zu zi zhu*" to refer to the time when the Han Chinese ruled their own land in the Sui and Tang dynasties (581–907).

sporadically appeared in the literature elsewhere.[43] This temporary retreat from the political arena and social movements allowed *zi-zhu* to reserve its original linguistic structure and semantic meaning. It later reappeared in Mao's writings in 1937 in the discussion of the CCP's stand on the Second United Front,[44] the alliance between the previously antagonistic CCP and the GMD (Nationalists) in resisting the Japanese invasion. In disagreement with the view in the revolutionary camp that suggested the CCP should be fully subject to the leadership of the Nationalist government for the sake of fighting the Anti-Japanese War, Mao insisted on the "independence and self-determination" (*duli zizhu* 独立自主) of the CCP in the United Front.[45] In a similar situation, Mao also criticized the view, once prevalent in the communist party, that the CCP should wholeheartedly receive the Russian-led Comintern's instructions on the Chinese revolution for the sake of uniting internationalism and communism against capitalism and fascism.[46] In using *zizhu* to characterize the CCP and Chinese revolution vis-à-vis the Nationalists and the Comintern, Mao manifested the CCP's effort of seeking independence and autonomy. During China's fight against Japanese imperialism, the term was employed to describe the Chinese nation's struggle against the Japanese invasion.[47] Given the broad use of this term, it can be presumed that in the context of the early 1940s, the legal workers of the SGNBR extended the term *zi-zhu* from the political realm to legal practice, for its connotation of self-determination fitted the autonomy practiced and demanded by local women.

[43] See Jin Guantao and Liu Qingfeng, *Guannian shi yanjiu*, 526. In the 1930s, most dictionaries of neologisms did not include the term *zi-zhu*, meaning that the compilers did not regard this term as either important or as an imported term. See Xing Moqing (comp.), *Xin mingci cidian*. In contrast, every dictionary in the same period up to the 1930s has collected the term "*ziyou*/*zi-you*."

[44] Li Huaxing and Wang Lingyi, "Lun Mao Zedong de duli zizhu he dui wai kai fang sixiang" (On Mao Zedong's Thoughts on Independence, Self-determination, and the Open Door), *Shi lin* 23(3) (March 1991): 22–30; also see You Lin (ed.), *Lun Yan'an jingshen* (On the Yan'an Spirit) (Beijing: Gaodeng jiaoyu chubanshe, 2008), 136–7.

[45] Mao Zedong, "Tongyi zhanxian zhong de du li zi zhu wenti" (The Issue of [the CCP's] Independence and Self-Determination in the United Front), *Mao Zedong xuanji*, vol. II, 502–05.

[46] Wang Hui, "*Difang xingshi, fangyan tuyu yu kang Ri zhanzheng shiqi de 'minzu xingshi' de zhenglun*" (Local Form, Vernacular Language, and the Debate on the National Form during the Anti-Japanese War), in *Yazhou shiye: Zhongguo lishi de xushu* (Asian Perspective: The Narration of Chinese History) (Hong Kong: Oxford University Press, 2010), 237–81.

[47] This term once again appeared in the 1940 *Cihai* (The Ocean of Words [Shanghai: Zhonghua shuju, 1940], 221) compiled by Shu Xincheng (1893–1960), a leftwing educator and compiler. This reemergence in *Cihai* should be considered within the circumstances of the surge of nationalism in the 1930s and the influence of the CCP's view on the compiler. However, it is another topic that needs more exploration at another time.

II. "Self-determination": a new principle for marriage through legal practice

Up to 1942, the official CCP view on women ranged from an illuminated idealism at the political top to a realistic pragmatism at the level of implementation. The 1939 marriage regulation had failed to provide a legal ground for many marriage disputes and related property quarrels, as shown in the previous chapters; instead, it put the solution into the hands of local judges and cadres, allowing them to settle disputes at their discretion. In the dynamics between an idealistic vision of women and local women's activities, workers in the legal system were the first group to recognize the social reality. The term *zi-zhu* began appearing in legal documents to remedy the misunderstanding caused by the term "freedom of marriage." From 1942 on, the term *zi-zhu* became dominant in most legal documents and gradually replaced *ziyou* at a practical level, though in Yan'an the official rhetoric on marriage reform retained the May Fourth discourse of "freedom." Moreover, as a result of rural women's activities and participation in the legal process, legal workers had to develop and adopt specific legal techniques in order to identify a woman's will.

Reconceptualizing and understanding rural women

When the May Fourth ideas on marriage were put into practice in a specific location, the communists began to perceive "real" rural women. Government officials and legal workers tried to play the role of savior to these local peasant women and lead them into an "idealized" marriage form, but soon found that their efforts and good intentions were twisted and manipulated in an environment in which family agency was still dominant and young women sometimes collaborated with their fathers for material benefit. Because of the controversial nature of the case of *Zuo Run v. Wang Yinsuo*, the High Court, now seeing women not only as agents for revolution but also the object of reform, sent out a lengthy instructive letter on divorce cases to county courts, advising them to:

> not operate the principle of freedom of marriage mechanically and apply the term of "incompatibility of emotional relations" [to all divorce cases indiscriminately], because in a region like northern Shaanxi [*Shaanbei*] where the economy and culture are so underdeveloped, the term of incompatibility of relations was frequently used as a pretext for some backward women to despise their poor husbands and want to marry rich men instead.[48]

[48] SPA 15–33, "Gao yuan zhishi xin 3: Chuli lihun anjian ying zhuyi ge jie" (The SGN High Court Instructive Letter Number 3: Please Pay Attention to All Details in Dealing with Divorce Cases).

The changing view of women from innocent victims of feudalism and imperialism to part of the "backward" society was reflected in the treatment of legal cases.

Although this letter held a moral judgment and urban elite bias, at least these legal experts began to realize that rural women were different from what they had previously imagined and how they had been portrayed in the May Fourth discourse and revolutionary ideology. In court, many of these women frequently claimed that their feelings toward their husbands were characterized by being "incompatible" (*bu he* 不合) or that they were "not getting along" (*bu hao* 不好), but when the court asked them to give more concrete examples, they turned to stating that their husbands did not provide enough food and clothing.[49] Some of them, mainly soldiers' wives/fiancées, simply used the absence of their men as justification. Food, clothing, and having their husbands present were these women's expectations for marriage and conditions to which the women believed they were fully entitled. For them, these elements were important, as well as basic indicators that defined the quality of their marriages. However, this concept of marriage differed significantly from that shaped by the New Culture and May Fourth movements in the urban environment, which solely emphasized the feeling of love or emotional relation as the cornerstone of marriage, attempting to encompass love, sex, marriage, and family in a homocentric circle. In the eyes of the court, influenced by the idealistic image of marriage spread by communist lawmakers, providing insufficient food and clothing did not seem like a legitimate reason for divorce, nor was the absence of soldier husbands.[50]

To a certain extent, they seemed sympathetic to those rural women who used marriage as a survival strategy, but they jumped to an extreme by denying rural women's love. They thought that for an ordinary woman, the purpose of marriage was to find a man she could live with for life. They stated that these women did not marry for "love"; in fact, they did not even care about love as long as they had food and clothing.[51] This statement was, in fact, contradicted by the fact that men and women in this area did experience strong feelings of love, as recorded in hundreds of folk songs and local legends later collected by the artists of Yan'an Lu Xun College of Arts (Lu Yi), which I discussed in Chapter 2. However, in this statement we can see the discrepancy between the idealistic image of Chinese women that originated from the New Culture movement and

[49] SPA 15–29, *Huang Guiying v. Gao Yuhe.*
[50] *Ibid.*
[51] SPA 15–33, "Gao yuan zhishi xin 3: Chuli lihun anjian ying zhuyi ge jie."

motivated the communist revolutionaries and the real women in the concrete social environment. Based on this encounter with "real" women, the revolutionary image of rural women that had originated from an urban milieu collapsed.

Up to 1944, after the review of judicial works, the High Court became clearer about the principles for marriage disputes that should be in accord with revolutionary principles of class division, with a certain amount of flexibility. The view of seeing rural women as part of "backward feudalism" now changed to a class perspective that showed much more sympathy to these women. By admitting women's agency, the High Court accepted the term that had been spread in legal practice, saying that under the new democracy the principle of "self-determination and self-willingness" (*zi-zhu zi-yuan* 自主自愿) should be more flexible and apply to marriage cases.[52] The then High Court believed that the social roots for buying/selling marriages were more environmentally and economically motivated than the reason of personal morality.[53] The High Court also believed that since marriage disputes occurred more frequently among the poor, it was poverty that led to marriage instability.[54] This diagnosis of the cause of marriage disputes was different from the 1942 one, which named women as the problem. Rather, this report attributed the source of marriage disputes to social and environmental problems.

Based on these diagnoses, legal workers and local cadres increasingly realized that an ex parte divorce was not a simple solution for women in the region because after a divorce, even if it was caused by a husband's abuse, the woman would immediately fall back into the hands of her parents. They saw in many cases that women became the object for the next arranged marriage for a higher price that would benefit the parents or a third party, thus increasing the flow of buying/selling marriage. During this period, the CCP also proposed the slogan of "harmonious family" (*hexie jiating* 和谐家庭) and/or "democratic family" (*minzhu jiating* 民主家庭) to complement its policy of family reform. However, this political slogan did not appear in any legal document as the principle for delivering divorce verdicts, showing a gap between the CCP's idealistic policy and legal practice. In dealing with divorce cases, the High Court tried to draw the line between cases brought merely for material gain by a patriarch through manipulating marriage and those that were true divorces, involving evidence of intolerable cohabitation. At the same

[52] SPA 15–26, "Bianqu panli huibian, 1944."
[53] SPA 15–72, "Hunyin wenti yu hunyin tiaoli."
[54] SPA 15–294, "Jiaxian hunyin faling zhixing zongjie."

time, the High Court also worked to correct family practices and change women's living conditions, as demonstrated below.

Ultimately, the High Court believed that women's misery in marriage was deeply embedded in their economic condition; thus, for true freedom of marriage, the state had to help women win economic independence and improve their position in the family.[55] In February 1943, the CCP Central Party Committee instructed that the women's movement should be redirected to organizing women to engage in economic productivity through various means.[56] Around the March 8th International Women's Day of the same year, Cai Chang 蔡畅 (1900–90), one of the most important female leaders in Yan'an, published an article responding to the Central Committee's instruction. The article emphasized the importance of women winning their economic independence through participating in productive work in handicrafts and agriculture.[57] Through mobilizing women to work in the fields, the party's women workers believed, women would become an important part of the labor force and would earn their independence, so that they would not need to depend on men to provide their food and shelter, thus eventually changing the power relations in the family.[58] During this period, many changes occurred in legal practice that had a profound influence on the CCP's legal system and further convinced people that women's autonomy should be recognized in marriage disputes.

Changing legal practices (1): definitions and techniques

As early as 1941, the High Court had already realized the problems caused by the 1939 regulation in its implementation and thus tried to develop some workable definitions to resolve any confusion stemming from the regulation. In October 1941, Director Lei Jingtian presented the annual report on the legal work of the BR, in which he admitted that the problems in legal practice were caused by the fact that there were

[55] See Stacey, *Patriarchy and Socialist Revolution*, 109.

[56] "Zhongguo Gongchandang zhongyang weiyuanhui guanyu kang Ri genjudi muqian funü gongzuo fangzhen de jueding, 1943" (The Central Committee of the CCP's Decision on the Recent Development of Women's Work in Various Revolutionary Base Areas, 1943), *Shaan-Gan-Ning bianqu funü yundong wenxian ziliao xuan*, 162–4.

[57] Cai Chang, "Yingjie funü gongzuo de xin fangxiang" (Facing the New Direction of Women's Work), *Shaan-Gan-Ning bianqu funü yundong wenxian ziliao xuan*, 167–71.

[58] Due to the limited length and the specific topic of this book, I do not deal with the change of women's economic condition. For the CCP's policy on changing women's economic status, see Stranahan, *Yan'an Women and the Communist Party* (58–86) which gives more details on women's participation in the Great Production Campaign as a means of attaining economic independence.

no clear definitions of legal terms such as "buying/selling marriage," "marriage by force," and "arranged marriage." He offered some tentative and brief definitions of the above terms by defining "buying/selling marriage" as "a third party taking some pelf to make the [privy] man and woman get married," "marriage by force" as one in which "a third party by taking some pelf forces a [privy] man and woman into a marriage to which one side of the [privy] man and woman dissents," and "arranged marriage" as one "under the condition that a [privy] man and woman who have never known each other are brought into a marriage by a third party."[59]

With further understanding of local communities and customs and recognizing that women exercised autonomy even under the patriarchy, legal officials realized that they needed women's cooperation to carry out their new ideas on marriage, while also adjusting their own ways of working with women. Thus, the BR's practice in marriage reform gradually shifted away from its previous focus on loosely granting ex parte divorce to empowering women in marriage disputes under the term "self-determination" (*zi-zhu*). This principle enabled women to decide which man they would prefer if there were any dispute among two or more men/families.

The empowerment of women started with courtroom techniques and strategies that were developed during the construction of the revolutionary judicial system, discussed in Chapter 3. The legal system and civil registration of marriage had already set up a practice that required the woman in question to be present in the courtroom or registration office to confirm her acknowledgment of her own marriage. However, as shown in previous chapters, this policy was often manipulated by fathers who accompanied their daughters to the site. Even under the principle of self-determination, there were still some cases in which a woman's family claimed that the marriage or dissolution was the woman's decision.[60] Therefore, the self-determination principle had to be supported by corresponding court techniques and strategies.

Under the directorship of Lei Jingtian in the early 1940s, the court attempted to perform a series of new techniques in courtroom investigation that differed from both imperial style and modern/Western style. The imperial courtroom order had required the litigants to kneel in the court for the majority of the time, in order to acknowledge the judge's authority. Moreover, in criminal cases, judges often used corporal

[59] SPA 15–175, "Lei Jingtian: Bianqu sifa gongzuo baogao."
[60] For example, in the case of Zhang Lawa and Liu Baoqing (SPA 15–891), mentioned in Chapter 2.

torture as interrogation techniques to intimidate the litigants into admitting their crimes.[61] The modern/Western courtroom style adopted by the Nationalist judicial system required both sides to meet face-to-face in the courtroom and submit to a cross-examination to discover the truth and expose lies. One can imagine that either style would be very intimidating to a rural woman or young girl and prevent her from speaking for herself, especially if her father, husband, or some influential third party (such as male relatives, even her mother) were on site. Even if she were able to overcome her shyness and fright and disclose her true wishes in the courtroom, she would then have to face the consequences at home. In another scenario, it would be difficult for a girl to bring herself to confront her father's word, making him lose face in public and portraying herself as a disobedient daughter. This was exactly the situation Peng'er faced when her father brought her to the ward office to cancel her previous engagement contract. It is very likely that her father did most of the talking and she simply nodded to confirm what he said, resulting in the record that she "strongly rejected" the engagement (see Chapter 1).

To eliminate the problems caused by these techniques, the BR courts developed a new style of courtroom investigation and interrogation, in which the judges sat at the same height as the litigants as a gesture of equality, while also prohibiting the use of intimidation (Figure 4.1 shows an SGNBR style of government office). The interrogation was conducted through a face-to-face conversation style, intended to make litigants feel relaxed and comfortable with the judge so that they were willing to tell him what they knew about the case. The courtroom interrogation also adopted a flexible style, in which judges sometimes called all litigants into the same room and at other times talked to them one by one in a separate room so that the judge could learn the facts of the case and compare testimonies. Based on this process, he would be able to make an inferential deliberation. Ideally, the adjudication should not be entirely based on the testimonies; instead, judges had to conduct a thorough investigation outside the courtroom and sometimes hold open courts in villages in order to involve the masses in the legal process, as shown in Chapter 5.

By understanding the particular autonomy that women enjoyed under the patriarchal system and their desire to make decisions in their own marriages as discussed in Chapter 2, the courts tried to break down the father-daughter alliance and win women over to their side. In this way,

[61] Spence, *The Death of Woman Wang*, 133–9.

Figure 4.1 Gu Yuan, "Qu zhengfu de bangongshi" [Township Government Office], *Jiefang ribao*, November 14, 1942

the judiciary would be able to recognize a woman's personhood, instead of seeing her as merely the attachment of her family. Correspondingly, women in marriage disputes greatly benefited from this reformed courtroom technique and strategy. In those cases in which one woman was betrothed to two or three families, or one woman married two men consecutively, local legal workers would question the woman in a separate room, away from her father, husband, or any third party, and ask her which man *she* wanted to be with. In this situation, a woman was more willing to tell the judge her wishes without openly defying one of the men in her life. Once it learned a woman's wishes, the court would make an adjudication favoring her preference. After the final ruling, she could shield herself behind the judge's authority and avoid a direct confrontation with her father or husband if the court's decision dissatisfied them. Legal records of the SGN High Court show a broad application of this strategy in courtrooms. The aforementioned cases of "one girl betrothed to two families" and other cases such as the Zhang Lawa and Liu Baoqing case in the previous chapters also followed the same principle and used the same court technique, as did the case of *Feng v. Zhang*, in which Ma's investigation in the village included asking Peng'er about her wishes in private.

The case *Gu v. Cai and Bai* exemplified this practice. Woman Bai (*Bai shi*) was engaged to Gu Jiayou in 1931 and soon became a *tongyangxi* of the Gu family. After fifteen-year-old Gu Jiayou left home as a migrant worker in 1935, his older brother engaged Woman Bai to Cai Mingqi for 50 silver *yuan*, and the wedding was held in 1939. One day in 1941 on the streets of the Dingbian County seat, Woman Bai ran into Gu Jiayou, who was by then a revolutionary soldier in the local military unit. Woman Bai initiated the greeting by asking if Gu recognized her and still wanted her. When Gu responded affirmatively and then brought her to the local government office to register for marriage, this attempt was prevented by a suspicious government official. A few days later, the Cais heard the news and came to fight for Bai; her case thus became a legal dispute between two men over a woman. Moreover, this case almost caused a military revolt, as Gu and his fellow soldiers, led by the unit officer, besieged the local government office asking for a favorable ruling. The petition was even sent up to Bai Zhimin 白治民 (1918–2007), the party secretary of the Sanbian Subregional committee, Gao Gan, the party secretary of the Northwest Bureau (*Xi bei ju* 西北局), and Xie Juezai, the president of the BR Council.[62] However, after stirring up all this trouble, when the court asked Woman Bai individually which man she wanted to be with, Bai decided to return to Cai Mingqi, regardless of Gu's wishes. Thus the court ruled according to Bai's decision and the case was closed.[63]

[62] SPA 4-2-170, "Bai Zhimin zhi Gao Gang han" (Bai Zhimin's Letter to Gao Gang).

[63] SPA 15-1293, *Gu Jiayou v. Cai Mingqi and Bai shi*. Woman Bai probably made her decision based on the fact that Gu was a military soldier and unavailable at home.

This practice was also embodied in many cases related to the implementation of banning minors' marriage and installing self-determined marriage. The practice of self-determination was related to a woman's marriageable age, as defined by the state. In this type of dispute, if a girl was not of statutory age, the court would simply invalidate the original engagement or marriage. The court also instructed that the girl could make her own decision once she reached eighteen. Sometimes, the court would issue a restraining order to prohibit her parents from engaging the girl to another family or marrying her away before reaching the statutory age, as was the case in *Zuo v. Wang* described in Chapter 2 and the case of Feng Run'er in Chapter 1. By adopting this strategy, the court skillfully utilized the nature of marriage disputes, in that the original fiancé's family did not want to lose its future daughter-in-law whom they had paid for, and would thus be alerted if they discovered any violation by the girl's parents, as in the case of *Feng v. Zhang*. Holding on the principle of "self-determination," the legal practitioners and government officials hoped to gradually exclude the influence of parents or third parties on women regarding their marriage decisions, and thus respect women's choices in their marriages.

Changing legal practices (2): detecting motives for divorce

In ex parte divorce cases, the High Court recognized the complications posed by both material motives and parental domination.[64] The same courtroom technique was also adopted in these divorce cases. In order to detect the true reasons for a divorce and the real problems in a marriage, the judges talked to the woman face-to-face during investigations and dealt with each divorce on a case-by-case basis by analyzing the motive for the couple's split. In doing so, they tried to exclude parental and/or third-party interests from the divorce.

In a discussion among county courts in 1943, it appeared that judges had tried to reach a consensus on the conditions for granting a divorce, in addition to what was listed in the 1939 regulation. The Suide County court believed that those who were abetted by their parents; those who used improper reasons such as aversion to the poor, the old, and the ugly; and those who became engaged and then proposed divorce or abandoned their spouse for material profit, should not be allowed to divorce. A divorce request based on affirmed domestic violence, on the other hand, should certainly be granted. Some also suggested that if the couple

[64] At the same time, the divorce with agreement was not restrained by these grounds in the regulation. Thus this type of divorce would not be included in our discussion.

had a good relationship but the wife suffered from abuse by in-laws, the court ought to help them divide the household and let the young couple live by themselves.[65] If one party in a couple were a dishonorable or ignoble person (such as a sorcerer, idler, gambler, or opium-smoker), and if it was evidentially a buying/selling or forced marriage, one should be allowed to divorce. In addition to what Suide County had listed, Jingbian County added that a court should also grant a divorce if a couple had concrete evidence for "incompatibility of relations," but this had to be confirmed through government investigation, a term that differed from the 1939 regulation but was in accord with the 1931 HJP regulation. This meant that the courts should not simply take the word of any party in an ex parte divorce. About those cases in which the court should not grant divorce, Jingbian County agreed with Suide County, only adding that if a woman's family abetted her divorce in order to gain material profit, or if a person committed adultery and sought the divorce in order to marry the third party, the divorce should not be granted.[66] Of course, this classification was built on the revolutionary state's principle on marriage. On the one hand, by classifying the motives behind the divorce and engagement dissolution, the court tried to cut off the connection between material profit and marriage and prevent parents' domination over young women's marriages. In Chapter 6, we will see that through creating an image of a rural young male, Zhu'er (based on the prototype of Zhang Bo), the revolutionary power tried to guide women to reshape their criteria in selecting male partners and their values in marriage.

Changing legal practices (3): conditions of family abuse and "intolerable cohabitation"

Regarding the most contentious term in the 1939 regulation, "incompatibility in emotional relations and intolerable cohabitation" (*ganqing bu he, buneng tongju* 感情不合, 不能同居), the court seemed to be gradually developing a clear consensus that a divorce on this basis required much more detailed and concrete evidence to receive the court's approval. As Huang points out, emphasizing "emotional relations" in marriage was indeed a communist invention and not listed in the Nationalist civil code,[67] or even in either the JCS marriage regulation/law or the HJPS

[65] SPA 15–43, "Ge xian taolun chuli lihun anjian jueding banfa ji hunyin zhengce, 1943" (County Courts' Discussion on Dealing with Divorce Cases and Policy on Marriage, 1943).
[66] *Ibid.*
[67] Huang, *Chinese Civil Justice*, 116.

regulation. There was thus no precedent for using this term. Moreover, as mentioned, in practice "incompatibility of relations" could be used by both women's families and by women themselves to obtain an expedient divorce. Huang discusses post-1949 divorce cases in which a married couple often used the term "*ganqing polie*" 感情破裂 (breaking up the relation) in filing for a divorce.[68] The word *polie* (breaks) must have been a term that appeared after 1950, because there is no trace of it in any of the SGN High Court documents; instead, they often used *bu he* (not getting along or not fitting well, incompatible) or *bu hao* (not good) to describe a couple's emotional relations (*ganqing*) (regarding the term *polie*, also see Chapter 7).

In practice, instead of searching for the definition of the elusive term *ganqing* and a yardstick by which to measure it, the SGNBR legal workers tried to prioritize the latter half of this term, "intolerable cohabitation," as a concrete ground for granting a divorce. Indeed, a common problem for women unable to live with their husbands was abuse by husbands and/or in-laws. In the corresponding discussion among local courts, there was a consensus that it was more important for the court to protect women from family violence than to examine a couple's "incompatibility of relations." Legal workers thus tried to develop a judicial strategy in order to prevent domestic violence against women. When a woman reported her husband's or in-laws' abuse and asked for a divorce, the court would conduct an investigation and also order the husband to produce a guarantee of stopping the abuse. Very often, the husband had to find neighbors, relatives, or family members who were neutral, or a respected public figure or village head, to vouch for him, which was a public humiliation. In some cases, in addition to forcing the husband to provide a warranty, the local government or court also jailed him for a few days in order to teach him a lesson and prevent the violence from re-occurring in the future.[69] If the situation was abuse by the husband's family, the court would support dividing the household so that the woman could escape from her in-laws' tyranny. If the court found that the abuse was more than an accident, it would warn the husband or in-laws that if the violence occurred again, the wife's divorce request would be immediately granted. This threat was significant because, as discussed in Chapters 1 and 2, divorce was a huge economic loss for husbands' families. If the abuse became frequent, the court would recognize it as evidence of "intolerable cohabitation" and thus grant the divorce.

During the process of investigation, the court also developed a discourse against family violence to let husbands or in-laws know that it

[68] Huang, *Chinese Civil Justice*, 12.
[69] SPA 15–1480, *Chang Baogui v. Liu Yinglan*.

was intolerable behavior by the government. In courtrooms, judges constantly and suspiciously questioned whether a husband or his parents beat his wife and stressed that beating a wife was a crime, which became the key for granting a wife's divorce request. The records show that the court repeatedly backed accused husbands into a corner with a series of questions, putting them on the defensive. Under this pressure, the husband either denied the charge or minimized his wrongdoing. This exact situation occurred in the case of Gao Lanying and the case of *Zhang v. Liang Fucheng*, as well as *Sun Changzen v. Li Xiuying*,[70] and many other cases. Judges believed that these concrete measures would help women improve their marriage conditions more effectively than simply granting a divorce.

On the other hand, there were also other reasons that a couple was in "intolerable cohabitation," for example, an incurable disease or mental disorder. In the cases of dissolution of an engagement or a marriage, "sexual impotence" and "mental disorder" were fully justifiable reasons (see Table 1.1). In the case of physical or mental problems, once the medical evidence was provided, the divorce was immediately granted. For example, in the case of *Liu Guanghan v. Bai Yulan* (in which the husband, Liu Guanghan, had gonorrhea), and the case of *Tong Xiangneng v. Chang Guiying* (in which the husband had syphilis), the wives' requests for divorces were approved.[71] In the case of Woman Hou-Zhang, Hou Dingmao's wife had been a *tongyangxi* but now requested a divorce based on her husband's mental disability. Hou Dingmao's father, serving as his son's proxy, insisted that Hou Dingmao was fine, and that the problems in their marriage were his daughter-in-law's fault. Upon summoning Hou Dingmao in person for examination, however, the local court found that at the age of twenty-seven, Dingmao could not count to ten, had the intelligence of a five-year-old, and could not understand the meaning of conjugal duty. Based on these facts, the court immediately granted a divorce to Woman Hou-Zhang.[72] All the above cases were appealed to the then-highest legal institution, but all courts unanimously rejected the husbands' appeals.

III. The marriage regulations in revision, 1944 and 1946

In order to deal with the incompatibility between the 1939 regulation and reality, and to ease the widespread discontent in local communities,

70 SPA 15–1576, "Shi Yude qi bei guaimai an"; and 15–1397, *Zhang Ying v. Liang Fucheng*.
71 SPA 15–1396, "Tuo Tianyuan shangsu an" (The Appeal of Tuo Tianyuan); and SPA 15–30, "Gaoyuan panjue shu."
72 SPA 15–1346, "Hou Dingmao shangsu an" (The Appeal of Hou Dingmao).

the BR legislature made an adjustment to the marriage statute in 1944. This revision adopted some local customs in order to remedy the unsuitability caused by a twisted understanding of the 1939 statute. The 1944 regulation was a trial program, and its implementation led to another extreme in practice that again compromised the principle of marriage reform. Thus, the marriage regulation was revised again in 1946, confirming the principle of "self-willingness/self-determination," but leaving enough room for local adaptation.

The 1944 regulation: a provisional change

Since 1943, the Border government had been overwhelmed with complaints from villagers, local cadres, and local legal practitioners about the marriage regulation. These complaints resulted in the promulgation of a revised regulation that made several changes aiming at closing up the loophole and redressing the incompatibility of the 1939 regulation. Moreover, the Amended Provisional Marriage Regulation (*Xiuzheng Shaan-Gan-Ning Bianqu Hunyin Zanxing Tiaoli* 修正陕甘宁边区婚姻暂行条例),[73] published in March 1944, presented certain tentative definitions to terms that had previously been unspecified.

It is worth noting several changes in the 1944 provisional marriage regulation. The most important one was that the term *zi-yuan* 自愿 (self-willingness or one's wish/volition toward a certain thing) was upgraded from an unnoticed position in a subordinate clause to the general principle of marriage, replacing the previous principle, *ziyou*. Compared to *ziyou*, the phrase *zi-yuan*, in a much more casual and vernacular style, signifies one's wish for a specific action, thus narrowing the unlimited possibilities hinted at by the phrase *zi-you*. On the other hand, compared to *zi-zhu* – which suggests a strong decision-making power in action – *zi-yuan* still retains the lingering meaning of expressing a subjective wish toward a specific choice, with a rather weak power of action/will. In terms of semantics, *zi-yuan* was not interchangeable or replaceable with either *zi-zhu* or *zi-you*, but its meaning is much closer to that of *zi-zhu* in limiting an actor and his/her volition to a specific goal. Nonetheless, neither the BR Council nor the High Court seemed prepared to explain the reason for this change until 1946, as discussed below. Meanwhile, *zi-zhu* was not included, either because it was still in casual use among legal practitioners, or because there was a serious

[73] "Xiuzheng Shaan Gan Ning Bianqu hunyin zang xing tiaoli" (The Amended Provisional Marriage Regulation in the SGNBR), *Shaan-Gan-Ning bianqu funü yundong wenxian ziliao xuanbian*, 192–4.

controversy between the ideologues and legal pragmatists among the top leaders. It is also possible that *zi-zhu* stayed as a practical term, and it continued to appear in legal documents, though only as a complementary parallel to either *zi-you* or *zi-yuan* (for example, *zi-you zi-zhu*, or *zi-yuan zi-zhu*).[74] In Chapter 7, we will see that the 1950 Marriage Law – which was dominated by a group of ideologues among the May Fourth female activists and the urban educated – excluded the legal pragmatists, and the principle of marriage subsequently returned to *ziyou*.[75]

The second important change in the 1944 revision was to recognize engagement as a premarital condition and make it subject to the rules of the marriage regulation. It stated that "a man or a woman who is engaged but dissents with the engagement prior to the wedding may dismiss his/her engagement at the local government; at the same time, both sides should return gifts [given by the other side] for the engagement." It also required the return of *caili* once the engagement was ended.[76] This shows that the High Court began to recognize local practice, as the term provided a legal foundation to regulate engagements and their related property issues.

The third important change occurred in the order of the conditions for granting a divorce, which has become the most controversial issue among Western feminist scholars in evaluating the CCP's policy. The 1944 regulation prioritized divorce conditions in the following order: (1) bigamy, (2) adultery, (3) criminal framing of one's spouse, (4) incurable disease or impotence, (5) ex parte abandonment, (6) spouse abuse, (7) total incompatibility of the couple's emotional relations and inability to live together, (8) one party's absence with no contact for over three years, (9) either husband or wife being an idler without improvement after being warned and disturbing the life of the other party, and (10) other important conditions.[77] Condition number two in the 1939 regulation, the "incompatibility of relations and intolerable cohabitation," seen as a significant indicator of women's liberation, was now moved to number seven. This move seemed to make the term "incompatibility of emotional relations" less important in ex parte divorce cases. However, it could be argued that this change may have reflected the CCP officials' understanding of the local culture and the local view of marriage, and thus developed a new criterion in judging divorce, as discussed above.

[74] SPA 15–72, "Hunyin wenti yu hunyin tiaoli" and SPA 15–26, "Bianqu panli huibian, 1944."

[75] As this work tries to display the marriage reform from an implementation approach, I would like to put the ideological disputes at the CCP leadership aside.

[76] "Xiuzheng Shaan-Gan-Ning Bianqu hunyin zan xing tiaoli."

[77] *Ibid.*

The fourth important change was adding a provision for the ex parte divorce/dissolution of soldiers' marriages/engagements. This term was basically copied from the "Instruction" discussed in Chapter 2, with a minor change in wording. It stated that if a soldier loses contact with his wife for at least five years or with his fiancée for three years, the government should grant a divorce/dissolution. In cases where a soldier stays in contact with his fiancée but is still unable to return for the wedding for over five years, the engagement dissolution should be granted. In cases where a civilian loses contact with his wife/fiancée for at least three years, dissolution will be granted.[78] Theoretically, the 1939 regulation seemed radical by treating soldiers' divorces in the same way as those of civilians; in reality, it created a situation in which local governments demanded unlimited dedication from soldiers' wives. In contrast, the 1944 regulation put it in clear terms by defining the waiting period, and provided evidence of progress as well as compromise between the demands of soldiers' wives/fiancées and the constraints of local governments.

Implementation of the 1944 regulation and its deficiency

In the early 1940s, local governments had a narrow definition for "buying/selling marriage" under the direction of the 1939 regulation. It led them to confiscate *caili* in any case brought to the government for resolution. This policy caused an even stronger reaction from the local residents, both the woman's side and the man's side.[79] Facing this widespread discontent, the High Court realized that a radical policy could result in an opposite effect, causing the government to lose control of the marriage system. To respond to the constant inquiries from local courts on how to deal with violations of the marriage regulation, in August 1942 the High Court admitted in an instructive letter that "the progress of a marriage system must be made concomitantly with the improvement of educational and cultural life [of a region]. Only in so doing is [the legal practice] able to reach the effective result." It also pointed out that "if the educational and cultural life [of a region] has not yet reached a certain advanced level and we rush it with a strict law, it would result in" a number of conditions that would create a contradiction between the law and the reality, making the law become an annoyance to the people.[80]

[78] *Ibid.*
[79] SPA 15–72, "Hunyin wenti yu hunyin tiaoli" and SPA 15–175, "Lei Jingtian: bianqu sifa baogao."
[80] SPA 15–33, "Gaodeng fayuan duiyu Chishui xian xunwen maimai hunyin jiaokuan yinfou moshou de yijian" (High Court's Answer to Chishui County's Inquiry on Whether the Money from Buying/Selling Marriage Should Be Confiscated).

Following this view, the High Court sent out an order, signed by Acting Director Li Mu'an, that two principles on the issue of *caili* should be followed: first, the government should not intervene unless the party in question filed a lawsuit (*bu gao bu li* 不告不理, *fei qin gao bu li* 非亲告不理); and second, even in those cases that had been confirmed as buying/selling marriages, the government should not confiscate *caili* as a means of punishment.[81] The High Court tried to explain that it was difficult for a legal system to intervene in a local custom that was so prevalent, and it was hard for the government to draw a line between what was a *caili* as a social protocol and what was buying or selling marriage prohibited by the law.[82] In fact, this instruction was a passive gesture at resolving a difficult issue: first, because it did not offer a solution to the practice of *caili*, and second, because it practicably recognized property transfer in a marriage and thus negated the effort of banning "buying/selling marriages." It was not until 1944 that engagement and the return of *caili* upon the abolition of an engagement were put into the amended regulation.

Although in 1942 the High Court still tried to dodge the issue, once a dispute was brought to court it became a problem for the government to deal with. This is why the solution to buying/selling marriages varied from county to county and time to time during the early 1940s. However, the 1944 regulation made the practice swing to another extreme. Under the 1944 regulation, many local authorities started to order the woman's side to repay an amount of grain (*nüfang pei mi* 女方赔米) to the fiancé's family, with the purpose of covering the devaluation of *caili* caused by inflation. Even so, this policy brought both practical troubles and theoretical challenges. The documents show that some county courts, such as Wubu, indiscriminately applied this rule to all cases of divorce or engagement dismissals, regardless of the conditions of each case. The court granted any divorce request, along with ordering compensation by the woman's side.[83] This practice seemed to be a punishment to those women who were eligible for an ex parte divorce and engagement dismissal without compensation. It obviously violated women's rights and the spirit of marriage reform, especially in those cases in which women were abused by their husbands or those in which lazy husbands refused to support the family. Even worse, it actually encouraged *more* buying/

[81] SPA 15–33, "Shaan-Gan-Ning bianqu gaodeng fayuan mingling: maimai hunyin kuan shifou moshou wenti" (SGNBR High Court Order: On the Issue of Whether or Not the Court Should Confiscate Money from Buying/Selling Marriages).

[82] SPA 15–33, "Gaodeng fayuan duiyu Chishui xian xunwen maimai hunyin jiaokuan yinfou moshou de yijian."

[83] SPA 15–365, "Wubu xian sifa panjueshu" (The Adjudication Writs of Wubu County).

selling marriages – once the woman's side compensated the previous fiancé, her father would have a motive to request a higher price from the next suitor, or even make the next suitor pay the compensation. In response, the High Court criticized Wubu County and instructed it to stop the indiscriminate practice of ordering compensation of grain by the woman's side.[84]

In reality, it was impractical to impose the compensation, because in most cases very little was returned to the fiancé's family. According to 1945 statistics, of a total of seventy-nine cases requesting engagement dismissal, seven engagements were dismissed without the return of *caili*, fifty-nine were dismissed with only the original *caili* returned, three were dismissed with *caili* returned and grain paid as compensation, and ten cases were not allowed to be dismissed.[85] In divorce cases, compensation was even harder to pursue because if a girl was not at the statutory marriage age, the local government often simply voided the marriage/engagement without dealing with the issue of *caili*, as in the aforementioned examples.

In fact, the requirement of compensation created more problems than it solved because it could form a challenge to the reform policy and government authority. First, since the rate of inflation varied in different regions, the two parties often disagreed about the amount of grain to be repaid to the fiancé's family. In the negotiation, government officials or court workers had to serve as mediators, and compensation was included in legal settlements. Second, when girls' families refused to pay compensation after the legal settlement, government officials could choose to either carry out the implementation of the verdict, which would take time and interrupt government operations, or ignore it, which would bring endless appeals to higher authority by the fiancé's family. Moreover, serving as mediators for compensation put government officials in a very awkward position. This practice led villagers to believe that the government allowed buying/selling marriages, and thus saw no reason to stop arranged and buying/selling marriages.[86] On the other hand, if the government did not rule for compensation, it would encourage more families with girls to end original engagements for material profit, while creating an unfair situation for those who paid for marriages. To get out of this theoretical and practical dilemma, the High Court thus called

[84] SPA 15–365, "Wang Ziyi: Bianhan, 1946.4.2" (Wang Ziyi's Memo to Chief-judge Wei of the Wubu County Office of Justice, April 2, 1946).
[85] SPA 15–72, "Hunyin wenti yu hunyin tiaoli."
[86] SPA 15–365, "Wei chuli hunyin anjian zhong bude zai you nüfang pei mi" (Instruction on Marriage Cases: It Should No Longer Make Women Repay Grain); and also SPA 15–72, "Hunyin wenti yu hunyin tiaolie."

a halt to the practice of "compensating grains" in 1946.[87] In reality, the High Court still regularly ordered returning the original *caili* without compensation, but tried to regulate this practice with a much clearer definition of *caili*, as discussed below. Although the policy was unable to fully eradicate *caili* practice even after 1949, under government pressure the locals gradually developed a protocol in compensation along with new practices under the marriage regulation and the Marriage Law, which I discuss in the epilogue.

The 1946 regulation: making law practicable

In December 1945, a legal conference in Yan'an gathered more than one hundred judiciaries, chief-judges (*tingzhang* 庭长), judges (*tuishi* 推事), and junior judges (*shenpanyuan* 审判员) from various local courts of the entire BR to discuss issues of law, the legal system, and legal practices. One of its tasks was to comment on the draft of the revised marriage regulation prepared by the High Court. Some considered the existing marriage regulation too conservative, while others thought it too radical. By the end of the conference, the High Court had admitted that it had learned some lessons from the previous implementation of the marriage regulation, in that the court's practices swung back and forth in regard to controversial issues – sometimes too harsh and sometimes too loose.[88]

With the opinion offered by the participants in the 1945 legal conference, the High Court scripted another revised marriage regulation that was promulgated in early 1946. Compared to the 1939 and 1944 regulations, it appeared to be a compromise between the idealists and realists, or dogmatists and pragmatists; it continued to use the term "self-willingness" (*zi-yuan*) to describe the principle of marriage, while restoring the priority for ex parte divorce by moving "incompatible relations" back to second place in the divorce conditions.[89] The most important modification of this revision was that along with the formal text of articles, the High Court offered a lengthy legal interpretation to smooth the disparity and the transformation from *ziyou* to *zi-yuan*. The interpretation made a connection but also a distinction between *ziyou* and *zi-yuan*, stating that "the so-called principle of '*zi-yuan*' emphasizes that both an engagement and/or a marriage must be based on the wills of both the man and woman in question … The spirit of *zi-yuan* is freedom

87 SPA 15–365, "Wei chuli hunyin anjian zhong bude zai you nüfang pei mi."
88 SPA 15–72, "Hunyin wenti yu hunyin tiaoli."
89 "Shaan-Gan-Ning Bianqu hunyin tiaoli, 1946" (Marriage Regulation of the SGNBR, 1946), in *Shaan-Gan-Ning bianqu funü yundong wenxian ziliao, xuji*, 422–4.

in substance (*zi-yuan er zi zhi jingshen, ji ziyou zhi shizhi* 自愿二字之精神，即自由之实质), but to avoid the people's misapprehension, [we therefore believe that] using the term of *zi-yuan* seems more appropriate."[90] This interpretation clearly indicates that the High Court recognized the problem in the term, in that *ziyou* was often used in the context of licentiousness or lawlessness. It also implies a controversy about the term *zi-yuan* replacing *ziyou*, as the High Court felt it necessary to emphasize the equality between the two. Equating *zi-yuan* to *ziyou* seemed like an answer to those who insisted on the principle of freedom. This may reflect some debates among different groups, or between pragmatic legal workers and urban intellectual idealists that led to a restoration of the term *ziyou* in the 1950 Marriage Law, as discussed in Chapter 7.

A further interpretation made by a High Court officer Lan Zuoxin 兰作馨 offers a key to understanding the principle of *zi-yuan* as stated in the 1946 regulation. In addition to restating the interpretation of the High Court on most issues, Lan stressed the importance of the *zi-yuan* principle in marriage by arguing that formality matters less than essence. He pointed out that it was not how a marriage was made, but rather the willingness of the man and woman in question that legitimized a marriage.[91] This interpretation indicated that instead of banning the old marriage practice in its formality, legal practice should focus on examining whether or not the marriage was consented to by both sides, even though the marriage might involve parental arrangement or other types of local practice. Based on this principle of self-willingness, the High Court even began to tolerate other local customs that were previously defined as vices, such as polyandry (*zhao fu yang fu*). In 1946, the High Court responded to an inquiry on how the 1946 regulation applied to a concrete case of polyandry, stating that in principle this practice should be prohibited; nonetheless, given the condition that the woman's former husband would have no means of survival after a divorce, the court should not intervene if there was no dispute inside the family. However, it still needed to gradually taper off this practice.[92]

Second, in terms of "prohibiting arranged and forced marriages and buying/selling marriages," the High Court offered official definitions to

[90] SPA 15–72, "Shaan-Gan-Ning Bianqu hunyin tiaoli jieshi" (An Interpretation of the SGNBR Marriage Regulation). This interpretation was a document prepared by the High Court at the legal conference in December 1945 for the forthcoming 1946 regulation.

[91] SPA 15–9, "Lan Zuoxin: Shaan-Gan-Ning bianqu hunyin tiaoli xiuzheng cao'an jieshi, 1946" (An Interpretation of the Draft of the SGNBR Marriage Regulation, 1946).

[92] SPA 15–40, "Han fu Guanzhong fenting Zhou Ming hunyin tiaoli jieda" ([High Court's] Letter Answering Zhou Ming of the Guanzhong Dispatched Court on the Marriage Regulation).

various conditions in marriage practices to make them practicable. It described an "arranged marriage" as an action in which "a third party decides on a marriage by ignoring the consent or dissent of the man and woman in a marriage." It defined "a marriage by force" as an action in which "[a third party] arranged a marriage based on his/her view by disregarding the opinion of the man and woman in a marriage." Most important, the High Court not only defined "buying/selling marriage" but also set up a parameter for measuring it:

A third party, for the purpose of gaining profit, makes a decision on a marriage based on the fact that a person could provide more merchandise/money or wealth (*caiwu he shili* 财物和实力) while ignoring the will of the man and woman in question. If the amount of *caili* brought a major financial upgrade to [this third party's] family, it should be considered to be a buying/selling marriage. Any gift-giving [for a marriage] or any *caili* should not have a major impact on the family's financial condition.

The High Court continued to instruct on dealing with buying/selling marriages:

[A court should] fine the buyer and seller mulct or penalize them for labor service, while the penalty is based on the circumstances of the offense. The [government should] confiscate 60 percent of the *caili* [in a buying/selling marriage] and return the rest to the buyer. The confiscated *caili* should be used for the commonweal of the local community ... However, if this type of marriage is based on the self-willingness of both the man and woman in question, their marriage should still be considered valid; it should not be ruled on for dissolution [even after the confiscation of *caili*].[93]

At the same time, the court also defined the behavior of instigating/abetting a divorce as "a person(s) who, for the purpose of making profit, abets a person [in a marriage] to marry oneself or a third party, and thus destroyed the good relations of a couple." The High Court suggested penalizing this type of behavior through criminal law. In a case in which divorce was instigated by another man in order for a woman to marry him, after the instigator had served his sentence, the marriage between the instigator and the woman should be allowed, based on their self-willingness. The High Court added that in some special circumstances, the court should prohibit the marriage between the instigator and the instigated.[94]

The High Court's interpretation of the 1946 regulation also offered a much more detailed definition and solution for cases of "marriage by

[93] SPA 15–72, "Shaan-Gan-Ning Bianqu hunyin tiaoli jieshi."
[94] *Ibid.*

force" and other conditions. It stated that "regarding those marriages through kidnapping or seduction, [the courts should] punish the part of violation of criminal law but support the wills of the man and the woman in the marriages."[95] Obviously, this regulation was in accord with Ma Xiwu's adjudication in the case of *Feng v. Zhang*; thus the 1946 regulation can be seen as an outcome of the legal practice in past years. To other marriage practices, such as *tongyangxi* and its male counterpart, *zhannianhan*, the High Court required them to meet two conditions: (1) being at the statutory age for marriage, and (2) self-willingness of both the man and woman in question. If these two conditions were fulfilled, the marriage should be considered valid.[96] Given the fact that in most cases a woman's choice became the decisive element in a marriage dispute, this regulation would benefit women more than men. Moreover, these new interpretations, which had the same legal authority as formal law terms, indicated that the legal practice would punish those parents who dominated their children's marriage, but would still permit the marriage if the young man and woman desired it.[97] This term seems also to have echoed Ma's adjudication of the case of *Feng v. Zhang* three years earlier. The High Court's interpretation largely differed from earlier legal practice, in that the government had previously invalidated any buying/selling marriage, regardless of the will of the man and woman involved. Through empowering young men and, especially, women, it would gradually create a generational gap, and thus make the tradition fade away with the old patriarchy. Combined with the legal strategy of excluding a third party's influence on women, this policy was conducive to disentangling the younger generation, particularly women, from the net of patriarchal power in the family by recognizing their individual personhood in marriage. This policy should be considered more radical in substance and more effective in practice than the 1939 regulation.

Like the 1944 regulation, the 1946 regulation also addressed the practice of engagement, but in a different way. Having learned from actual practice over the past two years, the 1946 regulation dropped the term from its formal text, instead putting it into the interpretation. It restated that in general, *caili* still needed to be returned when an engagement was dissolved; however, in reality when one party had no capacity to return the pelf, the court should suggest an alternative punishment.[98]

95 *Ibid.*

96 *Ibid.*

97 *Ibid.*

98 "Shaan-Gan-Ning Bianqu hunyin tiaoli, 1946"; and SPA 15–72, "Shaan-Gan-Ning Bianqu hunyin tiaoli jieshi."

The 1946 regulation reversed the order of the conditions for divorce from the 1944 regulation by listing "incompatibility of emotional relations and intolerable cohabitation" first rather than seventh.[99] On the other hand, the High Court's interpretation stressed that this term was applied to a condition in which there was no hope for a couple to continue to live together.[100] Lan Zuoxin's interpretation further confirmed that incompatibility of emotional relations indicated that a couple could no longer bear to live together.[101] It appears that in 1946, legal practitioners finally reached a consensus on the feasible criteria for the term "incompatibility of relations."

Conclusion

Through an analysis of the changing terminology in Ma's writ, we are able to understand the profound conflict behind these new terms in the CCP's marriage policy. From the early years in Jiangxi, the communist reform of marriage emphasized the principle of freedom, an idea shaped in an urban environment with a strong Western influence. This idealistic concept encountered difficulties in inland areas of northern China, where local tradition and newly imported ideas interplayed and interacted. The change from an idealized term, *ziyou*, to a practical term, *zi-zhu*, with the term *zi-yuan* serving as a bridge, was written into the official regulation, indicating the winding path of Chinese social reform in the twentieth century. The changing principle of marriage reform in legal practice was significant in that it not only involved a transformation of the connotations of linguistic terms, but also depended on legal practice and considerable deliberation in changing legal technique. Through legal practice, women were recognized for their personhood and were thus able to be separated from the patriarchal family to make their own decisions concerning marriage. The revised marriage regulations of 1944 and 1946 represented the fact that revolutionary legal practitioners gradually understood the social reality, the community, and the local culture. It was through this experience that a marriage could reach its practicable principle of self-determination.

99 "Shaan-Gan-Ning Bianqu hunyin tiaoli, 1946."
100 SPA 15–72, "Shaan-Gan-Ning Bianqu hunyin tiaoli jieshi."
101 SPA 15–9, "Lan Zuoxin: Shaan-Gan-Ning Bianqu hunyin tiaoli xiuzheng cao'an jieshi, 1946."

Part III

Politics and gender in construction

5 Newspaper reports

Casting a new democracy in village communities

Beginning in 1944, the case of *Feng v. Zhang* attracted more public attention thanks to a series of newspaper reports. *Liberation Daily* (*LD*, *Jiefang ribao*), the largest newspaper in the SGNBR and the official voice of the Border government and the CCP Central Committee, published an article on March 13, 1944, titled "Comrade Ma Xiwu's Way of Judging" (*Ma Xiwu tongzhi de shenpan fangshi*, 马锡五同志的审判方式 abbr. Ma's Way). The article used three cases to exemplify Ma Xiwu's judicial work. *Feng v. Zhang* represented marriage disputes, while the cases of *Wang v. Wang* and *Ding v. Chou* represented disputes over landownership. After the article's publication, other local newspapers in the BR, such as the *Longdong News* (*Longdong bao* 陇东报) and the *Border Region Masses Weekly* (*Bianqu qunzhong bao* 边区群众报), also followed suit in publishing reports, based on the *LD* article, of the case of *Feng v. Zhang*.[1]

On October 9, 1944, *LD* also published a woodcut (*muke hua* 木刻画) titled "Comrade Ma Xiwu in Mediation" (*Ma Xiwu tongzhi tiaojie susong* 马锡五同志调解诉讼) by Gu Yuan (1919–96), who was one of the renowned revolutionary artists of the Yan'an period. This picture, based on the previous report in *Liberation Daily*, reenacted a scene in open court in which Ma was mediating the case of *Feng v. Zhang*.[2] *Xinhua Daily* (*XD*, *Xinhua ribao*), a newspaper established by the CCP in Chongqing, the wartime capital of the Nationalist government as part of an agreement of the CCP's Second United Front with the Nationalist Party, also reported this story on October 22, 1944, under the title "A Real Case of Mediating a Marriage Dispute in the Border Region" (*Bianqu tiaojie hunyin de yi ge shili* 边区调解婚姻的一个实例). It singled out the story of *Feng v. Zhang* from the three cases reported in *Liberation Daily*.[3] The same story reappeared in *Xinhua Daily* six months later on April 11, 1945; one of its journalists,

[1] See Shaanxi sheng difangzhi bianzuan weiyuanhui (The Compiling Committee of Shaanxi Provincial Gazetteer), *Shaanxi sheng zhi – Bao kan zhi*, 241–8.

[2] Gu Yuan, "Ma Xiwu tongzhi tiaojie susong."

[3] "Bianqu tiaojie hunyin de yi ge shili."

Li Pu 李普 (1918–2010), retold the story with more details under the title "A Case of Marriage by Capture" (*Yi jian qianghun an* 一件抢婚案), based on previous reports from *Liberation Daily* and *Xinhua Daily*.[4]

With this series of publications, the case of *Feng v. Zhang* moved from a small village in the revolutionary frontier to the revolutionary center of Yan'an and even crossed the geographical space of the BR, reaching the urban audience in Chongqing in southwestern China. In the article and reports, however, the theme of the story shifted away from a local marriage dispute between two families to a case that exemplified the state's governance and working style, thus placing *Feng v. Zhang* in the political domain. On the one hand, the three cases selected for the original *LD* article attested to the party-state's attention to its major social reform programs focusing on marriage and land (i.e., family and property); on the other hand, they also reflected the major source of community dissatisfaction. When later reports in *Xinhua Daily* singled out the marriage dispute, they showcased a democratic government under which women enjoyed freedom in their marriages and were supported by the BR government when they opposed the domination of the local patriarchy.

However, the reality of the 1940s' SGNBR society was that the CCP's marriage reform policy encountered mixed reactions from villagers and caused many disputes, as demonstrated in previous chapters. The *LD* article, in fact, reveals the anxiety of the party's top leadership in facing the unease in villages;[5] Ma's Way was thus seen as the CCP's effort to search for a solution that would pacify the communities. For this purpose, the state not only called for its cadres to improve their work style, but also promoted mediation in the legal system and in the communities. In doing so, the state recognized local autonomy to a certain extent while reorganizing and reshaping local villages. The article also exposed an interesting phenomenon: in the process of imposing its reform and ideology on villagers, the revolutionary state was itself penetrated by the local culture through tolerating the concept of a "clear-sky" judge (*qing tian* 青天, see below section). A process of interaction, interplay, negotiation, and mutual penetration established the CCP's practice of a mass-line policy and its relationship with local communities. In this process, the CCP demonstrated its flexibility in implementing policies and use of a "cultural positioning" strategy, as Elizabeth Perry terms it, in winning the support of the masses.[6]

[4] Li Pu, "Yi jian qianghun an," 90–3.

[5] In fact, many disputes also occurred over landownership, and more frequently took place in Longdong subregion because of the coming of new immigrants (see Chapter 1).

[6] Perry, *Anyuan*, 4–6.

I. Ma Xiwu's way of judging: pacifying the local community

In his book *Seeing Like a State*, James Scott reveals his intent to search for the logic behind the disaster that the worldwide authoritarian state created in the modern era. He stresses the concept of "imperialistic" attitude, because he makes "a case against an imperial or hegemonic planning mentality that excludes the necessary role of local knowledge and know-how."[7] Scott provides an inspired approach to viewing the conflict between the revolutionary state and the local communities in the SGNBR. In previous chapters, I pointed out that the judicial system tried to learn from and adopt local knowledge and knowhow into its consideration of adjudications, even including these in its statutes on marriage. In responding to the community protests caused by the marriage reforms, the state seemed to show no "imperialistic mentality"; rather, it actively communicated and interacted with the communities, and sometimes even yielded to them by revitalizing local traditions, calling for a change in work methods, and gradually reshaping the community through these interactions.

The Yan'an Way or Ma's Way: an authoritarian state or New Democracy?

In a political sense, the CCP attributed its success in mobilizing the villagers and reorganizing the local communities to its mass-line policy, which was seen as the essence of Mao's New Democracy. Mark Selden's notable 1971 work agrees with this view by arguing that the party's idealistic view of egalitarianism, the policy for land revolution, the democratic government, working within the United Front, and cooperative production effectively mobilized peasants to support the CCP and its resistance movement. After the collapse of the United Front in 1942, the CCP launched a series of policies related to the mass-line that formed the essence of the "Yan'an Way." For Mark Selden, the mass-line was a powerful weapon for the CCP in mobilizing peasants to support the party in its war against the Japanese invasion, and achieve national power in 1949.[8]

However, this policy analysis-based research and its optimistic image of the CCP during the war have been challenged since the 1990s, when China opened its archives to academic research and made more documents available to Western scholars. Some studies demonstrate that

[7] Scott, *Seeing Like a State*, 6.
[8] Selden, *The Yenan Way in Revolutionary China*, 177–278.

the CCP's revolutionary policies were not unified, but instead showed strong regional diversity; others argue that the implementation of these policies revealed the CCP's authoritarian culture and coercive governance in the 1940s, contradicting the democratic nature of the mass-line in mobilization as described in Selden's book.[9] In 1995, Selden responded to this criticism by revisiting the subject and revising his argument, stating that he might have underestimated the "dark side of mobilization politics," the limitation of the mass-line policy, and the party's authoritarian culture. Yet, he also defended his original argument by stating that the party's authoritarian nature was still in nascent form in the 1940s.[10]

On the other hand, Pauline Keating points out that the limits of these works lie in the fact that they do not offer a convincing and complete explanation for the party's achievement of national power, and they do not focus enough attention on the relations between the party and the peasants.[11] Based on her 1997 study of two subregions of the SGNBR, Suide and Yanshu, from the perspective of village construction, Keating reaffirms Selden's basic argument but suggests that the success of the mass-line was limited because the CCP's uniform implementation of its policies brought varied results due to existing regional ecological and social differences.[12] It is thus necessary to reevaluate the revolution in the Yan'an period, particularly its marriage and legal practices, to see if there was an authoritarian state that coercively imposed its policies on the local villages, or a strategic state that presented a flexible image and used a tactic of cultural positioning to win the support of the masses.

Ma's Way: responding to an agitated village community

The communist cadres' coercive actions and "commandism" (*mingling zhuyi* 命令主义) did indeed exist in the SGNBR and became a major cause of community agitation, particularly in marriage reform, as shown in the verdict made by Huachi County in the case of *Feng v. Zhang* and

[9] Such as Stephen Averill, "The Origin of the Futian Incident," Gregor Benton, "Under Arms and Umbrellas: Perspectives on Chinese Communism in Defeat," Kathleen Hartford, "Fits and Starts: The Chinese Communist Party in Rural Hebei, 1921–1936," Timothy Cheek, "The Honorable Vocation: Intellectual Service in CCP Propaganda Institutions in Jin-Cha-Ji, 1937–1945," and others, in *New Perspectives on the Chinese Communist Revolution*, Tony Saich and Hans van de Ven (eds.) (London: M. E. Sharpe, 1994), 79–115, 116–43, 144–74, 235–62. Also see Benton, *New Fourth Army* on the CCP's accommodation of local culture in its policy implementation.

[10] See Selden, *China in Revolution*, 222–52.

[11] See Pauline Keating's review of *China in Revolution* and *New Perspectives on the Chinese Communist Revolution*, *The China Journal* 37 (January 1997): 219–23.

[12] See Keating, *Two Revolutions*. Also Pauline Keating, "The Ecological Origins of the Yan'an Way," *The Australian Journal of Chinese Affairs* 32 (July 1994): 123–53.

other cases presented in the previous chapters of this book. In view of James Scott's theory on the failed utopia summarized in his introduction, we may find some clues to explain why the party-state did not develop into an authoritarian power during this period but moved on to a national victory. In the SGNBR, the revolutionary state was not yet strong enough nor had intent to become an authoritarian power, and there were strong protests and expressions of discontent from village communities that prevented the state from taking extreme actions in imposing certain reform plans.

Indeed, the high percentage of marriage disputes among all civil disputes reflects the tension between the revolutionary government and the locals. The archival documents support this argument: of the 1,112 total surviving legal cases of the SGN High Court, 731 are criminal and 381 civil. Of these civil cases, 145 are marriage-related, 85 are land-related, 61 are debt disputes, and 21 are house-ownership disputes, as well as others related to civil matters such as inheritance, property, rent, and debt.[13] Meanwhile, another source reveals that from 1938 to 1943, all courts in the BR had dealt with 864 marriage-related disputes, among which only 84 were appealed to the High Court.[14] This number of marriage disputes is much greater than the number of cases that has survived in the High Court files. Moreover, the above categories of documents may not accurately reflect the nature of individual cases, because some criminal cases started as civil disputes and some civil disputes involved criminal actions. As discussed in previous chapters, many marriage disputes eventually developed into crimes such as kidnapping, abduction, assault, and even murder.[15] Furthermore, these surviving documents only offer a limited snapshot of community protests in the twelve years of the CCP's judicial rule over the BR, from 1937 to 1949. A larger number of documents were destroyed during the time that the Nationalist army, led by Hu Zongnan 胡宗南 (1896–1962), occupied Yan'an in 1947.[16] Finally, these files only contain those cases that were appealed to the High Court;

[13] The criminal cases include treason, soldiers' desertions, official corruption, opium smuggling, murders, assaults, banditry, and economic crimes. See Wang Shirong *et al.*, *Xin Zhongguo sifa zhidu de jishi*, 32–6.

[14] Zhang Shibin *et al.*, *Shaan-Gan-Ning bianqu gaodeng fayuan shiji*, 76.

[15] For instance, the case of Zhang Guiying, who was seriously injured in an assault by her former fiancé (SPA 15–294), and the famous case of Huang Kegong, a Red Army officer who shot and killed Liu Qian, a young female student after Liu rejected Huang's marriage proposal (SPA 15–543), as well as the murder cases caused by divorce (SPA 15–72). Although the SGNBR did not criminalize adultery, it often led to other criminal activities during this period.

[16] Liu Quan'e and Li Juan, "Shaan-Gan-Ning bianqu gaodeng fayuan dang'an ji qi xueshu jiazhi" (The Documents of the SGNBR High Court and Their Academic Value), *Falü kexue* (Science of Law) 1 (2006): 156–62.

a much larger number of cases that were settled in the county and subregional courts do not survive today.

In addition to these civil disputes, the community had another way to demonstrate its dissatisfaction, a practice called "unrelenting litigation" (*chansong* 缠讼) that had existed since the imperial era. Unrelenting litigation refers to a situation in which litigants on one (or both) side(s) of a legal case do not accept the result of either mediation or adjudication and repeatedly appeal to a higher authority for a more favorable outcome to achieve the justice that they believe is due. In this process, both parties mobilize all means to fight for the best result, making litigation last for years or even decades until one party has exhausted all resources and is thus forced to yield. One case cited in the *LD* article on Ma's Way, *Chou v. Ding*, provides an example of such unrelenting litigation (see below). This lawsuit lasted for almost a decade until it was settled in 1943 under the mediation of Judge Shi Jingshan. Xie Juezai expressed his concern over this rural phenomenon and discussed it in his 1942 column in *LD*, "A Piece of Thought" (*Yi de shu* 一得书). He viewed it from the perspective of class oppression, claiming that *chansong* was used as a legal strategy by the more powerful/richer party to prevent the weaker/poorer party from appealing. This enabled the rich to intimidate the poor in their pursuit of justice. He believed that the revolutionary government could eradicate this problem with three important measures: making the loser pay compensation to the winner; establishing a good primary trial institution; and creating social pressure against this corrupt practice in order to protect the poor.[17] It seems that Xie assumed that under the revolutionary judicial system, rich bullies would lose their lawsuits against the oppressed poor and should thus pay compensation to prevent them from continuing to appeal. In reality, however, this unrelenting litigation strategy was more commonly used by ordinary villagers than by the rich.

The High Court documents show that up until 1945, the BR judiciary was still unable to entirely solve the problem of *chansong*, particularly in marriage disputes. Many conflicts over marriage started in township and ward governments, then moved into the county court. In most cases, one party (usually the man's side, unwilling to accept the marriage dissolution) appealed to the subregional court and eventually to the High Court, and sometimes to the TCBG during its existence. For instance, the case of *Zuo Ren v. Wang Yinsuo* and Zhang Lawa's case mentioned in Chapter 2 were two of many examples that went through the mediation of village organization and township administration, and the adjudication

[17] Huan Nan (Xie Juezai), "Yi de shu: chan song" (A Piece of Thought: Unrelenting Lawsuits), *Jiefang ribao*, November 19, 1942.

of county courts, then brought to the subregional court and finally to the High Court in Yan'an City, making the trial and appeal last two years or more. According to incomplete statistics, among the 133 closed divorce cases that were appealed to the High Court from 1945 to 1948, the woman's side appealed in 32 cases while the man's side appealed in 101.[18] During the appeal process, all family members were mobilized to win the case and those involved had to spend time and money on travel, and then stay near the courts to wait for their court time and adjudication.

The CCP's top leaders were fully aware of this popular agitation and the tension between the government and the communities. The state's biggest anxiety about these unrelenting lawsuits was that during the time of the trial and appeal, the litigants were unable to engage in productive work, thus reducing their capacity to improve their family's living conditions and ability to pay taxes.[19] For the BR government, stabilizing the communities and securing tax resources were serious issues, because these unrelenting law suits also jeopardized the survival of the revolutionary state, especially in the time when the Nationalist army had blockaded the entire SGN Border Region. In addition, for a shorthanded judicial system, dealing with endless litigations and disputes, even when implementing adjudications, exhausted the manpower of the legal system and government workers, as discussed in Chapters 3 and 4.

Official documents reveal the anxiety of the BR government about the problems that threatened the CCP's survival. At the beginning of 1944, when President Lin Boqu published his annual report to the Border Council, in the section on judicial works he included a list of suggestions on how to make the judicial system able to support the Anti-Japanese War while also guarding democracy and people's rights in the BR. The list included the proposal to popularize community mediation (*minjian tiaojie* 民间调解), in which the ward and township governments would encourage local respected figures among the people (such as those who were labor models, *laodong mofan* 劳动模范, or enlightened members of the gentry, *kaiming shishen* 开明士绅) to mediate disputes in order to reduce litigation to a minimum (*xi song* 息讼). He also addressed the work of judicial enactments by asking legal workers to be more considerate of people's actual living conditions in issuing their penalties. The

[18] Zhang Shibin *et al.*, *Shaan-Gan-Ning bianqu gaodeng fayuan shiji*, 76.

[19] "Bianqu zhengfu guanyu puji tiaojie, zongjie panlie, qingli jiansuo zhishi xin" (The Instructive Letter of the BR Government on Promoting Mediation, Collecting Adjudication Samples, and Screening Detainees in Prisons), in *Tiaojie wei zhu shenpan weifu* (Using Mediation as the Dominant Way and Adjudication as an Assistant) (Yan'an: Shaan-Gan-Ning bianqu zhengfu bangongting [SGNBR Government General Office] print, 1944), 10–16.

courts should not jail any party in civil cases, or even in misdemeanors, in order that more laborers could work in the fields. He requested that legal procedures be simple, speedy, and convenient, as in Ma's Way, so that legal practice could serve as a means of educating the masses rather than simply punishing them.[20] All these suggestions were for the purpose of reducing the number of litigation cases. To echo Lin's report, the BR Council (*Bianqu canyihui*) also passed three propositions calling on all governments to follow Ma's Way of investigation and a democratic approach to solve community disputes, overcome their workers' subjectivism and cursory working style, and eliminate litigation and increase productivity.[21]

This annual report also revealed the problems of government in coercively implementing the party's policies and misconduct of officials, which were frequently exposed in *LD*, beginning in 1942. In December 1944, *LD* reported a number of dismissals of officials, including a village head who had embezzled funds, a ward party secretary who was guilty of misconduct out of arrogance, and a ward head (*qu zhang* 区长) who arbitrarily imposed fines on villagers.[22] As for the marriage reform, the most frequent complaint was that "everything the CCP has done is good except divorce [policy]."[23] In 1945, Xie Juezai gave a speech in a small rectification forum that addressed causes of popular dissatisfaction with the government, including unfair tax burdens, abusive government officials, and overworked township and ward workers, as well as too many meetings. He admitted that among all complaints, the most frequently mentioned issues were marriage, land, and debts.[24]

If the BR government is seen as an authoritarian state, it is assumed that the revolutionary party-state was a strong power with an omnipotent and omnipresent capacity for full control. The fact was that this revolutionary state, facing agitated communities, sought means of

[20] Lin Boqu, "Guanyu gaishan sifa gongzuo" (On Improving Judicial Works), *Tiaojie wei zhu shenpan weifu*, 1–4.

[21] SPA 15-13, High Court, "Tishi xin: zhixing bennian qiyue Bian can changzhu hui, zhengfu weiyuanhui lianxi huiyi tongguo de sifa ti-an" (A Letter of Reminder: Implementing the Propositions of Border Council Standing Committee and Government Committee on Judicial Work).

[22] "Huanxian Tianshui qu er xiang bamian tanwu de cun zhuren" (Township Number Two in Tianshui Ward of Huanxian County Dismissed a Corrupt Village Head), *Jiefang ribao*, December 14, 1944; "Zhenyuan ganbu jin xing xuexi hou, chufa qunzhong xianxiang jianshao, Mengba qu quzhang renyi chufa qunzhong, bu xuxin jieshou piping bei gezhi" (After Studying [the Policies], Zhenyuan Cadres Reduced a Number of Fines for the Masses; Ward Head of Mengba Ward Arbitrarily Fined the Masses But Rejected All Criticism, Thus He Is Dismissed), *Jiefang ribao*, December 17, 1944.

[23] SPA 15–72, "Hunyin wenti yu hunyin tiaoli."

[24] Xie Juezai, *Xie Juezai riji*, 814–15.

community autonomy through mediation and minimizing litigation to assuage the people's dissatisfaction. As for the marriage issue, in most cases government officials from outside the community may have been able to actively promote the policy rather than policing every marriage activity. It often happened that when a dispute occurred, the government/court would step in and insist on the implementation of its policy. In the absence of disputes, the government pursued a policy of non-intervention in marriage unless it was brought to the government, as mentioned in Chapter 4. Meanwhile, for the community, the state was often used either as a source of authority or as a referee in community disputes rather than a power that fully controlled villages across the board.

II. Ma Xiwu's Way: improving state relations with local communities

Though anonymous, the 1944 *LD* article was written in an authoritative tone and obviously came from the top BR leadership. It recapitulated the fact that Ma's Way was based on thorough investigations that involved interviewing the masses and respecting the community's opinions. When Ma dealt with village disputes, he used both mediation and adjudication as an effective means to finding a solution acceptable to all parties. The article also defined Ma's Way as government officials bringing the courts to the villages, as well as simplifying legal procedures through convenient and speedy trials. It pointed out that the "view of the masses" was the core value of "Ma Xiwu's Way," and praised it as being in accordance with the party's central policy of the mass-line. This article believed that the keys to achieving a peaceful community were to visit the villages (*xia xiang*), conduct thoughtful investigations, implement expedient procedures, establish an open court with mass participation, and exercise skillful methods (either adjudication or mediation or both) to settle problems. In reality, however, it was the dynamic relation between the state and community that was being shaped during this period.

Ma's Way in local context: achieving a peaceful community via mediation

The *LD* article emphasized one of Ma's tactics in settling community disputes. The article, following Lin Boqu's speech, encouraged judges to conduct mediation to solve local disputes; this mediation should be guided by revolutionary principles and the state's policies, but also take local customs into account.

However, mediation was neither an invention of Ma Xiwu nor a product of the communist movement. Studies of Chinese legal history have proven the existence of mediation in traditional rural communities prior to the communist revolution.[25] In the Ming period (1368–1644), the state intentionally encouraged local autonomy by supporting the custom of "senior judgment" (*laoren zhi* 老人制) in community disputes.[26] Fei Xiaotong's research on Chinese villages in the 1930s showed that most local disputes went through a mediation process led by clan elders or other authoritative persons, thus minimizing the number of lawsuits.[27] Huang believes that during the late imperial period, mediation was often conducted by leaders of clans in order to reduce litigation.[28] In building a modern judicial system, however, the Nationalist government did not totally reject the idea of community mediation, stipulating that mediation could proceed through either the society or the courts,[29] though how widely it was practiced is still unknown.

Mediation through both the administrative and judicial systems had existed in the SGNBR for years, even before the establishment of the formal judicial system in 1937 and before the introduction of Ma's Way. According to the 1941 report of the High Court, most wards (*qu*), the administrative districts below counties, had established a "People's Committee for Mediation" (*Renmin tiaojie weiyuanhui* 人民调解委员会) for most civil disputes.[30] In 1942, *LD* published a woodcut picture, "Mediation" (*Tiaojie* 调解), by Gu Yuan.[31] In the picture, a young woman is telling her story to a man sitting behind a desk, likely a village leader (see Figure 5.1). A man and an older woman, likely the young woman's husband and his mother, stand at the other end of the desk. The print

[25] Jerome A. Cohen, "Chinese Mediation On the Eve of Modernization," *Journal of Asia and African Studies* 2(1) (April 1967): 54–76; Franz Michael, "The Role of Law in Traditional, Nationalist and Communist China," *China Quarterly* 9 (1962): 124–48; Stanley Lubman, "Mao and Mediation: Politics and Dispute Resolution in Communist China," *California Law Review* 55 (1967): 1284–359; Hsiao Kung-Chuan, *Compromise in Imperial China* (Seattle: School of International Studies, University of Washington, 1979); Philip Huang, "Court Mediation in China, Past and Present," *Modern China* 32(3) (July 2006): 275–314.

[26] Yoshiaki Nakajima, *Mingdai de xiangcun jiufen yu zhixu* (Village Disputes and Order during the Ming Era), Guo Wanping and Gao Fei (trans.) (Nanjing: Jiangsu renmin chubanshe, 2010), 86–167.

[27] Fei Xiaotong, *Xiangtu Zhongguo* (Village China) (Shanghai: Shanghai renmin chubanshe, 2006), 45–8.

[28] Huang, "Court Mediation in China," and *Chinese Civil Justice*, 14–17, 87–123.

[29] See Xie Donghui, "Nanjing guomin zhengfu minshi tiaojie zhidu kaolun" (An Examination of Mediation in Civil Litigation by the Nanjing Government), *Nanjing shehui kexue* (Nanjing Social Sciences) 10 (2009): 86–93.

[30] SPA 15-175, "Lei Jingtian: Bianqu sifa gongzuo baogao."

[31] Gu Yuan, "Tiaojie" (Mediation), *Jiefang ribao*, December 19, 1942.

Figure 5.1 Gu Yuan, "Tiaojie" [Mediation], *Jiefang ribao*, December 19, 1942

seems to be depicting a family dispute that is now undergoing mediation conducted by the village leader. In the background, a crowd at the doorway observes the process. Mediation, long a widespread tradition, was now being conducted and celebrated by the revolutionary government.

In June 1943, when Ma was processing the case of *Feng v. Zhang*, the Border Region government issued a statute, the "Regulation of Mediation on Civil and Criminal Cases" (*Shaan-Gan-Ning bianqu min xing shijian tiaojie tiaoli* 陕甘宁边区民刑事件调解条例), that listed the types of civil litigations and minor criminal offenses eligible for mediation.[32] The

[32] "Shaan-Gan-Ning bianqu min xing shijian tiaojie tiaoli" (The Statute of the SGNBR on the Mediation Used in Criminal and Civil Cases) in Gansu sheng shehui kexueyuan lishi yanjiu suo (comp.), *Shaan-Gan-Ning geming genjudi shiliao xuanji*, vol. I (Selected Documents on the History of the SGN Revolutionary Base, vol. I) (Lanzhou: Gansu renmin chubanshe, 1981), 317–20. It is also possible that this statute was issued under the influence of the Nationalist legal code, because the Nationalist government promulgated a statute for regulating mediation in 1930 and a revised civil code in 1935 that stipulated the procedure of mediation. It established a special committee in each jurisdiction to be in charge of mediation, although mediation could also go through the court system. See Xie Donghui, "Nanjing guomin zhengfu minshi tiaojie zhidu kaolun."

regulation strongly encouraged mediation for civil disputes, and standardized the procedure by stipulating that both sides of the dispute could invite neighbors, relatives, or community organizations "to the site to determine right from wrong" (*cong chang pingyi qu zhi* 从场评议曲直) while "advising both sides on ending the dispute" (*quandao shuangfang xi zheng* 劝导双方息争).[33] This can be viewed as mediation outside the court that encouraged the participation of the community.

Community involvement in the process was important for all types of mediation, including the second step: mediation led by the court or government if community mediation failed. In this process, the government/court could invite grassroots cadres, representatives from various mass associations, and local gentry with a neutral stance to assist in the mediation. It is obvious that during this period, mediation was viewed as a legal technique that had proven useful in settling cases. The mediation was voluntary for both sides of the case, and once the two reached an agreement, the resolution was written into a reconciliatory agreement by either the community or the court.[34] The archival documents of the SGN High Court also show that mediation was frequently used in civil disputes during this period. Of the three cases mentioned in the *LD* article, two had gone through mediation before Judge Ma and his assistant became involved. This situation thus begs the question: since mediation was already a widespread technique in dealing with community quarrels, why did the BR government (via the *Liberation Daily* article) take care to highlight it as a method for solving civil disputes? What was the government's purpose in popularizing Ma's Way and how did Ma's Way differ from previous mediation?

Of course, it was clear that winning popular support for the state was the major concern when seeking to minimize litigation in communities. This motive was clearly stated in an official 1944 letter from the BR government (drafted by Xie Juezai)[35] sent to all administrative jurisdictions and courts. It explained that promoting mediation and Ma's Way could help reduce litigation to a minimum.[36] As Xie Juezai put it, mediation "is able to make a big dispute into a small one and a small dispute into none (*dashi hua xiao, xiaoshi hua wu* 大事化小，小事化无); it prevents a small dispute from growing into a big issue and from nothing into a trouble; it will increase the harmony of villages, thus saving labor and energy for production."[37] From this point, we are able to see how the

[33] "Shaan-Gan-Ning bianqu min xing shijian tiaojie tiaoli," 317–20.
[34] *Ibid.*
[35] See *Xie Juezai riji*, 620–30.
[36] "Bianqu zhengfu guanyu puji tiaojie, zongjie panli, qingli jiansuo zhishi xin," in *Tiaojie wei zhu shenpan wei fu*, 10–16.
[37] Xie Juezai, *Xie Juezai riji*, 621.

CCP judicial branch inherited the Qing idea of legal minimalism and community autonomy.[38]

Ma's Way in practice: pushing the party-state to improve its working style

Some contemporary scholars view Ma's Way solely through the lens of law by using the Western judicial system and legal concepts as their points of reference. These studies often reduce Ma's Way to mediation, which in their eyes is simply an informal mode of judicial procedure, a judicial technique, or a judicial improvisation during the revolution.[39] In fact, Ma's Way included many other important aspects, such as the judge visiting villages and conducting on-site investigations, listening to the masses' opinions on the case, conducting mediation, simplifying legal procedure, establishing an open court for the final conclusion or adjudication, and spreading modern legal knowledge to the masses. The *LD* article presented mediation as only one step toward a better resolution of a dispute, depending on the judge's discretion and his tactics in the application of either mediation or adjudication.

According to the statute on mediation issued by the BR government, mediation required both sides of a dispute to be voluntarily on site. However, the *LD* article revealed that the case of *Feng v. Zhang* cannot be viewed as a simple mediation because in the first two steps, investigation and learning the masses' opinion, Ma did not involve either the Zhangs or Feng. In the last step, which took place in open court, the original litigants, Feng Yangui and the Zhangs, were summoned to the site to receive the final adjudication. In the open court, Ma gave a speech on the law and delivered the new adjudication, which was obviously based on a series of efforts that went beyond the mediation process stipulated by the 1943 regulation.

The second case discussed in the *LD* article, *Wang v. Wang*, was a land dispute that occurred in Heshui County of Longdong subregion. According to the article, the dispute started with the greedy attempt of

[38] See Huang on imperial legal minimalism in his *Chinese Civil Justice*, 17–19, 81–6.

[39] Fan Yu,"Jian lun Ma Xiwu shenpan fangshi" (A Preliminary Discussion on Ma Xiwu's Way of Judging), *Qinghua falü pinglun* (Qinghua Law Review) 2 (1999): 221–31; Huang, "Court Mediation in China, Past and Present," and also *Chinese Civil Justice*; Qiang Shigong, "Quanli de zuzhi wangluo yu falü de zhilihua." Qiang Shigong also simplifies Ma's Way as mediation and merely a legal technique, but one that could be powerful in improving the CCP's governance when integrated into its political network in local communities. For criticism of Ma's Way in contemporary scholarship, see Xiaoping Cong, "Ma Xiwu's Way of Judging: Villages, the Masses, and the Legal Construction in Revolutionary China of the 1940s," *The China Journal* 72 (July 2014): 29–52.

a farmer, Wang Zhikuan, to dig a trench on the land of his neighbor, Wang Tongyi (not related to Wang Zhikuan). The dispute was first settled through community mediation under the supervision of the ward cadres, but after the mediation, Wang Zhikuan appealed to the county court. The judges of the county court did not visit the village to check out the story, but simply took Wang Zhikuan's word on the matter and thus ruled in his favor. Wang Tongyi then appealed to the subregional court, at which time Chief-Judge Ma sent his assistant, Judge Shi Jingshan 石静山, to the village for a thorough investigation. After discovering the source of the dispute, Judge Shi held an open court in a public venue to deliver his final decision. Given the facts revealed by the investigation, and under pressure from the judge and community members, Wang Zhikuan eventually admitted his wrongdoing and apologized to Wang Tongyi. In this case, mediation was used but did not solve the problem; it was the court adjudication and strong public pressure that eventually settled the case and reconciled the parties.

The third case, *Chou v. Ding*, also occurred in Heshui County and can be considered a mediated case. Beginning in the mid-1930s, both Chou and Ding had pushed the borderlines of their fields toward each other, which eventually resulted in a land dispute. The primary trial of the case was held at the Nationalist county court and appealed in the Nationalist district's appellate jurisdiction, but the primary trial and the appeal resulted in completely opposite judgments. According to the *LD* article, neither the county court nor the district appellate jurisdiction visited the fields, but simply declared the winner based on the size of the litigants' bribes. When the CCP took over power in the county, Chou, who had lost the case at district court, appealed to the revolutionary subregional court. Ma Xiwu sent Judge Shi to the village, where he investigated the history of the case and examined the plots in person. After conscientious deliberation, he held an open court in a community venue and persuaded them to meet in the middle for a solution. The case was closed with a peaceful ending that satisfied both sides.

In these cases, Ma's Way sometimes took the form of mediation and sometimes judicial adjudication, but the two were never mutually exclusive; instead, Ma's Way was more inclusive. For adjudication, he needed to do a thorough investigation; for mediation, he had to be considerate and persuasive. As a judge, Ma had to follow the form of the law, but the goal of settling the case had to accord with revolutionary principles; and also, as a local leader, he had to look for a way to satisfy all parties in the dispute. Thus, Xie Juezai emphasized that "the combination of adjudication and mediation is Comrade Ma Xiwu's way of judging."[40] The goal

[40] Xie Juezai, *Xie Juezai riji*, 621.

was to maintain a peaceful community by offering a solution acceptable to all. This method seemed certain to receive success in that when Ma Xiwu reviewed the SGNBR's judicial work in 1955 he stressed that the most important practice was the mass-line.[41]

The 1944 *LD* article presented Ma's Way as a wake-up call for government officials to improve their working style in order to serve the people better. For legal workers, a simple adjudication could rest on dogmatism and commandism that could invite antagonism from the community. According to the article, in all three cases the original disputes were made worse by irresponsible or dogmatic workers in county courts. For example, in the case of *Feng v. Zhang* the Huachi County court did not conduct a thorough investigation, but rather believed Feng and punished the Zhangs without giving consideration to the fact that the father of the Feng family had sold his daughter into marriage against her wishes. A similar situation occurred in the two land disputes, in that the county courts failed to conduct any investigation and based the adjudications on the word of the plaintiff.

It is obvious that by praising Ma, the *LD* article was also responding to issues raised in previous judicial reforms, bureaucratization, professionalization, and formalization, the issues contested in the 1943 review of judicial works discussed in Chapter 3. One way to reduce the state's coercive enforcement and pacify discontented villages was to encourage judges and government workers to visit villages in person and conduct a full investigation in order to understand the history and the source of a dispute. The investigation enabled legal workers to gain a better understanding of all elements involved in a dispute, which would greatly help mediation and application of the spirit of the law. This was far preferable to staying in courtrooms and formalistically applying the words of the law, as discussed in Chapters 3 and 4.

The article applauded Ma for his handy procedures and for using an open court with community participation. By contrasting Ma's way to the court-centered judicial system and to the imperial *yamen* style that waited for people to bring their disputes to the court and made adjudications through courtroom interrogation, the article stressed that Ma's Way

[41] See "Xin minzhu zhuyi geming jieduan zhong Shaan-Gan-Ning bianqu renmin sifa gongzuo" (People's Judicial Works in the SGNBR during the Period of the New Democratic Revolution) in Zhang, *Ma Xiwu shenpan fangshi*, 80–100. A speech made by Kang Sheng in 1958 also praised how Ma's legal practice assisted in building a close relation between the judicial sector and the masses. See "Kang Sheng tongzhi baogao jilu zhaiyao" (The Note of Comrade Kang Sheng's Speech) (*Zhongyang zhengf ganxiao shehuizhuyi jiaoyu fudao zu zhengli*, Beijing, 1958, 1–8). Here I would like to express my sincere gratitude to Professor Michael Schoenhals who generously shared this document with me from his precious collection.

belonged to the community and the people (*min jian* 民间). The article emphasized that Ma was willing to meet litigants wherever and whenever it was convenient for them, either day or night, in hilly fields or at the riverside, so that anyone could sit down with him and get help for their problems. Using the case of *Feng v. Zhang* to illustrate this, the article stressed that Peng'er ran into Prefect Ma under a tree near the village, where she appealed her case.[42]

The article also praised Ma's Way in dealing with disputes by traveling a circuit through his jurisdiction. According to another report on Ma published in *LD*, each year Ma spent little time in his office but traveled frequently to counties and villages in his jurisdiction in order to discover possible mistakes made by local judicial workers.[43] The *LD* reporter followed up by publishing another report on Ma's work circuit in August and September 1944, in which Ma discovered that many cases had been appealed repeatedly and were also impossible to be solved simply by mediation or adjudication. Ma invited some influential figures from the local communities to become involved in mediation, then followed this with court adjudication.[44] At almost the same time, *LD* published another piece on the work of the Longdong subregional court, which had adopted the method of mediation in most of its cases; Quzi County and Huanxian County won high evaluations. The same report also presented the Zhenyuan County court as a negative example, because its judge failed to conduct on-site investigations or adopt mediation to settle cases.[45] Ma's work circuit had exposed this problem. In this way, Ma's style seemed very similar to that of the enlightened officials in imperial culture, which I discuss below.

Following the 1944 article, the BR government began to encourage the use of Ma's Way across a broader region by promoting the new slogan "Mainly use mediation while assisted by adjudication" (*tiaojie wei zhu, shenpan wei fu* 调解为主, 审判为辅) in both civil disputes and minor criminal cases.[46] For a while, mediating community disputes became a political campaign in which many people, such as judges, cadres, labor

[42] To create an idealistic image of Ma, the article seems to overlook the fact that Peng'er had visited Ma's residence in the Qingyang administrative center before they ran into each other in the field (see Chapter 2).

[43] "Ma Xiwu tongzhi shenpan fangshi."

[44] "Ma Xiwu tongzhi chuxun shen'an jingyan" (Comrade Ma Xuwu Doing Trials in His Circuit), *Jiefang ribao*, December 20, 1944.

[45] "Longdong gaodeng fenting chuli anjian duo yong tiaojie fangshi, Zhenyuan chuli anjian duo wei xiaxiang diaocha" (Longdong Dispatched-High Court Uses Mediation for Most Cases, But Zhenyuan County Failed to Do On-site Investigation in Dealing With the Majority of Cases), *Jiefang ribao*, December 19, 1944.

[46] Wang Ziyi, "Shenpan yu tiaojie."

models, and individuals, were involved. After March 1944, *LD* devoted considerable space to reporting on mediation cases. For example, on June 14, *LD* published the BR governmental instructive that called on all courts to adopt Ma's Way.[47] By presenting Ma's working style and its spread, the state, though with a high-modernist ideology, displayed its intent to remedy its coercive style and commandism, as concrete measures to present itself as a democratic power. It was in response to the pressure of community protests and the state's concern for its survival that it sought to achieve harmony and balance in its relationship with the villages.

Ma's Way in practice: the state negotiating with and reshaping the local community

Some Western historians have argued that under the influence of the West at the turn of the twentieth century, a Habermasian "public sphere" and "civil society" began to develop among educated elites in China's urban areas. These historians believe that the rise of print publications in coastal and urban areas brought about a "public opinion" that represented the awakening consciousness of the urban populace in modern politics.[48] If the public sphere Habermas describes as a phenomenon of eighteenth-century Germany did indeed occur in twentieth-century China, it could only be built on the foundation of urban print culture and among a modern educated population. The active print media and basic education created a base for the populace's participation in public affairs that would, in theory, pave the way for political democracy. The question that follows is: was it possible for public opinion or civil society to arise in rural communities such as the SGNBR of the 1940s, where the illiteracy rate was over 95 percent? If print culture was indeed the vehicle for public opinion in urban areas, in what ways could this opinion be expressed in a rural region like the SGNBR? In such a community, how could mass participation in public affairs become possible, and how was public opinion shaped? Moreover, what types of public affairs

[47] "Bian fu zhishi ge fenqu sifa gongzuo duoduo caiyong minjian tiaojie, shenpan yao xuexi Ma Xiwu tongzhi de fangshi" (Border Government Instructs the Judicial Works of Each Subregion to Adopt People's Mediation, and [Their] Adjudication Should Learn from Comrade Ma Xiwu's Way of Judging), *Jiefang ribao*, June 14, 1944.

[48] Mary Backus Rankin, *Elite Activism and Political Transformation in China, Zhejiang Province, 1865–1911* (Stanford, CA: Stanford University Press, 1986); Joan Judge, *Print and Politics: "Shibao" and the Culture of Reform in Late Qing China* (Stanford, CA: Stanford University Press, 1996); David Strand, *Rickshaw Beijing: City, People and Politics in the 1920s* (Berkeley: University of California Press, 1989).

concerned the populace, and what role did the state play in shaping public opinion on such affairs?

In confronting the urban-oriented study of modernization, Philip Huang keenly grasps the problematic assumption of a Habermasian civil society in China. Huang redefines the dynamic interplays between state power and the rural community by proposing the theory of the "third realm" that he believes existed in late imperial society, especially in the sphere of civil disputes during the Qing period. According to him, the state and rural communities each had their own domain, but only for the purpose of settling a civil dispute would they meet in this third realm during negotiation. In the third realm, the imperial state (represented by local government) was able to use its informal influence on both sides of a civil dispute. The state urged solutions through community mediation, while the communities could also bargain with the state, to their benefit.[49] However, in Huang's work the term "rural communities" often refers to those places where clan-based organizations dominated local affairs and clan elites led negotiations with the state. We still do not know how mass involvement in community affairs affected the results of legal cases, especially in a region like Longdong where weak clans (if any) barely tied the community together (see Chapter 1).

In the 1940s, the revolutionary forces in the SGNBR attempted to establish a democratic polity based on mass participation;[50] nonetheless, the expression of public opinion through print media was obviously unrealistic. Although Yan'an had more than ten newspapers and each subregion had its own publications,[51] they could hardly be used to shape any kind of public opinion that could influence the massive number of illiterate farmers. At best, these publications reached only a small group of educated people such as government cadres, party leaders, and intellectuals/students in various cultural institutions in Yan'an. At worst, many of these newspapers were the official media of government at all levels; the newspapers were used by the party-state as an instrument for political mobilization, ideological inculcation, or for posting the party's instructions and propagating its achievements.

On the other hand, the party attempted to use newspapers for policy feedback, urging both government workers and newspaper reporters to

[49] Philip Huang, "Between Informal Mediation and Formal Adjudication: The Third Realm of Qing Civil Justice," *Modern China* 19(3) (1993): 251–98.

[50] Selden, *China in Revolution*, 99–143; Rong Jingben, Luo Yanming, and Ye Daomeng, *Lun Yan'an de minzhu moshi* (On the Model of Yan'an Democracy) (Xi'an: Xibei daxue chubanshe, 2004), 288–96.

[51] Wang Jing (comp.), *Yan'an Jiefang ribao shi* (History of Liberation Daily in Yan'an) (Beijing: Xinhua chubanshe, 1998), 5–6.

submit observations of the grassroots voices of the village in order to discover problems that could threaten social stability. This type of voice was assigned a special term, "the mass opinion" (*qunzhong yijian* 群众意见), that was derived from and supported by the party's mass-line. The mass opinion differs from the term "public opinion" that Mary Rankin uses to describe a phenomenon in the late Qing political movements in which the intellectual elite expressed their dissenting opinions against Manchu rule. In this case, public opinion, as a self-conscious activity, represented intellectuals constructing an abstract social space opposite state power, in which an elite view of public affairs was articulated through print.[52] Rankin's "public" was an imaginary community defined by the educated elite, who tried to assemble a force for reform or revolution.

The mass-line may have been permeated by the party-state's intent of top-down dominance of the masses; from a bottom-up perspective, it could also serve as the political source for some grassroots cadres to legitimize their compromises with and concessions to local communities. Moreover, as archival documents have shown, it could provide a source for ordinary farmers or women to bargain with the state, as discussed in Chapters 1 and 2. In the environment of the SGNBR, it would be misleading to say that the illiterate masses/farmers were completely mobilized by CCP's ideology. They may not have fully comprehended the political rhetoric of communism and the new terms that were imported to the region. In contrast to what Chalmers Johnson believes,[53] they may not have even cared deeply about nationalism, because the threat of the Japanese invasion was still far from their region. However, this does not mean that farmers were indifferent to public affairs or had no opinion on the party's policies and governance. In this view, Lucien Bianco might be right that in many cases peasants' cooperation with the revolutionary forces was more a matter of "compliance" than "support,"[54] if they believed that a policy was acceptable. What they cared about were those things most closely related to their lives, such as marriage practice and landownership (or rental), in which they sought a legal system that would help them achieve justice and fairness if any dispute occurred. A legal case also provided a chance for the state to negotiate and interact with communities: when the state merely tried to calm communities but did not listen to popular concerns, unhappy litigants from villages would force the state to bend

[52] Backus Rankin, *Elite Activism and Political Transformation in China*.
[53] See Chalmers Johnson, *Peasant Nationalism and Communist Power* (Stanford, CA: Stanford University Press, 1962).
[54] Bianco, "Peasant Responses to CCP Mobilization Polices," 175–87.

its rules a little for the litigants' benefit and for the sake of a peaceful community (see below).

However, as a revolutionary party that aimed to reform "backward" local customs, the CCP brought some alien ideas into the locality and intended to overturn the original order of society. Therefore, in the CCP's view, mass opinions needed to be led by party officials or party trained activists, and the masses needed to be inculcated with revolutionary ideas. This was one of the purposes of the open court, in which a revolutionary judge would encourage and guide favorable opinions from the participants in order to reach an outcome that did not compromise the revolutionary goal.

This point was manifested in Ma's way of dealing with *Feng v. Zhang*. Ma interviewed a number of villagers in the neighborhood to determine the "popular inclination/opinion" (*yiban yulun quxiang* 一般舆论趋向) in the case. Through discussing the case with villagers and local cadres, Ma found that the "general masses" (*yiban qunzhong* 一般群众) disliked the previous adjudication made by Huachi County and sympathized with the "young couple" (*yidui shaonian fufu* 一对少年夫妇).[55] In the two cases on land disputes, Judge Shi strictly followed Ma's Way by conducting a thorough on-site investigation and discussed the case with various people in the villages in order to learn the mass opinion. It was the masses' knowledge of the history of a specific case, their awareness of the litigants' motives, their basic conscience in judging right from wrong, and their common sense in terms of fairness that would produce the acceptable result of a case. Sometimes, the state could also use community pressure to force the litigants to give in and reach an agreement. Thus, Ma's Way became an example of the mass-line because he made his new adjudication by taking the mass opinion into account. However, we will see that this mass opinion, though sometimes given the chance to be expressed, was also shaped and judged by the state as part of the process of the state's penetration into and interaction with the community.

The last step of Ma's Way was to hold an open court that invited mass participation and to serve the state's purpose of educating the people. Open court became the "community public site" where the revolutionary state and the masses of the village community met directly. Differing from the "public sphere," which was filled by urban bourgeoisie, or the "third realm," which was dominated by clan elites, this community public site was a local venue such as a village temple or threshing floor where villagers frequently met for events and/or entertainment.[56] This public

[55] "Ma Xiwu tongzhi de shenpan fangshi."

[56] According to one study, Ma held the open court in a local temple that was used as village office. See Lu Di, *Zhongguo xiandai banhua shi* (A History of Modern Chinese Woodcuts)

venue became the place where the revolutionary state met with local villagers to hold political meetings, to mobilize villagers for state reform programs, rental reduction, and to announce the tax levy. Villagers gathered at this public site because they had concerns about their interests and the outcome of local affairs. In these assemblies, some villagers had the chance to voice their opinions. Although it was a way for the state to interact with the local community, the deficiencies of this type of public site were several: the articulations of the locals were limited to oral expression and took place on a small scale, and additionally, this site was created and led by the state, with the intent of allowing the state to push its will into villages.

It was the leading role of the revolutionary state in community affairs and its direct interaction with villages that made community mediation different from that of the Qing period. *Liberation Daily* gives us a glimpse into how these open courts operated and how the mass view was expressed. As previously mentioned, a woodcut, Gu Yuan's "Comrade Ma Xiwu in Mediating Litigation," was published in *LD* on October 9, 1944. The artist specifically indicated that this picture was inspired by Ma Xiwu's way of dealing with the case *Feng v. Zhang*. The picture vividly depicts a scene in an open court, in which Ma stands at the center guiding the discussion, while other litigants and locals are either responding or listening to him (see Figure 5.2). Contemporary art historian Wu Xueshan analyzes this picture, pointing out that the composition obviously divides the masses into two camps: the "victors" on the left side, who have joyful expressions, and the "punished" on the right side, who are being addressed.[57] However, this view stresses that the CCP was responsible for creating antagonism among villagers. This interpretation intends to criticize the dogmatic CCP theory of class struggle, which was carried out from 1947 but in fact was not at the center of the CCP's concerns before the mid-1940s when the CCP did not plan to split with the Nationalists in the United Front so soon.

If we place the picture in the original story, there is much more than simply the victors and the punished. The background of the woodcut locates the court in an open space in the village, indicating that the

(Beijing: Renmin meishu chubanshe, 1987), 209. On the other hand, the situation may have varied in different subregions. For instance, in Suide subregion, where patriarchal clans played an important role in village affairs, this type of assembly would likely have been held in the front of a clan hall.

[57] Wu Xueshan, "Cong Ma Xiwu tongzhi tiaojie susong dao Liu Qiao'er: geming hunyin de huayu jiangou" (From Comrade Ma Xiwu Mediating a Litigation to Liu Qiao'er: Constructing a Revolutionary Discourse on Marriage), in *Wu Xueshan Zhongguo meishu shi yanjiu wenji* (A Collection of Wu Xueshan's Research on Chinese Art History) (Beijing: Zhongyang minzu daxue chubanshe, 2009), 135–72.

Figure 5.2 Gu Yuan, "Ma Xiwu tongzhi tiaojie susong" [Comrade Ma Xiwu in Mediating Litigation], *Jiefang ribao*, October 9, 1944

court went to the village rather than bringing the dispute to a courtroom located in a city. On the left side of the foreground stand a young woman and man, presumably Peng'er and Zhang Bo, and a middle-aged woman who could be Peng'er's mother or a female leader of the village, as I discuss in the next chapter. Another group of people, including two older men, likely Feng Yangui and Zhang Jincai, are listening to Ma's speech. This picture does indeed construct a tension between the state and the local patriarchy, demonstrating that the state, represented by Ma facing the two fathers, encountered and prevented the local patriarchy from interfering in the lives of their daughters/sons. However, we can see from the facial expressions and the standing gesture that the two fathers are not intimidated by Ma, but rather seem to be defending themselves with smiles. Other villagers are either observing or discussing the case, and their opinions could also be presented. This picture, although the representative of the state as the central figure, provides a vivid image of open court as a state-created public site where local voices could be heard.

Incorporating mass opinions into the judicial process and holding an open court did indeed offer a chance for mass participation in community affairs and state-building. However, if the opinions from the villagers were accepted uncritically and unscrupulously, it could compromise the goal of reform and weaken the revolutionary government as an effective state power. Thus, the state needed to guide the mass opinion in open court so that the final result would not diverge from revolutionary principles.

An *LD* report by Qian Feng on a Qingyang case, "Auditing a Divorce Case" (*Pangting lihun an* 旁听离婚案), offers us a glimpse of a seminar-like open court and how the mass opinion was shaped in this court.[58] It stated that the various locals actively observed the case by packing the hall temporarily used for the courtroom. Local notables, such as a member of a standing committee of the BR Council, a former member of a provincial assembly, the vice-chair of the Qingyang Council, and the director of the Association for Resisting Japan and Saving China of Longdong Subregion, filled both sides of the courtroom. The litigant was a young woman, Zhang Xiu'er, who was filing for divorce. She stated that her husband had been ill and lost the ability to father a child. Moreover, she claimed that both her husband and father-in-law had abused her. The husband, Chen Jixiang, told his side of story: they had been married for four years and had good relations as he recovered from his illness. Several months before, his wife had suddenly demanded a divorce after she returned from visiting her natal family; thus, he had reason to believe that her parents were behind this divorce plot. The man admitted wrongdoing in hitting her once, but claimed it had been triggered by his wife's verbal attack. He also swore that it was the only incident of abuse in the four years of their marriage.

The woman's father, Zhang Zhichang, was called to explain his role in the divorce. The father admitted that for the past four years, the Chens had treated his daughter very well and she had never had any trouble, but his daughter brought up the subject of divorce because of her husband's illness. When the judge asked if he still wanted his daughter to divorce when his son-in-law recovered, Zhang, facing the audience's gaze, spoke evasively but eventually agreed with reluctance that his daughter should return to her husband if her husband recovered. He also added that it should be his daughter's decision. When the audience turned to the young woman, she insisted on the divorce. At the conclusion of the questions, the judge stood up and read two documents. One was a letter from a hospital stating that the husband's illness was totally curable and that he was currently recovering; the second document included two letters from the

[58] Qian Feng, "Pangting lihun an" (Auditing a Divorce Case), *Jiefang ribao*, March 5, 1946.

woman's natal village and the husband's village, respectively. One letter stated that the couple had had good relations in their four years of marriage, but it was Zhang's father who had instigated the divorce because he wanted to sell his daughter for a higher price. The second letter stated that the woman's father was considered a bad character in the village, while the Chens were regarded as honest and industrious people.

After introducing the case and the documents, the judge opened the court to discussion. It is intriguing that the local leaders began by criticizing the father. Some female leaders, such as the director of the village women's organization, tried to persuade Zhang Xiu'er to drop the case because her husband was a good man. On the other hand, there were also some audience members who argued that the Chens needed to take some responsibility for not treating the man's illness earlier. A jumble of views was voiced in the courtroom, but support for the divorce seemed to dim. Then the judge stood up and announced the adjudication: the conditions for divorce were not sufficient, and the husband was at fault for hitting his wife. Since it had happened only once, it could not yet be considered domestic abuse. The court instructed the woman's father to persuade his daughter to return to her husband. The report observed that Zhang accepted the result with embarrassment. To show that this was the correct outcome, the article offered a warm ending that the husband approached his wife and comforted her, then the two walked out of the court together.[59]

This report, though romanticized, described an open court likely very similar to that in the case of *Feng v. Zhang*, the details of which were covered only briefly in the *LD* article. Based on carefully selected "mass opinion," a judge could reach a conclusion that fitted the revolutionary principle, and the adjudication would be based on this opinion. At the same time, an open court provided a public site where "incorrect opinion" or behavior would be criticized and "correct opinion" would be encouraged and even included in the adjudication. CCP leaders viewed this type of occasion as a good opportunity to educate people and mobilize the masses.[60] In this process of legal construction and state-building, the revolutionary state actively promoted a grassroots "public space/site" (hardly in the Habermasian sense) in the rural community among illiterate farmers, though this public opinion was guided and judged by the state and its new trained elites. The results of this public discussion

[59] Qian Feng, "Pangting lihun an."

[60] In this process, the CCP trained new local elites such as village heads, the director of the village women's organization, the deputy of the local militia, and activists as the new generation's leaders in the public arena. Due to the limits of the topic of this book, this group of people will be discussed in future work.

would favor state-led reform projects, but still left enough room for public expression. This particular model, in which the state promoted public opinion in order to lead social reform, could help us to understand the situation in the SGNBR.

At the same time, this process also provided a chance for the state to compromise with the community. It is important to note that although Zhang Bo played a major role in the kidnapping in the case of *Feng v. Zhang*, the state did not want to spoil the masses' expectation of the young couple's happiness and thus bent the rules, sparing him from criminal charges.[61] Moreover, there was a postscript to this case that had not been revealed, but which can be seen as a good example of the state's compromise with the locals in order to reduce antagonism between the two. After the open court that settled the case, Prefect Ma filed this case with a letter and sent it to the High Court on July 1, more than a month after the settlement. During this period, the Zhang family had been pleading for a reduction in the sentence. To update this new development of the case, on July 11 Ma wrote another report to the High Court, which detailed his concerns about the penalty. He also asked for instructions on whether it was appropriate to confiscate the 7,000 *yuan fabi* from Zhu Shouchan, and whether the sentence for Zhang Jincai and his brother, Zhang Jingui, one of the participants in the kidnapping, was too harsh.[62]

The High Court sent back a quick response, dated July 16 and received by Longdong District Branch Office on July 25. The High Court believed that Feng Yangui's sentence of three months labor service was appropriate. Regarding the forfeiture, the High Court instructed that it depended on whether Zhu Shouchang was an innocent third party. If Zhu did not know about the previous engagement and the continuing dispute between Zhang and Feng, he should be viewed as innocent and his money and goods returned. Regarding the Zhang brothers' sentence, the High Court commanded:

> Although their [the Zhangs] behavior disturbed the social order, it was their ignorance and their hotheaded emotions that led to their act. In the condition that the marriage has been validated, we should show some leniency to their criminal action. But you should determine the Zhangs' everyday behavior in the community. If they are indeed ordinary good people, you should allow them to have an early parole, or put them on probation in order to show the leniency and for the purpose of education (*yi shi kuanda er zi jiaoyu* 以示宽大而资教育).[63]

[61] SPA 15–842, *Feng v. Zhang*.

[62] SPA 15–842, "Wei cheng qing dui Feng Zhang hunyin an zhi chuli pi da" (Asking for a Response [from the High Court] on the Adjudication of the Case of *Feng v. Zhang*).

[63] SPA 15–842, "Shaan-Gan-Ning gaodeng fayuan pi da: Feng Yangui yu Zhang Jincai wei er nü hunyin yi an keyi cong kuan chuli."

This process can be seen as part of the community's negotiation with the state, while the state had to cover its concession with the rhetoric of "leniency" and "for the purpose of education" in order to maintain peace with the community. On the other hand, the revolutionary state also tried to play the role of educator rather than punisher, and wanted to use this case to educate villagers, since legal adjudication could be a means of reshaping communities, as discussed in the following chapters.

III. Ma's Way: local communities in the shaping of state discourse

The *LD* article reemphasized the significance of Ma's Way in the end by stating that Ma's Way belonged to the "community" (*min jian*), explicitly indicating that Ma dealt with local disputes in the framework of the community and through the form of mediation that originated from local tradition. This statement also implicitly admitted that the party was bringing local values, such as the "clear-sky" judge (see below), into its revolutionary discourse to promote good governance. Thus, it was the tactical resistance of local communities and their interactions with the state that impeded the party-state's drive for absolute power.

Reestablishing the order of the community

As for the origin and significance of Ma's Way, Zhang Xipo sees it as an inevitable and necessary part of the revolutionary institutions that were produced along with the revolution. It represented the CCP's efforts to make the legal system available to all people.[64] Huang believes that as mediation, Ma's Way was a mixture of (imperial) rural tradition and CCP revolutionary practice. Based on his examinations of mediation in the post-1949 legal system, Huang points out that this mixed legal practice composed the most important part of the so-called "Mao's legal legacy" in the contemporary (post-1949) civil litigation system.[65] Other scholars believe that Ma's Way originated from the economic shortage and judicial plight faced by the Border Region in the 1940s.[66] Some scholars argue that in its legal construction, Ma's Way was an innovation

[64] Zhang Xipo, *Ma Xiwu shenpan fangshi* (Ma Xiwu's Way of Judging) (Beijing: Falü chubanshe, 1983), 41–54.

[65] Huang, "Court Mediation in China, Past and Present," and also *Chinese Civil Justice*, 113–16.

[66] Li Juan, "Ma Xiwu shenpan fangshi chansheng de beijing fenxi" (An Analysis of the Historical Context of Ma's Way), *Falü kexue* (Legal Science) 2 (2008): 163–9.

of the CCP, diverging from the model of the Nationalist implantation of the Western-style judicial system.[67]

The birth of Ma's Way in the Longdong subregion was not a coincidence, but the result of a combination of regional history and the revolutionary process that led state power to play an important role in community civil disputes. It was mainly a historical product of a particular social and cultural setting in which disintegration of local communities, state-building, and revolution that reshaped communities occurred synchronously. As discussed in Chapter 1, each subregion had its own ecological and social conditions. Suide and Guanzhong were more populated, richer, and developed, but Yanshu, Longdong, and Sanbian were areas of vast hilly and barren land with sparse population. Due to the fact that the land revolution in Longdong and a large part of Yanshu proceeded before the GMD–CCP Second United Front in 1937, the social conditions became different in these subregions as the revolution unfolded.[68] Longdong subregion was an area in which revolutionary forces had maintained a strong presence since 1930. The land reform carried out in the mid-1930s won the loyalty of the local farmers for the revolutionary government, allowing revolutionary leaders to play an active role in reorganizing the disintegrated communities.

In contrast to the strong revolutionary forces, Longdong region had a long history of weak community solidarity and autonomy, since rebellions and natural disasters had destroyed most of its villages, as discussed in Chapter 1. In most of Longdong, as well as in Yanshu and Sanbian subregions (see map), communities gradually took shape as immigrants continued to pour in in the 1930s and 1940s. The revolutionary government had to deal with many disputes between the earlier residents and the newcomers. The drastic social upheavals and natural disasters in this area during the late Qing and the Republican periods also destroyed the credit system based on morality, social norms, means of communication, and local authority in the villages. This type of mixed community differed from traditional communities where people had known each other for generations and which were built on a mutual trust system with shared moral and social norms.

Moreover, a traditional community naturally produced its own authoritative persons who could play key roles in village mediation.

[67] Qiang Shigong, "Quanli de zuzhi wangluo yu falü de zhilihua"; Hou Xinyi, *Cong sifa wei min dao renmin sifa – Shaan-Gan-Ning bianqu dazhong sifa zhidu yanjiu* (From Judicial Works for the People to the People's Judicial System – A Study on the Judicial System of the SGNBR) (Beijing: Zhongguo zhengfa daxue chubanshe, 2007), 260. For details, see Xiaoping Cong, "'Ma Xiwu's Way of Judging': Villages, Law, and Legal Modernity."

[68] Keating, *Two Revolutions*, 35–64.

Huang's research indicates that traditional community mediation often centered on either villages or clans and required certain local authoritative figures to deal with civil disputes.[69] Since Longdong region was characterized by the small size of families, weak clan ties, and declining domination of village communities (see Chapter 1), there was little possibility of such authorities existing. Additionally, the previous small landlords were forced out of the villages, eliminating them as potential authorities for mediation. As Chapter 1 has discussed, as this region had been marginalized in the imperial political map for a long time since the early Qing leading to the weak presence of imperial power and the chaos of the post-imperial period, the communists' political and legal power established in this void had to deal directly with various civil disputes instead of being a lofty but influential power like the Qing state, which existed above community disputes and mediation. These circumstances enabled Ma Xiwu or people like Ma, as representatives of state power, to become involved in village disputes along with promoting the state's social reform programs.

Keating believes that the CCP made a positive contribution to constructing village communities, especially in the Yanshu subregion[70] next to Longdong subregion, which shared similar ecological and social conditions. However, by relying on Johnson and other early works on the marriage reform, she falls into an assumption that sets failed marriage reform in the context of successful village construction.[71] This is disproved by the facts that villagers could manipulate the new concept of marriage while the judicial system delivered divorce adjudication, altering community norms. Meanwhile, it was village construction that produced a group of new local elites such as village heads, labor models, organizers of mutual assistance groups, and deputies of local councils, as well as heads of village militias, associations for resisting Japan, and women's associations. In the community mediation of civil cases, these elites would back the new concept that was gradually reshaping villagers' views of marriage. In my 2005 interview with Feng Zhiqin, I asked her how she learned about the idea of "freedom of marriage."[72] She told me that it was a labor model in her village, Zhang Zhencai, who introduced the idea to her. Zhang learned all kinds of new ideas from attending a conference for labor models held in Yan'an and brought them back to the village.[73] Moreover, as mentioned in Chapter 1, Feng Zhiqin's father also

69 Huang, "Court Mediation in China," 281–2.
70 Keating, *Two Revolutions*, 5–6.
71 Keating, *Two Revolutions*, 7.
72 During this time, I haven't discovered the term *zi-zhu* used in legal documents, thus presumed it was "freedom of marriage."
73 Interview with Feng Zhiqin, July 21, 2005.

became this type of local new elite. We thus see that village construction and marriage reform could be mutually supportive.

Local autonomy and culture under the revolutionary state

In its interplay with the locals, and especially in promoting Ma's Way, the state showed a certain respect for local knowledge, know-how, people, and autonomy. The *LD* article cited Ma's words that "the power of mass opinions [in judging the disputes] is stronger than the power of the law. It can be proved by a byword that '[the wisdom/judgment of] three senior farmers can compete with that of a county magistrate.'"[74] With these words, Ma equated local knowledge and the masses' views with the authority of law and elevated them to a position that would be unthinkable from the perspective of legal formalism. By citing Ma, the article also showed a willingness to seek the wisdom of local elders to solve disputes, and demonstrated respect for the traditional local autonomy.

Keating confirms that the CCP allowed a certain degree of local autonomy in village construction and as a means to reenergize local government.[75] In many mediated cases reported by *LD*, influential local elders and "enlightened gentry" (*kaiming shishen* 开明士绅) were invited to participate in the discussion. Promoting community mediation and encouraging local elders to contribute their wisdom in disputes helped build popular acceptance of the judicial system by integrating local customs into legal construction. However, for a revolutionary state with a high-modernist ideology, allowing local autonomy could compromise the state's goal of reforming and mobilizing the community according to the state's designs. It was necessary for the state to bring up a group of new elites under its revolutionary programs to counter the influence of community elders. In the balance between traditional elders and new revolutionary elites, the state could play the role of mediator, pushing the reform program toward its intended direction.

In reviewing the process of state-building in twentieth-century China, it is worth noting that local elites sometimes involved themselves in and penetrated local state power, merging the state and society into a space for their activities.[76] This occurred in communist regions in the 1940s; many ward and county officials came from local elites, and Ma Xiwu was one of them. Ma Xiwu could play a key role in community affairs not

[74] "Ma Xiwu tongzhi shenpan fangshi."
[75] Keating, *Two Revolutions*, 6.
[76] My study of local educational associations and local educational bureaucrats demonstrates this. See Xiaoping Cong, *Teachers' Schools and the Making of the Modern Chinese Nation-State, 1897–1937* (Toronto: University of British Columbia Press, 2007), 83–7.

only because of his position as a state representative, but also because of his long history with the region and close ties with the local communities. This dual status allowed him to enjoy a certain authority and respect from the locals. Ma Xiwu came from an ordinary farming family in Bao'an (today's Zhidan), the home county of Liu Zhidan and a county adjacent to the Longdong region. He received only three years of literacy education in a traditional school (*sishu*) in his village, and was a farmer into his thirties.[77] In the chaotic period of the 1920s, he engaged in the activities (and may have become a member) of the Elder Brothers Society (*Gelaohui*) in his hometown and the nearby Longdong region. In 1930, when Liu Zhidan extended his activities into the Longdong region, Ma joined the revolutionary enterprise, becoming a member of the CCP in 1935. Because of his close connection with local secret societies, in December 1936 the CCP assigned Ma the special task of calling a meeting of all doyens (*daye* 大爷) from the *Gelaohui* in Longdong and the northwestern Shaanbei area. At this meeting, Ma presented himself as a "*daye*" of the Red Gang (*Hong bang* 红帮), sent to lecture on the CCP's policy in the Anti-Japanese War and seek support from the meeting's attendees for the newly arrived CCP Central Committee.[78] Beginning in 1937, he worked in Longdong as the highest authority and then as the chief-judge of the subregional court until 1946, when he moved to Yan'an to serve as the director of the High Court. Ma's previous experience of working in rural communities definitely influenced the way he handled his administrative and legal duties. Ma's personal history and his influence before the revolution helped establish his revolutionary authority as a state representative who reinforced state power. In some sense, Ma's dual identities and his work of presenting the interests of both the local community and the state indicated a new dynamic between the revolutionary state and the local community.

At the time when the state was constructing its discourse for good governance, by adopting a cultural positioning strategy, it also took in some ideas from the local community. The *LD* article presented the penetration of local values into the state's view. It ended with an intriguing remark: "This is why Comrade Ma was called 'Ma the Clear-sky' (*Ma Qingtian* 马青天) by the masses."[79] Calling certain government

[77] Liu Fengge *et al.* (comp.), *Qingyang diqu Zhonggong dangshi renwu* (The Historical Figures of CCP Members in Qingyang District) (Qingyang: The District Office of CCP History, 1992 [print]), 65–73.

[78] Liu, *Qingyang diqu Zhonggong dangshi renwu*, 65–73; *Qingyang diqu zhi*, 500–502; *Huanxian zhi*, 54. Ma Xiwu's relationship with the *Gelaohui* seems to be a sensitive issue that is avoided in most of Ma's biographies.

[79] "Ma Xiwu tongzhi de shenpan fangshi."

officials "clear-sky" has a long history in Chinese culture, and the term "*qingtian*" was mostly used for those imperial officials who demonstrated their intelligence in judging complicated cases through thorough investigations, sagacious deliberation, and fair and just verdicts. Their good judgment cleared up the temporary clouds (i.e. corrupt and incompetent judges who wrongfully convicted innocent people) in the sky and brought heavenly justice (clear sky) back to the people. The most famous clear-sky images in traditional popular culture are "Judge Bao" (Bao Zheng 包拯) and "Judge Di" (Di Renjie 狄仁杰), who are still well known as Rhadamanthus-like characters in contemporary television series, local operas, and films.[80] Ma's activities, such as circuit visits, examining prisons, personal investigation, and meeting litigants outside the courts, followed this cultural legacy of enlightened imperial judges that deliver justice.

However, from the viewpoint of revolutionary dogma, it was a bit odd for the state to accept villagers' praise of Ma as a clear-sky judge. The communist party saw the working classes as the vanguard of the revolution, rather than victims to be saved by sage-saviors. Moreover, it was the traditional image of a clear-sky official as a heroic individual that was quite contradictory to the CCP idea of organizational power in revolution. Third, the image of a clear-sky official often implied a ruling model that between a good emperor and corrupt local officials, the clear-sky official would bring imperial justice to victims, thus sweeping away the clouds created by corrupt officials.

Local communities' expectations for a clear-sky judge involved several points. First, as a strategy for resistance, the villagers may not challenge the highest authority of state, but blame the injustice they suffered on the immorality and corruption of local officials. Second, the clear-sky image represents the locals' ideas of justice and fairness – that the judge must have great integrity to conduct an investigation and to make a wise judgment. It not only demanded a high moral standard from the state at the local level, but also required it deliver justice and fairness according to local beliefs. By praising Ma as a "clear-sky" judge, *LD* was communicating an acquiescence of the party-state to local values, and encouraging other local cadres to follow Ma's model. This article also revealed the state's concern about how to deliver justice in the eyes of the local

[80] Wilt L. Idema, *Judge Bao and the Rule of Law: Eight Ballad-Stories from the Period 1250–1450* (Cambridge, MA: Harvard University Press, 2010). See unknown author, *Di Gong An* (Judge Di and the Law) (Ji'nan: Qi Lu shushe, 1993 reprint). Also see the recent Chinese television series *Judge Bao the Clear-sky* (Bao Qingtian) (director Sun Shupei, 1993) and *Genius Judge Di* (Shen tan Di Renjie) (director Qian Yanqiu, 2004–10).

people while still constructing a revolutionary legal system. By negotiating with local communities and meeting their expectations, the state, for the purpose of playing the role of educator, was willing to revive a century-old community tradition and adapt the concept of a clear-sky judge as a compromise.

Ma's Way as a judicial example and political model was not unquestioned during its time. In 1945, when the SGNBR held a legal conference, some judges questioned the definition and practice of Ma's Way as well as its effectiveness, while others criticized it as "guerrilla-warfare style" (*youji zuofeng* 游击作风).[81] Some judges demanded to clarify the line between adjudication and mediation, while others assumed that the two were complementary, and could be applied flexibly in dissolving community conflicts.[82] It was possible that geographic differences produced this variety of views on Ma's Way. However, due to the rapid victory of the CCP in national battles in the following years, discussion of these important issues and of the possible extension of Ma's Way to a much broader geographical region and more complicated social conditions was cut short. At the same time, its practice, along with the different interpretations of it by each individual judge, was directly implemented in the post-1949 judicial system.

IV. *Xinhua Daily*: showcasing SGN democracy and a prelude to a new heroine

While the *LD* articles focused on pacifying the BR by reporting exemplary cases of good governance, the story of *Feng v. Zhang* took another turn. On October 22, 1944, a half-year after the *Liberation Daily* article, *Xinhua Daily* also published a report on this case. The article was titled "A Real Case of Mediating a Marriage Dispute in the Border Region" (*Bianqu tiaojie hunyin de yi ge shili*). It singled out the story of *Feng v. Zhang* from the three cases reported in *Liberation Daily* and reworded it for its "Women's Road" column. Although *Xinhua Daily* almost duplicated the *Liberation Daily* article, the *XD* story emphasized the fact that Prefect Ma respected the woman's choice in marriage. It was not presented as a case of a woman resisting patriarchal forces, as it would be in its next stage of artistic works. However, the tone of the report introduced a dual

[81] SPA 15–73, "Bianqu tuishi, shenpanyuan lianxi huiyi fayan jilu" (The Records of the Presentations at the Joint Conference of Judges and Assistant-judges in the BR).

[82] SPA 15–79, "Bianqu tuishi, shenpanyuan lianxi huiyi fayan jilu" (The Records of the Presentations at the Joint Conference of Judges and Assistant-judges in the BR). For the details of this conference and its debate over Ma's Way, please see Cong, "Ma Xiwu's Way of Judging."

theme: a woman insisting on marrying the man of her choice, while Ma helped to settle the case by respecting the woman's decision.[83] It is obvious that a democratic state was emphasized in the story.

In the same column, another article titled "Divorces in the Border Region"[84] contextualized the previous report. This article stated that "under the democratic polity, men and women enjoy freedom of marriage." Another report on women in the Border Region covered women involved in productive work and their role in cooperative organizations and community improvement. It portrayed the women in the Border Region as living lives of self-reliance and mutual assistance, freed from old social bondage such as arranged marriages under the "democratic polity" of Yan'an. Through editing, the case of Peng'er was easily placed in the bigger picture and used to demonstrate that women in the Border Region were able to resist arranged marriages and choose their own mates with the help of the democratic government. The column drew a contrast between women under the "democratic polity" of the Border Region and those living under the gloomy "autocratic" GMD region.[85] Mediation in the legal system was thus seen as the way of democracy and mass participation in legal practice.

This slight turn in the development of the case must also be understood in another context: Yan'an, confined and isolated in China's most poverty-stricken region, was competing with its rival, the Chongqing government, to win the support of women at the national level. In the case that women, workers, and educated youth composed 70 percent of *XD*'s readers,[86] *Xinhua Daily*'s showcase of Peng'er's story certainly set up Yan'an as an example of the CCP's good governance and democratic practices to the outside world. *Xinhua Daily* also contrasted the happy picture of women in the Border Region with articles on women in Nationalist-controlled areas, where women's conditions were incredibly miserable and still suffering from old family oppression.

A half-year later, on April 11, 1945, *Xinhua Daily* journalist Li Pu again published an article on Peng'er, which covered her story in a

83 "Bianqu tiaojie hunyin de yi ge shili."

84 "Bianqu de lihun wenti" (Divorces in the Border Region), *Xinhua ribao*, October 22, 1944.

85 To highlight this point, in the same column series there were another group of articles on the plight of women in GMD region that included the story of a woman who had lost her job. See Li Jin, "Wo you shiye le – Ji yi ge nü gongwuyuan de zaoyu" (I Lost My Job Again – The Life of a Female Civil Servant), *Xinhua ribao*, October 4, 1944.

86 Xiong Fu, "Guanyu Xinhua ribao de lishi diwei jiqi tedian" (On the Historical Position of Xinhua Daily and Its Characters), *Xinhua ribao de huiyi, xuji* (A Recollection of the Xinhua Daily, A Continued Collection), Shi Ximin and Fan Jianya (eds.) (Chengdu: Sicuan renmin chubanshe, 1983), 61–74.

much more detailed manner. This story, titled "A Case of Marriage by Capture," gave more attention to Peng'er than to the fathers of the two families.[87] Written in a literary style, the article recounted the story of Peng'er's success in resisting an arranged marriage with the help of Prefect Ma, as well as the practice of open court. The additional details presented in this story included praise for the democratic nature of the BR's judicial system, which did not require a written complaint for filing a lawsuit. Moreover, it offered an egalitarian picture of the BR, a society in which everyone knew that there were no "officials" (*guan* 官) but only "men for the public [service]" (*gongjia ren* 公家人), who would serve the people. The description of the open court extolled the participation of the locals in the legal process and their ability to express their opinions, providing a strong contrast not only to the Nationalist political system, under which the majority of the people had no right to speak, but also to its judicial system, which was dominated by lawyers and legal experts. Given the environment in 1945 on the eve of victory in the war, the future of postwar China was everyone's concern. This vivid interpretation of the "New Democracy" proposed by Mao was being promoted to the educated masses in the Nationalist region.

[87] Li Pu, "Yi jian qianghun an."

6 The Qin opera and the ballad

From rebellious daughters to social mothers

In the fall of 1944, Yuan Jing, a young female teacher from Longdong Middle School (*Longdong zhongxue* 陇东中学), was called to Yan'an for her political background check. While in Yan'an she read the article "Ma Xiwu's Way of Judging" and was deeply attracted to the story of the marriage dispute. She subsequently drafted a libretto based on this article and titled it *Liu Qiao'er Goes to the Law* (*Liu Qiao'er gaozhuang*).[1] The libretto was immediately set to music by a group of young students who were lovers of local opera (*Qinqiang* 秦腔, Shaanxi opera) and staged in early 1945. In the following years, the opera was performed many times in Yan'an and its surrounding areas. Shortly after, a blind local troubadour named Han Qixiang (1915–89), who listened to someone recount the opera, created his own version of the story of Liu Qiao'er in ballad form and brought it to an even broader region of the SGNBR. Han not only changed the title to "Liu Qiao's Reunion" (*Liu Qiao tuanyuan*) but also modified the story with his own interpretations.[2] This ballad, combined with Yuan's version, later became the foundation for a new opera and a film in the 1950s, which will be discussed in Chapter 7.

The appearance of these cultural products indicates that the case of *Feng v. Zhang* was not confined within legal realm as a "pure" legal issue, but extended to a broader social sphere for a new interpretation. Yuan Jing reshaped Peng'er's story into a cultural model of womanhood in the political and cultural environment of the 1940s' SGNBR. The activities of Yuan and many other educated youth were the part of the CCP's cultural positioning project, as in Anyuan,[3] helping the party to promote the idea of self-determination and to mobilize rural women for the marriage reform. Moreover, by using various forms of cultural products for the revolutionary purpose, the party also was able to attract a number of

[1] Yuan Jing, *Liu Qiao'er gaozhuang*. The earliest publication of this libretto was by Yan'an Xinhua Bookstore in 1946 but there seems to be no trace of this original edition.

[2] Han Qixiang, *Liu Qiao tuanyuan* (Liu Qiao's Reunion) (Hong Kong: Haiyang Bookstore, 1947).

[3] See Perry, *Anyuan*.

talented youth to cultural production. Thus this chapter also addresses how this model reflected the mentality of the educated youth of the post-May Fourth generation in viewing the relationship between family and state, and their identity in the revolutionary state.

From the late 1930s to the 1940s, tens of thousands of urban-educated youth went to Yan'an. To distinguish them from those established intellectuals who gained fame in the New Culture and May Fourth Movements, I label this group of not-yet-established youth the "post-May Fourth generation"; they absorbed the spirit of the May Fourth culture but were still developing their interests and searching for their future in the 1940s' social and literary movements. Different from those established writers, this post-May Fourth generation of educated youth shaped their political views and cultural tastes under the direction of the Communist Party and were thus willing to believe in the power of the party-state and support the CCP's social reform efforts. Suffering from material shortages and political bitterness, they still held on to their faith and spirit in supporting the social reform programs and state-building projects of the CCP during the time of national crisis. Yuan Jing belonged to this group of youth, and her life trajectory and her literary path tell us much about this post-May Fourth generation. The characters she created in *Liu Qiao'er Goes to the Law* conveyed Yuan's ideas about family relations and the relationship between people and the state, ideas that were characteristic of this generation.

In the libretto, Yuan Jing created a story that successfully transformed the focus of the legal case involving two families disputing a marriage contract and the newspaper article exemplifying Ma's Way into a drama in which a young woman resists an arranged marriage with the help of the state. Most importantly, she moved the spotlight from male figures, the two fathers and Ma Xiwu to female figures, particularly to a new heroine, Liu Qiao'er, a character based on Feng Peng'er. The title *Liu Qiao'er Goes to the Law* also reveals its dual theme of a woman (Liu Qiao'er) resisting patriarchal domination and needing the support of the revolutionary state (goes to the law). She believed that a revolutionary state could and would overpower patriarchal domination and correct this local malpractice. Moreover, this revolutionary state was not solely a patriarchal or masculine power, but a state that contained matrilineal and feminine space, opposed to what Judith Stacey believes.[4] Yuan's work implied that the revolutionary state could contain a feminized space in which women

[4] Judith Stacey believes that the CCP's policy on "democratic family" was in fact the reestablishment of patriarchal domination, which she named as "patriarchal socialism." See her *Patriarchy and Socialist Revolution in China*, 108–57, 203–47.

leaders play the role of "social mother" to help younger women, thus continuing the mother–daughter genealogy and carving out women's space in the public domain.

In contrast, Han Qixiang's version of the story emphasized a heroine who faced a miserable fate but luckily achieved a happy ending (a reunion) with the help of a good government official (a clear-sky judge). It provided a competitive, comparative, even contending view of how the revolution was brought to the locals and to what degree the indigenous culture was changed under the new power.

I. The post-May Fourth generation of urban-bred youth in Yan'an: searching for their national roots and devotion to the revolution

Yuan Jing did not belong to the circle of highbrow female writers in 1940s' Yan'an, where Ding Ling 丁玲 (1904–86) and Chen Xuezhao 陈学昭 (1906–91) occupied the center of attention. Ding was a well-known female writer in the urban literary circle of the May Fourth period even before coming to Yan'an, and Chen, already famous in China's journalism with her French Ph.D. degree in literature, held a high position in *Liberation Daily*. Born at the beginning of the New Culture Movement, Yuan looked up to and was nurtured by the female writers of the May Fourth period. Like many other urban-educated youth of this time, she came to Yan'an simply to work for national salvation. It was writing the libretto of *Liu Qiao'er Goes to the Law* that permitted her entrance into Yan'an's cultural circles. Reading into this libretto and the characters it created allows us to have a better understanding of the post-May Fourth generation youth, their path, and their outlook.

Established intellectuals versus educated youth in Yan'an

Previous scholarship on intellectuals in the Yan'an period does not make a clear differentiation between the established intellectuals and the educated youth, who were still in school when the Anti-Japanese War broke out; rather, these studies have focused solely on a small group of high-profile writers such as Ding Ling and Wang Shiwei 王实味 (1906–47).[5] Moreover,

[5] For example, Merle Goldman, *Literary Dissent in Communist China* (Cambridge, MA: Harvard University Press, 1967), 1–50; Dai Qing, *Wang Shiwei and "Wild Lilies": Rectification and Purges in Chinese Communist Party, 1942–1944* (New York: M. E. Sharpe, 1994); Charles J. Alber, *Enduring the Revolution: Ding Ling and the Politics of Literature in Guomindang China* (Westport, CT: Praeger, 2001), and *Embracing the Lie: Ding*

Western scholars often emphasize the implacable relations between the party and these urban-bred writers.[6] This elitist perspective ignores the thousands of urban-educated students, both male and female, who arrived in Yan'an at the height of the national crisis. The people with urban educations who came to Yan'an in the late 1930s and 1940s can be divided into three groups: those who had already worked for the party before arriving in Yan'an; those who were previously established urban professionals, writers, and artists who worked in Yan'an's cultural institutions; and those who were young urban students with a level of education ranging from primary school to early college. Of these three groups, the first and second were very small in number. The third group, on the other hand, composed the main body of Yan'an's educated population. They were often labeled "young students" (*qingnian xuesheng* 青年学生) or "educated youth" (*zhishi qingnian* 知识青年) by the party, differentiating them from a small number of established intellectuals, such as Ding Ling, Xiao Jun 萧军 (1907–88), Wang Shiwei, and others.

Between 1938 and 1947, tens of thousands of young students from urban areas arrived in Yan'an. Based on incomplete data, from 1937 to 1939 alone, more than 6,000 youths were sent to Yan'an via the various communist organizations in just three cities, Lanzhou, Wuhan, and Chongqing. Around 1938 and 1939, of the 20,124 students in Kangda 抗大 (*Kang Ri junzheng daxue* 抗日军政大学, Military and Political Academy for Resisting the Japanese) alone, more than 60 percent were educated youth from urban areas.[7] The Yan'an leaders promoted the rural base area as the center of resistance to attract urban youth, and set up channels for students to go to Yan'an. The war shattered the dream of many youth in continuing their secondary and tertiary educations, and so the BR government established a number of schools and training programs to recruit them. Kangda, the Academy of Marxism-Leninism (*Ma-Lie zhuyi xueyuan* 马列学院), Yan'an Women's University (*Yan'an nüzi daxue* 延安女子大学), Lu Xun Academy of the Arts (*Lu Xun yishu xueyuan* 鲁迅艺术学院, or *LuYi* 鲁艺), Shaanbei Public Schools (*Shaanbei gongxue* 陕北公学), Yan'an University (*Yan'an daxue* 延安大学), and many other short training programs (*qing xun ban* 青训班) were opened to these urban youths during this time. Particular attention was given to female students: in the short period between its establishment in 1939 and its

Ling and the Politics of Literature in the People's Republic of China (Westport, CT: Praeger, 2004).

[6] Goldman, *Literary Dissent in Communist China*, 1–50.

[7] Wang Feng, "Kang zhan shiqi 'zhishi qingnian ben fu Yan'an' xianxiang" (On the Phenomenon of 'Educated Youth Going to Yan'an' During the Anti-Japanese War Period), *Ershi yi shiji* (Twenty-First Century) (Hong Kong) 114(8) (August 2009): 51–8.

merger with Yan'an University in 1941, the Yan'an Women's University trained more than 1,000 students from urban areas.[8]

From May 1941 to June 1942, the CCP Central Committee issued many theoretical documents, reviewing its history while examining the previous "failures" in the revolution. Beginning in 1942, the so-called "rectification campaign" (*zhengfeng yundong* 整风运动) spread in the SGN Border Region, mainly aimed at cadres at each level of both the party and the government. At the same time, the campaign was also extended to the cultural institutions in which intellectuals were concentrated, such as *Liberation Daily* and Yan'an Lu Yi. In the campaign, most cadres and intellectuals bore the brunt of criticism for their "dogmatism," "factionalism," and their elitist attitude toward ordinary people; their loyalty to the party was questioned as well.[9]

In academic studies of intellectuals of this period, Ding Ling and Wang Shiwei receive special attention because of their panache, daring, and satirical writing style that fitted China's urban culture of the time, which had been largely influenced by the West. Merle Goldman sees these figures as China's dissenting writers who had a strong presence in opposing the party.[10] Like many others, Dai Qing's sympathetic study also focuses on Ding and Wang.[11] Chen Yung-fa emphasizes the strategies and processes that Mao used in the rectification campaign to realize the goal of reforming, and to gain the power of, the party that formed the "shadow" of the Yan'an period.[12] Gao Hua follows suit in his book that simplifies the entire rectification campaign into a power struggle in which Mao manipulated everyone in order to reach his goal.[13] However, the model

[8] Yan'an shi funü yundong zhi bianzuan weiyuanhui (comp.), *Yan'an shi funü yundong zhi* (Historical Records of the Women's Movement in Yan'an City) (Xi'an: Shaanxi renmin chubanshe, 2001), 108.

[9] Qiang Xiaochu, *Yan'an zhengfeng yundong huiyilu* (My Recollection of the Yan'an Rectification Campaign) (Harbin: Heilongjiang renmin chubanshe, 1958); Yang Junchen, *Huiyi Yan'an zhengfeng yundong* (Recalling the Yan'an Rectification Campaign) (Changsha: Hunan renmin chubanshe, 1957); *Yan'an zhengfeng yundong bianxiezu, Yan'an zhengfeng yundong jishi* (The Chronicle of the Yan'an Rectification Campaign) (Beijing: Qiushi chubanshe, 1982); Gao Xinmin and Zhang Shujun, *Yan'an zhengfeng shi lu* (The Historical Records of the Yan'an Rectification Campaign) (Hangzhou: Zhejiang renmin chubanshe, 2000); Gao Putang and Zeng Luping, *Yan'an qiangjiu yundong shimo – 200 ge qinlizhe de jiyi* (On the Whole Yan'an Campaign History of Rescuing Delinquents – The 200 Person Experience Person's Recall) (Hong Kong: Time International, 2008). The English title of the last book is from its own translation.

[10] Goldman, *Literary Dissent in Communist China*, 1–50.

[11] Dai, *Wang Shiwei and "Wild Lilies."*

[12] Chen Yung-fa, *Yan'an de yingying* (Yan'an's Shadow) (Taipei: Institute of Modern History, Academia Sinica, 1990).

[13] Gao Hua, *Hong taiyang shi zengyang shengqi de? Yan'an zhengfeng yundong de lailongqumai* (How Did the Sun Rise over Yan'an? –The Origin and History of the Rectification Movement) (Hong Kong: Chinese University Press, 2000).

of the party versus intellectuals described by Goldman and others hardly explains Ding Ling's life and her work in the 1940s.[14] In some studies, Ding's life is split into two periods with two identities: a brave fighter against the GMD regime, and a liar after the Yan'an period, leaving a complete blank in her life in the 1940s.[15] These studies take the intellectual life of Yan'an out of historical context, and view it through an ahistorical lens of Cold War ideology.

It was during the Yan'an period that this group of young students made themselves into party and military leaders, as well as government cadres, and some of them became writers, journalists, and artists. Their works and reports mirrored their lives in the SGNBR, as they absorbed folk culture to create a new literature that reflected their understanding of Chinese society, their achievements, loves and marriages, and the pain of life and politics.[16] Without including these young students and their life experiences in Yan'an, we cannot achieve a complete picture of both the Chinese revolution and Chinese literature.

Yuan Jing came from a very wealthy family in Beijing, much like the one described in Ba Jin's novel *Family*, in which an extended family of multiple generations lived under the same roof. The males of the family had a long history of holding imperial official positions, and the women they married also came from equally outstanding backgrounds.[17] Inspired by the May Fourth movement and radical social theories, Yuan became involved in communist-led student movements and then became a CCP member in 1935. While participating in these social movements, she fell in love with Zhao Meisheng 赵梅生 (aka Zhao Changyuan or Zhao Zuolin, 1906–45) and married him. Zhao graduated from Beiping (Beijing) University (Beida) and became a college teacher in the 1930s. He was also the leader of the Beiping student movement and the

[14] Goldman, *Literary Dissent in Communist China*, 1–50.

[15] Alber, *Enduring the Revolution* and *Embracing the Lie*.

[16] A collection of memoirs of this group of people was published in 1992. After forty years, though they had experienced a series of political campaigns since the late 1950s, the authors still wrote about their Yan'an experience with a joyful tone and appreciation. See Yan'an Lu Yi huiyi lu bianweihui (comp.), *Yan'an Lu Yi huiyilu* (A Collection of Memoirs from the Yan'an Lu Xun Academy of the Arts) (Beijing: Guangming ribao chubanshe, 1992). This ethos also surprised Zhu Hongzhao, who observed that in his 1990s' interviews with the members of this group, the eyes of the former young students shone when they talked about their life in Yan'an. See Zhu Hongzhao, *Yan'an: Richang shenghuo zhong de lishi*, 309–10. Other contemporary authors who interviewed this group also offered the same observation. See Huang Renke, *Lu Yi ren – hongse yishujia men* (People of Lu Yi – Red Artists) (Beijing: Zhonggong zhongyang dangxiao chubanshe, 2001); Wang Peiyuan, *Yan'an Lu Yi fengyun lu* (The History of Time at Yan'an Lu Yi) (Guilin: Guangxi shifan daxue chubanshe, 2004).

[17] See "Yuan Xiaoyuan," Wikipedia: http://zh.wikipedia.org/wiki/袁晓园 (accessed May 9, 2012).

communist party organization in the city. In 1934, the Nationalist government arrested Yuan and Zhao for their radical activities, but they were soon released with the help of Yuan's family connections.[18] Both were clearly children of the New Cultural and May Fourth movements and activists in the urban communist movements. Their marriage perfectly fitted the model of "revolution plus love" that represented the ideal relationship for radical, urban, educated women outside the family during this period.[19]

After the Japanese-occupied Beiping in 1938, Yuan and her husband drifted from place to place, promoting resistance movements, and eventually arrived in Yan'an in 1940. During their travels they both lost their proof of party membership and their connection with the party organization. Once they arrived in Yan'an, due to Zhao's educational credential and his fame in the urban student movement, he was assigned to the position of deputy-headmaster for the newly established Longdong Middle School. As his wife, Yuan was assigned to be a teacher of literature in the same school.[20]

From 1942 to 1943, Yuan was working for the famous 359 Brigade of the Eighth Route Army near the Longdong area and assisting its propaganda team in staging small *yangge* (秧歌) plays.[21] During the 1940s, *yangge* was a very popular performing art in the SGN region because it was viewed as the reinvention of rural culture and a national form of art. The advantage of the *yangge* play was that it consisted of one scene with a few characters for a quick view of one piece of a story.[22] It appears that Yuan's

[18] Yuan Zhaoxiu (comp.), *Longdong zhongxue xiao shi* (History of Longdong Middle School) (Lanzhou: Gansu wenhua chubanshe, 2000), 180–1; Jiang Changren, "Zhao Zuolin," in Wang Xiaoting *et al.* (comp.), *Beida yinglie* (The Heroic Alumni of Beijing University), ser. 3 (Beijing: Beijing daxue chubanshe, 1997), 183–94; Gu Zhuoxin, Wang Xinsan, Yuan Jing, Yuan Junshi, and Zhao Zuowei, "Huainian Zhao Meisheng tongzhi" (In Memory of Comrade Zhao Meisheng), *Renmin ribao*, August 10, 1986; San Mu, "Beida xuesheng Zhao Meisheng de chuanqi rensheng" (The Legendary Life of a Student of Beida, Zhao Meisheng) *Dangshi bolan* (Broad View of the Party's History) 2 (February 2006): 25–7.

[19] See Liu Jianmei, *Revolution Plus Love: Literary History, Women's Bodies, and Thematic Repetition in Twentieth-Century Chinese Fiction* (Honolulu: University of Hawai'i Press, 2003).

[20] See Ma Wenrui, "Chuang ban chuqi de Longdong zhongxue" (Longdong Middle Schools in Its Early Years), in *Qingyang xian wenshi ziliao, di yi ji* (Historical and Cultural Documents of Qingyang County), series 1 (publisher unknown, 1999), 153–7; Yuan Jing, "Zai Longdong zhongxue de rizi li" (Life at Longdong Middle School), in *Qingyang xian wenshi ziliao*, di yi ji, 161–2; Yuan Zhaoxiu, *Longdong zhongxue xiao shi*, 154–5.

[21] Yuan Zhaoxiu, *Longdong zhongxue xiao shi*, 180–1.

[22] Hung Chang-tai, *War and Popular Culture: Resistance in Modern China, 1937–1945* (Berkeley: University of California Press, 1994), 230–1; Ellen R. Judd, "New Yangge: The Case of 'A Worthy Sister-in-Law'," *CHINOPERL Papers* 10 (1981): 167–86; David Holm, *Art and Ideology in Revolutionary China* (Oxford: Clarendon Press, 1991).

literary interest was awakened at this time. In fall 1944, Yuan and Zhao were sent to Yan'an separately to undergo political background checks in the Security Department of the Border Region (*Bianqu bao'an chu* 边区保安处).[23] The major issues to be clarified in this background check were probably their prison experiences in the early 1930s, the political issues in the regional party organization under Zhao's leadership, their drifting from place to place, their short stay on Lushan Hill 庐山,[24] Yuan's family connections with the Nationalist Party,[25] and the fact that they had no proof of Communist Party membership.[26] Yan'an was a place of heartbreak for Yuan: Zhao Meisheng died from a recurrence of tuberculosis that resulted from poor living conditions in the cold winter of early 1945 during his political background check.[27] But it was also the outset of Yuan's new life. In Yan'an, Yuan Jing became a writer and started to develop her literary career from which she gained a new marriage. The publication of the libretto and the performance of *Liu Qiao'er Goes to the Law* made her well known in Yan'an's literary and art circles.[28]

Yuan Jing's literary career and the national form: from Liu Qiao'er *to* The Story of New Heroic Sons and Daughters

In May 1942, Mao Zedong gave a speech at the Yan'an Forum on Literature and Art (*Yan'an wenyi zuotanhui* 延安文艺座谈会), which was published in *Liberation Daily* in October 1943 as one of the guiding documents for the rectification campaign. This speech called for literary and artistic workers to go out among the people and use their creativity to serve the working class and the revolution.[29] Mao's speech is

[23] Hao Zaijin, "Pingju Liu Qiao'er yu san wei nüxing de chuanqi jingli" (Ping Opera Liu Qiao'er and the Legendary Experience of Three Women), *Dangshi bolan* 2 (2005): 25–7.

[24] Around the end of 1937, Zhao and Yuan stayed at a rest home in Lushan Hill for months during Zhao's TB recurrence. See *Beida yinglie*, ser. 3, 183–94. In the 1930s, Chiang Kaishek built his summer alcove in Lushan Hill; many Nationalist programs for training special agents for penetrating the BR were also located there at this time. This was probably the reason that the political background check was conducted.

[25] Yuan Jing's eldest sister, Yuan Xiaoyuan, her husband, and his father all held high positions in the Nationalist government.

[26] Ma Wenrui, "Chuang ban chuqi de Longdong zhongxue."

[27] See San Mu, *Jiu rizi, jiu renwu* (The Old Days and the People of that Time) (Guangzhou: Huacheng chubanshe, 2007), 28; and *Beida yinglie*, 183–94.

[28] Gao Minfu and Yuan Jing, "Zanmen sui bian sui chang ba" (Let's Sing while Composing), in Shaan-Gan-Ning xiezuo qu (comp.), *Yan'an diqu geming wenhua shiliao ji* (A Collection of the Historical Documents on Revolutionary Culture in Yan'an Region) (Yan'an: Yan'an diqu wenhua wenwu ju print, 1991), 71–84.

[29] Mao Zedong, "Zai Yan'an wenyi zuotan hui shang de jianghua" (Speeches at the Yan'an Forum on Literature and Art), *Mao Zedong xuanji* (Selected Works of Mao Zedong) (Beijing: Renmin chubanshe, 1963), 804–35.

often viewed as a turning point in the history of modern Chinese literature and art. However, Chinese scholars have noted that even before the speech, there was already an ongoing debate in literary circles regarding the national form of literature and art, how to eliminate the colonial influence, and the search for a national literary form for China.[30] In fact, Mao's speech should be seen as the conclusion of this debate, rather than the beginning of a new one.

According to Wang Hui, the political intention of this movement was to emphasize the national characteristics of literary form and to use local languages in literary works, thus establishing Chinese subjectivity in literature and politics against the colonial urbanity that had dominated Chinese literary style and aesthetic concept since the early twentieth century. It also embodied Mao's desire to win self-determination from the international communist movement dominated by the USSR and the Comintern, thus making the CCP a more independent party.[31] The movement began with questioning the urban literature produced since the beginning of the twentieth century, because this type of literature was inextricably linked to intellectuals' previous urban experiences in a semi-colonial environment, in which these writers often expressed frustration with their subaltern status.[32] The movement encouraged writers to search for a national form by absorbing the vitality of popular culture, rural culture, and local languages. In this way, intellectuals could rediscover the roots of the Chinese nation's culture and connect with the people.[33] The Yan'an movement further helped intellectuals to disentangle themselves from their previous colonial complex, their urban-oriented tastes, and victim mentality, in order to gain strength from the spring of the national culture.

If we look at Yuan Jing's literary path as well as that of her second husband, Kong Jue 孔厥 (1914–66), we see the transformation of Yuan and Kong from young urban students to stars in the literary and artistic fields during this period.[34] They voluntarily combined state ideology with local ethical values in their writings, searching for a national form

[30] Wang Hui, "Difang xingshi, fangyan tuyu yu kang-Ri zhanzheng shiqi 'minzu xingshi' de zhenglun," 237–81.
[31] *Ibid.*
[32] Hershatter, "The Subaltern Talks Back."
[33] Wang Hui, "Difang xingshi, fangyan tuyu yu kang-Ri zhanzheng shiqi 'minzu xingshi' de zhenglun."
[34] In the same period, a constellation of new writers appeared among this group of the post-May Fourth generation, such as Zhao Shuli, Sun Li, Liu Baiyu, Li Ji, Yang Shuo, Zhou Erfu, and Ma Feng. See Liu Zengjie (comp.), *Zhongguo jiefang qu wenxue shi* (History of Literature in the Liberated Region) (Zhengzhou: Henan daxue chubanshe, 1988), 147–71.

to present their works. After finishing *Liu Qiao'er Goes to the Law*, Yuan began to work with the group of writers, artists, and poets she used to admire before she came to Yan'an.[35] She soon fell in love with one of them, Kong Jue, and married him in fall 1946. At that time, Kong was a rising star in Yan'an literary circles. Born into a poor family in Suzhou, Kong had financial difficulty completing his secondary education but held on to a dream of creative writing. After the outbreak of the war, he came to Yan'an and entered Lu Yi in 1938. During his study and work at Lu Yi, he became a party member and published a number of short stories; most famous were "The Suffering One" (*Ku ren'er* 苦人儿) and "A Story of a Woman Whose Life Turned Around" (*Yi ge nüren fanshen de gushi* 一个女人翻身的故事). These stories are about women who suffered under the old "feudal" family system and changed their lives under the CCP's leadership.[36] Both were first published in *LD* and then included in the collection *The Suffered* (*Shou ku ren* 受苦人), published by Yan'an Xinhua Bookstore, which was considered a great honor for a writer at that time.

In 1946, Yuan and Kong continued their professional collaboration by co-authoring a musical drama, *Lan Huahua*,[37] which seemed like a perfect gift to themselves upon their wedding in August 1946.[38] It is possible that the success of *The White-Haired Girl* (*Bai mao nü* 白毛女) in Yan'an inspired them to adapt this folktale into a modern melodrama. Unlike the drama of *The White-Haired Girl*, which originated from a real story and later became a revolutionary legend,[39] the story of *Lan Huahua* was already well known in the region, as discussed in Chapter 2. The melodrama was performed by the newly established Central Orchestra (*Zhongyang guanxian yue tuan* 中央管弦乐团) of Yan'an in early 1947, and critical reviews of it were published in *LD* on February 23.[40] Following the basic structure of the folktale but adding political elements and meaning, this melodrama tells the story of a rich and bullying landlord who forces his tenant's beautiful daughter, Lan Huahua, to marry his

[35] See interview with Qin Wenhu, June 26, 2012 (Qin was Yuan's secretary from the 1970s to 1980s). See Gao Minfu and Yuan Jing, "Zanmen sui bian sui chang ba," 71–84.

[36] Lu Zonglin and Wang Zaijue, "Kong Jue shi lue" (Short Biography of Kong Jue), *Xin wenxue shiliao* (Historical Documents on New Literature) 3 (1985): 165–8.

[37] "Lan Huahua jijiang yanzou" (The Forthcoming Performance of Lan Huahua), *Jiefang ribao*, August 20, 1946.

[38] See *Xie Juezai riji*, p. 964.

[39] See Meng Yue, "Baimaonü yanbian de qishi – jianlun Yan'an wenyi de lishi duo zhi xing" (The Revelation from the Evolution of White-Haired Girl – On the Multi-dimensional Nature of Yan'an Literature in Historical Context), in Meng Yue, *Ren, lishi, jiayuan: wenhua piping san diao* (Humans, History, and Homeland: Cultural Critics in Three Tones) (Beijing: Renmin wenxue chubanshe, 2006), 251–76.

[40] "Bitan Lan Huahua" (A Review of Lan Huahua), *Jiefang ribao*, February 23, 1947.

son. Huahua suffers in the landlord's home and gives birth to a child in a pigpen, which leads to the death of the child. This suffering turns Huahua from a beautiful girl to a blind madwoman. In the end, the coming of communist power saves her and her father from their suffering.[41]

The highly critical reviews seem to indicate that this musical drama was not very successful. We should remember that 1947 was no longer the time of the United Front; instead, the CCP and the GMD were embroiled in civil war. While landlords had formerly been tolerated, by 1947 the CCP had launched the land reform that aimed to eliminate the landlord class. Against this background, reviewers pointed out that though *Lan Huahua* served the purpose of supporting the ongoing land reform, it failed to cast strong models of resistance in both the father and the daughter. The review compared its structure, characters, and acts to *The White-Haired Girl*, pointing out many similarities.[42] In comparing Yuan and Kong's work to *The White-Haired Girl*, it appeared to be a duplicate.

After this show, Yuan and Kong continued their search for a national form of literature by going to the central Hebei revolutionary base area (*Ji zhong genjudi* 冀中根据地) to help the land reform campaign. Here their literary life reached a new peak. In 1949, they finished a novel, *The Story of New Heroic Sons and Daughters* (*Xin er nü yingxiong zhuan* 新儿女英雄传),[43] based on the true story of a woman cadre from the village in which they worked.[44] This novel tells the story of ordinary men and women fighting to protect their land in the war and revolution; the hero and heroine, who share similar values, fall in love. The novel's success was due not only to its borrowed model of "revolution plus love" but also its shift from the city to a rural ground, as well as its traditional writing form. Its title echoes a popular Qing novel, *The Story of Heroic Sons and Daughters* (*Er nü yingxiong zhuan* 儿女英雄传) by Wen Kang 文康 (1820s?–1870s?) that portrayed the loves and adventures of a group of sons and daughters from literati-official families.[45] What was new about Yuan-Kong's story was that the heroes and heroines in the title were a group of ordinary farmers; the authors praised their courage in the Anti-Japanese War and told their romantic story. Moreover, in writing a contemporary novel they abandoned the prevalent urban elite style introduced from the West,

41 *Ibid.*
42 *Ibid.*
43 Yuan Jing and Kong Jue, *Xin ernü yingxiong zhuan* (The Story of New Heroic Sons and Daughters) (Beijing: Renmin wenxue chubanshe, 2006 reprint).
44 San Mu, *Jiu rizi, jiu renwu*, 32–3.
45 Liu Zengjie, *Zhongguo jiefang qu wenxue shi*, 179–85; Yuan Xingpei (chief comp.), *Zhongguo wenxue shi* (History of Chinese Literature), vol. IV (Beijing: Gaodeng jiaoyu chubanshe, 1999), 464–6.

instead adopting the "traditional chapter-structured novel" (*zhanghui ti xiaoshuo* 章回体小说) that originated from story-telling (*shuo shu* 说书) among the rural populace. Thus Yuan and Kong combined content and form in writing a perfect Chinese story of rural men and women.

The novel was well received when it was first published as a serialized story in the *People's Daily* (*Renmin ribao* 人民日报) in 1949; it was immediately printed by the Haiyan Bookstore in Shanghai in September 1949, then several other publishing houses followed suit. In 1956, China's top publisher of literature, the People's Literature Press (*Renmin wenxue chubanshe* 人民文学出版社), printed over 3.8 million copies. It was translated into more than ten languages and developed into a film that received many international and national prizes in the 1950s.[46] This was the peak of Yuan's literary life; none of her later works surpassed it.

II. New images of women under the revolutionary party-state

Yuan's libretto, *Liu Qiao'er Goes to the Law*, should be understood in light of this historical context and her experience in the revolutionary base area. By crafting a motherless heroine (though contrary to the actual story, see below), Yuan not only carried on the legacy of the May Fourth daughters as rebels against patriarchal family, but also demonstrated her elitist view of rural mothers, who were often portrayed as backward and fatuous by Yuan and other revolutionary writers. Given her view of rural biological mothers, Yuan needed to invent a "social mother" who represented the revolutionary state, carving a feminine space inside the masculine state.

New images of women: the rebellious daughter

Yuan Jing's work was welcome not only because it fitted the needs of revolutionary reform, but also because it catered to local tastes to a certain extent. Yuan Jing's literary writing reflected the ideas circulated by the publication of Mao's 1942 talk at the Yan'an Art Forum. In *Liu Qiao'er*

[46] Yuan Zhaoxiu, *Longdong zhongxue xiao shi*, 180–1; Song Naiqian and Wu Xiu, "Suiyue wuhen, shengming buxi – fangwen zhuming nü zuojia Yuan Jing" (No Trace of Time but Life Has Never Stopped – Interview with Famous Female Writer Yuan Jing), *Hua Xia changshou* (Longevity in China) 5 (1999): 38–9; San Mu, *Jiu rizi, jiu renwu*, 32–3; also see Tianjin tushuguan (library), "Jin men qun xing: Yuan Jing," http://dlibrary.tjl.tj.cn/jmqx/renwu/yj.htm (accessed May 12, 2012); "Yuan Jing and Xin ernü yingxiong zhuan" (Yuan Jing and the Story of New Heroic Sons and Daughters), http://news.enorth.com.cn/system/2005/09/06/001111863.shtml (accessed May 12, 2012).

Goes to the Law, she tried to combine the revolutionary idea of marriage with certain forms and values from popular culture.[47] Meng Yue's study of *The White-Haired Girl* shows that its reinvention also included the adoption of local culture, mixing revolutionary ideology with local values that would be acceptable to the villagers.[48]

The true heroine in the libretto, of course, is Liu Qiao'er.[49] Unlike the pale urban bourgeois women straying in their pursuit of love[50] or the New Women struggling in their stressful urban lives,[51] Qiao'er is presented as a young rural woman who is beautiful, healthy, smart, courageous, and industrious, but also longing for a happy marriage. By following the revolutionary spirit of "self-determination," she bravely protests her arranged marriage and the unjust ruling by the local government. The story centers on the dynamics between Qiao'er and her father, Qiao'er and the horrendous landlord, and Qiao'er and Prefect Ma. Through these dynamics, the themes of anti-patriarchy and class tension between the rich and the poor (not yet a political struggle until the period covered in Chapter 7) are brought into the marriage decision, thus defining the heroine's revolutionary political character.

At the beginning, Qiao'er's industriousness is embodied in her weaving work, which she took up as a response to the BR government's call for self-reliance in the Grand Productive Campaign. While on the way to turn in her finished cotton yarn to the government-run cooperative, she is harassed by landlord Wang Shouchang, learning that her father has betrothed her to this disgusting man. In a supposedly chance meeting actually arranged by her neighbor, Auntie Li, Qiao'er sees her former fiancé, Zhu'er 柱儿 (modeled on Zhang Bo), and discovers that he is not mentally disabled, as her father had claimed. She finds out that he is in fact the leader of a production team (*bian gong dui* 变工队), a handsome and healthy young man with the same diligent spirit as her own. Qiao'er's choice of marriage mate is based on both revolutionary principles and the local tradition: after comparing the ugly old landlord to Zhu'er, she was more in favor of the latter's young and strong physique, as well as his diligent and decent character, the value and aesthetics

47 Hao Zaijin, "Pingju Liu Qiao'er yu san wei nüxing de chuanqi jingli."

48 Meng Yue, "Baimaonü yanbian de qishi – jianlun Yan'an wenyi de lishi duo zhi xing," 251–76.

49 Yuan Jing, *Liu Qiao'er gaozhuang*. In the following, all references come from this libretto unless otherwise specified.

50 Such as Ms. Sophie in Ding Ling's "Ms. Sophie's Diary." See *Ding Ling wenji* (The Collected Works of Ding Ling) (Changchun: Jilin sheying chubanshe, 2004), 44–84.

51 See the 1930s' leftwing films, such as *New Women* (Xin nüxing) (directed by Cai Chusheng, 1934).

often presented in traditional dramas and folklores, and championed by the revolutionary government.

Qiao'er's strong character and rebellious image are established by the confrontation with her father, Liu Yangui, indicating a woman resisting patriarchal power. In reality, Feng Yangui was an ordinary farmer who benefited from the communist land reform and worked for the government, as explained in Chapter 1. However, in the play Liu Yangui is portrayed as a cunning and calculating itinerant vendor, a scalawag, and a drunkard. This change had a certain significance in both revolutionary discourse and popular culture. In an agricultural society, a vendor and drunken scalawag belonged to a marginalized and rootless group who lived by taking advantage of others. They also represented a negative image in the BR Grand Productive Campaign in the 1940s, in which everyone was mobilized to be productive. This character represented the traditional image of small vendors, who were usually mercenary in nature, demonstrated by the way he treated his own daughter as a commodity. At the beginning of the scene in which the matchmaker visits him, he is drunk in a messy home that indicates his meager financial conditions. He tricks both naïve Qiao'er and Zhu'er's short-tempered father with lies to get them to agree to the dismissal of the engagement. Through the unfolding of Liu's scheme, a vivid image of a village wretch is presented on the stage. This negative image of the father also fitted the state's purpose of attacking the patriarchal family while providing the daughter with a good reason for rebellion. His pursuit of more betrothal gifts signifies his patriarchal identity and positions him in the old feudal system.

Qiao'er's class consciousness is concentrated in her abhorrence of a parasitic and ugly landlord, and her rejection of his lustful harassment and addiction to opium smoking and gambling. The character of Wang Shouchang is based on a real person, Zhu Shouchang, to whom Peng'er's father had engaged her in March 1943. In reality, there is no mention of Zhu's age, family background, occupation, or appearance in any official documents and even newspaper reports. According to Feng Zhiqin's 1982 memoir, she heard that Zhu was more than ten years older than herself,[52] which would still make Zhu younger than forty, but this has not been officially confirmed. The only thing we know about him from legal documents is the fact that he (or his family) had the plentiful resources to offer a higher amount of *caili* to Peng'er's father. The case file states that the government confiscated this property as a penalty for purchasing

[52] Feng Zhiqin, "Huiyi Ma Xiwu tongzhi," 145–53.

a marriage, but it was also possible that the property was later returned to him, as discussed in Chapter 5.

However, Yuan's libretto portrays Wang Shouchang as a rich landlord (*lao cai* 老财) who is not only old (forty-eight), but also lewd, an opium smoker, and a crippled man with a pockmarked face. In defiance of the BR's policy of prohibiting buying/selling marriage, he secretly conducts a purchased marriage through a matchmaker, believing that his money allows him do anything he wants, including buying Qiao'er's youth and beauty. This character embodies everything disgusting to both revolutionary ideas and local folk culture. Wang's opium smoking and gambling could potentially corrupt the revolutionary spirit of the BR. Wang belonged to an enemy camp only temporarily tolerated by the revolutionary state at the time of the United Front. Creating a contrast between an old, ugly, lewd man and a pretty young woman appealed to the locals, who always sympathized with beautiful young women in ill-matched marriages, as in "Lan Huahua." Wang's harassment of Qiao'er and bragging about his fortune expose his evil nature in contrast to Qiao'er's belief in state policy, which encouraged citizens to lead a hardworking and self-reliant life. Here revolutionary ideas penetrate the local values that contribute to Qiao'er's principled image. Given the fact that Yuan's creation of this image occurred during the Second United Front, Qiao'er's aversion to Wang Shouchang mainly focuses on his appearance, age, and morality, rather than his class background, which would become the main target in the changing political environment after 1947, as discussed in Chapter 7.

The idea that Qiao'er follows the principle of self-determination is enriched by her choice of Zhu'er, who contrasts strongly with Wang Shouchang in all aspects, including age, physical features, family conditions, and moral values, all of which have local roots, as discussed in Chapter 2. In the original legal writ and *LD* article, Zhang Bo existed in his father's shadow. We have no knowledge of him, except that he was two years older than Peng'er, met Peng'er at a local event, and participated in the kidnapping. In Yuan Jing's libretto, Zhu'er has already escaped his father's shadow and has become a leader of a youth team for the production campaign. This new image of Zhu'er shows both the physical and moral qualities of his character. He rejects his father's idea of kidnapping Qiao'er and refuses to take part in it; instead, he urges his father to resort to the law and government for a solution, a detail totally opposite to the historical fact. This alteration not only makes Zhu'er a productive worker but also an obedient citizen, part of a young generation of rural males rejecting old and brutal traditions that had been banned by the revolutionary state. It is these exact qualities that attract Qiao'er. Needless to say, this new value of preferring a marriage mate on the basis of emotional affection and good moral quality also substantiated the state's call for marriage based on "emotional relations" (*gan qing*) between men and women. At the same time, through the image of Liu Qiao'er, it urged young women to make their choices based on such values instead of collaborating with their fathers for money-oriented marriages. The new image of Qiao'er places her choice against the outdated practices of feudalism and manifests the new spirit of self-determination.

The new image of middle-aged women: a social mother

In the same libretto, Yuan created another character, a middle-aged woman, Auntie Li (*Li shen* 李婶). Her role is to assist and guide the rebellious Qiao'er like a mother, but she is more than a mother – she also represents the state. Auntie Li is not only Qiao'er's neighbor, but also the director of the village women's association (*funü zhuren* 妇女主任). She cares about Qiao'er and frequently offers comfort to this "motherless child" (*mei niang de haizi* 没娘的孩子).[53] In the libretto, when Qiao'er accidentally learns from Wang Shouchang about their betrothal, she is shocked. Facing her father's betrayal and the possibility of marrying this disgusting man, Qiao'er seeks help from her substitute mother. Due to Auntie Li's political status, she not only comforts Qiao'er, as a biological mother would, she also provides Qiao'er with assistance and guidance under state policy. Following the government injunction against buying/selling marriage, and promoting self-determination in marriage, Auntie Li arranges an occasion that enables Qiao'er to see Zhu'er working in the field, where he can display all his good qualities. Seeing Zhu'er with her own eyes quells Qiao'er's doubts and makes up her mind. In this case, Auntie Li plays the role of social mother, guiding a young woman to find the correct path.

Yuan Jing made Qiao'er a motherless woman whose marriage is decided solely by her father, but she receives assistance, protection, and guidance from someone outside the family, a female representative of the revolutionary state. However, the historical reality was quite different. In her 1982 memoir, Feng Zhiqin recalled that it was her mother who brought her to that decisive event where she was introduced to Zhang Bo. Her mother supported her decision to marry Zhang Bo and even informed the Zhangs about Peng'er's wishes.[54] This point was also

[53] Yuan Jing, *Liu Qiao'er gaozhuang*.
[54] Feng Zhiqin, "Huiyi Ma Xiwu tongzhi."

confirmed in my 2005 interview with Feng Zhiqin.[55] It was obvious that Peng'er's mother disagreed with her husband regarding their daughter's marriage and played an active role in helping her daughter get out of it. Bringing Peng'er to that local event seems to have been part of her mother's plan, and the kidnapping might have been a mother–daughter conspiracy against the father's faithless decision. Although the newspaper reports did not mention Peng'er's mother, in a fictional work an author could always invent a character to fit into his/her intended plan. Some sources even claim that Yuan interviewed Ma Xiwu when composing her libretto.[56] If this was the case, she would have been informed about the actions of Peng'er's mother. It is obvious that the absence of the mother character was her intention. This raises the question: why did Yuan Jing omit Peng'er's mother and instead create a motherlike character to offer assistance and guidance to Qiao'er in her struggle for a good marriage?

III. A revolution that transformed the mother–daughter relationship

If Qiao'er represents a rebellious daughter who echoes her urban counterpart in the May Fourth discourse, the character of Auntie Li had no equivalent in the literature of the same period. The conventional study of May Fourth literature often follows the meta-theory of Western feminism that defines gender in terms of power relations between males and females. This perspective has overlooked how Chinese women defined their positions and gender identities in dynamic relations with multiple layers in the network of family. In the multi-dimensional relations, women cast their identities not only in relation to fathers and husbands, but also mothers, brothers, sons, and daughters. Thus the character of Auntie Li represents a sign of the important transformation of the mother–daughter relationship in twentieth-century Chinese society, which occurred on the foundation of isomorphic and correlative relations between family and state, extending the family relationship to state and public domains. By transferring the mother–daughter bond from the domestic to the public domain, Auntie Li also offers an example for Chinese female political leaders who sought to create a feminine space within the masculine modern state.

[55] Interview with Feng Zhiqin, July 21, 2005. Also see Hao Zaijin, "Pingju Liu Qiao'er yu san wei nüxing de chuanqi jingli."

[56] See Hao Zaijin, "Pingju Liu Qiao'er yu san wei nüxing de chuanqi jingli." This is highly possible, since Yuan was in Yan'an during the time that Ma frequently stayed there.

The May Fourth daughters: leaving their mothers behind

The revolution of the family in the twentieth century was a multi-dimensional transformation that involved not only changes in love relations between young females and males, but also in the bonds between parents and children. The New Culture and May Fourth Movements spawned a large number of literary works that emphasized the antagonism between the patriarchal family, dominated by old-fashioned fathers, and a young generation of educated men and women armed with newly introduced ideas. In these social conflicts, the image of the father bore the brunt of the attack, while the mother's changing relations with her children, particularly with her daughters, in the social domain was neglected.

The image of mothers became ambiguous in the anti-traditional and anti-patriarchal movements of the 1910s and 1920s. Sally Taylor Lieberman suggests that in the literature of the early twentieth century, the character of the mother was often depicted as a gentle, loving, and caring woman devoted to her children, especially her sons.[57] To the phenomenon that some urban female writers attacked the patriarchal family, while still emotionally attaching to their mothers, Meng Yue and Dai Jinhua suggest that rebellious daughters in the May Fourth period had not shaped their independent subjectivity and thus projected their emotional needs onto the image of the mother. Through their writing, they revived the mother's love as a supplement to their immature subjectivity.[58] Many contemporary critics propose that it was daughters' love for their mothers that created the daughters' modern identity and maintained the mother–daughter bond in early twentieth-century China.[59]

However, this type of mother–daughter bond in the writings of female authors during the May Fourth period had some limits in social reality and practice. First, for most female writers, the loving bond between a mother and a daughter was restricted to an emotional expression in literary articulation that emphasized the daughters' emotional needs. Second, in these writings the mothers remained in their homes and were confined

[57] But Lieberman also observes that with the rise of the image of the "New Woman," this portrayal of mothers lost its position in literature. See Sally Taylor Lieberman, *The Mother and Narrative Politics in Modern China* (Charlottesville: University of Virginia Press, 1998), 19, 104–33.

[58] Meng Yue and Dai Jinhua, *Fu chu lishi dibiao* (Emerging from the Horizontal) (Luoyang: Henan renmin chubanshe, 1989), 14–20.

[59] Meng Yue and Dai Jinhua, *Fu chu lishi dibiao*, 14–20; Lingzhen Wang, *Personal Matters: Women's Autobiographical Practice in Twentieth-Century China* (Stanford, CA: Stanford University Press, 2004), 61–139; Ray Chow, *Women and Chinese Modernity: The Politics of Reading between West and East* (Minneapolis: University of Minnesota Press, 1991), 168–70.

to the domestic domain, in contrast to the daughters, who moved to cities and involved themselves in social movements. In fact, this was a situation of a New Culture daughter portraying an old-fashioned mother, manifesting a split between their emotional needs and their rational pursuit of modernity. In some cases this so-called "loving mother" reinforced the traditional patriarchal power that sometimes led to the death of the daughter in resisting an arranged marriage.[60] These female writers failed to create a new model of a mother who was no longer restricted to her home duties but was involved in public affairs so that the mother's image would have a new significance in social practice. In the rapidly changing society of twentieth-century China, new ideas not only transformed daughters but also required change of the mother so that the mother–daughter bond would be built on a common ground that would sustain their connection.

In fact, the image of the mother created by the rebellious daughters of the May Fourth period had already fallen behind the social reality, as shown, for example, in the case of Cai Chang's mother, Ge Jianhao 葛健豪 (1865–1943). Ge, already a mother of six, bravely walked out on her elite family and engaged in overseas studies and social movements with her sons and daughters in the early decades of the twentieth century.[61] It is likely that the articulation of motherly love by May Fourth writers was a reflection of a lonely daughter's nostalgia which, however, did not help to bring mothers out of domesticity and into the rapidly changing social domain. In these writings, mothers and daughters were set in two worlds of social transformation, and the daughters' emotional articulation could be seen as a warning sign and painful cry of the breaking of the mother–daughter bond.

Traditional Chinese literature and historical documents contain rich writings about the mother figure, though mostly about the mother–son relationship, in which Mencius' mother was a great Confucian model. Their bond was both emotional and significant in social practice because

[60] Although Wang argues that the daughters' articulation of their love for their mothers was a modern phenomenon, she might overstate the nature of this "love," because it is hard to tell if it was a modern "love" or the daughter's filial piety expressed by the new term "love." In one of Feng Yuanjun's short stories discussed in Wang's work, the heroine's mother lures her daughter from an urban school and from her lover and forces her daughter to accept an arranged marriage. This eventually leads to her daughter's suicide. It seems there was no change on the mother side, while daughters adopted the modern urban concept of love. Wang, *Personal Matters*, 72–81.

[61] Luo Shaozhi, "Cai mu Ge Jianhao" (Mother of the Cai Family, Ge Jianhao), in *Zhonggong dangshi renwu zhuan* (Biographies of the CCP Members), vol. VI, Hu Hua (comp.) (Xi'an: Shaanxi renmin chubanshe, 1982), 47; Li Lingling, *Ge Jianhao zhuan* (Biography of Ge Jianhao) (Beijing: Zhongguo funü chubanshe, 2005).

she pushed her son(s) to become accomplished in the public domain, which in return recognized her accomplishments and status in the society. Many literati-officials during the Ming and Qing periods writing their autobiographies recalled how their mothers, especially widowed ones, suffered a great deal in raising them to be men of achievement; these writers shared strong emotional ties with their mothers.[62]

In the environment of the highly competitive civil service examination during the late imperial period, mothers in elite families had high expectations for their sons that differed from those for their daughters, though this does not mean they loved their daughters any less.[63] Dorothy Ko proposes that in premodern China, a solid tie existed between a mother and her daughter in both emotional needs and social practice that lay the groundwork for forming a strong nexus for women's culture.[64] Studies on women's lives also document mothers' efforts to promote the education of their children, both boys and girls. The education that mothers provided to girls included basic literacy, moral training, household training, knowledge of sexuality, and childrearing.[65] Some talented women in elite families inherited skills of literary writing and art from their natal families, and some women even became the genealogical link to important academic schools in the development of Confucianism.[66] Learning to weave and embroider also reinforced the tie between mothers and daughters.[67] In marrying, a daughter marked her separation from her natal family, but the customs of periodically visiting her natal family and exchanging gifts, letters, and literary works helped maintain a certain level of communication between mother and daughter that sustained their bond throughout their lives.[68]

The social changes in the twentieth century subverted traditional family relations and the mother–daughter relationship. The domestic activities

[62] Hsiung Ping-chen, "Constructed Emotions: The Bond between Mothers and Sons in Late Imperial China," *Late Imperial China* 15(1) (June 1994): 87–117.
[63] Xiaoping Cong, *Teachers' Schools and the Making of the Modern Chinese Nation-State*, 32–3.
[64] Dorothy Ko, "Pursuing Talent and Virtue: Education and Women's Culture in Seventeenth- and Eighteenth-Century China," *Late Imperial China* 13(1) (1992): 9–39.
[65] Susan Mann, "The Education of Daughters in the Mid-Ch'ing Period," in *Education and Society in Late Imperial China, 1600–1900*, Benjamin A. Elman and Alexander Woodside (eds.) (Berkeley: University of California Press, 1994), 19–49. Mann, *Precious Records*.
[66] See Benjamin Elman, *Classicism, Politics, and Kinship: The Ch'ang-chou School of New Text Confucianism in Late Imperial China* (Berkeley: University of California Press, 1990).
[67] Susan Mann, "Learned Women in the Eighteenth Century," in *Engendering China: Women, Culture and the State*, Christina K. Gilman, Gail Hershatter, Lisa Rofel, and Tyrene White (eds.) (Cambridge, MA: Harvard University Press, 1994), 27–46.
[68] Ko, "Pursuing Talent and Virtue."

that had previously bonded mothers and daughters[69] seemed outdated to a new generation of young women who had received a modern education and wanted to open up a social space for themselves. In the atmosphere of May Fourth radicalism, which promoted the nuclear family, the conjugal family, public education for girls, scientific knowledge in raising children, and eugenics through modern textbooks, journals and magazines, mothers' knowledge and experience regarding women's bodies, sexuality, and childrearing became useless.[70] Lieberman also observes that with the rise of the image of the "New Woman," the positive portrayal of mothers lost its position in literature.[71] On the other hand, the negative image of mothers frequently related to the dark side of the family, such as arranging marriages (along with fathers), binding daughters' feet, the habit of opium smoking, being idle, and being superstitious.[72] Beginning in the 1930s, the image of traditional mothers gradually became more negative when portrayed in literature and social discourse.

Yuan Jing herself belonged to a family with a legendary maternal lineage involved in literature, the arts, and even the medical fields. Both Yuan's great-grandmother and grandmother belonged to the circle of talented women (*cai nü* 才女) in the nineteenth-century Jiangnan area that has been studied by Dorothy Ko, Ellen Widmer, Susan Mann, and many others.[73] The Jiangnan literary women were transformed in various ways during the twentieth century;[74] a similar situation occurred in Yuan's family. The preeminent carriers of this tradition in the twentieth century are probably Yuan Jing's eldest sister, Yuan Xiaoyuan 袁晓园

[69] See Mann, *Precious Records* and "Grooming a Daughter for Marriage."

[70] See Bray (*Technology and Gender*) and Mann (*Precious Records*) on the traditional knowledge of motherhood. See Tani Barlow, *The Question of Women in Chinese Feminism* (Durham, NC: Duke University Press, 2004) on the discussion of eugenics; and Glosser (*Chinese Visions of Family and State*) on the idea of the nuclear and conjugal family.

[71] Lieberman, *The Mother and Narrative Politics in Modern China*, 19, 104–33.

[72] For instance, Ba Jin's *Family* and Zhang Ailing's works.

[73] Ko, *Teachers of the Inner Chambers*; Susan Mann, *The Talented Women of the Zhang Family* (Berkeley: University of California Press, 2007); Ellen Widmer and Kang-I Sun Chang (eds.), *Writing Women in Late Imperial China* (Stanford, CA: Stanford University Press, 1997).

[74] See Hu Ying, "'Tossing the Brush'? Wu Zhiying (1868–1934) and the Uses of Calligraphy;" Grace Fong, "Reconfiguring Time, Space, and Subjectivity: Lü Bicheng's Travel Writing on Mount Lu;" Xiaoping Cong, "From 'Cainü' to 'Nü Jiaoxi': Female Normal Schools and the Transformation of Women's Education in the Late Qing Period, 1895–1911;" Nanxiu Qian, "The Mother *Nü xuebao* versus the Daughter *Nü xuebao*: Generational Differences between 1898 and 1902 Women Reformers;" Xia Xiaohong, "Tianyi bao and He Zhen's Views on 'Women's Revolution,'" in *Different Worlds of Discourse: Transformations of Gender and Genre in Late Qing and Early Republican China*, Nanxiu Qian, Grace S. Fong, and Richard J. Smith (eds.) (Boston, MA: Brill, 2008), 57–86; 87–114; 115–44; 257–92; 293–314.

(aka Yuan Xingjie, 1901–2003),[75] and her paternal cousin's daughter, Qiong Yao 琼瑶 (1938–), a popular novelist.

Foregrounded by the historical tradition of an elite family and a glorious maternal lineage, Yuan Jing's creation of a motherless daughter in her work seems to contradict her family background, but the omission of the mother–daughter bond in her writing has a basis in both the social and literary worlds. The new urban life in the coastal areas and big cities, where modern educational institutions were concentrated and the print culture was flourishing, opened up a new space for this generation of rebellious daughters. In the 1920s and 1930s, a group of young women resided in these cities without their mothers. For example, Ding Ling's famous "Ms. Sophie's Diary" portrays a lonely and self-pitying young woman who left her family for the freedom of the city.[76] Ms. Sophie was not simply a literary character but a social reality; female writers such as Ding Ling, Lu Yin 庐隐 (1898–1934), Xiao Hong 萧红 (1911–42), Shi Pingmei 石评梅 (1902–28), and Bing Xin 冰心 (1900–99), among many others, were living a similar life. They had come from the old familial and social order but had left their mothers behind in their hometowns to pursue their education, freedom, and advancement. Like this group of female writers, the geographic and social distance made these young women de facto "motherless daughters." Under this circumstance, as Lieberman points out, the mother's gentle and caring image in early twentieth-century literature only represented the male youths' nostalgia for the rustic life after their struggle in modern cities;[77] similarly, these rebellious daughters also became nostalgic when they felt lost and lonely in their urban lives.

Social mother versus biological mother (1): rural mothers as others

The image of motherless daughters in the May Fourth era represented the reality of some educated women in the urban areas of the 1920s and 1930s, but this situation would change when female students from the cities moved to revolutionary base areas, such as the SGNBR, where they began to observe mother–daughter relations and family bonds in rural communities. Facing the reality that some rural mothers were deeply involved in, even dominated, their daughters' marriages and schemed to profit from the unions (see previous chapters), these educated women may have felt they should offer guidance to "save" young rural women.

[75] See http://zh.wikipedia.org/wiki/袁晓园(accessed May 9, 2012).
[76] Ding Ling, "Ms. Sophie's Diary."
[77] Lieberman, *The Mother and Narrative Politics in Modern China*.

The image of the rural mother was also compromised by the revolutionary reality of reforming the family. In the rural revolution seeking to liberate women from family oppression, the revolutionary state faced opposition not only from fathers and husbands, but also from mothers and mothers-in-law. In the early period of the SGNBR, in order to mobilize women to participate in political movements, female cadres frequently responded to young women's requests and engaged in the struggle against abusive mothers-in-law and husbands, as discussed in Chapters 1 and 2.

Thus revolutionary writers, both male and female, found it difficult to present a progressive image of rural (biological) mothers. The negative image of rural mothers was also reflected in Yuan Jing's later work with Kong Jue. Different from *Liu Qiao'er Goes to the Law*, which featured a motherless daughter, Yuan's and Kong's new novel, *The Story of New Heroic Sons and Daughters*, created an image of a feudal rural mother for the heroine Xiaomei. Xiaomei's mother was depicted very negatively in terms of revolutionary standards: she clearly knew that her daughter was fond of the hero, Daniu, but still sold her to a Japanese collaborator from a rich and politically corrupt family. Similarly, the male author Zhao Shuli 赵树理 (1909–70), in his *Xiao Erhei's Marriage* (*Xiao Erhei jiehun* 小二黑结婚), portrays the heroine Xiaoqin's mother as a sorceress who tries to sell her daughter for material gain.[78] These rural biological mothers of young women seemed to embody backward feudalism and were targeted as objects of social reform.

Since rural (biological) mothers were corrupted, it became necessary to create an image of the social mother to provide guidance to young women. As biological mothers could not pass on new ideas of social reform and revolution to their daughters, saving young rural women and launching a family revolution thus became the task of social mothers, who possessed social status and revolutionary spirit. Young women's reproductive processes (puberty, menses, marriage, and childrearing) inevitably required the guidance of a mother, but traditional biological mothers were not qualified in the eyes of the revolutionary state, since they did not have modern scientific knowledge of women's bodies.[79] This

[78] Zhao Shuli, "Xiao Erhei jiehun" (Xiao Erhei's Marriage), in *Zhao Shuli zuopin xin bian* (A New Compilation of Zhao Shuli's Works) (Beijing: Renmin wenxue chubanshe, 2011), 6–21.

[79] See Gail Hershatter's work on reforming midwives in the 1950s: the state organized the programs of training new midwives and reforming older midwives. See "Birthing Stories: Rural Midwives in 1950s China," in *Dilemmas of Victory: The Early Years of the People's Republic of China*, Jeremy Brown and Paul G. Pickowicz (eds.) (Cambridge, MA: Harvard University Press, 2007), 337–58. In fact, this program of training midwives and reforming old rural midwives began in the 1940s' SGNBR as one of the social reform projects. See Qin Yan and Yue Long, *Zhou chu fengbi*, 189–205.

required a social mother with a modern education or training by the revolutionary state, which had equipped her with new ideas and new knowledge to offer care, protection, and guidance to young rural women.

Envisioning themselves as social mothers could also express educated women's self-perception, their goal of saving more women, their engagement in social work, and their desire to win a position equal to that of men. Because of their education, their dedication to the revolutionary cause, and their participation in state-operated programs, they were an organized force backed by public resources. Moreover, by aligning with the revolution, their status was sanctioned by the state and even became part of the nexus of state power. As female social workers and political leaders, they could understand the physical and spiritual needs of young women. Guided by a social mother, a rebellious daughter like Qiao'er would no longer be lonely in her resistance to patriarchy, as Zi Jun in Lu Xun's work[80] and Cousin Qin in Ba Jin's novel. With a social mother's help, Qiao'er did not need to escape from her family like those urban women, but could stay at home, following revolutionary principles and gaining her deserved happiness.

The social mother versus the biological mother (2): sexuality, reproduction, and class

Yuan's invention of the character Auntie Li is critical to understanding the tension between the roles of the biological mother and the social mother during this period. The emphasis on the mother–daughter relationship's transformation from biological to social mother reflects the change in women's position from the domestic to the public domain, and their struggle between these two identities in twentieth-century China. Meng Yue suggests that revolutionary discourse, movements, and communist state ideology may have suppressed and circumscribed women's physical and psychological desires for love, sexuality, and even procreation,[81] thus making the role of the biological mother inferior to that of the social mother. However, this suppression should not be fully blamed on the revolution, because the phenomenon that separated the identities of biological mother and social mother had a historical origin. The revolution continued this traditional practice of the late imperial elite family and imbued it with new political significance.

[80] See Lu Xun's short story "Shang shi" (Regret for the Past), in *Selected Stories of Lu Hsun*, 197–215.

[81] Meng Yue, "Female Image and National Myth," in *Gender Politics in Modern China, Writing and Feminism*, Tani E. Barlow (ed.) (Durham, NC: Duke University Press, 1993), 118–36.

Research shows that due to the hardship and danger of delivering children, many elite women during the Ming and Qing periods tried to avoid giving birth to more children[82] and transferred this physical burden to concubines, who were physically stronger but socially of a lower class.[83] According to Hsiung Ping-chen's research, instead of being the biological mother of her own children, an elite woman became a "socially recognized mother" (*di mu* 嫡母) to the children born under her husband's name, based on her status as her husband's primary wife. The status of this socially recognized mother was endorsed by the imperial state, thus integrating a family matter into the state political order. The major responsibilities of a socially recognized mother to her children, mainly sons (both those she herself gave birth to and those from her husband's former wife or concubines), was to oversee their education, moral integrity, and behavior, as well as encourage their future achievements and family glory.[84] Differentiating the social status of recognized mothers and biological mothers created a division of labor within the domestic domain. However, it was the later social movements and revolution that offered a new version of this division of labor on the basis of class status. This version not only created a warning to women regarding their bodies that could transgress class lines, but also related the social mother's status to state power.

Beginning in the late Qing, a strong reformist discourse urged women to change their role and take on more responsibility for the society and for the nation. This discourse, starting with Liang Qichao 梁启超 (1873–1929), expected women to be citizens of the nation and to be mothers of citizens,[85] thus demanding that the mother's supposed duty be transformed from the domestic to the public realm. Educated women moved to the public domain, where they became teachers and engaged in other professions.[86] By the 1940s, the educated women of the post-May Fourth generation were facing a critical juncture: these previously rebellious daughters were about to enter a new stage of life, motherhood. This group of urban women formed a view of motherhood that was influenced by the traditional elite family model. Women's role

[82] Hsiung Ping-chen, "Constructed Emotions."

[83] See Francesca Bray, *Technology and Gender: Fabrics of Power in Late Imperial China* (Berkeley: University of California Press, 1997), 351–68.

[84] Hsiung Ping-chen, "Constructed Emotions"; Bray, *Technology and Gender.*

[85] Liang Qichao, "Lun nü xue" (On Women's Schooling), in *Yinbingshi heji: wenji* (Collected Works from Drinking Ice Studio: Article Collection) (Shanghai: Zhonghua shuju, 1932), 37–8.

[86] Xiaoping Cong, *Teachers' Schools*; also see Qian Nanxiu, Grace Fong, and Rich Smith (eds.), *Different Worlds of Discourse: Transformations of Gender and Genre in Late Qing and Early Republican China* (Boston, MA: Brill, 2008).

as biological mothers to their children, especially to daughters, seemed to be overshadowed by their glorious public identities and social duties, because being a biological mother meant responsibility for many family duties and would thus again bind a young woman to the family that she had struggled to leave. This historical discontinuity and social change split women between the two identities of biological mothers and social workers, and between the two domains of the private sphere and public space, which created anxiety for women from the 1940s onward. In the 1940s, these educated young women were also affected by the harsh environment of the SGNBR, which caused serious physical problems and brought difficulties to their family life.

This troubling issue not only originated from women's biological nature, but also their social and political identity in marriage and procreation. In twentieth-century revolutionary cultural products, the image of mother has been infiltrated by the theme of class oppression. For example, the aforementioned "A Mother as a Slave" by Rou Shi portrays a mother from a poor peasant family as a "borrowed womb" for a rich landlord family, implying that the mother is part of an exploited class deprived of control over both her body and reproduction. Similarly, the famous 1950s' novel *The Song of Youth* (*Qingchun zhi ge* 青春之歌) tells a story of a young revolutionary woman whose mother, a daughter of a tenant family, became the concubine of a landlord. After giving birth, this mother was abandoned by her husband and forbidden from seeing her daughter who was raised by her socially recognized mother.

In the 1940s, revolutionary literature and artistic works created by educated women had a tendency to terminate the biological mother's status at birth to prevent the perpetuation of villainous bloodlines created through class transgressions. In *The White-Haired Girl* and Yuan Jing's work *Lan Huahua*, both heroines are sexually violated by class enemies and give birth to children, but both babies are stillborn. Here, the biological body of the woman makes motherhood a problem because their children result from illicit sexual relations between classes.[87] For this reason, the birth of a child immediately puts the heroine into the position of mother with an ambivalent identity.

The discourse of praising the role of the social mother and denouncing/victimizing the biological mother began in the Ming-Qing era and was then strengthened by revolutionary discourse and taken up by this group of educated women. The mother–child relationship created a dilemma between sexuality in the private domain and the revolution in the public domain that becomes hardly reconciled, and had been

[87] Meng Yue, "Female Image and National Myth," 118–36.

troubling young educated women since the beginning of the twentieth century. This discourse required young women's wholehearted devotion to social movements and the revolution, while devaluing or postponing the status of biological mother. Scholarship shows that during this period, young women in the revolutionary camp in Yan'an faced pressure to delay or avoid motherhood, due to both environmental hardships and revolutionary discourse. The harsh life in this region made it difficult to be a healthy mother, while the revolutionary discourse had no room for a young woman to be a proud mother.[88] The revolutionary discourse praised young women's vigor, but the environment and ideology discouraged them from having children. Although Deng Yingchao 邓颖超 (1904–92), one of the CCP female leaders, gave a speech in Yan'an calling for respecting women's right to motherhood and understanding the hardships involved in raising a child,[89] she herself refused to become a mother in her early years under the influence of the May Fourth radicalism and revolutionary ideology.[90] However, it should be pointed out that this ideology in fact affected only educated women and those who were trained as rural female leaders. Ordinary rural women continued their usual practices of motherhood, thus leaving us to wonder if the division of labor for childbirth present since the late imperial time continued.

Yuan Jing herself was the example of this tension of dual identities. Though married three times, she never became a biological mother.[91]

[88] Qin Yan and Yue Long, *Zou chu fengbi*, 212–24. Also see Qin Yan, "Cong shehui xingbie shijiao dui Yan'an shiqi xin nüxing de yanjiu" (A Study of New Women in Yan'an Period from the View of Gender), *Funü yanjiu luncong* (Collection of Women's Studies) 75(5) (September 2006): 38–42.

[89] Jin Tao, "Women duiyu haizi he muqin de taidu – Ji Deng Yingchao tongzhi de tanhua, 1942" (Our Attitude Toward Children and Mothers – Report on the Conversation with Comrade Deng Yingchao, 1942), *Shaan-Gan-Ning bianqu funü yundong wenxian ziliao xuji*, 322–6.

[90] Deng had an abortion during her first pregnancy because she wanted to devote herself to revolutionary work; her second pregnancy ended with dystocia which led to her sterility. See Yin Jiamin, *Guo Gong wangwshi fengyunlu: cong Huangpu dao Beifa* (The Old Stories of Time between the Nationalist Party and Communist Party: From Huangpu Academy to the North Expedition) (Beijing: Dangdai Zhongguo chubanshe, 2012), 147.

[91] In the late 1970s and the early 1980s, Yuan Jing told her secretary, Qin Wenhu, that the reason she did not have her own child was the hardship in the SGNBR and her emotional trauma from the death of her first husband Zhao Meisheng in 1945. These conditions resulted in her sterility (interview with Qin Wenhu, June 26, 2012). However, this explanation may require some examination. Yuan and Zhao married before 1934 and it is hard to believe that there was no chance for her to have a child if she wanted one in ten years of marriage. After they arrived in Yan'an in 1940, they were assigned to teach at Longdong Middle School for four years, which offered a peaceful time to have a family. It is possible that at this time she was under the influence of the revolutionary discourse and was reluctant to have a child, but regretted that choice decades later, or that Zhao's long-term TB had led to their childlessness.

In the mid-1950s, Yuan divorced Kong Jue and married her third husband, the party secretary of the Tianjin City committee. With this marriage came a stepdaughter, and Yuan Jing started to learn how to be a mother. However, she had a particular way of showing her motherhood: by becoming a children's story writer and publishing a number of prize-winning children's books dedicated to her stepdaughter.[92] In this way, she seemed to be meeting her responsibility for social motherhood.

Feminine space in the masculine party-state: recasting the relationship between state and family

The most interesting part of Yuan Jing's libretto is its ending, in which Qiao'er and Zhu'er marry, with Prefect Ma presiding. This wedding – sanctioned by the state – is held on site at the open court when the final judgment is announced. This scene is very similar to traditional dramas in popular culture that always have a happy ending, with family members or a young couple reunited under the good judge's just verdict.[93] Most importantly, state power is represented by a male figure, Prefect Ma. However, women's activities in the revolution and their participation in creating their own space within the revolutionary state should not be forgotten. Through redefining the position of males and females in state and society, the state and family acquired a new correlative relationship, mirroring those of traditional political philosophy and the cosmological relation of *yin* and *yang*.

In twentieth-century China, modern state-building was often seen as a process of masculine and rational modernization. Eugenia Lean suggests that the emotional expression of the public represents the feminine side of modernity that coexisted within the masculine public sphere.[94] However, this feminized public is very likely disconnected with its previous structure of family and state order, thus resulting in a historical discountiuity of women's culture. Creating the image of Auntie Li could be an effort to position women in the social domain while going beyond the biological identity of a mother while expanding her sense of motherhood to the public. Thus it was in the revolutionary period that literary works tried to rebuild a positive image of the mother and provided a model for social practices in which the mother–daughter genealogy in the public sphere could be continued.

[92] Yuan Zhaoxiu, *Longdong zhongxue xiao shi*, 180–1; interview with Qin Wenhu (June 26, 2012).

[93] For example, many of Feng Menglong's short stories, as well as traditional dramas.

[94] Lean, *Public Passions*, 4–13.

In the traditional Chinese family, patriarchal power very often appeared to dominate, while in practice maternal power played an important role in softening or supplementing hard masculine authority. In some cases, however, as in that of Peng'er, maternal power could subvert patriarchal authority. Moreover, the image of the social mother and her social institution indicates a feminine agent for social activities connected to women's issues and women's work. Wang Zheng argues that in studying the communist state, many ignored the important role of women leaders in policy-making and implementation. These female leaders, most of whom belonged to the All-China Women's Federation organization (*Quan guo funü lianhehui* 全国妇女联合会, abbr. Fulian 妇联), represented women's interests and fought for women's rights whenever male leaders neglected them in their state plans. Wang regards the workers of the All-China Women's Federation as "state feminists" who affiliated with Fulian in promoting China's "state feminism."[95] This institution, as part of state power and as state representative, feminized the rigidity of a masculine state and opened up a space for women's protection and benefit. In the post-1949 PRC, the biggest institutional "social mother" for women was the Women's Federation and its subsidiary organizations, which were called women's "natal/maternal family" (*niang jia* 娘家), as substitutes for women's biological natal families. The account of revolutionary literature that believes victimized women were rescued by men and represented by a patriarchal state may not consider that the state could also incorporate a feminine aspect, represented by a motherlike figure. In this presentation, the mother–daughter genealogy continued but had been transformed from family to society.

When the absence of the biological mother becomes a special device in literature, it puts the focus on the young woman as an individual fighting patriarchal domination. Institutionally speaking, women's associations showed the feminine side of state power and created a solid foundation for the isomorphic and correlative relations between state and family in local communities. The social mother, that is, the director of the local women's association, connected the individual woman to a revolutionary institution. This type of social organization was part of the state's power nexus, and the directors of village women's associations carried out the state's reform programs, such as training midwives in rural areas, and particularly promoting marriage reform.[96] Many literary and artistic works presented the director of the local women's association as a middle-aged

[95] Wang Zheng, "'State Feminism'? Gender and Socialist Formation in Maoist China," *Feminist Studies* 31(3) (Fall 2005): 519–51; Wang Zheng, "Dilemmas of Inside Agitators: Chinese State Feminists in 1957," *The China Quarterly* 188 (2006): 913–32.

[96] See Hershatter, "Birthing Stories."

woman taking care of young women like a mother,[97] epitomizing the older generation of women who passed down their care, wisdom, and life experience to the next generation while also offering guidance to younger females. In the conflict between young females and the patriarchal family, women's associations would provide organizational power, though state power was intended to be the final arbiter in disputes. Although the happy ending had to be affirmed by the state, it included female leaders' work and participation. Yuan presented this image of a revolutionary state that stood behind women's fight against the old patriarchy.

IV. Remaking the story for the locals: Han Qixiang and the ballad "Liu Qiao's Reunion"

Yuan Jing's writing embodied the imagination of the post-May Fourth generation regarding the reconstruction of the isomorphic relationship between the state and family through the promotion of young women's self-determination in their marriages and the feminine image of the state in the village. However, a local artist interpreted this story differently. Han Qixiang, a blind roaming storyteller, was inspired by Yuan's opera and adapted it into a traditional ballad story (*shuo shu*), "Liu Qiao's Reunion," which leaned more to local tastes.[98] Yuan's *Liu Qiao'er Goes to the Law* was performed mainly in Yan'an and its adjacent areas, but Han's ballad reached a much broader audience, even extending into some parts of the Longdong region.

Han Qixiang and the transition of local culture

Han Qixiang was a native of Hengshan County and a blind local artist. According to an *LD* report, Han had received government assistance when he was suffering from illness and hunger, leading him to express his gratitude by creating "new ballads" (*xin shu* 新书). He fashioned some pieces that praised the communist leadership and endorsed government policies such as anti-superstition campaigns.[99] In the 1940s, the CCP

97 For example, Yuan-Kong's novel *The Story of New Heroic Sons and Daughters*; Lüju (Shandong opera) musical film *Remarriage of Li the Second Sister-in-Law* (*Li ersao gaijia*, directed by Liu Guoquan, Changchun Film Studio, 1957); and Li Qun's woodprint cartoon series in the 1940s, *Xiao gu xian* (A Good Sister-in-law), in *Jiefang qu muke lianhuanhua* (Woodprint Cartoon Series Produced in the Liberation Areas), vol. IV (Harbin: Heilongjiang meishu chubanshe, 2001). Also see the case presented in Chapter 7.

98 Han Qixiang, *Liu Qiao tuanyuan*.

99 "Yan xian shujiang Han Qixiang zhuanbian shuo xin shu" (Yan'an County Minstrel Han Qixiang Turned to Telling New Stories), *Jiefang ribao*, July 23, 1945.

government systematically organized a campaign to reform local folk artists, one of several projects seeking to transform local society, in the name of banning superstitious and feudalist propagation.[100] Han became the leading local artist embracing this policy, and the revolutionary power showered praise on him for his work.[101] When he performed in Yan'an in July 1945, he brought a number of stories to the populace based on traditional operas. It was during this 1945 trip that Han met a cadre from the Central Party School, who narrated the story of *Liu Qiao'er Goes to the Law* to him. Han was inspired to adapt the story into a ballad,[102] and might have begun to perform this ballad sometime around the fall of that year.[103] By the time he arrived in Mizhi County in June 1946, his program already included "Liu Qiao's Reunion," indicating that he had completed the adaptation of this story by then.[104]

As a reeducated storyteller, Han represented a success in the state's program to reform local culture. Xie Qing's review in *Liberation Daily* pointed out that he was well received by the audience because his vivid language was based on a deep understanding of local culture, society, and characters of stories. Han was not confined to the old ballad style, but able to create his own style. At the same time, his performances provided a chance for revolutionary writers and artists to learn from him.[105] For example, artists Lin Shan and Gao Minfu from Lu Yi worked with him to record his ballads. The two revolutionary artists were deeply impressed by his performance and his rich and vivid language,[106] and also astounded by his fluid presentation. In the process of recording, Han spontaneously changed the story each time, exhausting the two recorders.[107] While elites and the state tried to standardize his oral performance and reform the local culture, Han demonstrated the autonomy of popular culture and the deep-rooted local values in his presentation by refusing to follow a set script. Interestingly, although

[100] Lin Shan, "Shuo shu xunlianban de shouhuo" (The Achievement of Training Program for Storytelling), *Jiefang ribao*, November 23, 1945; Zhou Erfu, "Hou ji" (Epilogue), in *Liu Qiao tuanyuan*, 139–43; Chang-tai Hung, "Reeducating a Blind Storyteller: Han Qixiang and the Chinese Communist Storytelling Campaign," *Modern China* 19(4) (October 1993): 395–426; "Liangge shuoshu ren, zou de liangtiao lu" (Two Story-tellers on Two Different Paths), *Jiefang ribao*, September 2, 1946.

[101] Zhou Erfu, "Hou ji," 143–7.

[102] Xie Qing, "Ping Liu Qiao tuanyuan" (A Review of Liu Qiao's Reunion), *Jiefang ribao*, September 4, 1946. Also see Zhou Erfu, "Hou ji," 146.

[103] Zhou Erfu, "Hou ji," 146.

[104] "Han Qixiang dao Mizhi shuoshu" (Han Qixiang Comes to Mizhi for a Performance), *Jiefang ribao*, June 20, 1946.

[105] Xie Qing, "Ping Liu Qiao tuanyuan"; Zhou Erfu, "Hou ji," 146.

[106] Fu Ke, "Ji shuoshu ren Han Qixiang."

[107] Chang-tai Hung, "Reeducating a Blind Storyteller."

Figure 6.1 Xiao Su, "Shaanbei shuoshu" [Shaanbei Story-telling], *Jiefang ribao*, August 5, 1945[108]

[108] This is an illustration of Han Qixiang. See Lin Shan, "Gaizao shuoshu" (Reforming Story-telling), and Fu Ke, "Ji shuoshuren Han Qixiang" (Local Folk Artist Han Qixiang), *Jiefang ribao*, August 5, 1945.

Han was receptive to the state reform and praised the state, he continued providing one of his routine services by performing fortune-telling, satisfying village women's desire for children but rejecting the CCP's judgment of fortune-telling as a feudal and superstitious practice.[109]

"Liu Qiao's Reunion": moving toward local taste

When Han adapted Yuan's story, he unconsciously depoliticized the theme of anti-patriarchy. Although "Liu Qiao's Reunion" basically followed the narrative line of *Liu Qiao'er Goes to the Law*, the emphasis of Han's early version shifted to an immoral father's mistreatment of his daughter after the death of her mother, as occurred in many folk songs that had been passed around the region for generations. A clever judge eventually works out the problems and saves the pitiful daughter. As Chang-tai Hung points out, the story clearly followed folk tradition by creating conflict between good and evil,[110] but this good and evil is not focused on the father–daughter conflict. A local Shaanbei audience would be offended by a daughter's direct defiance of her father's authority; thus, the confrontation of daughter against father in Yuan's version has been shifted to a daughter's misfortune, a way of winning sympathy from the audience. It shows that when she discovers that her father has betrothed her to a disgusting old man, Liu Qiao bemoans her ill fate and grieves over the fact that she is without a mother's protection. After the county judge invalidates her marriage, instead of actively appealing the case, as in Yuan's version, she is passive, sobbing under a mulberry tree near a road. It is Prefect Ma who detects the problems in the case file and decides to visit Liu Qiao's village for clarification. On the road to the village, he runs into the sobbing Liu Qiao and asks about her story. In contrast to Yuan Jing's version, in which a strong woman dares to sue her father and seek help from a higher authority, in Han's version Liu Qiao is comparatively weak and simply cries about her problems to a senior authority.

Han's version also differs from Yuan Jing's in the relationship between Liu Qiao and Auntie Li. In Yuan's libretto, it is unclear how a mother's absence affects a daughter's fate, but the concern of a social mother fills this absence. In Han's ballad, Auntie Li, a softhearted woman, is simply Liu Qiao's neighbor who sympathizes with Liu Qiao as a motherless child. Han states that "Auntie Li and Liu Qiao seem like a real

[109] Ke Lan, "Rechen de panwang: Bianqu nongcun fu ying weisheng wenti zhi yijiao" (Cordial Expectation: The Hygienic Problems for Women and Children in the BR), *Jiefang ribao*, March 7, 1946.
[110] Hung, "Reeducating a Blind Storyteller."

(biological) mother and daughter" (*haoxiang qin niang qin nü yiban* 好像亲娘亲女一般).[111] His ballad entirely erases Auntie Li's political identity as a leader of a women's association, and instead she plays a role more like Qiao's biological mother. When young educated women in Yan'an tried to reestablish family relations in their literary works to legitimate the local structure of state power, they recast motherhood with a strong social identity, indicating that the family ought to be open to the state's direction. Their ideas left room for later political campaigns for family reform based on the state ideology. On the other hand, the local culture presented by Han depicts this biological relationship as an ever-solid one that should not be penetrated by the politics of state power.

The two versions of the same story also differ in their dealing with the details of sexuality. Of the characters, the most evil was the landlord, Wang Shouchang. In Yuan Jing's version, Wang was physically repellent and engaged in bad habits, and his age was a disadvantage when compared to Zhu'er. Although Yuan Jing labels him as lewd, no details about Wang's disgusting sexual behavior are provided; instead, it is Wang's belief that his money could buy young Qiao'er's beauty that makes him evil. Yuan Jing does not explain why he needs a wife at the age of forty-eight, assuming that a forty-eight-year-old man wanting to marry an eighteen-year-old woman was itself a symbol of his lewd desires. In contrast, Han exaggerated Wang's sexual lewdness to the point that any woman in the audience would be morally and physically repulsed. In "Liu Qiao's Reunion," Han details Wang's evil sexual behavior as including harassing even his daughter-in-law, humuliating his wife so much that led her to commit suicide by hanging. This extreme evil nature creates a strong contrast between evil/ugly and good/beauty, and also creates suspense regarding Liu Qiao's fate if the plot succeeded. Compared to Yuan Jing's version, this depiction better fitted the taste and expectations of the villagers, who always sympathized with ill-fated pretty women. In terms of the state image presented at the local level, Han also expressed his own view, seeing the CCP and its officials from a local and traditional perspective. According to the memoir of General Zhang Caiqian 张才千 (1911–94), who was the commander-in-chief of the Eighth Route Army stationed in the Longdong region during the 1940s, the theme of Han's early ballad-story focused on how Prefect Ma, as a "clear-sky" judge, discovered the malpractice of local officials and helped an unfortunate woman. When Prefect Ma Xiwu later heard about Han's story, he met Han in person and advised him to revise the

[111] Han Qixiang, *Liu Qiao tuanyuan*, 47.

story by emphasizing the government's policy on new marriage rather than praising him as an individual. Han accepted Ma's suggestion and made slight changes accordingly.[112] In fact, the title of the ballad story, "Reunion," implies that after going through all her suffering, the heroine eventually achieves her happy ending by reuniting with her husband, an outcome delivered by a good judge.[113] Even after his revision, Han's version continues praising Ma as "the clear sky" in various places. His ballad story fitted popular tastes regarding a "clear-sky" judge who delivers a fair result, an everlasting view that could fit any regime and bring order, prosperity, and justice to the people.

[112] Zhang Caiqian, *Liushou Longdong* (Stationing in Longdong) (Lanzhou: Gansu renmin chubanshe, 1984), 200–01.

[113] This format is typical of Feng Menglong's short stories produced in the eighteenth century, which continued to exist in popular culture in rural communities. See Arkush, "Love and Marriage in North Chinese Peasant Operas."

7 The Ping opera and film

Nationalizing the new marriage practice and politicizing the state-family, 1949–1960

From 1949 to 1956, the story of Liu Qiao'er departed from its spatial and social roots in the SGNBR and was brought to the national stage. The route of the story from Yan'an to the nation between the late 1940s and early 1950s was closely associated with the CCP's rapid political and military victories in China. After the People's Liberation Army (PLA) gained control of Manchuria, the CCP made that region the most important revolutionary base for marching toward inner China. Yuan Jing's libretto of *Liu Qiao'er Goes to the Law* was republished in 1947 by Dongbei Bookstore, a revolutionary publisher in Manchuria. In the same year, Han Qixiang's ballad script, *Liu Qiao's Reunion*, was also published by Haiyang Bookstore, a leftwing press in Hong Kong, as an example of the national form of artistic works. In 1949, Han's ballad script was again republished by Xinhua Bookstore, the official publishing agency of communist-led China, indicating that this ballad was to be sold through the bookstore's newly established national network.

In 1948, when the CCP could foresee its upcoming national victory, the top leaders began their construction of a new state that included extending the party's reform of marriage and the family throughout the country. By the time the CCP entered Beijing in early 1949, the drafted Marriage Law was already awaiting approval by the newly established legislature; in the meantime, the CCP's female leaders turned to preparing a campaign for its promulgation. Elizabeth Perry suggests that during the early communist movement, the CCP adopted a "cultural positioning" policy toward mass mobilization, while after 1949, the party-state applied a "cultural patronage" strategy.[1] In fact, in the 1950s, the CCP used both cultural positioning and cultural patronage in promoting the Marriage Law. On the one hand, the state adopted and adapted various forms of popular culture in supporting the marriage reform campaign; on the other hand, the state also constantly revised and recast the

[1] By "cultural patronage," Perry means that the state recasts and manipulates certain cultural images for mobilization and legitimation. See Perry, *Anyuan*, 11–13.

cultural symbols from Yan'an for reconstructing its historical narrative. The image of Liu Qiao'er, which originated from the legal case *Feng v. Zhang*, also became a part of this cultural positioning and patronage project.

In this project, Xin Fengxia, a young actress of the Ping opera, rose quickly from among the ranks of popular artists. Her low social origin and excellent performance as Liu Qiao'er, as well as her new-style marriage, made her a successful story of the CCP's liberation of women. Moreover, with the participation of elite professionals, the opera *Liu Qiao'er* was revised to contribute to the presentation of the revolutionary experience in Yan'an and the story of self-determination. The newly revised opera was frequently staged over a large part of northern China, including Beijing, Hebei, and Tianjin, from 1950 to 1958, and its music was recorded and broadcast nationwide on the radio, penetrating into daily life of the people. In northwest China, Liu Qiao'er was re-adapted in 1958 into Qin (Shaanxi) opera (*Qin qiang* 秦腔) based on the Pingju version, and performed widely.[2] In 1956, the opera was put on screen by the Changchun Film Studio; the story thus reached all corners of the country.

The 1949 victory brought the communists back to cities and granted them national power. The political and women's leaders were thus distanced from local communities. When drafting the new Marriage Law, they returned to the urban radical term *ziyou*. Along with the campaign for land reform, however, the social reform program for marriage and the family had been politicized with the help of artists. On the other hand, at the local level the term *zizhu* maintained its momentum, in that the opera and film brought a strong message to youth. The icon of Liu Qiao'er and many other female models set influential examples in mobilizing women for the political campaigns of the 1950s. These models of new women also served as examples of the cultural resources, through state patronage, for women to use in fighting for their new position in society and self-determined marriage.

I. The changed term in the 1950 Marriage Law: departing from locality

The promulgation of the 1950 Marriage Law was of great significance in twentieth-century China, but this event should not be seen simply as

[2] Wang Yiqun, "Preface," *Liu Qiao'er* (Shaanxi Qinqiang shiyan jutuan gaiwei Qinqiang ben [Adopted Libretto for Qin Opera by Shaanxi Provincial Experimental Theater]) (Xi'an: Chang'an shudian, 1958).

the work of a group of female leaders fighting for women's rights, or the modern agenda of a masculine state. The Chinese revolutionary state was not a united entity; instead, there was a conflict between how to insist on the ultimate, idealistic goal of women's emancipation and how to effectively implement the law in a concrete locality, especially given that it was a high-modernist policy to be installed across the vast land of the country. As a political campaign executed on a large scale and in a short time span, the Marriage Law became a project that was pushed from the top, often leaving little room for local adjustment, flexibility, or assimilation.

Tracing the contestation: returning to urban idealism

The 1950 Marriage Law was inherited only partially from the 1944 and 1946 regulations, but reads more like a refurbished combination of the 1931/1934 and 1939 marriage law/regulations. For the general principle of marriage, the 1950 Marriage Law set up the standard of "practicing freedom of marriage between male and female" (*shixing nan nü hunyin ziyou* 实行男女婚姻自由), which applied to both entering and dissolving a marriage. At the same time, the term "self-willingness" (*zi-yuan*) was again degraded to the much more specific condition of a man and woman entering a marriage.[3] There was still no trace of the term *zi-zhu* in the formal text of the 1950 Marriage Law.

This reversal may have roots that trace back to the 1940s. In its interpretation of the 1946 regulation, the High Court recognized the disparity of opinions on the term, as discussed in Chapter 4. In the documents prepared for the 1945 legal conference, the High Court admitted that the radical marriage regulation encountered local resistance that endangered the rule of the revolutionary government. On the other hand, young intellectuals, educated women, and cadres strongly supported absolute freedom in marriage and unconditional ex parte divorce. Facing these two extremes and reviewing the history of the policy, the High Court admitted that legal implementation had swung back and forth between rigid and harsh responses to any offense in the early years, and tolerance and even complicity with local tradition in the two years after the 1944 regulation. The High Court believed that the new (1946) marriage regulation, as a corrective to the previous two extremes, acknowledged

[3] "Zhonghua renmin gongheguo hunyin fa, 1950" (Marriage Law of the People's Republic of China, 1950), in Zhongyang renmin zhengfu fazhi weiyuanhui (Legislature Committee of the Central Government, comp.), *Hunyin fa ji qi youguan wenjian* (The Marriage Law and Related Documents) (Beijing: Xinhua shudian, 1950), 1–9.

the reality of local "backward" practices, while also making an effort to minimize them.[4] In searching for a middle way between the radical 1939 regulation and the problematic 1944 regulation, and a balance between rural reality and urban idealists' demands, the High Court merged two terms together, announcing that the marriage principle under New Democracy was free and self-determined (*ziyou zi-zhu* 自由自主).[5]

The return to the phrase *hunyin ziyou* in the 1950 Marriage Law was closely related to the fact that the CCP had become the national leading party and sought to draw in various social classes and strata. Now stationed in urban areas, the CCP chose to use the term "freedom of marriage" to be more attractive to educated youth. This also reflected the CCP's mentality of the time: it was returning to an urban base, because China's modernization required the support of the urban population. The High Court responded to this change of mentality by issuing a document in July 1949. It stated that since the situation had flipped, with the revolution advancing from "the rural besieged the urban" to "the urban led the rural," the marriage regulation should correspondingly be revised.[6] In 1948, one of the CCP's top leaders, Liu Shaoqi 刘少奇 (1898–1969), had directed the CCP's female leaders, including Deng Yingchao and others, to organize a special committee for drafting a new marriage law for the entire nation that could be implemented after the CCP's coming victory in China.[7] In Liu's instructions, he argued that the existing marriage regulations in various revolutionary base areas were not unified and powerful enough in combatting feudalism. He suggested that the 1934 Soviet Marriage Law represented a firm stand against feudalism and should be used as the basis for drafting a new law.[8] The term underlying the principle of marriage reverted to *ziyou*, and the policy became more radical.

[4] SPA 15–72, "Hunyin wenti yu hunyin tiaoli."

[5] *Ibid.*

[6] SPA 15–9, "Dui Xibei nan nü hunyin wenti yijian, 1949.7.27" (An Opinion Regarding the Marriage Issue in the Northwest Area, July 27, 1949).

[7] Ge Yabo, "Xuanchuan di yi bu Hunyin fa" (Promoting the First Marriage Law), in Quanguo fulian lao ganbu ju (comp.), *Jinguo huihuang: jinian Zhonghua quanguo funü lianhehui chengli wushi zhounian* (Glorious Heroines: Celebration of the Fiftieth Anniversary of the All-China Women's Federation) (Beijing: Zhongguo funü chubanshe, 1999), 60–7. Ge Yabo served as a female cadre in the newly established All-China Women's Federation beginning in 1951.

[8] Ge Yabo, "Xuanchuan di yi bu Hunyin fa". However, Huang Chuanhui, a reporter who interviewed Luo Qiong, wrote that Liu stated that the 1931 Chinese Soviet Marriage Regulation should be used as the basis for the new Marriage Law. See Huang Chuanhui, *Tianxia hunyin – Gongheguo san bu hunyin fa jishi* (Marriages under Heaven: A Report on the Three Marriage Laws of the PRC) (Shanghai: Wenhui chubanshe, 2004), 38–9. In either way, the New Marriage Law was made on the basis of the Jiangxi revolutionary period rather than the experience of the SGN period.

Readopting this term also reflected the preference of the individuals who drafted the marriage law, and was much more convenient for most political elite women in the CCP. As discussed in Chapter 4, in the 1940s the term *zizhu* was used as both a principle in legal practice and a political principle in the party's independence from the Comintern and the nation's war against the Japanese invasion. Even during the Yan'an period, the use of *ziyou* in the CCP's political and ideological rhetoric for the women's movement had not changed in the top political group. This term was favored by the drafting committee of the Marriage Law that was established in late 1948 and composed of a group of female communists.[9] The director was Deng Yingchao, and the committee included another six members, of whom most were wives or widows of the CCP top leaders.[10] Of this group, all except Kang Keqing 康克清 (1911–92)[11] had received a very good modern education in urban areas and were heavily influenced by the May Fourth Movement; some of them had participated in student protests in 1919.[12] Soviet Russia-trained Chen Shaoyu 陈绍禹 (1904–74, aka Wang Ming 王明), the director of the legislature committee of the PRC central government, presented the drafted Marriage Law and its interpretation to the People's Central Government Committee for approval in April 1950.[13] After its approval, the law was officially issued to the public in May 1950.

Although the group of women who composed the 1948 drafting committee had engaged in the women's movement and become female leaders, in fact, this group of idealistic leaders of the communist women's movement had little experience in actually implementing marriage regulations. Their activities and experiences focused primarily on urban settings and political campaigns centered in Yan'an and Chongqing. For example, Deng Yingchao, Zhou Enlai's wife, was stationed with her husband in Chongqing for most of the 1940s as Yan'an's representative to the United Front. Other female leaders lived in Yan'an, the headquarters of the CCP, or in urban areas working undercover in the Nationalist government and leading the communist women's movement in Nationalist regions. In contrast, both the 1944 and 1946 marriage regulations were

9 Huang Chuanhui, *Tianxia hunyin*, 33–49.

10 The members included Shuai Mengqi, Yang Zhihua, Kang Keqing, Li Peizhi, Luo Qiong, and Wang Ruqi. See Huang Chuanhui, *Tianxia hunyin*, 35–49.

11 Among them, Zhu De's wife Kang Keqing may have been the only exception, in that she was a rural women's leader with no modern education.

12 For example, Deng Yingchao was one of the student leaders in the May Fourth Movement in Tianjin in 1919.

13 Chen Shaoyu, "Guanyu Zhonghua Renmin Gongheguo Hunyin Fa qicao jingguo he qicao liyou de baogao" (The Report on the Process and the Rationale of Drafting the Marriage Law), in *Hunyin fa ji qi youguan wenjian*, 33–97.

drafted by a group of legal practitioners from the SGN High Court. These legal workers had experience in practicing the law and were fully aware of the importance of term differentiation. It was their legal practice and daily contact with various litigants that led them to develop a practical principle for a more effective implementation of the regulation. When the top party leadership pushed through the Marriage Law in a short period of time and set about implementing it across the country, it was difficult for legal workers to apply the delicate strategies and skills that they had developed over the past decade.

Regularizing marriage reform

Along with land reform, which granted women property rights, the Marriage Law became a powerful weapon for eradicating old customs and rearranging the local social order. If party leaders had examined the experience of the CCP in the SGNBR, they would have seen that it was both the idealistic direction and the practical compatibility blended with a certain flexibility that made CCP policies work more effectively in that locality. Instead, marriage reform became a state campaign and a high-modernist project pushed down from the top onto the localities. To show the quick effect, this high-modernist campaign deprived young women and men of agency, given that in many rural areas marriage was still a family business and that most women were still enmeshed in the net of patriarchal families. The SGNBR had achieved success by establishing a connection with women's autonomy through a flexible legal strategy that tactically separated women from the patriarchal family net and appealed to community sympathy and support rather than mobilizing women to confront their families and communities directly.

History began to repeat itself as a result of the party's radicalism. The implementation of the new Marriage Law brought a wave of divorces and local opposition in rural communities, similar to the situation that had occurred in the SGN Border Region in the early 1940s. In the vast rural areas, the Marriage Law was viewed as a divorce law; the number of divorce cases in the courts reached more than 1,170,000 nationwide in the single year of 1953.[14] According to Liu Jingfan 刘景范 (1910–90), the deputy-director of the Office for Implementing the Marriage Law in the Central Government, the radical movement in rural areas resulted in strong local resistance, and some young men and women were killed as a result of their confrontations with old patriarchal families and community

[14] Huang Chuanhui, *Tianxia hunyin*, 64–6, 92.

customs.[15] Indeed, this law was also seen as benefitting another small group of people, the male revolutionary cadres of rural origin who now served as government officials in urban areas. The law offered them a chance to divorce their rustic, illiterate, and old-fashioned wives, who had made sacrifices for their husbands' revolutionary cause. After divorcing their wives, the cadres were free to marry fashionable and educated urban women in the name of "freedom of marriage."[16]

Given this situation, the tone of the central government in promoting the Marriage Law started to change in 1953. Both the CCP Central Committee and the state department of the central government, led by Prime Minister Zhou Enlai 周恩来 (1898–1976), issued special instructions respectively to address the problems. These instructions first blamed the problems on the backwardness of local feudal culture and the incorrect working methods of local cadres in implementing the law, but also clarified that this struggle represented a conflict among the people (*renmin neibu maodun* 人民内部矛盾), differentiating it from the struggle against the class enemy such as the landlord in the land reform campaign.[17] The central government hoped that this would calm agitated local communities. Liu Jingfan's speech also attempted to soothe the localities by redirecting the goal of implementing the Marriage Law to the establishment of a harmonious family, and stated that divorce should only be used as a last resort when other attempts at reconciliation had failed.[18]

Due to this change, some scholars believe that the Marriage Law was put on hold, thus postponing a change in women's status in society and the family.[19] This conclusion implies that the Marriage Law was primarily

[15] Liu Jingfan, "Guanche hunyin fa shi dang qian ge ji renmin zhengfu he quan guo renmin de zhongyao zhengzhi renwu" (Implementing the Marriage Law Is an Important Political Task for All Governments at Each Level and the People Nationwide), *Guanche hunyin fa yundong de zhongyao wenjian* (The Important Documents of the Campaign of Implementing the Marriage Law) (Beijing: Renmin chubanshe, 1953), 23–34.

[16] Zhang Zhiyong, "1950 niandai chuqi Zhonggong ganbu hunyin wenti chu tan: Yi 1950–1956 Hebei sheng ganbu qunti wei li" (Examining the Marriage Issue of the CCP Cadres in the Early 1950s: The Cadres in 1950–1956 Hebei Province), *Ershiyi shiji* 60(3) (March 2007), www.cuhk.edu.hk/ics/21c/index.html.

[17] Zhou Enlai, "Zhongyang renmin zhengfu zhengwuyuan guanyu guanche hunyin fa de zhishi" (An Instruction from the State Department of the Central Government on Implementing the Marriage Law), *Guanche hunyin fa yundong de zhongyao wenjian*, 1–5; "Zhongguo gongchandang zhongyang weiyuanhui guanyu guanche hunyin fa yundong yue gongzuo de buchong zhishi" (The Supplementary Instruction from the CCP Central Committee on the Campaign Month of Promoting the Marriage Law), *Guanche hunyin fa yundong de zhongyao wenjian*, 6–11.

[18] Liu Jingfan, "Guanche hunyin fa shi dang qian ge ji renmin zhengfu he quan guo renmin de zhongyao zhengzhi renwu."

[19] Johnson, *Women, the Family and Peasant Revolution in China*; Stacey, *Patriarchy and Socialist Revolution*; Andors, *The Unfinished Liberation of Chinese Women*.

carried out through a political campaign; once the campaign ended, the marriage reform was suspended. However, various scholarly works have proved that was not the case, as pointed out in the Introduction. Similar to the 1930s, when the judicial system concretized the modern concept of gender equality stimulated by the 1920s social movement,[20] in the 1950s it was also the judicial system that continued carrying out the legal issue of marriage reform after the political campaign was over.[21] Neil Diamant, through fieldwork researching the implementation of the 1950 Marriage Law and the marriage conditions of both urban and rural women in the 1950s, also strongly opposes the assumption of the suspension of marriage reform and women's rights in 1953. Instead, he offers a much more dynamic picture of state power at the local level, in which village cadres had no intent or authority to hinder women's divorce actions but rather turned problems over to the higher authority, which pursued a much stronger revolutionary action of helping women escape their unhappy marriages.[22] Philip Huang's study of legal cases of divorce in both rural and urban areas during the 1950s and 1960s also proves that the implementation of the Marriage Law continued after 1953 through both the judicial system and the administrative system, mostly dealt with by courts and work units rather than women's organizations. Judicial workers and administrators dedicated themselves to thorough investigations in the divorce process, trying to discover the motive and cause behind each divorce case,[23] following the practice of the SGNBR courts in the 1940s. The reality, similar to the situation in the SGNBR, was that once again marriage problems were assigned to the judicial system and administrators, while top women's organizations often following the party's shifting theme of political campaigns such as land reform, Korea War mobilization, rural cooperative movements, people's communes, and the Great Leap Forward.[24]

Although the term *zizhu* was not explicitly used in the formal text of the Marriage Law, it definitely existed in practice at local levels and in the informal interpretation of formal text, representing a latent sign of past revolutionary experience. The new outline for promotion

[20] See Kuo, *Intolerable Cruelty*, 3–17.

[21] See Judd, "Reconsidering China's Marriage Law Campaign."

[22] Diamant, "Re-examining the Impact of the 1950s Marriage Law." Also see his *Revolutionizing the Family*.

[23] Philip Huang, "Divorce Law Practices and the Origins, Myths, and Realities of Judicial 'Mediation' in China," *Modern China* 31(2) (April 2005): 151–205. Huang also points out that investigating each individual divorce was a time- and energy-consuming process dedicated to finding a workable solution. The judicial workers in the post-Mao period preferred legal adjudication because it saved time and energy.

[24] Wang Zheng, "State Feminism?" and "Dilemmas of Inside Agitators."

of the law stated that freedom of marriage meant young men and women should make their own decisions regarding marriage (*ziji zuo zhu* 自己做主),[25] a spelled-out form of "self-determination." In his speech, Liu Jingfan also stated that marriage should be based on the self-determination (*zizhu*) of men and women.[26] It is worth noting that as younger brother of Liu Zhidan, Liu Jingfan had experience in working in the SGNBR judicial system. It is possible that Liu's SGNBR experience alerted him to this term. Some official interpretations from one locality claimed "*zizhu ziyuan* (自主自愿) for a marriage between a man and a woman" as an alternative interpretation for the principle of *hunyin ziyou*.[27]

We also frequently see the term *zizhu* in various magazines, newspapers, and other sources. For example, in 1957 a series of correspondence on marriage problems was published in the national magazine *Chinese Women* (*Zhongguo funü*), among which an article categorized existing marriages into four types that included "self-determined and self-willing marriage" (*zi zhu zi yuan*) based on the man and woman's choice. The author pointed out that "semi-self-determined marriage" (*ban zizhu* 半自主) also existed, indicating a union initiated by the parents but consented to by both the man and woman in question. Other types were more old-fashioned marriages.[28] At the same time, the literary and artistic works that originated in the SGNBR, including *Liu Qiao'er*, continued to use the term *zi-zhu* in calling for women to have the right to a happy marriage. This shows that although the principle of *ziyou* shadowed the practical principle of *zi-zhu*, in fact it created a dual layer and a discrepancy between the idealistic presentation and the social reality of marriage reform after 1953. In political rhetoric, it retained the urban term of "freedom of marriage," while the previous legal practice of "self-determination" inherited by the judicial system in post-1949 China was broadly acknowledged by the populace.[29]

25 "Guanche hunyin fa xuanchuan tigang" (The Outline of Promoting the Marriage Law), *Guanche hunyin fa yundong de zhongyao wenjian*, 12–22.
26 Liu Jingfan, "Guanche hunyin fa shi dang qian ge ji renmin zhengfu he quan guo renmin de zhongyao zhengzhi renwu," 28.
27 Wang Xicong (comp.), *Xin hunyin fa wenti jieda huibian* (A Collected Interpretation of the New Marriage Law) (Shanghai: Lianying shudian, 1950), 22.
28 Xiong Xianjue, "Lue tan dangqian lihun de yuanyin wenti" (A Brief Discussion of the Cause of Divorce in the Present Days), *Zhongguo funü* (*Chinese Women*) 8 (1957): 16–17.
29 Evidence of the term *zizhu* used in the localities was provided by Dr. Sharon Wen, who was born in Taiyuan, Shanxi Province in the 1950s and is a professor at the University of Houston. She still remembers that the term *hunyin zizhu*, not *hunyin ziyou*, was painted on the surface of a mirror that was a wedding gift to her parents in 1951 (interview with Sharon Wen, April 20, 2013).

II. The Ping opera *Liu Qiao'er*: the image of new women

The period 1948 to 1949 was also the time that Manchuria and Hebei fell into the hands of the PLA. The most significant aspect of the story of *Liu Qiao'er*, after Yuan Jing's creation and Han Qixiang's revision, was its adaptation in a new locality. This adaptation was no coincidence: Pingju is a local form of opera with large audiences in the vast areas of Manchuria, Hebei, Tianjin, and Beijing. Unlike Beijing opera, which was widely regarded as fine art by both the general populace and elites, Pingju, a low-culture performing art, survived among the people at the bottom of society. It is this characteristic of Pingju that served a political purpose in promoting the new Marriage Law. This political campaign also created a new chapter for a Pingju actress, Xin Fengxia, who became the heroine in her own marriage inspired by the character she played, Liu Qiao'er.

Adapting Liu Qiao'er *to Ping opera, 1949–55*

Xin Fengxia was born in Tianjin in 1927. Her father was a street peddler and her mother a *tongyangxi* from a poor peasant family. Although they lived in a large city, Xin did not have a chance to receive any literary education. From childhood, she followed a troupe in Hebei and Tianjin to receive training in Ping opera as an apprentice. She gradually learned to read some characters through memorizing her lines during her internship in the troupe. Under her mother's protection and help, and due to her own talent, Xin grew up to be a promising young actress after dodging dangers in the slum district of Tianjin.[30] Xin's family background offered a favorable ground for her to rise as a model of women's liberation in the revolutionary theoretic framework.

Xin's new chapter in Beijing started with the party-state's cultural positioning project in promoting the Marriage Law. In 1947, Xin Fengxia became a new star in Tianjin's Pingju circle and then moved to Beijing, trying to find a better environment for the development of her troupe.[31] In Beijing, she became close to the newly arrived communist women cadres. Xin's adaptation of Liu Qiao'er's story into Pingju was in response to a request from Zhang Xiaomei 张晓梅 (1911–68), the director of the Women's Federation of Beijing City. In 1949, Zhang learned

[30] Xin Fengxia, *Xin Fengxia de huiyi* (The Recollection of Xin Fengxia) (Beijing: Beijing chubanshe, 1982), 3–128; Xin Fengxia, *Wo jiao Xin Fengxia* (I Am Xin Fengxia) (Beijing: Beijing chubanshe, 1998), 200.

[31] A Pingju troupe often centered with its leading actress, using her name to attract audiences.

of Xin's growing fame and asked her to help the new government. Xin was already excited about new forms of revolutionary art, such as *yangge*. She thus staged two new plays, *Liu Qiao'er* and *Xiao Erhei's Marriage*,[32] in late 1949 in the Tianqiao Market Theater in Beijing, all for the purpose of promoting the Marriage Law.[33]

According to Xin, the early version of her play was based completely on Han Qixiang's ballad script *Liu Qiao's Reunion*,[34] as Zhang Xiaomei had given her a copy.[35] Xin and her musicians worked together to transform the ballad story into a form suitable for Pingju performance. Xin admitted that this story fitted the nature of Pingju, in which all performances centered on a strong female character – in this case, Xin herself. In early 1950, with the help of the director of the Beijing City Bureau of Culture and Arts, the troupe invited a dramatist of Beijing opera, Wang Yan, and a director of modern spoken drama (*hua ju* 话剧), Xia Chun, to help refine the libretto and performance of this play (see below).[36]

This new version of *Liu Qiao'er* won great success; many female leaders in Beijing, such as Deng Yingchao, Cai Chang, and Kang Keqing, came to see it. In spring 1950, Xin and her troupe were invited to the theater in Zhongnanhai, the official complex of the new central government for the PRC and the headquarters of the CCP, to perform *Liu Qiao'er* for a group of China's top leaders, including Mao Zedong, Zhu De, Liu Shaoqi, and Zhou Enlai.[37] Receiving this glory, Xin continued to perform the play in Beijing, as well as many other important theaters in the Beijing and Tianjin area. After one performance, she was introduced to Ma Xiwu and Xie Juezai, who had come to see *Liu Qiao'er* because of its fame.[38] In 1952, this play was brought to the renowned China Grand Theatre in Tianjin at the First National Theater Festival, where Xin Fengxia's outstanding performance of Liu Qiao'er received even greater honors and awards.[39] Her success with this play inspired many traditional artists to begin adapting revolutionary dramas into Pingju, as well as stage *Liu Qiao'er* in their own theaters.[40] In 1953, Xin joined a

[32] *Xiao Erhei's Marriage* was written by the communist writer Zhao Shuli, based on a story that occurred in the Shandong revolutionary base area in the late 1940s. It was also adapted into a musical film in the 1950s.

[33] Xing Fengxia, *Xin Fengxia huiyi lu* (Memoir of Xin Fengxia) (Tianjin: Baihua wenyi chubanshe, 1980) 117; Xin Fengxia, *Wo jiao Xin Fengxia*, 200–01.

[34] Xin Fengxia, *Wo jiao Xin Fengxia*, 200–01.

[35] Xin Fengxia, *Xin Fengxia huiyi lu*, 183–5; Xin Fengxia, *Wo jiao Xin Fengxia*, 200–01.

[36] Xin Fengxia, *Xin Fengxia huiyi lu*, 185–91.

[37] *Ibid.*; Xin Fengxia, *Wo jiao Xin Fengxia*, 201.

[38] Xin Fengxia, *Xin Fengxia huiyi lu*, 190–2; Xin Fengxia, *Wo jiao Xin Fengxia*, 201.

[39] Xin, *Xin Fengxia huiyi lu*, 101, 208.

[40] Xin Fengxia, *Xin Fengxia de huiyi*, 146; Xin Fengxia, *Xin Fengxia huiyi lu*, 133.

delegation of artists on the frontlines of Korea, where she performed the opera for many soldiers.[41] This play thus became a piece of representative work in the campaign for promoting the Marriage Law.

A new heroine in reality: Xin Fengxia's marriage

In the 1950s, Xin Fengxia also represented a new model for those women whose lives were turned around by the communist revolution and the marriage reform. Remarkably, her own marriage was a realization of the spirit of self-determination inspired by Liu Qiao'er, and a variation derived from Liu Qiao'er. After she performed *Liu Qiao'er*, Xin became famous as a member of the circle of renowned revolutionary writers and artists. She also became the protégée of women leaders in Beijing city and high-level leaders, such as Zhang Xiaomei, and even Deng Yingchao, as well as some famous writers and dramatists such as Zhao Shuli, Lao She 老舍 (1899–1966), and Ouyang Yuqian 欧阳予倩 (1889–1962).[42] Gaining entrance to this circle, she was introduced to her future husband, the leftwing playwright and dramatist Wu Zuguang 吴祖光 (1917–2003), who was an absolute opposite to Xin in every respect. Wu came from an old elite family; his grandfather was the curator of the National Forbidden City Museum in the 1920s, and Wu had received a good college education and published a series of drama librettos beginning at the age of twenty. Xin recalled that she had seen a number of Wu's modern dramas staged in Tianjin and came to admire Wu for his artistic cultivation and talent.[43] Wu also expressed his appreciation of Xin's excellent performance, as well as her frank and pure character.[44]

Their relationship was never smooth; however, it was the opera characters Xin had drawn the strength from to overcome the obstacles to their love and marriage. According to Xin, Wu was a gentle and patient man with many attractive qualities, but he showed his love for Xin in subtle ways. When their relationship seemed not to be progressing, Xin decided to propose to him, a bold and unconventional action for a woman of her time. To control her nervousness, she repeatedly recited the aria from *Liu Qiao'er*. Two of the sentences she repeated were the most famous arioso of *Liu Qiao'er*: "I fell in love with him" and "This time I want to choose my marriage mate myself."[45] After their marriage in 1951, Xin began to

41 Xin Fengxia, *Wo jiao Xin Fengxia*, 31.
42 Xin Fengxia, *Wo jiao Xin Fengxia*, 5–17.
43 *Ibid.*, 3–16.
44 *Ibid.*
45 Xin Fengxia, *Yi ku wei le: Xin Fengxia yishu shenghuo* (Enjoying the Bitterness: The Artistic Life of Xin Fengxia) (Beijing: Zhongguo xiju chubanshe, 1983), 418–19; *Wo*

receive an education and cultivate her intellectual tastes with Wu's assistance. Wu helped her enhance her artistic quality and also wrote operas particularly for her.[46]

The bigger ordeal in their life and marriage came later, following a change in the political winds. In 1957, Wu was labeled a Rightist, removed from his government position, and sent to the countryside in northeast China for three years of reeducation. During this period, Xin resisted pressure to divorce Wu, which mainly stemmed from others' concern regarding her marriage as well as the threat it might pose to her political future. During this period, her courage in rejecting all advice to divorce came from another female character she had played, Wang Baochuan, a legendary woman who insisted on her own choice of marriage and waited alone for eighteen years for her husband.[47] Ironically and paradoxically, although Xin served as a symbol of the new Marriage Law and a new image for women's liberation, she also gained courage from a traditional female heroine like Wang Baochuan. The values and faith that supported her in her marriage came from both traditional and revolutionary models.

III. From Ping opera to a film: politicizing popular culture

From 1950 to the 1960s, the image of Liu Qiao'er was constantly recast to respond to the political atmosphere and to serve state political goals. Meanwhile, the state also launched a project to reform other kinds of

jiao Xin Fengxia, 10–20. The original words were "to choose my mother-in-law's house" (*po jia*); some may argue that this indicates that a woman was still under the domination of her mother-in-law. In rural areas, a customary way of saying that a woman will enter into a marriage is "finding a mother-in-law's home" (see the documentary film *Small Happiness*, directed by Carma Hinton, 1984). It is true that this term reflected the situation in China at that time, as most marriages were virilocal, but it was primarily used simply as an idiom in this situation. It also reflected the reality of the time that marriage was still a family matter, not yet an individual matter. Language change is always behind social changes; by the 1970s, the phrase had turned into "looking for a mate" (*zhao duixiang*). In fact, looking at the context of the sentence, the emphasis is on "I myself" and "choose," indicating a self-determined marriage. This term is thus more rhetorical than substantial, and my translation is not literal but based on the context.

46 Xin Fengxia, *Yi ku wei le*, 421–5; Xin Fengxia, *Wo jiao Xin Fengxia*, 24–7.

47 Xin Fengxia, *Wo jiao Xin Fengxia*, 30–46. Wang Baochuan was a popular character in various traditional operas. She was based on a historical story from approximately the sixth or seventh centuries. Wang came from a rich family but believed in a fated marriage because she had tossed a silk embroidered ball that hit her later husband, a poor young man. When her family disapproved of this marriage, she disowned her parents and lived faithfully and alone in poverty, waiting for her soldier husband's return. After eighteen years, when her husband returned with wealth, an honored title, and a new wife, she had to swallow her bitterness and accept the situation. On the other hand, this story also portrays a woman who stood firmly by her own decision regardless of pains or gains.

popular culture for the same purpose, while in return raising the social status of these popular artists to balance out elite arts such as Beijing opera. The modification and recasting of the image of Liu Qiao'er was also a process in which old intellectuals embraced the new political ideology and the elite incorporated and refined popular culture to serve the new regime. These politicized intellectuals inserted their understanding of new political ideas into revolutionary cultural products.

A campaign for reforming the performing arts

An important cultural project of the 1950s involved reforming the popular arts, such as local operas and other types of low-class performing arts. Xin's rise as a new star and the upgrade of Pingju to the status of upper-class art was closely related to her use of Pingju to serve the new Marriage Law and other political campaigns in the 1950s as the CCP sought to reform the performing arts. Beginning in the 1950s, many previously low-class art forms such as *xiangsheng* 相声 (comedians' talk, or cross-talk)[48] and *Quyi* 曲艺,[49] as well as Pingju and various other local operas, received sponsorship from the new revolutionary state. In his study of *xiangsheng* art, Perry Link points out that due to its satirical nature, *xiangsheng* was crushed in a series of political campaigns staged before 1957.[50] In contrast, both Xin and Pingju proved very useful in promoting new ideas, survived political campaigns and continued performing on stage up to the Cultural Revolution in the mid-1960s.

Most Pingju actors and actresses came from the lower social classes and troupes drifted among various marketplaces and performed on shabby village stages, as in *xiangsheng*. Xin and many other performers resented their previously low social status, and thus had great hopes for the communist regime. Xin felt herself doubly oppressed, both as a popular artist and as a woman, and viewed the Liberation in romanticized terms that she later articulated in a letter to her fans.[51] Xin's dedication to helping the new regime promote the Marriage Law was rewarded dearly by the government: Pingju received official recognition by the state. In addition to Xin entering the high artists' circle and marrying a member

[48] "*Xiangsheng*" performers usually appear onstage in pairs. It uses a conversational style to tell comedic stories.

[49] A general title for all types of oral art that combine singing and speaking, accompanied by simple musical instruments.

[50] Perry Link, "The Crocodile Bird: *Xiangsheng* in the Early 1950s," in *Dilemmas of Victory: The Early Years of the People's Republic of China*, Jeremy Brown and Paul G. Pickowicz (eds.) (Cambridge, MA: Harvard University Press, 2007), 207–31.

[51] Xin Fengxia, "Da xie re ai 'Qiao'er' de guanzhong men" (My Gratitude to the Audience Who Love 'Qiao'er'), *Zhongguo qingnian bao* (*Chinese Youth Daily*), February 16, 1957.

of it, Xin's troupe, previously a private enterprise was now upgraded into a group chartered by the state. Its name was changed to "The Experimental Pingju Theater in the Capital" (*Shoudu Shiyan Pingju Tuan* 首都实验评剧团), and the troupe was assigned to a permanent theater in the nation's new capital by the Beijing city government.[52] In her memoir, Xin Fengxia recalled that a senior actress, Xiao Bai Yushuang, who had great achievements in Pingju but died young, wanted Xin someday to realize her dream of performing Pingju on the stage of the China Grand Theater in Tianjin, which normally accepted only high-class performing arts such as Beijing operas and modern spoken dramas (*hua ju*). In 1952, when Xin brought *Liu Qiao'er* to this auditorium, she could not thank the CCP enough for putting Pingju on the same stage as Beijing opera.[53]

Compared to Beijing opera, the flexibility of various local operas and *quyi* helped them to respond promptly to the changing society and cater to a broader audience. On the other hand, Beijing opera had a close relationship to the imperial court and the upper classes, and often presented stories of male-centered imperial houses, courtrooms, and literati officials. Xin believed that Pingju centered primarily on female characters, presenting the life of ordinary women from the bottom of society.[54] Xin also pointed out that Beijing opera had already formed a fixed audience and was thus shaped around a series of formulaic melodies and character stereotypes, making it difficult to adopt ideas from other arts and present newly emerging social themes and events. In contrast, Pingju's elastic melodies and versatile characters willingly adopted any new theme to promptly respond to social changes. From late 1949 to 1950 she also quickly adopted various *yangge* plays brought by artists from the previous revolutionary base areas,[55] showing the flexibility of popular arts in catering for the audience in the social changes. In addition to *Liu Qiao'er* and *Xiao Erhei's Marriage* mentioned above, she also adopted *The White-Haired Girl*, *Xianglin's Wife* (*Xianglin sao* 祥林嫂), and others.[56]

For the CCP, the popular arts like Pingju and other local operas were very helpful in promoting its new policies. These arts had a broad audience among the lower social classes which were the targeted audience for the CCP social movements, and were strongly motivated to adopt revolutionary themes for social reform as they sought state recognition for their works. Nevertheless, in the eyes of the elites and the new state, the

[52] Xin Fengxia, *Wo jiao Xin Fengxia*, 24–5.
[53] Xin Fengxia, *Xin Fengxia de huiyi*, 131–4.
[54] Xin Fengxia, *Xin Fengxia huiyi lu*, 290.
[55] Xin Fengxia, *Xin Fengxia de huiyi*, 159–61.
[56] *Xianglin's Wife* was adapted from one of Lu Xun's famous short stories.

popular arts, such as *xiangsheng*, *quyi* and local operas, also had shortcomings because the performers and musicians, who were often illiterate or semi-literate like Xin, had difficulty in understanding the political core of social reform and were thus not able to present the political themes well. They also insisted on their old views of the new regime, which limited their openness to new themes brought by the revolution. Meanwhile, the vulgar taste and erotic content of their works also became a big obstacle to their consideration as high-class art and use in serving the idealistic goals of politics. It was the involvement of intellectuals and elites that made *Liu Qiao'er* into a piece of fine art that fitted the revolutionary reform agenda.

Transforming popular culture: intellectuals under the new revolutionary ideology

In the cultural patronage, the revolutionary narrative needed to be retold through a fine cultural presentation and artistic details that would further legitimate the revolution and its principles. However, the version of *Liu Qiao'er* that Xin Fengxia staged in late 1949 was an unstructured interpretation that used Han's ballad as an outline. Without an actual libretto, this version was very simple and largely depended on the individual performer's improvisations and was based on the actors' or actresses' understanding of their roles, or a spontaneous response to other performers in mid-act.[57] However, this unstructured opera was not refined enough to fit the purpose of promoting the Marriage Law, thus it needed big surgery.

The first *Liu Qiao'er* revision in early 1950 was written by Wang Yan 王雁 (?–?) and Xia Chun 夏淳 (?–?), and this script was later published as a libretto in 1952. Wang Yan was a traditional dramatist of Beijing opera who often selected historical stories for his libretto writing. Xia Chun was the director of modern spoken drama at the Beijing Modern Drama Theatre (*Beijing Huaju Tuan* 北京话剧团). The new director and dramatist restructured the play and recomposed the content by bringing Yuan Jing's version back.[58] Merging Yuan's libretto with Han's ballad, as well as Wang's and Xia's participation in recreating the Pingju libretto, embodied an important political sign of intellectuals combining with the populace, both spiritually and physically, very much like Xin's marriage.

[57] Xin Fengxia, *Xin Fengxia huiyi lu*, 184–5.
[58] Han Qixiang and Yuan Jing (original authors), *Liu Qiao'er* (Shoudu shiyan Pingju tuan jiti gai bian, Wang Yan zhi bi [collectively revised by the Experimental Pingju Troupe in the Capital, recorded by Wang Yan]) (Beijing: Wenbaotang shudian, 1952).

Their version was again modified and published in 1954, and became the basis for the 1956 film.

According to Xin, the 1950 revision by Wang Yan and Xia Chun can be viewed as a model of the combination of artistic elites and mass performers. Under the direction of both Wang and Xia, the entire troupe engaged in an analytic discussion so that everyone could present their ideas on the revision while receiving a thorough understanding of the story's theme, what purpose it served, and what social effect it should achieve.[59] Obviously, Xin's early version, which still used the title *Liu Qiao's Reunion*, was influenced by Han's ballad and fitted the popular taste. In this version, Liu Qiao, though the heroine, was not a strong character but a self-pitying figure who often sang long arias complaining about her unlucky fate and heartless father. The theme followed Han's design, emphasizing the protest against the unfair ruling of the county court and demanding the official recognition of the reunion between Qiao'er and Zhu'er. There was no anti-patriarchal theme. Wang suggested that the title be changed to simply *Liu Qiao'er*, which eliminated both Yuan Jing's theme of "going to law" and Han's theme of "reunion," instead placing a brave woman center stage.

Xia and Wang also helped the troupe alter the simple and straightforward presentation of the opera. According to Xin Fengxia, in the early version the story only included a few major scenes, such as Qiao'er's complaint about her father arranging a bad marriage, her conflict with Wang Shouchang on the road, and her meeting with Prefect Ma, which resulted in a happy ending. In this version, after being harassed and humiliated by Wang Shouchang, Qiao'er ran directly to Zhu'er's home and lived with him, an action of lawlessness. A revolutionary judge, Prefect Ma, appeared to rescue her, but his appearance had no context; he was simply a tool used to deliver a happy ending for the story. However, the revised version not only added additional scenes but also highlighted the revolutionary background of the story. For example, the opening was changed from Qiao'er complaining about her father to Qiao'er weaving in a cave-room with a particular style of window, a type of house design that only existed in the SGN region.[60] Xin recalled that every time the curtain opened, the audience immediately burst into applause because at the time admiring the Yan'an lifestyle was in fashion.[61] This revision and design thus ingeniously embedded the story of Liu Qiao'er and her pursuit of self-determined marriage into the revolutionary narrative.

[59] Xin Fengxia, *Xin Fengxia huiyi lu*, 186.
[60] Xin Fengxia, *Xin Fengxia huiyi lu*, 185–6.
[61] *Ibid.*

Second, the new version added more content that stressed the values behind Qiao'er's choice. In Xin's early version, Qiao'er did not explain why she insisted on marrying Zhu'er, which largely weakened the concept of love-based marriage promoted by the Marriage Law. With director Xia's suggestion, a new scene was added that dramatized Qiao'er falling in love with a labor model, Zhao Zhenhua, at a political meeting, but not knowing that he was her former fiancé Zhu'er, which was only his "milk name," not his official name. The idea of Zhu'er being a labor model (*laodong mofan* 劳动模范) was absolutely Xia's and Wang's innovation, in which another revolutionary symbol was carefully woven into the artistic details of *Liu Qiao'er*. Men and women being labor models was a practice initiated in the Yan'an period, and thus presenting a labor model established a new image of young males under the revolutionary state. According to Xin's memoir, Xia wanted her to understand that love is based on hard work to create a happy family. Thus they composed a long aria to show that the young woman was in love and longed to be together with her lover, the model laborer Zhao Zhenhua.[62]

Third, the new version reintroduced the character of Auntie Li and her political identity as the director of the village women's association, as in Yuan Jing's version.[63] In Han's version, the character of Auntie Li was simply a motherly middle-aged woman who cared about Qiao'er. As a male wandering singer, Han may not have fully understood the role of village director of the women's association as a local representative of the revolutionary state. Xin was also unable to appreciate the political significance of Auntie Li, and thus the character was entirely omitted in her early version.[64] Reintroducing this character signified that Qiao'er was not alone in her fight, but was aided by the guidance of a systematic organization of state power that supported women's resistance to arranged marriage, and offered help to women who encountered troubles.

There was another change in the scene in which Qiao'er ran into Prefect Ma, and the way the story concluded. In Xin's early version, the last scene of Prefect Ma settling the case was very brief, which differed from both Yuan's and Han's versions. Also, in Xin's version Qiao'er's appeal to Ma occurred not immediately after the kidnapping but much later, when Qiao'er had already given birth to her son. In the scene, Ma was simply an authoritative figure, like the judge in traditional opera, to whom Qiao'er presented her grievance about her fate and complained about her father's decision, hoping for approval of her actions. It appears

62 Xin Fengxia, *Xin Fengxia huiyi lu*, 186–8.
63 Wang Yan, *Liu Qiao'er*, 1952.
64 Xin Fengxia, *Xin Fengxia huiyi lu*, 185.

that this act closed very abruptly, with Prefect Ma's announcement of her legal marriage to Zhu'er.[65] In the modified version, the ending became an important scene featuring another long aria, in which Qiao'er told Prefect Ma about her avaricious father, the covetous matchmaker, and the vicious landlord, while expressing her determination to marry Zhu'er.[66] In order to show how Prefect Ma reached his decision and carried out the policy of the mass line, the new version extended the scene to show Prefect Ma investigating the case and determining community opinion prior to delivering his judgment in an open court,[67] all details that made revolutionary narrative more appealing to the populace.

Regarding the specific term used for the principle for marriage, in the 1950 modified version, the term *zi-zhu* was spread throughout the text; the main characters, including Qiao'er's father, Auntie Li, Qiao'er, and Prefect Ma, all articulate that the principle of marriage was *zi-zhu*, a term also used in Yuan Jing's version.[68] It seems that the use of this phrase was not only an inheritance from SGNBR practice, but also well explained the Marriage Law in the term of popular culture (see the discussion of the origin of this term in popular culture in Chapter 4). In all subsequent publications of Liu Qiao'er's libretto, and the film, this term was maintained.

Politicizing popular culture

After the opera was staged in 1950, Wang continued to refine the libretto with minor changes and published the revised libretto in 1952, 1954, and 1958 with different publishers. The 1954 version was used for the film in 1956. In the 1954 version, Wang strongly articulated the goal of this opera as being an instrument for promoting the idea of new marriage and propagating the Marriage Law. In its preface, Wang Yan justified the new modifications by stating that since fighting feudalism in marriage was a long-term project, this new opera was well-suited for the war against it. By applying new political theory to his work, Wang pointed out the deficiencies of all the previous versions that they did not adequately expose arranged marriage as the remains of the old ruling class, and did not sufficiently emphasize the idea of freedom of marriage.[69] According to Wang, in both Yuan's and Han's versions, the foundation for Qiao'er's

[65] Xin Fengxia, *Xin Fengxia huiyi lu*, 183–5.
[66] Xin Fengxia, *Xin Fengxia huiyi lu*, 189–91.
[67] Wang Yan, *Liu Qiao'er*, 1952.
[68] Wang Yan, *Liu Qiao'er*, 1952.
[69] Wang Yan, "Guanyu Liu Qiao'er de gaibian" (Regarding the Revision of Liu Qiao'er), in *Liu Qiao'er* (Beijing: Baowentang shudian, 1954), 1–3.

insistence on marrying Zhu'er was their previous engagement. Both versions showed that once Qiao'er learned that Zhu'er was not mentally disabled, she regretted that she had believed her father and ended the original engagement. Wang Yan argued that this left room for justifying arranged marriage, because one could say that Qiao'er could have been happy if she had not abolished the original engagement. Wang believed that the new version should present Qiao'er's decision to end her engagement as due to her belief that the old practice blindly forced two people together, regardless of whether the result was good or bad. The new version deleted Qiao'er's expression of her regret, thus fully preventing the possibility of arranged marriage being presented in a positive light.[70] This marked a radical vision of marriage practice that fortified the new form of marriage but entirely excluded the slightest possibility of involving local custom in marriage as presented in the judicial practice of the 1940s. Wang's new version thus included a long aria describing Qiao'er's disagreement with her old engagement and the excitement of her new love. Her rejection of the prior engagement was justified because "I have never known him and never met him, how could we be happy together?"[71] This aria later became the classic piece of *Liu Qiao'er*.

To reinforce this point and to base the young couple's marriage on the solid ground of love, Wang rewrote the scene in the field so that Qiao'er, who in previous versions only saw Zhu'er from a distance, now had a chance to talk to him, and express her love. Having learned from Auntie Li that Zhu'er was the labor model she admired and having seen him working skillfully in the field, she made her decision not because of the previous engagement but because of her feelings for this man and his good qualities.[72] This alteration thus confirmed that Qiao'er's marriage was based on mutual affection. Wang Yan was convinced that this was the true spirit of the new Marriage Law.[73]

Wang Yan also believed that the old versions retained much of their prototype from the legal case and were not sufficiently focused on the issue of marriage. They leaned too much on the sagacious Prefect Ma and his working style of mass mobilization, which provided a happy ending for the couple. In the revised version, Wang deliberately created Qiao'er as a strong character. The help of Prefect Ma was necessary, but it was Qiao'er's courage in pursuing her true love that brought about the happy ending. In doing so, Wang hoped to encourage more women to

[70] *Ibid.*
[71] Wang Yan, *Liu Qiao'er*, 1952.
[72] Wang Yan, "Guanyu Liu Qiao'er de gaibian."
[73] *Ibid.*

follow the spirit of freedom in marriage and seek true love. The new version preserved the mass meeting at the end because it served the purpose of educating people. As Wang Yan explained, retaining this section was useful for spreading the idea of freedom of marriage among the masses and encouraging criticism against arranged marriage.[74] This alteration totally eliminated the dual themes in Yuan's version and the admiration of the "clear-sky" judge in Han's version.

At the same time, the image of Wang Shouchang became even more wicked, with a strong political connotation at the height of land reform. First, Wang Shouchang's status as a landlord now became the key to understanding his behavior. Neither Yuan's nor Han's version explicitly linked politics to his behavior. Although Wang Shouchang was a rich and wicked man, his moral malevolence and sexual deviance regarding Qiao'er originated from his wealth, not his political status. However, Wang Yan pointed out that the previous versions were produced during the time of the United Front, when the SGNBR government had not yet launched the land reform campaign against the landlord class. In the current period, the propagation of the new Marriage Law sought to teach people that landlords as a counter-revolutionary class represented backward social customs in marriage.[75] As discussed in Chapter 6, in previous versions it was Qiao'er's avaricious father who wanted to find a high-priced suitor for his daughter and listened to a greedy matchmaker to do so, but in Wang Yan's version this arranged marriage was initiated by Wang Shouchang. The purchase of Qiao'er was a conspiracy launched by this lecherous landlord targeting a young and beautiful woman, and a vicious witchlike matchmaker who was looking for financial gain. Wang Yan thus implied that this arranged marriage represented not only the remaining elements of old social practices, but the dying struggle of a moribund class that preyed on the vigor of working-class women.[76]

Changchun Film Studio began to film this Pingju version of *Liu Qiao'er* in 1954 as a musical film of the same title, with Xin Fengxia playing the leading role.[77] Beginning in late 1956, the film was shown nationwide and advertised in various popular magazines and newspapers such as *The Masses' Movies* (*Dazhong dianying* 大众电影, no. 18, 1956), *Chinese Youth Daily* (*Zhongguo qingnian bao* 中国青年报, February 5, 1957), and *Popular Cartoons* (*Lianhuan huabao* 连环画报, no. 3, 1957), which used Liu Qiao'er's picture on its back cover. This film raised the image of Liu Qiao'er to a

[74] *Ibid.*
[75] *Ibid.*
[76] *Ibid.*
[77] Yi Lin (director), *Liu Qiao'er*.

national symbol for new women fighting for happy marriages. At the same time, Xin Fengxia rose from being a regional opera star to a nationally famous actress with a large number of fans. To respond to this honor, in 1957 Xin Fengxia published an open letter in *Chinese Youth Daily* that expressed her gratitude for the support from her fans nationwide and for their appreciation of her performance of *Liu Qiao'er*.[78]

The still photos, advertisements, and stage performances of each opera also showed a gradual politicization that injected heroism into Qiao'er's struggle with the landlord. In the scene where Qiao'er ran into Wang Shouchang on the road and learned that she was to marry this ugly old man, both Yuan and Han made it a surprise to Qiao'er, who was shocked and humiliated. In Xin's version, a physical struggle occurred between Wang Shouchang and Qiao'er because Wang tried to sexually harass her. Qiao'er was kicked to the ground by Wang and humiliated. But after Wang Yan's revision, this scene was drastically reversed: Qiao'er slapped Wang's face, showing her to be angry rather than humiliated, and thus making Qiao'er the winner of the confrontation.[79] The film also adopted this version. However, when Wang Yan's libretto was readapted into Shaanxi (Qin) opera, the confrontation became even more dramatic: Qiao'er not only slapped the landlord's face but also kicked him to the ground. A cover page of the libretto of the Qin opera showed a still picture of Wang on the ground, frightened of Qiao'er (see Figure 7.1).[80] It is worth noting that the Shaanxi opera adaptation was done in 1958, when the ideology of class struggle was especially prominent in the context of the Great Leap Forward.

Wang Yan's idea of emphasizing class struggle in the implementation of the Marriage Law was fully reflected in the film's advertisements. The advertisement described the plot as "a doglike landlord tries to pick up the moon on the sky[81] with his stinky money, but a good woman eventually marries her lover through her shrewdness and courage."[82] In the film, the story completed its full transformation from a drama with dual themes to focusing solely on a woman achieving her ideal marriage through "her shrewdness and courage." The film also presented the political message that arranged marriage, though seen as an old practice,

[78] Xin Fengxia, "Da xie re ai 'Qiao'er' de guanzhong men."

[79] Xin Fengxia, *Xin Fengxia huiyi lu*, 186.

[80] *Liu Qiao'er* (Shaanxi Qinqiang shiyan jutuan gaiwei Qinqiang ben [Adopted Libretto for Qin Opera by Shaanxi Provincial Experimental Theater]).

[81] In Chinese, "doglike" is a very negative term that describes a filthy person of very low morals and dignity and no independence. The metaphor "picking up the moon on the sky" describes the landlord's attempt to marry Qiao'er, i.e an impossibility.

[82] *Zhongguo qingnian bao*, February 5, 1957.

Figure 7.1 Still photo of Shaanxi opera (*Liu Qiao'er*, 1958)

would be used by the "doglike" landlord class to infringe on the happiness of the working people.

IV. Feng Zhiqin and "Liu Qiao'er": the new models of women

These operas and films created a strong image of womanhood and a political model for women. In China, the state's patronage of moral and political models for both men and women has a long history. Since the Han Dynasty (206 BCE–220 CE), when the stories of a group of exemplary women were put into collections for the purpose of educating women, every dynasty, from central governments to local governments, sought exemplary women and made them into moral models for other women to serve as a means of social control or as an ideological instrument for remolding people's views.[83] On the other hand, elite social organizations

[83] For example, Liu Xiang (77–6 BCE), *Lienü zhuan* (Biographies of Exemplary Women) (Harbin: Harbin chubanshe, 2009 reprint).

were also able to promote exemplary women to spread their views of women's role in society in times of reform in the late Qing and the early Republic.[84] During the May Fourth period, traditional images of women, such as Hua Mulan, became examples for some educated women who were brave enough to leave home for their education and to set up their goal of fighting for women's interests.[85]

The Chinese revolutionary state in Yan'an also adopted this traditional practice by applying it to its construction of villages and the Grand Production Campaign in the 1940s.[86] In the 1950s, one of the female models was the tractor driver,[87] but in the 1970s, the state promoted "iron girls" (*tie guniang* 铁姑娘) as the models in factories and rural production teams.[88] After studying the female icons of the 1950s' PRC, Tina Mai Chen argues against the view that sees official feminism as a one-dimensional effort serving the party's goals without considering women's place in society; rather, she believes that state-sponsored female model workers had multilayered experiences in the multifaceted interactions between these women and the state's representation of them. Female models lived in a different dimension from the state image of women, and were thus still able to maintain their subjectivity.[89] Likewise, Feng Peng'er enjoyed her own life experiences in both family and public affairs, while the character of Liu Qiao'er, based on Peng'er's story, inspired its followers to assert agency in their actions.

From Feng Peng'er to Feng Zhiqin: rural women in the public domain

While the case of *Feng v. Zhang* experienced this series of transformations from being brought to the then political center of Yan'an, reinvented as the opera *Liu Qiao'er*, and then moving even farther to Beijing

[84] Judge, *The Precious Raft of History*.
[85] Wang Zheng, *Women in the Chinese Enlightenment*, 119–356.
[86] See Patricia Stranahan, "Labor Heroines of Yan'an" *Modern China* 9(2) (April 1983): 228–52.
[87] Yu Minling, "Nüren fu li? – Nü tuolaji shou zai Zhongguo" (Women Ploughing? – Female Tractor Drivers in China), in *Liang an fen tu: leng zhan chu qi de zheng jing fazhan* (Divided Roads on the Two Sides of the Taiwan Strait: Political and Economic Development of [the Mainland and Taiwan] in the Early Cold War Period), Yu Minling (ed.) (Taipei: Zhongyang yanjiuyuan jindashi suo, 2006), 1–29.
[88] Naihua Zhang, "In a World Together Yet Apart: Urban and Rural Women Coming of Age in the Seventies," in *Some of Us: Chinese Women Growing Up in the Mao Era*, Xueping Zhong, Wang Zheng, and Bai Di (eds.) (New Brunswick, NJ: Rutgers University Press, 2001), 1–26.
[89] Tina Mai Chen, "Female Icons, Feminist Iconography? Socialist Rhetoric and Women's Agency in 1950s China," *Gender & History* 15(2) (August 2003): 268–95.

for a national campaign, it left the initial protagonist, Peng'er, behind in her small village.

Peng'er appreciated the CCP and the communist revolution for allowing her to achieve a happy marriage, a feeling that came from the bottom of her heart. In the late 1940s, when the communist military forces were on the cusp of winning all of China, the CCP asked for more manpower from its former base areas to win the civil war. Peng'er actively responded to this call by encouraging her husband, Zhang Bo, to enlist in the PLA; he was discharged with an injury a year later.[90] During Zhang Bo's absence, Peng'er expressed her appreciation for the PLA by granting a special honor to a PLA officer, Zhang Xuan 张宣. In my interview with him, Zhang Xuan told me that when his unit arrived at a small village on the way to their designated location in 1948, the village head came to him, stating that a young woman had particularly asked for a fortunate military man of the Eighth Route Army (former title of PLA) to be her son's sworn father (*gan da* 干大) and offer actual/virtual protection to her one-year-old son.[91] As a unit officer, Zhang responded to the call. The village head, who had apparently heard about the opera of *Liu Qiao'er* showing in Yan'an, told Zhang that the woman's story had been recounted in the opera *Liu Qiao'er Goes to the Law*. Officer Zhang had seen the opera in Yan'an in 1946 and was excited to meet this legendary young woman. He followed the local custom by bringing a small gift, a piece of red thread to tie on the boy's wrist, which supposedly holds protective powers for the child.[92]

The establishment of the PRC in 1949 also brought drastic changes to Peng'er's life. First, she was no longer known by her "milk name," Peng'er, but given the new official name Feng Zhiqin, like a man, as part of the local population registration. The middle character of her name followed her (paternal cousin-) sister, indicating that they belonged to the same generation, which was a traditional way of naming males who were brothers or paternal cousins.[93] This name gave Peng'er an official identity, indicating that she was no longer limited to the family

[90] Feng Zhiqin told me that the village head tried to mobilize Zhang Bo's younger brother to join the army, but she encouraged her husband to go instead. Interview with Feng Zhiqin, July 21, 2005.

[91] According to the local custom, once a child reached one year old, his/her parents had to find a sworn father or sworn mother for extra protection for the child. It is an honor for a person to be granted the position of sworn father/mother of a child.

[92] Interview with Zhang Xuan, June 25, 2006. Unfortunately, this boy passed away about a year later. Peng'er gave birth to two daughters but no more sons, so in the early 1950s she decided to adopt a son from her husband's clan. Interview with Feng Zhiqin, July 21, 2005.

[93] Interview with Feng Zhiqin, July 21, 2005.

domain but officially capable of participating in public affairs. In the early 1950s, she became the director of the village women's association, a role that represented the party's authority in the village as well as serving as women's natal agent.[94] In 1956, she joined the Chinese Communist Party.[95]

Although the film *Liu Qiao'er* had already been shown nationwide, given her location in a remote village of the northwestern region, Feng probably only saw it some time between 1957 and 1960.[96] Before seeing this film, Feng Zhiqin had only a vague idea about the image that had been created based on her story and the importance of this symbol in women's liberation. In 1955, Ma Xiwu, now the deputy director of the National Highest (Supreme) Court, returned to his hometown and Longdong region for a visit and informed Feng in more detail about the famous Pingju *Liu Qiao'er* and that it was going to be made into a film. Feng told Ma that her family had joined the cooperative and that she had been elected a member of its agricultural committee.[97] Through Ma's introduction, Feng Zhiqin and Xin Fengxia got to know each other and exchanged several greeting letters in the 1950s.

Feng Zhiqin received great honors for her past experience as the prototype of a revolutionary model and her active participation in public affairs. Beginning in the late 1950s, Feng served as the people's representative of the Fourth, Fifth, and Sixth Congresses of Yuele Township, the representative of the Seventh Congress of Huachi County, and the representative of the Fourth Congress of Gansu Province. Up to 1965, Feng served as the deputy director of the Women's Federation in the Yuele Township Commune.[98] Moreover, she had been interviewed by a number of newspapers and her picture was published in various magazines as the story of *Liu Qiao'er* brought people back to learn the original legend.

[94] Yang Zhengfa, *Feng Zhiqin, Liu Qiao'er*, 119.

[95] From the tablet in front of Feng's new home.

[96] The local gazetteer may be wrong about the time that the film was shown in Huachi in 1956 (*Huachi xian zhi*, 1250) because the film was officially released in December 1956 and it should have taken several months to reach remote places such as Huachi. Yang Zhengfa believes that it was much later in the 1960s that the film was first shown in Yuele Township where Feng Zhiqin lived (Yang, *Feng Zhiqin, Liu Qiao'er*, 86). In the interview, Feng Zhiqin remembered vaguely that it might have been some time after 1957 (interview July 21, 2005).

[97] Yang, *Feng Zhiqin, Liu Qiao'er*, 101.

[98] The gazetteer recorder believed that it was after the film that Feng received all kinds of honors. However, as I have discussed, if the film was shown in Huachi in 1957 it was possible for the government officials to select her for this honor. See *Huachi xian zhi*, 1250.

"Liu Qiao'er" as a model for rural women

During the 1950s, a number of artistic works similar to *Liu Qiao'er* were published expressly for the purpose of promoting the Marriage Law. In addition to *Xiao Erhei's Marriage*, there were *Xiao nüxu* 小女婿 (Child Husband), *Li Ersao gaijia* 李二嫂改嫁 (Remarriage of Li the Second Sister-in-Law), *Liushu jing* 柳树井 (Willow Well), and *Luohan qian* 罗汉钱 (Luohan Coin), all local operas then adapted into films, that attacked the traditional arranged marriage and praised young men and women for selecting their own marriage mates.[99] Among these artistic works, the image of Liu Qiao'er became a model that women could copy; Liu Qiao'er thus did not only inspire Xin Fengxia alone, but reached women across rural China.

Liu Qiao'er as a model also created followers in rural communities. In 1951, a young woman, Li Zhiru from Mancheng County, Hebei Province, repeated Peng'er's and Liu Qiao'er's actions. During the land reform and the promulgation of the Marriage Law, Li became actively involved in a literacy campaign through which she learned the new idea of self-determined marriage, possibly the story of Liu Qiao'er. In these activities she fell in love with a young man, Jia Jincai. However, her father and elder brother strongly objected to her choice in marriage and then immediately arranged another marriage for her. To prevent her from contacting Jia and prepare her for this arranged marriage, her father confined her at home. With the help of a friend, she was able to send a letter to the county court and the women's association asking for help. The judge of the county court and the director of the women's association promptly came to her rescue. Due to the involvement and intervention of the government, a marriage tragedy was avoided and Li was eventually able to marry the man she loved. Her story was included in the promotion documents of the Marriage Law and known widely as "Liu Qiao'er in Hebei" (*Hebei de Liu Qiao'er* 河北的刘巧儿) during the 1950s. In a contemporary interview with her, Li still remembers this as an exciting moment in her life and she never regretted fighting for her ideal marriage.[100] In this case, the idea of self-determination was an inspiration and the woman became an embodiment of Liu Qiao'er. Meanwhile, the assistance for women coming from both the county judge and the director of the women's association also showed a similarity to the story of Liu Qiao'er. It was a successful case of state cultural patronage using Liu Qiao'er as the symbol for self-determined marriage.

[99] *Zhongguo xiqu quyi cidian* (An Encyclopedia of Chinese Operas and Other Oral Performing Arts) (Shanghai: Shanghai cishu chubanshe, 1981), 614–15.

[100] Huang Chuanhui, *Tianxia hunyin*, 68–73.

The image of Liu Qiao'er as a cultural symbol developed since the Yan'an period encapsulated the CCP's experience in legal practice and represented its mode of political governance during this period. In the 1950s, when the CCP, after taking over national power, spread its way of governance across the whole country, its previous revolutionary experience was legitimated through cultural patronage in which the cultural symbols developed from its revolutionary period, such as Liu Qiao'er, were revised and recast as national models. Through promoting these revolutionary symbols, the state had the chance to narrate its revolutionary past. Meanwhile, the lives of the inspirations for this image – the prototype (Feng Zhiqin), the creator of Liu Qiao'er (Yuan Jing), and performer of Liu Qiao'er (Xin Fengxia) – continued on their own life paths after 1960.

Epilogue

"Liu Qiao'er," law, and *zizhu*: beyond 1960

The reform of marriage and family in twentieth-century China was an important project that involved various social forces and a multilayered and multifaceted process. This social movement produced its own images and neologisms that demonstrate the dynamics between imported urban ideas and the adaptive process that evolved in the implementation. In return, these images, symbols, and neologisms reconstructed the state ideology and guided social practice.

The historical trajectory, in which the marriage dispute of *Feng v. Zhang* was transformed from a local instance to the making of the image of Liu Qiao'er as a national icon, and from a legal case to a cultural symbol, epitomized the changing relationship of Chinese women to family and state in the twentieth century. If Feng Peng'er's action represented women's agency that spontaneously challenged patriarchal domination, as many rural women did before her, the ending of her case can be seen as a turning point in which the revolutionary state worked with women to empower them. By creating the image of Liu Qiao'er, the state set up a political/moral model for women, encouraging them to engage with their agency. In mobilizing women to participate in social reforms, the state reshaped gender relations between the family and state, and the individual and society. Thus the image of Liu Qiao'er symbolizes the revolutionary power that integrated female agents into its agenda for social reform. It was in this process that neologisms such as *zi-zhu* began to emerge, which crystalized and conceptualized the revolutionary experience in its social practices that also recast the dynamics between the state and family. As the society and the life of the protagonists have moved on, the image of Liu Qiao'er and the neologism, as a part of revolutionary legacy, continued to play their roles even after the 1960s by making new history in contemporary China.

I. The ongoing story of Liu Qiao'er: Feng Zhiqin, Yuan Jing, and Xin Fengxia

From the 1950s onward, the three women involved in the making of the image of Liu Qiao'er experienced varied paths. In the 1960s Feng Zhiqin continued to enjoy the honor brought by the image of Liu Qiao'er and her dedication to public service; she served as the people's representative and director of the women's association until the beginning of the Cultural Revolution in 1966. As an official model, she was labeled a supporter of the old system; many other officially promoted models suffered similar persecution.[1] From the late 1960s to the early 1980s, Feng Zhiqin, Xin Fengxia, and "Liu Qiao'er" disappeared from the public eye.

In the early 1980s after suffering as the target of criticism along with many other artists during the Cultural Revolution, Xin Fengxia returned to the national stage as the "empress" of Pingju, and reclaimed her past glory in the performing arts.[2] The media and entertainment circles began to recall the outstanding characters she had created, including Liu Qiao'er. Xin's fame also brought attention to Feng Zhiqin. In this new wave of praise for Liu Qiao'er, Feng Zhiqin was recalled by the local government and granted new honors. In 1983 she became a provincial labor model and attended a conference in Lanzhou. Xin Fengxia and Feng Zhiqin met twice in the 1980s, the first time in 1983 and the second time in 1986 when Feng Zhiqin and her husband, Zhang Bo visited Beijing.[3] Zhang Bo passed away at the age of sixty-eight in 1991.[4]

In contrast to Feng and Xin, who received public attention when the play/film was shown nationwide and during the reform era after 1980, Yuan Jing, though the original author of the libretto and the creator of the image of Liu Qiao'er, was totally disconnected from these social events. In the 1950s she was not involved in either the reinvention of the image of Liu Qiao'er or the campaign promoting the Marriage Law. The publication of *The Story of New Heroic Sons and Daughters* brought her great honor and made her one of the most famous revolutionary writers.[5] Yuan continued working on her creative writing in Beijing, but

[1] Yang Zhengfa, *Feng Zhiqin, Liu Qiao'er*, 209–26.

[2] "Pingju huanghou Xin Fengxia xiju rensheng liu jiahua" (The Wonderful Life Story of Xin Fengxia as the Empress of Pingju), http://bjyouth.ynet.com/3.1/1204/18/6999091.html (accessed November 15, 2014).

[3] The content of the tablet on the front of Feng's new home.

[4] Yang Zhengfa, *Feng Zhiqin, Liu Qiao'er*, 133.

[5] Chunming chubanshe xin mingci cidian zu (comp.), *Xin ding xin mingci cidian* (Newly Revised Dictionary of Neologisms) (Shanghai: Chunming chubanshe, 1952), 9056.

her personal life took a turn in the early 1950s. The romance between Yuan and Kong and their cooperation in the field of creative literature came to an end because of Kong's extramarital affairs.[6] After marrying her third husband, Yuan moved to Tianjin[7] and wrote children's stories for her stepdaughter (see Chapter 6). From the 1960s to the 1970s she also published a series of mediocre novels on subjects ranging from Tianjin's water project to the story of a CCP secret agent in northern China, but their influence was very limited.[8]

As the central figures of the tale who had enjoyed public fame, both Feng Zhiqin and "Liu Qiao'er" continued their stories in the reform era. The wave of economic reforms and the withdrawal of state power from villages weakened the grassroots power structure and left a space for the revival of many old practices.[9] In 1983 the state official newspaper, *People's Daily*, published a reader's indignant letter complaining that in his hometown, Huachi County, where the image of Liu Qiao'er had originated, the old practices of teenage marriage, *caili*, and buying/selling marriage had returned. He wondered, "Where is Prefect Ma?" and demanded that the state react to the resurgence of these backward customs.[10] In the 1990s when economic development eroded the revolutionary spirit as well as the principle of self-determined marriage, this revival of old practices continued, especially in rural areas. Although her story was used to create a new model opposing arranged marriage and buying/selling marriage, Feng Zhiqin herself could not escape the trend of reviving old traditions. A 2000 report once again located the prototype of Liu Qiao'er and visited Feng Zhiqin, trying to explore more details of the story and its aftermath. In the interview, the reporter discovered that Feng was troubled by a family matter: her granddaughter had run away

6 See Lu Zonglin and Wang Zaiyu, "Kong Jue shi lue."

7 Lou Xiyuan, "Zoufang Yuan Jing yi xi tan" (An Interview with Yuan Jing), Kaidi shequ (Kaidi net), http://club.kdnet.net/dispbbs.asp?boardid=5&id=6834049&page=1&1=1#6834049 (accessed May 13, 2012); and interview with Qin Wenhu, June 28, 2012.

8 Sun Geli, "Pei tong zhuming zuojia Yuan Jing caifang yishi" (Some Anecdotes on Accompanying Famous Writer Yuan Jing for Interviews), http://203xcd.blog.sohu.com/187599463.html (accessed May 9, 2012); also interview with Qin Wenhu, June 28, 2012.

9 After 1949 and up to the reform period in the 1990s some old customs of marriage continued to exist, especially in rural and remote regions. However, under the state authority's close watch from the 1950s to the late 1970s, many old practices in rural areas went underground. The state's withdrawal of its supervision of villages in the 1980s brought these practices back into the public view.

10 Ma Yanglin, "'Ma zhuanyuan', ni zai nali?" (Prefect Ma, Where Are You?), *Renmin ribao*, July 13, 1983.

because Feng Zhiqin and her entire family disapproved of the man her granddaughter had chosen to marry.[11]

Based on this new development, in 2004 the Chinese Pingju Theater (*Zhongguo pingju yuan* 中国评剧团) produced and staged a new drama, *The New Story of Liu Qiao'er* (*Liu Qiao'er xin zhuan* 刘巧儿新传). This drama became another instance in which the CCP used its cultural positioning policy to respond to the revival of old issues. In this "new" story, Qiao'er falls in love with her neighbor, the widower Yu Laoshuan, after her husband, Zhu'er, dies in the Korean War. However, she is disturbed by the villagers' disparagement of her neighbor and thus suppresses her desire to remarry. To fulfill her unrealized wish to marry Yu, she arranges for her grandson to marry Yu's granddaughter, but the two young people vigorously object. Meanwhile, she also tries to create obstacles to her widowed son's remarriage to a widow because she is the granddaughter of Wang Shouchang, her former foe. With the help of the younger generation who inherited the true spirit of Liu Qiao'er, and armed with knowledge of the new marriage law, Qiao'er eventually comes to the understanding that she should let her son and grandson decide their own marriages (*zizhu*). Furthermore, she also overcomes her concerns and accepts Yu Laoshuan's proposal.[12] Consciously or unconsciously, the new story of Liu Qiao'er portrays the rural conditions of the early 1990s: old practices were revived and eroded the revolutionary legacy, and there was no state power or women's organization to guide resistance to the resurgence of these old customs. However, the dramatist still pinned the hope of carrying on the revolutionary spirit on the new generation.

The view of marriage and its practice have made a turn since the 1990s in face of further economic development. As Yunxiang Yan shows in his study, the concepts of family relations, private life, and love had experienced a drastic transformation in Chinese villages from 1949 in that the younger generation enjoyed much more freedom in their private lives.[13] Due to the deepening economic reforms and the nationwide expansion

[11] Teng Yuhong, "San ge nüren de gushi" (The Stories of Three Women), *Zhongguo dianshi bao* (Chinese Television Weekly) 10 (March 9, 2000).

[12] Zhou Heng, "'Liu Qiao'er' you you dongren xinzhuan" (Liu Qiao'er Once again Has a Touching New Story), *Renmin ribao*, haiwai ban (People's Daily, overseas version), September 27, 2004; "'Liu Qiao'er' you xinzhuan, liangxiang Beijing da wutai" (Liu Qiao'er Making a New Story and Showing on Beijing's Grand Stage), "Qianlong wang" (Qianlong website), http://culture.qianlong.com/6931/2004/05/11/1340@2047123.htm (accessed January 24, 2005).

[13] See Yunxiang Yan, *Private Life under Socialism: Love, Intimacy, and Family Change in a Chinese Village, 1949–1999* (Stanford, CA: Stanford University Press, 2003).

of compulsory education to nine years in the 1990s, many young men and women left their home villages and their parents' control to work in factories in coastal cities, which changed their views of love and marriage profoundly.[14]

In the new millennium, both Feng Zhiqin and Liu Qiao'er made contributions to local economic development. In the national wave of remaking revolutionary legends to stimulate tourism and improve the local economy, the Huachi County government designated Feng Zhiqin and her home as a site for "Red Tourism" (*Hongse lüyou* 红色旅游).[15] When I visited Feng Zhiqin for the first time in 2005, I found that in 2003 the local government had built a new house for her next to her old house, and attached an exhibition hall for a collection of cultural works including photos, newspapers, books, librettos, calligraphies, signatures of political leaders and celebrities, and many other items about Feng Zhiqin, Liu Qiao'er, and Xin Fengxia to showcase their local heroine. For the purpose of attracting tourists, the county government built a *basso-relievo* wall of cultural exhibits near the civic center that included important images from ancient times, through the revolutionary period, to contemporary events and figures. One of these emblems portrays local celebrities Feng and her husband as a marker of the past revolution. A new road was extended from the Huachi County seat out to the villages, passing by Feng Zhiqin's new house. Three huge signs have been built along the road to Feng Zhiqin's house, beginning miles away, that read, "Here is the home of Liu Qiao'er who is the model for women's liberation in New China," "Liu Qiao'er, the vanguard of anti-feudalistic arranged marriage: Her home is here," and "The spirit of Qiao'er represents the brightness and honor of [Chinese] women." Another sign has been set on the roadside across from Feng's new house, and two more signs have been placed in front of the homes that read "Liu Qiao'er's old residence" and "Liu Qiao'er's new residence" (see the following figures). The county government also

[14] See *Qingyang diqu zhi*, 919–24; *Huachi xian zhi*, 881–82. However, a recent report on the marriage condition in Qingyang region exposed the problems in the local marriage market. The shortage of young females brought a rapid increase of *caili* that made young males and their families fall into financial trouble. The imbalanced sex ratio in local population is partially caused by the one child policy and partially attributed to the recent urban development that brought a large number of young females to cities while young males had to follow the tradition by returning villages to take care of their parents. See CCTV, "Xinwen diaocha: Longdong hunshi" (News Investigation: Marriage Issues in Longdong), February 7, 2015. See http://tv.cntv.cn/vodplay/603a16aff11b480192d5b8ab4d519edc/860010-1102010100 (accessed on May 12, 2015).

[15] "Red Tourism" is the tourism program promoted by various local governments that uses previous revolutionary sites in their jurisdictional territories to attract tourists for economic gain.

Figures 8.1 and 8.2 The signs near to Feng Peng'er's home

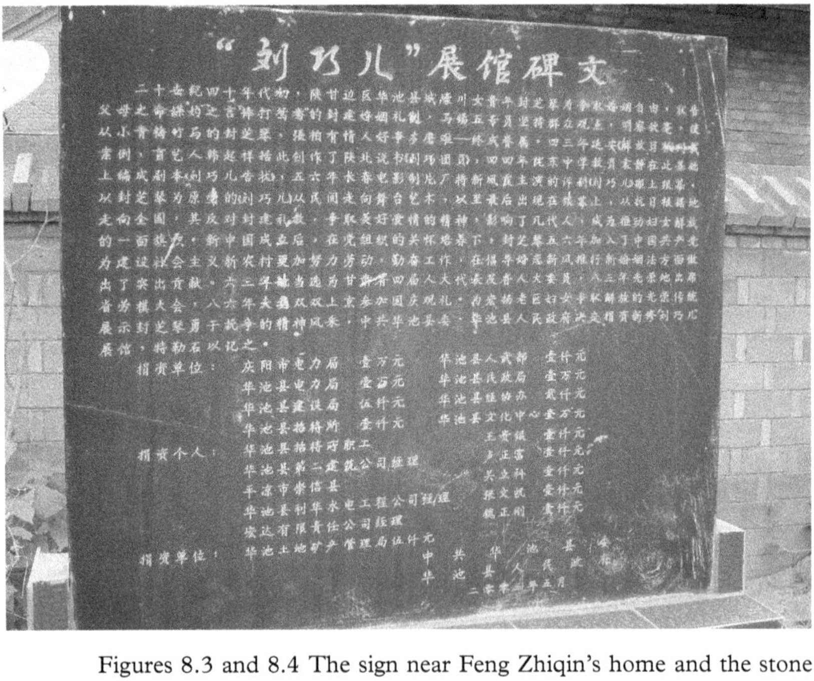

Figures 8.3 and 8.4 The sign near Feng Zhiqin's home and the stone tablet in front of her new house

installed a stone tablet in front of Feng's new residence that narrates the story and the reason the house was built for Feng. Most of the signs include Feng Zhiqin's smiling picture, but her name is no longer listed as Feng Peng'er or Feng Zhiqin – she is known only as Liu Qiao'er. As a national symbol, the name Liu Qiao'er covers her historical origins in Feng Peng'er and the later name of Feng Zhiqin. Although Feng Peng'er or Feng Zhiqin existed in the shadow of "Liu Qiao'er" in the official discourse and system, she still maintained her local and economic identity throughout the social changes.

II. The law and marriage: progress and practice beyond 1960

After the promulgation of the 1950 Marriage Law, marriage reform continued through both the judicial and administrative systems and thus concretized the principle of new marriage in institutionalized practice. Since then, the law and its implementation gradually changed local marriage practice and individual behavior. In 1980 a new marriage law was issued that revised the 1950 law. The major change was the term on divorce, which added one condition to ex parte divorce. The 1950 law sanctioned ex parte divorce only after the failure of court mediation, but the 1980 law allowed the procedure of court mediation to be omitted. It stipulated that the court could directly grant an ex parte divorce once it verified that the couple's emotional tie had been broken (*ganqing polie* 感情破裂).[16] In the 1939 regulation the condition for ex parte divorce was "incompatibility" of emotional relations (*ganqing bu he*), but the 1950 law did not include any terms on "emotional relations." This may have come from the assumption that the majority of existing marriages in the early 1950s were not based on affection or love; thus a request for an ex parte divorce was self-evident proof of an incompatible marriage. In the 1980 law the use of the term "*polie*" implied that the legislature believed that most divorcees had started their marriages with a certain emotional connection – an achievement of the 1950 law that eradicated any type of loveless marriage – but ended with broken relations. The 1980 law set up a condition that allowed judges to determine the degree of a couple's affection for each other – an almost impossible mission, as discussed in Chapter 2. Once again, the policy swung back to a radical

[16] "Zhonghua renmin gongheguo hunyin fa, 1980" (The Marriage Law of the People's Republic of China, 1980), in Zhonghua quan guo funü lianhe hui (comp.), *Hunyin fa xuanchuan shouce* (Pamphlet for Promoting the Marriage Law) (Beijing: Falü chubanshe, 1980), 6.

extreme that offered a much speedier divorce procedure but left problems in its implementation.

The term *zizhu* appeared for the first time as a formal legal lexis in the 1978 PRC Constitution. To date, the PRC legislature has produced four versions of the constitution. The earliest, the 1954 constitution, emphasizes the equal rights of men and women, leaving the liberal principle of marriage and the issues of family duties and property to a special law, the Marriage Law. The 1975 Constitution follows the tone of the 1954 constitution in terms of gender and family relations, but after three years, in the post-Cultural Revolution constitution of 1978, the legislature moved this term into its Article 53 (see Introduction). The current constitution was issued in 1982 and was amended in 1988, 1993, and 1999. Although still emphasizing the equal rights of men and women, the 1982 constitution removes the term *zizhu*, and in regard to the marriage issue uses the phrase "prohibiting the violation of marriage freedom" (*jinzhi pohuai hunyin ziyou* 禁止破坏婚姻自由),[17] returning to the term "*ziyou*." On the other hand, in 1986 when the Chinese legislature promulgated the PRC Civil Law, the "right of self-determination in marriage" (*hunyin zizhu quan*)[18] was formally written into the text, thus finally legally recognizing the term *zizhu* and its spirit. Freedom of marriage was thus set as a general and value-oriented principle, while the principle of self-determination was the de facto right of individuals in marriage practice.[19] After more than four decades of struggle and social practice, the urban-born and imported ideal of "freedom of marriage" and the legal principle based on local practices, "self-determined marriage," eventually reached a reconciliation that has changed marriage customs and practices in twentieth-century China. In 2001 China again renewed the marriage law, which allowed an ex parte divorce if the couple had been separated for two years, a proof of a broken relation, a term similar to the condition of "intolerable cohabitation" in the practice of the 1940s.

17 "Zhonghua Renmin Gongheguo Xianfa, 1982" (The Constitution of PRC, 1982), Article 49, www.gov.cn/gongbao/content/2004/content_62714.htm (accessed September 20, 2014).

18 See "Zhonghua renmin gongheguo minfa tongze" (The General Civil Law of the People's Republic of China, promulgated on April 12, 1986). For the Chinese version, see "Falü tushuguan" (Law Library website), www.law-lib.com/law/law_view.asp?id=3633 (accessed October 21, 2010). For an English version see "Dongfang fa yan," www.dffy.com/faguixiazai/msf/200701/20070119171429.htm. Article 103 of the Civil Law states that "citizens shall enjoy the right of marriage by choice [*zizhu quan*]. Mercenary marriages, marriages [based] on arbitrary decision by any third party and any other acts of interference in the freedom of marriage shall be prohibited."

19 "Hunyin ziyou yu hunyin zizhu quan de qubie" (The Difference between Freedom of Marriage and the Right of Self-determination), *Hunyin falü wang*, www.lihun99.com/jh/hyzzq/1007011263.html (accessed August 8, 2011).

After detailing these divorce terms, the 2001 law as well as a 2013 law focus more on property division and family relations after the divorce (see below).

After the revision of the 2001 marriage law, the Supreme Court promulgated "Judicial Explanation on Marriage Law Number Two" (*Hunyin sifa jieshi 2* 婚姻司法解释 2) in 2003 to provide implementable details on the issue of *caili*. It leaned toward the view in the 1930s' Nationalist code on betrothal gifts, as well as the 1946 High Court Explanation that defined *caili* as a special gift of good faith for marriage. On the other hand, it should not make any important impact on the payer's (normally the man's side) economic condition. In the event of an engagement/marriage being dissolved, the woman's side must return the *caili*.[20] In 2011 the Supreme Court issued a newly revised Judicial Explanation on Marriage Law (*Hunyin Fa sifa jieshi* 3 婚姻法司法解释 3) on the property before and in a marriage that caused heated debate.[21] People reacted strongly to the newest provisions on gendered property rights.[22] However, due to the improvement in economic and educational conditions, as well as the younger generation moving out of villages and away from their parents' supervision, the importance of *caili* in marriages has gradually been reduced; it has largely been transformed into a gift to the young couple starting a new life or a dowry for the bride to bring to her new home.[23]

III. *Zizhi* discourse: from marriage to state and society

In the twentieth-century Chinese revolution for social reform, the CCP's political and legal practice in the 1940s produced a series of neologisms and cultural symbols that strongly influenced the society in the post-1949

[20] Zui Gao Renmin Fayuan (People's Supreme Court), "Hunyin sifa jieshi, 2" (Judicial Explanation on Marriage Law, no. 2), *Lihun fawang* (website on Divorce Law), www.lihunfa.org/59w9.html (accessed January 15, 2014).

[21] Zui Gao Renmin Fayuan, "*Hunyin Fa sifa jieshi* 3" (2011-8-9) (Judicial Explanation on Marriage Law, no. 3, August 9, 2011), see *Xinhua baoye wang* (Xinhua News Web): http://news.xhby.net/system/2011/08/12/011448797.shtml (accessed December 20, 2014).

[22] The most controversial issue of this legal provision concerns premarriage property; according to the term, neither the property per se nor its increased value during a marriage can be divided in divorce. When I discussed the 2011 provision of legal interpretation no. 3 with people during my trip to China in summer 2014, some opposed it, stating that it protects rich people's property from being taken away by divorce; others supported it, saying that it warns women to watch out for their own interests and earn their own living instead of depending on men, thus encouraging women's independence. This debate is still ongoing, and it will take some time to see the effect of this newest provision.

[23] It appears that the custom of *caili* has spread more broadly in the last decade. According to my observations, most *caili* received by women's parents was given to the bride as a dowry, as the law expected.

era. In the process of inventing the term *zizhu*, the revolutionary practice reshaped the relationship between state and family but the isomorphic and correlative structure between state and family inherited from the past still has an effect. By creating the image of Liu Qiao'er that was used as a cultural instrument for women to participate in social movements, the intent of the revolutionary state in mobilizing women and reforming them for the goal of strengthening the nation has not yet altered. However, the use of the term *zizhu* legalized women's personhood and their agency in social movements that has empowered women to fight for their own interests.

During the Cold War period this cultural symbol was highly politicized under the theory of class struggle; as a result, the importance of the term *zizhu* as a political term[24] was downplayed in the early 1950s when the CCP looked to urban elites for its domestic construction and leaned toward the USSR for its international policy. This term returned to the political domain after China split with the USSR, serving the purpose of promoting China's sovereign and economic independence from the 1960s to the 1970s.[25] When China faced a time of economic reform and opened up to the world in the 1980s, most Western countries welcomed China's open door policy. However, the then paramount leader of China, Deng Xiaoping, constantly reminded the nation that China should hold on to its independent and self-determined policy in its diplomatic relations with the world powers and in its industrial and economic development, defining it as "socialism with Chinese characteristics."[26] After the clampdown of the 1989 movement, China faced economic sanctions from the Western world that led to difficulties for Chinese economic and technological improvements. This term experienced new momentum in technological and scientific research. From the 1990s up to today, the state has emphasized independence and self-determination in China's economic and technological development. In this atmosphere, the term *zizhu* as a political vocabulary and social idiom has acquired broad use in society, spreading from issues of sovereignty and economic development into much broader realms such as the legal code, educational experiments (*zizhu zhaosheng* 自主招生/recruitment autonomy), diplomatic

[24] For the term *zizhu* as a political term for state sovereignty, see Chapters 4 and 5.

[25] Mao Zedong gave a speech in 1959 in which he insisted on self-determination and independence in China's international relations after China split with the USSR. See Zhonggong zhongyang wenxian yanjiushi (comp.), *Mao Zedong nianpu, 1949–1976* (The Chronicle of Mao Zedong, 1949–1979), vol. IV (Beijing: Zhongyang wenxian chubanshe, 2013), 238.

[26] Deng Xiaoping, *Deng Xiaoping wenxuan* (Selected Works of Deng Xiaoping), vol. III (Beijing: Renmin chubanshe, 1993), 191, 131, 382, 223, 254.

principles (*zizhu waijiao* 自主外交/[state] self-determined diplomacy), and scientific research (*zizhu yanfa* 自主研发/invented and produced by China). The economic sanctions of Western countries on high technology and military weaponry from 1990 inspired the further expansion of the term into the technological fields, describing the circumstances in which China, through independent research and experimentation, had developed a high-tech product or sensitive weapons that largely inspired national pride in the younger generation. On the other hand, the extensive application of the term *zizhu* also brought linguistic changes in which the term was often restructured from a subject-predicate phrase to an adjective to define an abstract concept such as "*zizhu xing*" 自主性 (self-determination), or combined with legal words to define certain rights such as "*zizhu quan*" 自主权 (right for self-determination). This alteration reflects the increasing consciousness of the autonomy of the individual person or unit in domestic affairs in China.

The Chinese revolution occurred at the time of Western colonization in Asia. The CCP reemerged in the 1930s at a critical moment of national crisis, making the communist movement part of the national revolution for independence from foreign invasion. This revolution also integrated with the global trend of many Asian countries of struggling to build a modern nation-state. In the current postcolonial time, the Eurocentric discourse remains in the historical narratives of postcolonial and underdeveloped societies. In the case of China, when the communist revolution has faded into the historical background, how do we view the revolutionary legacy in the post-revolutionary era? How do we understand the historical context of the terms when we are still using this revolutionary legacy in contemporary society? Most importantly, how do we narrate the history of this period in terms of its own logic, respecting the subjectivity of actors of history so that we will be able to go beyond the postcolonial discourse and the Eurocentric domination of history? These questions will continue emerging in the twenty-first century; however, the term *zizhu*, originating from the twentieth-century revolution, has definitely left its imprint on the Chinese social movement of the changing position of women, marriage, and family.

Bibliography

I. ARCHIVAL DOCUMENTS

SPA 4-1-65, "Shaan-Gan-Ning bianqu hunyin wenti huiji, 1943" (The Collection on the Issue of Marriage in the Shaan-Gan-Ning Border Region, 1943).

SPA 4-1-66, "Hunyin wenti cailiao, 1944" (Documents on the Issue of Marriage, 1944).

SPA 4-2-170, "Bai Zhimin zhi Gao Gang han" (Bai Zhimin's Letter to Gao Gang).

SPA 4–65, "Guanyu lihun de zhiyi" (Questioning the Issue of Divorce).

SPA 15–9, "Lan Zuoxin: Shaan-Gan-Ning bianqu hunyin tiaoli xiuzheng cao'an jieshi, 1946" (An Interpretation of the Draft of the SGNBR Marriage Regulation, 1946).

SPA 15–9, "Dui Xibei nan nü hunyin wenti yijian, 1949.7.27" (An Opinion Regarding the Marriage Issue in the Northwest Area, July 27, 1949).

SPA 15–13, High Court, "Tishi xin: zhixing bennian qiyue Bian can changzhu hui, zhengfu weiyuanhui lianxi huiyi tongguo de sifa ti-an" (A Letter of Reminder: Implementing the Propositions of Border Council Standing Committee and Government Committee on Judicial Work).

SPA 15–26, "Bianqu panli huibian, 1944" (A Collection of Case Files in Border Region, 1944).

SPA 15–26, "Li Lian lihun an" (Li Lian's Divorce Case), in "Bianqu panli huibian, 1944."

SPA 15–26, *Li Rongchun v. Lei Shangzhi* in "Bianqu panli huibian, 1944."

SPA 15–26, *WangYingde v. Cao Xiuying*, in "Bianqu panli huibian, 1944."

SPA 15–27, "Bianqu gaoyuan: pan an shili kuolu, 1945" (The BR High Court: a Summary of Selected Cases, 1945).

SPA 15–27, "Qiang hun'an" (The Case of Liu Lian Kidnapping Shi Xiuying), in "Bianqu gaoyuan: pan an shili kuolu, 1945."

SPA 15–27, "Zichang xian qiang hun an" (Kidnapping Cases in Zichang County), in "Bianqu gaoyuan: pan an shilu kuolu, 1945."

SPA 15–29, "Sa wu niandu panjueshu cunben" (Preserved Copy of Adjudications for 1946).

SPA 15–29, *Han Wenguang v. Li Guihua/Sun Guilin*, in "Sa wu niandu panjueshu cunben."

SPA 15–29, *Huang Guiying v. Gao Yuhe*, in "Sa wu niandu panjueshu cunben."
SPA 15–29, *Wang Mingxuan v. Liu Zhiban*, in "Sa wu niandu panjueshu cunben."
SPA 15–29, *Zhang Piyou v. Wu Meixiang*, in "Sa wu niandu panjueshu cunben."
SPA 15–30, "Gaoyuan panjueshu huiji zhi er, 1946, er" (Collected Documents on the High Court Adjudications, 1946, vol. II).
SPA 15–30, *Zhao Zhixiang v. Liu Fenglan/Wen Yi*, in "Gaoyuan panjueshu huiji zhi er, 1946, er."
SPA 15–33, "Chishui xian sifachu qingshi guanyu zaohun ji maimai hunyin wenti, 1942" (Chishui County Office of Justice Requesting Instruction on Minor Marriages and Buying/Selling Marriages, 1942).
SPA 15–33, "Gao yuan zhishi xin 3: Chuli lihun anjian ying zhuyi ge jie" (The SGN High Court Instructive Letter Number 3: Please Pay Attention to All Details in Dealing with Divorce Cases).
SPA 15–33, "Gaodeng fayuan duiyu Chishui xian xunwen maimai hunyin jiaokuan yinfou moshou de yijian" (High Court's Answer to Chishui County's Inquiry on Whether the Money from Buying/Selling Marriage Should Be Confiscated).
SPA 15–33, "Shaan-Gan-Ning bianqu gaodeng fayuan mingling: maimai hunyin kuan shifou moshou wenti" (SGNBR High Court Order: On The Issue of Whether or Not the Court Should Confiscate Money from Buying/Selling Marriages).
SPA 15–39, "Wei cheng qing mai mai hunyin ruhe chuli" (Request Instruction from the High Court on How to Deal with Purchased Marriages).
SPA 15–40, "Han fu Guanzhong fenting Zhou Ming hunyin tiaoli jieda" (High Court's Letter Answering Zhou Ming of the Guanzhong Dispatched Court on the Marriage Regulation).
SPA 15–40, "Zenyang jinzhi mai mai hunyin?" (How to Stop Purchased Marriages?).
SPA 15–43 "Hunyin zhengce" (Marriage Policy).
SPA 15–43, "Ge xian taolun chuli lihun anjian jueding banfa ji hunyin zhengce, 1943" (County Courts' Discussion on Dealing with Divorce Cases and Policy on Marriage, 1943).
SPA 15–57, "Ge xian youguan de fengsu xiguan" (The Relevant Customs in All Counties).
SPA 15–72, "Hunyin wenti yu hunyin tiaoli, 1945" (The Issue of Marriage and the Marriage Regulation, 1945).
SPA 15–72, "Shaan-Gan-Ning Bianqu hunyin tiaoli jieshi" (An Interpretation of the SGNBR Marriage Regulation).
SPA 15–72, SGN High Court, "Shaan-Gan-Ning bianqu hunyin wenti yu tiaoli" (Issue of Marriage and Marriage Regulation in the SGN Border Region, 1945).
SPA 15–73, "Bianqu tuishi, shenpanyuan lianxi huiyi fayan jilu" (The Records of the Presentations at the Joint Conference of Judges and Assistant-judges in the BR).
SPA 15–79, "Bianqu tuishi, shenpanyuan lianxi huiyi fayan jilu" (The Records of the Presentations at the Joint Conference of Judges and Assistant-judges in the BR).

SPA 15–80, "Bianqu tuishi shenpan yuan lianxi huiyi fayan jilu, 5" (Collection of Presentations on the Legal Conference, Volume 5).
SPA 15–81, "Bianqu tuishi shenpan yuan lianxi huiyi fayan jilu, 7" (Collection of Presentations on the Legal Conference, Volume 7).
SPA 15–81, "Bianqu tuishi, shenpanyuan lianxi huiyi fayan jilu, 6" (Collection of Presentations on the Legal Conference, Volume 6), 42.
SPA 15–96, "Gaodeng fayuan Li Mu'an Lei Jingtian yuanzhang guanyu sifa gongzuo de jiantao huiyi fayan jilu" (Speeches of the Directors Li Mu'an and Lei Jingtian on the Meetings for Legal Review).
SPA 15–175, "Lei Jingtian: Bianqu sifa gongzuo baogao, 1941.10" (The Report on the Border Legal Works, October 1941).
SPA 15–220, "Qingjian liang xiang kangshu hunyin" (The Marriage Problems of Soldiers' Wives/Fiancées in Two Townships in Qingjian County).
SPA 15–294, "Jiaxian hunyin faling zhixing zongjie" (A Report on the Implementation of the Marriage Regulation in Jiaxian County, 1945).
SPA 15–294, "Jingbian xian hunyin jiufen cailiao" (The Document on Marriage Disputes in Jingbian County).
SPA 15–294, "Zhang Guiying an" (The Case of Zhang Guiying).
SPA 15–365, "Wang Ziyi: Bianhan, 1946.4.2" (Wang Ziyi's Memo to Chief-judge Wei of the Wubu County Office of Justice, April 2, 1946).
SPA 15–365, "Wei chuli hunyin anjian zhong bude zai you nüfang pei mi" (Instruction on Marriage Cases: It Should No Longer Make Women Repay Grain).
SPA 15–365, "Wubu xian sifa panjueshu" (The Adjudication Writs of Wubu County).
SPA 15–543, "Huang Kegong sharen an" (The Huang Kegong Murder Case).
SPA 15–806, "Bi Shenghua shangsu an" (The Case of Bi Shenghua's Appeal).
SPA 15–842, "Shaan-Gan-Ning gaodeng fayuan pi da: Feng Yangui yu Zhang Jincai wei er nü hunyin yi an keyi cong kuan chuli" (SGN High Court Response: Lenient Consideration May Be Given to Feng and Zhang in the Case of Their Marriage Dispute).
SPA 15–842, "Wei cheng qing dui Feng Zhang hunyin an zhi chuli pi da" (Asking for a Response [from the High Court] on the Adjudication of the Case of *Feng v. Zhang*).
SPA 15–842, *Feng v. Zhang.*
SPA 15–842, *Li Yucheng v. Liu Zhenhai and Chen Yu.*
SPA 15–842, "Chen Yu lihun an" (The Case of Chen Yu's Divorce).
SPA 15–842, "Zhang Dehou qi bei Hu Haiqing kuazou an" (The Case of Zhang Dehou's Wife Stepping Away with Hu Haiqing).
SPA 15–842, "Gao Wufeng zisha an" (The Case of Gao Wufeng's Suicide).
SPA 15–845, "Gao Yingcai shangsu an" (Gao Yingcai's Appeal).
SPA 15–847, *Li Yongchang v. Jia Yingui.*
SPA 15–891, "Zhang Lawa Liu Baoqing an" (The Case of Zhang Lawa and Liu Baoqing).
SPA 15–946, "Gao Zhangbao He Siwen kangshu hunyin an" (The Case of Gao and He Regarding a Soldier's Marriage).
SPA 15–946, "Dang Xiuying an" (The Case of Dang Xiuying).

SPA 15–948, "Zhao Pinglan bei bang an" (The Case of Zhao Pinglan's Kidnapping).
SPA 15–1076, "Liu Youfu Zhang Guihua an" (The Case of Liu Youfu and Zhang Guihua).
SPA 15–1076, "Li Zengzhi qi bei Li Zhongxun guaizou" (The Case of Li Zengzhi's Wife Being Brought Away by Li Zhongxun).
SPA 15–1133, "Li Fucai you guai ren qi an" (Li Fucai Abducted Someone's Wife).
SPA 15–1293, *Cao Jingui v. Jing Furong.*
SPA 15–1293, *Gu Jiayou v. Cai Mingqi and Bai shi.*
SPA 15–1332, *Zhang Weijin v. Bai Fenglin.*
SPA 15–1333, *Jia Yingui v. Zhang Fengliang.*
SPA 15–1334, *Cao Cuncheng v. Fu Jincai.*
SPA 15–1335, "Cheng Taohua an" (The Case of Cheng Taohua).
SPA 15–1336, *Zuo Run v. Wang Yinsuo.*
SPA 15–1340, *Chen Zhifang v. Li Hancheng.*
SPA 15–1340, "Wu Guojun v. Dong Shaolin in Yan'an, 1942."
SPA 15–1346, "Hou Dingmao shangsu an" (The Appeal of Hou Dingmao).
SPA 15–1396, "Tuo Tianyuan shangsu an" (The Appeal of Tuo Tianyuan).
SPA 15–1397, *Zhang Ying v. Liang Fucheng.*
SPA 15–1407, *Lian Shenghai v. He Xianglin.*
SPA 15–1470, *Zhang Huaibao v. Du Guirong.*
SPA 15–1471, "Zhu Jinhua an" (The Case of Zhu Jinhua).
SPA 15–1480, *Chang Baogui v. Liu Yinglan.*
SPA 15–1495, "Sun Shanwen shangshu an" (Sun Shangwei's Appeal).
SPA 15–1495, *Sun Shanwen v. Wang Shenggui.*
SPA 15–1497, *Zhao Fanshen v. He Shengchang.*
SPA 15–1498, "Guo Jungao zhao fu yan fu an" (The Case of Guo Jungao Having One Husband to Support Another).
SPA 15–1574, "Cao Huaihou Liang Wenlin an" (Cao Huaihou v. Liang Wenlin).
SPA 15–1574, "Ma Fugui mai renkou an" (The Case of Ma Fugui Selling a Woman).
SPA 15–1576, "Shi Yude qi bei guaimai an" (The Case of Shi Yude's Wife Being Abducted and Sold).

II. HISTORICAL DOCUMENTS, FILMS, AND SCHOLARLY WORKS

Akira Kurosawa (director), *Rashomon* (film), 1950.
Alber, Charles J., *Embracing the Lie: Ding Ling and the Politics of Literature in the People's Republic of China*, Westport, CT: Praeger, 2004.
Enduring the Revolution: Ding Ling and the Politics of Literature in Guomindang China, Westport, CT: Praeger, 2001.
Anagnost, Ann, "Transformation of Gender in Modern China," in Sandra Morgen (ed.), *Gender and Anthropology: Critical Reviews for Research and Teaching*, Washington, DC: American Anthropological Association, 1989, pp. 313–29.

Andors, Phyllis, *The Unfinished Liberation of Chinese Women, 1949–1980*, Bloomington: Indiana University Press, 1983.

Arkush, R. David, "Love and Marriage in North Chinese Peasant Operas," in Perry Link, Richard Madsen, and Paul G. Pickowicz (eds.), *Unofficial China: Popular Culture and Thought in the People's Republic*, Boulder, CO: Westview Press, 1990, pp. 72–87.

Averill, Stephen, "The Origin of the Futian Incident," in Tony Saich and Hans van de Ven (eds.), *New Perspectives on the Chinese Communist Revolution*, London: M. E. Sharpe, 1994, pp. 79–115.

Bao Qingtian (Judge Bao the Clear-sky) (television series), director Sun Shupei, 1993.

Barlow, Tani E., "Asian Perspective," *Gender and History* 1(3) (Autumn 1989): 318–30.

"Theorizing Woman: Funü, Guojia, Jiating [Chinese Women, Chinese State, Chinese Family]," in Angela Zito and Tani E. Barlow (eds.), *Body, Subject and Power in China*, Chicago, IL: University of Chicago Press, 1994, pp. 253–89.

The Question of Women in Chinese Feminism, Durham, NC: Duke University Press, 2004.

Barlow, Tani E. (ed.), *Gender Politics in Modern China, Writing and Feminism*, Durham, NC: Duke University Press, 1993.

Beauvoir, Simone de, *The Second Sex*, trans. and ed. H. M. Parshley, New York: Knopf, 1953.

Belden, Jack, *China Shakes the World*, New York: Harper & Brothers, 1949.

Benton, Gregor, *New Fourth Army: Communist Resistance Along the Yangtze and the Huai, 1938–1941*, Berkeley: University of California Press, 1999.

"Under Arms and Umbrellas: Perspectives on Chinese Communism in Defeat," in Tony Saich and Hans van de Ven (eds.), *New Perspectives on the Chinese Communist Revolution*, London: M. E. Sharpe, 1994, pp. 116–43.

Bernhardt, Kathryn, "A Ming-Qing Transition in Chinese Women's History? The Perspective from Law," in Gail Hershatter, Emily Honig, Jonathan N. Lipman, and Randall Stross (eds.), *Remapping China: Fissures in Historical Terrain*, Stanford, CA: Stanford University Press, 1996, pp. 42–58.

Women and Property in China, 960–1949, Stanford, CA: Stanford University Press, 1999.

"Women and the Law: Divorce in the Republican Period", in Kathryn Bernhardt and Philip Huang (eds.), *Civil Law in Qing and Republican China*, Stanford, CA: Stanford University Press, 1994, pp. 187–214.

Bernhardt, Kathryn and Philip Huang (eds.), *Civil Law in Qing and Republican China*, Stanford, CA: Stanford University Press, 1994.

"Bian fu zhishi ge fenqu sifa gongzuo duoduo caiyong minjian tiaojie, shenpan yao xuexi Ma Xiwu tongzhi de fangshi" (Border Government Instructs the Judicial Works of Each Subregion to Adopt People's Mediation, and [Their] Adjudication Should Learn from Comrade Ma Xiwu's Way of Judging), *Jiefang ribao*, June 14, 1944.

Bianco, Lucien, "Peasant Responses to CCP Mobilization Policies, 1937–1945," in Tony Saich and Hans van de Ven (eds.), *New Perspectives on the Chinese Communist Revolution*, London: M. E. Sharpe, 1994, pp. 175–91.

"Bianqu dangwei guanyu bianqu funv qunzhong zuzhi de jueding, 1937" (The Decision of the BR Party Committee on Women's Mass Organizations in the BR, 1937), in Shaanxi sheng fulian (comp.), *Shaan-Gan-Ning bianqu funü yundong wenxian ziliao xuan bian* (A Documentary Collection on the SGN Women's Movement), Xi'an: Shaanxi Provincial Women's Federation (print), 1982, pp. 3–6.

"Bianqu de lihun wenti" (Divorces in the BR), *Xinhua ribao*, October 22, 1944.

"Bianqu tianjie hunyin de yige shili" (Marriage Mediation in the BR), *Xinhua ribao*, October 22, 1944.

"Bianqu tiaojie hunyin de yi ge shili" (A Real Case of Mediating a Marriage Dispute in the Border Region), *Xinhua ribao*, October 22, 1944.

"Bianqu zhengfu guanyu puji tiaojie, zongjie panlie, qingli jiansuo zhishi xin" (The Instructive Letter of the BR Government on Promoting Mediation, Collecting Adjudication Samples, and Screening Detainees in Prisons), in Shaan-Gan-Ning bianqu zhengfu bangongting (comp.), *Tiaojie wei zhu shenpan weifu* (Using Mediation as the Dominant Way and Adjudication as an Assistant), Yan'an: Shaan-Gan-Ning bianqu zhengfu bangongting (print) 1944, pp. 10–16.

Bing Wen, "Hunyin ziyou" (Freedom of Marriage), in Quanguo fulian funü yundong yanjiu lishi yanjiushi (comp.), *Wu si shiqi funü wenti wenxuan* (Collections on Women's Issues Published in the May Fourth Period), Beijing: Sanlian shudian, 1981, pp. 233–5.

Birge, Bettine, "Levirate Marriage and the Revival of Widow Chastity in Yuan China," *Asia Major* 8(2) (1995): 107–46.

"Bitan Lan Huahua" (A Review of Lan Huahua), *Jiefang ribao*, February 23, 1947.

Bourgon, Jerome, "Rights, Freedoms, and Customs in the Making of Chinese Civil Law, 1900–1936," in William C. Kirby (ed.), *Realms of Freedom in Modern China*, Stanford, CA: Stanford University Press, 2004, pp. 84–112.

"Uncivil Dialogue: Law and Custom did not Merge into Civil Law under the Qing," *Late Imperial China* 23(1)(June 2002): 50–90.

Bray, Francesca, *Technology and Gender: Fabrics of Power in Late Imperial China*, Berkeley: University of California Press, 1997.

Brown, Jeremy and Paul G. Pickowicz (eds.), *Dilemmas of Victory: The Early Years of the People's Republic of China*, Cambridge, MA: Harvard University Press, 2007.

Butler, W. E. (ed.), *The Legal System of the Chinese Soviet Republic, 1931–1934*, New York: Transnational, 1983.

Cai Chang, "Yingjie funü gongzuo de xin fangxiang" (Facing the New Direction of Women's Work), in Shaanxi sheng fulian (comp.), *Shaan-Gan-Ning bianqu funü yundong wenxian ziliao xuan* (A Documentary Collection on the SGN Women's Movement), Xi'an: Shaanxi Provincial Women's Federation (print), 1982, pp. 167–71.

Cai Chusheng (director), *New Women* (Xin nüxing) (film), Shanghai, Lianhua Film Company, 1934.

CCTV, "Xinwen diaocha: Longdong hunshi" (News Investigation: Marriage Issues in Longdong), February 7, 2015. See http://tv.cntv.cn/vodplay/603a16aff11b480192d5b8ab4d519edc/860010-1102010100 (accessed May 12, 2015).

Cheek, Timothy, "The Honorable Vocation: Intellectual Service in CCP Propaganda Institutions in Jin-Cha-Ji, 1937–1945," in Tony Saich and Hans van de Ven (eds.), *New Perspectives on the Chinese Communist Revolution*, London: M. E. Sharpe, 1994, pp. 235–62.

Chen Jianhua, *"Geming" de xiandaixing: Zhongguo geming huayu kao lun* (The Modernity of Term "Revolution": An Examination of the Discourse of Chinese Revolution), Shanghai: Shanghai guji chubanshe, 2000.

Chen Shangmin, "Qingdai Gansu jinshi de dili fenbu" (The Geographical Distribution of *jinshi* Degreeholders in Gansu during the Qing), *Zhongguo lishi dili luncong* (Chinese Historic-Geography Journal) 24(4) (October 2009): 71–80.

Chen Shaoyu, "Guanyu Zhonghua Renmin Gongheguo Hunyin Fa qicao jingguo he qicao liyou de baogao" (The Report on the Process and the Rationale of Drafting the Marriage Law), in Zhongyang renmin zhengfu fazhi weiyuanhui (Legislature Committee of the Central Government) (comp.), *Hunyin fa ji qi youguan wenjian* (The Marriage Law and Related Documents), Beijing: Xinhua shudian, 1950, pp. 33–97.

Chen Yung-fa, *Yan'an de yingying* (Yan'an's Shadow), Taipei: Institute of Modern History, Academia Sinica, 1990.

Chen, Tina Mai, "Female Icons, Feminist Iconography? Socialist Rhetoric and Women's Agency in 1950s China," *Gender & History* 15(2) (August 2003): 268–95.

Chong xiu Zhenyuan zhi (Zhenyuan County Gazetteer, recomp.), Lanzhou: Chengwen Publisher, 1935.

Chow, Ray, "Violence in the Other Country: China as Crisis, Spectacle, and Women," in Chandra Talpade Mohanty, Ann Russo, and Laurdes Torres (eds.), *Third World Women and the Politics of Feminism*, Bloomington: Indiana University Press, 1991, pp. 81–100.

Women and Chinese Modernity: The Politics of Reading between West and East, Minneapolis: University of Minnesota Press, 1991.

Chunming chubanshe (comp.), *Xin mingci cidian* (A Dictionary of Neologisms), Shanghai: Chunming chubanshe, 1954.

Chunming chubanshe xin mingci cidian zu (comp.), *Xin ding xin mingci cidian* (Newly Revised Dictionary of Neologisms), Shanghai: Chunming chubanshe, 1952.

Cihai bianji weiyuanhui (comp.), *Cihai* (Ocean of Lexicons), Shanghai: Shanghai cishu chubanshe, 1979 [1980 reprint].

Cohen, Jerome A., "Chinese Mediation on the Eve of Modernization," *Journal of Asia and African Studies* 2(1) (April 1967): 54–76.

Discovering History in China: American Historical Writing on the Recent Chinese Past, New York: Columbia University Press, 1984.

Cong Xiaoping, "Zuo Run su Wang Yinsuo: 20 shiji 40 niandai SGN bianqu de funü, hunyin yu guojia jian gou" (*Zuo Run v. Wang Yinsuo*: Women, Marriage and State-building in the 1940s' SGN Border Region), *Kaifang shidai* (Open Times) 208(10) (October 2009): 62–79.

Cong, Xiaoping, "From 'Cainü' to 'Nü Jiaoxi': Female Normal Schools and the Transformation ofWomen's Education in the Late Qing Period, 1895–1911," in Nanxiu Qian, Grace S. Fong, and Richard J. Smith (eds.), *Different Worlds of Discourse*, Boston, MA: Brill, 2008, pp. 115–44.

"Ma Xiwu's Way of Judging: Villages, the Masses, and the Legal Construction in Revolutionary China of the 1940s," *The China Journal* 72 (July 2014): 29–52.

Teachers' Schools and the Making of the Modern Chinese Nation-State, 1897–1937, Toronto: University of British Columbia Press, 2007.

Coontz, Stephanie, *The Social Origins of Private Life: A History of American Families, 1600–1900*, New York: Verso, 1988.

"Da huoji" (Taking a Partner), in Lu Xun Yishu xueyuan (Yan'an Lu Xun Artist Academy) (comp.), *Shaanbei minge xuan* (Selected Folk Songs from the North Shaanxi Region), Yan'an: Xinhua shudian, 1949, pp. 69–76.

Dai Qing, *Wang Shiwei and "Wild Lilies": Rectification and Purges in Chinese Communist Party, 1942–1944*, New York: M. E. Sharpe, 1994.

Dang Yinzhi (comp.), *Xintianyou wu bai shou* (A Collection of 500 Songs-of-wandering-in-the-sky), Xi'an: Shaanxi renmin chubanshe, 1993.

Davin, Delia, *Woman-Work: Women and the Party in Revolutionary China*, New York: Oxford University Press, 1980.

Deng Xiaoping, *Deng Xiaoping wenxuan* (A Selected Works of Deng Xiaoping), vol. III, Beijing: Renmin chubanshe, 1993.

Deng Yingchao, "Kang Ri minzu tongyi zhanxian zhong de funü yundong" (The Women's Movement in the United Front of the Anti-Japanese War, 1939), in Shaanxi sheng fulian (comp.), *Shaan-Gan-Ning bianqu funü yundong wenxian ziliao xuan bian* (A Documentary Collection on the SGN Women's Movement), Xi'an: Shaanxi Provincial Women's Federation (print), 1982, pp. 61–73.

Diamant, Neil, "Re-examining the Impact of the 1950 Marriage Law: State Improvisation, Local Initiative and Rural Family Change," *The China Quarterly* 161 (March 2000): 171–98.

Revolutionizing the Family: Politics, Love, and Divorce in Urban and Rural China, 1949–1968, Berkeley: University of California Press, 2000.

Diamond, Norma, "Collectivization, Kinship, and the Status of Woman in Rural China," in Rayna R. Reiter (ed.), *Toward an Anthropology of Women*, New York: Monthly Review Press, 1975, pp. 372–95.

"Dianjia shi nü" (Inn's Owner Lost His Daughter), in Lu Xun Yishu xueyuan (Yan'an Lu Xun Artist Academy) (comp.), *Shaanbei minge xuan* (Selected Folk Songs from the North Shaanxi Region), Yan'an: Xinhua shudian, 1949, pp. 94–5.

Ding Ling, "Ms. Sophie's Diary," in *Ding Ling wenji* (The Collected Works of Ding Ling), Changchun: Jilin sheying chubanshe, 2004, pp. 44–84.

Ding Ling wenji (The Collected Works of Ding Ling), Changchun: Jilin sheying chubanshe, 2004.

Ding Shiliang and Zhao Fang (comp.), *Zhongguo difang zhi minsu ziliao huibian: Xibei juan* (A Collective Selection of Local Gazettes on Social Customs: Northwestern Region), Beijing: Beijing Tushuguan chubanshe, 1989.

Ebrey, Patricia, *The Inner Quarters: Marriage and the Lives of Chinese Women in the Sung Period*. Berkeley: University of California Press, 1993.

Elman, Benjamin, *Classicism, Politics, and Kinship: The Ch'ang-chou School of New Text Confucianism in Late Imperial China*, Berkeley: University of California Press, 1990.

Esherick, Joseph, "Deconstructing the Construction of the Party-State: Gulin County in the Shaan-Gan-Ning Border Region," *The China Quarterly* 140 (December 1994): 1052–79.

Fan Yu, "Jian lun Ma Xiwu shenpan fangshi" (A Preliminary Discussion on Ma Xiwu's Way of Judging), *Qinghua falü pinglun* (Qinghua Law Review) 2 (1999): 221–31.

Fei Xiaotong, *Xiangtu Zhongguo* (Village China), Shanghai: Shanghai renmin chubanshe, 2006.

Fei, Hsiao-tong, *Peasant Life in China: A Field Study of Country Life in the Yangtze Valley*, London: Kegan Paul, Trench, Trubner & Co., 1939.

Feng Zhiqin (Peng'er), "Huiyi Ma Xiwu tongzhi" (In Memory of Comrade Ma Xiwu), in *Gansu wenshi ziliao xuanji, di 12 ji* (Selected Documents of Gansu History and Culture, vol. XII), Lanzhou: Gansu provincial committee of political consultative conference [zhengxie] print, 1982, pp. 145–53.

Fong, Grace, "Reconfiguring Time, Space, and Subjectivity: Lü Bicheng's Travel Writing on Mount Lu," in Nanxiu Qian, Grace S. Fong, and Richard J. Smith (eds.), *Different Worlds of Discourse*, Boston, MA: Brill, 2008, pp. 87–114.

Fu Ke, "Ji shuoshuren Han Qixiang" (Local Folk Artist Han Qixiang), *Jiefang ribao*, August 5, 1945.

Fu Xueli, *Qingyang fu zhi* (1557) (Qingyang Prefecture Gazetteer), Lanzhou: Gansu renmin chubanshe, 2001 (reprint).

Fung, Edmund S. K., "The Idea of Freedom in Modern China Revisited: Plural Conceptions and Dual Responsibilities," *Modern China* 32(4) (October 2006): 453–82.

Galbiati, Fernando, *P'eng P'ai and the Hai-Lu-Feng Soviet*, Stanford, CA: Stanford University Press, 1985.

Gansu sheng funü lianhehui Qingyang diqu bianshichu fuyunshi xiaozu, "Longdong gedi fulian gongzuo jielue" (A Briefing on the Works of the Women's Federation in the Longdong Region), in Gansu sheng funü lianhehui Qingyang diqu bianshichu fuyunshi xiaozu (comp.), *Longdong funü yundong shi ziliao huibian* (A Collection of Historical Documents on the Women's Movement in the Longdong Region), Qingyang: Gansu sheng funü lianhehui Qingyang diqu bianshichu fuyunshi xiaozu (print), 1982, pp. 69–70.

Gansu sheng funü lianhehui Qingyang diqu bianshichu fuyunshi xiaozu (comp.), *Longdong funü yundong shi ziliao huibian* (A Collection of Historical Documents on the Women's Movement in the Longdong Region), Qingyang: Gansu sheng funü lianhehui Qingyang diqu bianshichu fuyunshi xiaozu (print), 1982.

Gansu sheng shehui kexueyuan lishi yanjiu suo (comp.), *Shaan-Gan-Ning geming genjudi shiliao xuanji*, vol. I (Selected Documents on the History of the SGN Revolutionary Base, vol. I), Lanzhou: Gansu renmin chubanshe, 1981.

Gansu sheng zhengxie (ed.), *Gansu wenshi ziliao xuanji*, 12 (A Series of Collections of Documents on Gansu's Culture and History, ser. 12), Lanzhou: Gansu zhengxie, 1981.

Gao Haishen and Ai Shaorun (comp.), *Shaanxi sheng zhi: shenpan zhi* (Shaanxi Provincial Gazetteer: Volume on the Judicial System), Xi'an: Shaanxi renmin chubanshe, 2007.

Gao Hua, *Hong taiyang shi zengyang shengqi de? Yan'an zhengfeng yundong de lailongqumai* (How Did the Sun Rise over Yan'an? –The Origin and History of the Rectification Movement), Hong Kong: Chinese University Press, 2000.

Gao Minfu and Yuan Jing, "Zanmen sui bian sui chang ba" (Let's Sing while Composing), in Shaan-Gan-Ning xiezuo qu (comp.), *Yan'an diqu geming wenhua shiliao ji* (A Collection of the Historical Documents on Revolutionary Culture in Yan'an Region), Yan'an: Yan'an diqu wenhua wenwu ju print, 1991, pp. 71–84.

Gao Putang and Zeng Luping, *Yan'an qiangjiu yundong shimo – 200 ge qinlizhe de jiyi* (On the Whole Yan'an Campaign History of Rescuing Delinquents – The 200 Person Experience Person's Recall), Hong Kong: Time International, 2008.

Gao Wen, Gong Shifeng and Gao Han (comp.), *Longdong geming geyao* (Revolutionary Lyrics in Longdong), Lanzhou: Gansu renmin chubanshe, 1982.

Gao Xinmin and Zhang Shujun, *Yan'an zhengfeng shi lu* (The Historical Records of the Yan'an Rectification Campaign), Hangzhou: Zhejiang renmin chubanshe, 2000.

Ge Yabo, "Xuanchuan di yi bu Hunyin fa" (Promoting the First Marriage Law), in Quanguo fulian lao ganbu ju (comp.), *Jinguo huihuang: jinian Zhonghua quanguo funü lianhehui chengli wushi zhounian* (Glorious Heroines: Celebration of the Fiftieth Anniversary of the All-China Women's Federation), Beijing: Zhongguo funü chubanshe, 1999, pp. 60–7.

Geertz, Clifford, "Introduction," "From the Native's Point of View," "Common Sense as a Cultural System," and "Art as a Cultural System," in Clifford Geertz, *Local Knowledge: Further Essays in Interpretive Anthropology*, New York: Basic Books, 1983, pp. 9–13, 55–120.

"Local Knowledge: Fact and Law in Comparative Perspective," in *Local Knowledge: Further Essays in Interpretive Anthropology*, New York: Basic Books, 1983, pp. 167–234.

Local Knowledge: Further Essays in Interpretive Anthropology, New York: Basic Books, 1983.

The Interpretation of Cultures: Selected Essays, New York: Basic Books, 1973.

Geng Yunzhi, Zheng Dahua, and Yu Zuhua, "Lishi weishenme mei you xuanze ziyou zhuyi" (Why History Did Not Select Liberalism), in Zheng Dahua and Zou Xiaozhan (eds.), *Zhongguo jindai shi shang de ziyou zhuyi*, Beijing: Shehui kexue wenxian chubanshe, 2008, pp. 1–10.

Genius Judge Di (Shen tan Di Renjie) (television series), director Qian Yanqiu, 2004–10.

Gilmartin, Christina, *Engendering the Chinese Revolution: Radical Women, Communist Politics, and Mass Movements in the 1920s*, Berkeley: University of California Press, 1995.

Glosser, Susan L., *Chinese Visions of Family and State, 1915–1953*, Berkeley: University of California Press, 2003.

Goldman, Merle, *Literary Dissent in Communist China*, Cambridge, MA: Harvard University Press, 1967.

Goodman, Bryna and Wendy Larson (eds.), *Gender in Motion: Divisions of Labor and Cultural Change in Late Imperial and Modern China*, New York: Rowman & Littlefield, 2005.

Goodman, David S. G., "The Licheng Rebellion of 1941: Class, Gender, and Leadership in the Sino-Japanese War," *Modern China* 23(2) (April 1997): 216–45.

Social and Political Change in Revolutionary China: The Taihang Base Area in the War of Resistance to Japan, 1937–1945, New York: Rowman & Littlefield, 2000.

Grieder, Jerome B., *Hu Shih and the Renaissance: Liberalism in the Chinese Revolution, 1917–1937*, Cambridge, MA: Harvard University Press, 1970.

Gu Yuan, "Ma Xiwu tongzhi tiaojie susong" (Comrade Ma Xiwu in Mediation) (woodcut), *Jiefang ribao*, October 9, 1944.

"Qu zhengfu bangongshi" (Township Government Office), *Jiefang ribao*, November 14, 1942.

"Tiaojie" (Mediation) (woodcut), *Jiefang ribao*, December 19, 1942.

Gu Zhuoxin, Wang Xinsan, Yuan Jing, Yuan Junshi, and Zhao Zuowei, "Huainian Zhao Meisheng tongzhi" (In Memory of Comrade Zhao Meisheng), *Renmin ribao*, August 10, 1986.

"Guanche hunyin fa xuanchuan tigang" (The Outline of Promoting the Marriage Law), *Guanche hunyin fa yundong de zhongyao wenjian* (The Important Documents of the Campaign of Implementing the Marriage Law), Beijing: Renmin chubanshe, 1953, 12–22.

Guanche hunyin fa yundong de zhongyao wenjian (The Important Documents of the Campaign of Implementing the Marriage Law), Beijing: Renmin chubanshe, 1953.

Gudai Hanyu cidian bianxiezu (comp.), *Gudai hanyu cidian* (A Dictionary to Classical Chinese Language), Beijing: Shangwu yinshuguan, 2006.

Guo Songyi, *Lunli yu shenghuo: Qing dai de hunyin guanxi* (Ethics and Life: Marriage Relations in the Qing), Beijing: Shangwu yin shu guan, 2000.

Guo Yuhua, "Xinling de jitihua: Shaanbei Ji cun nongye hezuohua de nvxing jiyi" (Collectivization of the Soul: Women's Memories of Agricultural Collectivization in Ji Village, Shaanbei), *Zhongguo shehui kexue* (Social Sciences in China) 4 (2003): 79–92.

Habermas, Jürgen, *The Structural Transformation of the Public Sphere: An Inquiry into a Category of Bourgeois Society*, trans. Thomas Burger and Frederick Lawrence, Cambridge, MA: MIT Press, 1989.

Han Nicai (comp.), *Xin mingci jieshi cidian* (A Dictionary of Neologisms with Detailed Connotations), Shanghai: Xinguang chubanshe, 1949.

Han Qixiang and Yuan Jing (original authors), *Liu Qiao'er* (Shoudu shiyan Pingju tuan jiti gai bian, Wang Yan zhi bi [Collectively revised by the Experimental Pingju Troupe in the Capital, recorded by Wang Yan]), Beijing: Wenbaotang shudian, 1952.

"Han Qixiang dao Mizhi shuoshu" (Han Qixiang Comes to Mizhi for a Performance), *Jiefang ribao*, June 20, 1946.

Han Qixiang, *Liu Qiao tuanyuan* (Liu Qiao's Reunion) (recorded by Gao Minfu), Hong Kong: Haiyang shuwu, 1947.

Hanyu da cidian (Grand Dictionary of Chinese), Shanghai: Shanghai cishu chubanshe, 2001.

Hanyu da cidian bianji weiyuanhui (comp.), *Hanyu da cidian* (The Grand Chinese Thesaurus), Shanghai: Hanyu dacidian chubanshe, 2000.

Hanyu da cidian, pu ji ben (Grand Chinese Dictionary, Popular Version), Beijing: Hanyu da ci dian chubanshe, 2000.

Hao Zaijin, "Pingju Liu Qiao'er yu san wei nüxing de chuanqi jingli" (Ping Opera Liu Qiao'er and the Legendary Experience of Three Women), *Dangshi bolan* 2 (2005): 25–7.

Hartford, Kathleen, "Fits and Starts: The Chinese Communist Party in Rural Hebei, 1921–1936," in Tony Saich and Hans van de Ven (eds.), *New Perspectives on the Chinese Communist Revolution*, London: M. E. Sharpe, 1994, pp. 144–74.

He Xiaoming, "Jindai Zhongguo ziyou zhuyi: Bu jie guoshi de jingshen zhi hua" (Liberalism in Modern China: A Spiritual Flower without Fruit), in Zheng Dahua and Zou Xiaozhan (eds.), *Zhongguo jindai shi shang de ziyou zhuyi*, Beijing: Shehui kexue wenxian chubanshe, 2008, pp. 14–26.

Hershatter, Gail, "Birthing Stories: Rural Midwives in 1950s China," in Jeremy Brown and Paul G. Pickowicz (eds.), *Dilemmas of Victory: The Early Years of the People's Republic of China*, Cambridge, MA: Harvard University Press, 2007, pp. 337–58.

Dangerous Pleasures: Prostitution and Modernity in Twentieth-Century Shanghai, Berkeley: University of California Press, 1997.

"The Gender of Memory: Rural Chinese Women and the 1950s," *Signs: Journal of Women in Culture and Society* 28(1) (2002): 43–70.

The Gender of Memory: Rural Women and China's Collective Past, Berkeley: University of California Press, 2011.

"The Subaltern Talks Back: Reflections on Subaltern Theory and Chinese History," *Positions* 1 (1993): 103–30.

"Virtue at Work: Rural Shaanxi Women Remember the 1950s," in Bryna Goodman and Wendy Larson (eds.), *Gender in Motion: Divisions of Labor and Cultural Change in Late Imperial and Modern China*, New York: Rowman & Littlefield, 2005, pp. 309–28.

Hershatter, Gail, Emily Honig, Jonathan N. Lipman, and Randall Stross (eds.), *Remapping China: Fissures in Historical Terrain*, Stanford, CA: Stanford University Press, 1996.

Hinton, Carma (director), *Small Happiness* (film), 1984.

Ho, P'ingti, *The Ladder of Success in Imperial China: Aspects of Social Mobility, 1368–1911*, New York: Columbia University Press, 1962.

Holm, David, *Art and Ideology in Revolutionary China*, Oxford: Clarendon Press, 1991.

Holmgren, Jennifer, "The Economic Foundation of Virtue: Widow Remarrying in Early and Modern China," *The Australian Journal of Chinese Affairs* 13 (1985): 1–27.

Hou Xinyi, *Cong sifa wei min dao renmin sifa – Shaan-Gan-Ning bianqu dazhong sifa zhidu yanjiu* (From Judicial Works for the People to the People's Judicial System – A Study on the Judicial System of the SGNBR), Beijing: Zhongguo zhengfa daxue chubanshe, 2007.

"Faxue de Zhongguo xuepai: Yuanyin, fangfa ji houguo – yi Yan'an xin faxuehui wei zhongxin de kaocha" (Chinese Legal School: The Origin, Method and Result – Examining the Society of New Law for China in Yan'an), *Zhengfa luntan* (Zhengfa Forum) 6 (2006): 13–16.

Hsiao, Kung-Chuan, *Compromise in Imperial China*, Seattle: School of International Studies, University of Washington, 1979.

Hsiung, Ping-chen, "Constructed Emotions: The Bond between Mothers and Sons in Late Imperial China," *Late Imperial China* 15(1) (June 1994): 87–117.

Hu Hua (comp.), *Zhonggong dangshi renwu zhuan* (Biographies of the CCP Members), vol. VI, Xi'an: Shaanxi renmin chubanshe, 1982.

Hu Shi, "Zhencao wenti" (The Issue of Women's Chastity), in Quanguo fulian funü yundong yanjiu lishi yanjiushi (comp.), *Wu si shiqi funü wenti wenxuan* (Collections on Women's Issues Published in the May Fourth Period), Beijing: Sanlian shudian, 1981, pp. 115–23.

Hu Qizhu, "Wan Qing 'ziyou' yuci de shengcheng kao lue" (The Formation of the Term "Ziyou" in the Late Qing, the 1820s–1900s), in Zheng Dahua and Zou Xiaozhan (eds.), *Zhongguo jindai shi shang de ziyou zhuyi*, Beijing: Shehui kexue wenxian chubanshe, 2008, pp. 127–45.

Hu, Ying, "'Tossing the Brush'? Wu Zhiying (1868–1934) and the Uses of Calligraphy," in Nanxiu Qian, Grace S. Fong, and Richard J. Smith (eds.), *Different Worlds of Discourse*, Boston, MA: Brill, 2008, pp. 57–86.

Hu Yongheng, "1943 nian Shaan-Gan-Ning bianqu tingzhi yuanyong *Liu fa quan shu*zhi kaocha – zhengfeng, shengan dui bianqu sifa de yingxiang" (On the Suspension of Invoking the Six Codes in the 1943 SGNBR), *KangRi zhanzheng yanjiu* (Studies on the Anti-Japanese War) 4 (2010): 90–102.

Huachi xian zhi (Huachi County Gazetteer), Lanzhou: Gansu renmin chubanshe, 2004.

Huan Nan (Xie Juezai), "Lu bian xian hua" (A Small Talk at the Side of Stove), *Jiefang ribao*, March 16, 1942.

(Xie Juezai), "Yi de shu: bu jin ren qing" (A Piece of Thoughts: Things are Lacking Human Sense), *Jiefang ribao*, August 4, 1942.

(Xie Juezai), "Yi de shu: chan song" (A Piece of Thought: Unrelenting Lawsuits), *Jiefang ribao*, November 19, 1942.

Huang Chuanhui, *Tianxia hunyin – Gongheguo san bu hunyin fa jishi* (Marriages under Heaven: A Report on the Three Marriage Laws of the PRC), Shanghai: Wenhui chubanshe, 2004.

Huang Kewu, "Jindai Zhongguo de ziyou zhuyi: yuan qi yu yan bian" (Liberalism in Modern China: Its Origin and Evolution), in Zheng Dahua and Zou

Xiaozhan (eds.), *Zhongguo jindai shi shang de ziyou zhuyi*, Beijing: Shehui kexue wenxian chubanshe, 2008, pp. 27–43.

Huang Renke, *Lu Yi ren – hongse yishujia men* (People of Lu Yi – Red Artists), Beijing: Zhonggong zhongyang dangxiao chubanshe, 2001.

Huang Zhenglin, *Shaan-Gan-Ning bianqu xiangcun de jingji yu shehui* (Rural Economy and Society in the Shaan-Gan-Ning Border Region), Beijing: Renmin chubanshe, 2006.

Shaan-Gan-Ning bianqu shehui jingji shi, 1937–1945 (Socio-economic History of the SGN Border Region, 1937–1945), Beijing: Renmin chubanshe, 2006.

Huang, Martin, *Desire and Fictional Narrative in Late Imperial China*, Cambridge, MA: Harvard University Press, 2001.

"Sentiments of Desire: Thoughts on the Cult of Qing in Ming-Qing Literature," *Chinese Literature: Essays, Articles, Reviews* (December 20, 1998): 153–84.

Huang, Philip, "Between Informal Mediation and Formal Adjudication: The Third Realm of Qing Civil Justice," *Modern China* 19(3) (1993): 251–98.

Chinese Civil Justice, Past and Present, New York: Rowman & Littlefield, 2010.

Code, Custom, and Legal Practice in China: The Qing and the Republic Compared, Stanford, CA: Stanford University Press, 2001.

"Court Mediation in China, Past and Present," *Modern China* 32(3) (July 2006): 275–314.

"Divorce Law Practices and the Origins, Myths, and Realities of Judicial 'Mediation' in China," *Modern China* 31(2) (April 2005): 151–205.

"Women's Choices under the Law: Marriage, Divorce, and Illicit Sex in the Qing and the Republic," *Modern China* 27(1) (2001): 3–58.

"Huanxian Tianshui qu er xiang bamian tanwu de cun zhuren" (Township Number Two in Tianshui Ward of Huanxian County Dismissed a Corrupt Village Head), *Jiefang ribao*, December 14, 1944.

Huanxian zhi (Huanxian County Gazetteer), Lanzhou: Gansu renmin chubanshe, 1993.

Hung, Chang-tai, "Reeducating a Blind Storyteller: Han Qixiang and the Chinese Communist Storytelling Campaign," *Modern China* 19(4) (October 1993): 395–426.

War and Popular Culture: Resistance in Modern China, 1937–1945, Berkeley: University of California Press, 1994.

Hunt, Lynn, "Introduction," in Lynn Hunt (ed.), *The New Cultural History*, Berkeley: University of California Press, 1989, pp. 1–14.

Hunt, Lynn (ed.), *The New Cultural History*, Berkeley: University of California Press, 1989.

"Hunyin ziyou yu hunyin zizhu quan de qubie" (The Difference between Freedom of Marriage and the Right of Self-determination), *Hunyin falü wang*, www.lihun99.com/jh/hyzzq/1007011263.html (accessed August 8, 2011).

Idema, Wilt L., *Judge Bao and the Rule of Law: Eight Ballad-Stories from the Period 1250–1450*, Cambridge, MA: Harvard University Press, 2010.

Interview with Feng Zhiqin, July 21, 2005 (the protagonist of the case *Feng v. Zhang*).

Interview with Feng Zhiqin, July 5, 2007.

Interview with Qin Wenhu, June 28, 2012 (Yuan Jing's secretary in the 1970s and 1980s).

Interview with Sharon Wen, April 20, 2013 (professor at University of Houston).
Interview with She Xingfa, July 21, 2005 (the director of the Huachi County Bureau for Cultural Development).
Interview with Zhang Xuan, June 25, 2006 (former PLA officier who had contact with Feng Zhiqin in 1948).
Jacka, Tamara, *Women's Work in Rural China: Change and Continuity in an Era of Reform*, New York: Cambridge University Press, 1997.
Jiang Changren, "Zhao Zuolin," in Wang Xiaoting, Jiang Changren, and Huang Wenyi (comp.), *Beida yinglie* (The Heroic Alumni of Beijing University), ser. 3, Beijing: Beijing daxue chubanshe, 1997, pp. 183–94.
Jiang Ping, "Si de dao bi sheng de duo: Ansai weisheng shiyan qu diaocha" (Deaths Exceed Births: A Survey in Ansai Public Health District), *Jiefang ribao*, March 4, 1942.
Jiangxi sheng fulian and Jiangxi sheng dang'an guan (comp.), *Jiangxi Su qu funü yundong shiliao xuanbian* (Selected Documents of the Women's Movement in Jiangxi Soviet Region), Nanchang: Jiangxi renmin chubanshe, 1982.
Jin Guantao and Liu Qingfeng, *Guannian shi yanjiu: Zhongguo xiandai zhongyao zhengzhi shuyu de xingcheng* (A Study on the History of Views: The Formation of Important Political Terminology in Modern China), Beijing: Falü chubanshe, 2009.
Jin Tao, "Women duiyu haizi he muqin de taidu – Ji Deng Yingchao tongzhi de tanhua, 1942" (Our Attitude Toward Children and Mothers – Report on the Conversation with Comrade Deng Yingchao, 1942), in Shaanxi sheng fulian (comp.), *Shaan-Gan-Ning bianqu funü yundong wenxian ziliao xuji* (A Documentary Collection on the SGN Women's Movement), Xi'an: Shaanxi Provincial Women's Federation (print), 1982, pp. 322–6.
Johnson, Chalmers, *Peasant Nationalism and Communist Power*, Stanford, CA: Stanford University Press, 1962.
Johnson, Kay Ann, *Women, the Family and Peasant Revolution in China*, Chicago, IL: University of Chicago Press, 1983.
Judd, Ellen R., "New Yangge: The Case of 'A Worthy Sister-in-Law'," *CHINOPERL Papers* 10 (1981): 167–86.
"Reconsidering China's Marriage Law Campaign: Toward a DeOrientalized Feminist Perspective," *Asian Journal of Women's Studies* 4(2) (1998): 8–26.
Judge, Joan, *Print and Politics: "Shibao" and the Culture of Reform in Late Qing China*, Stanford, CA: Stanford University Press, 1996.
"Talent, Virtue, and the Nation: Chinese Nationalisms and Female Subjectivities in the Early Twentieth Century," *The American Historical Review* 106(3) (June 2001): 765–803.
The Precious Raft of History: The Past, The West, and The Women Question in China, Stanford, CA: Stanford University Press, 2008.
"Kaichuang shehuizhuyi yidai xinfeng" (Pioneering the New Life Style in Socialist Society), *Renmin ribao*, March 7, 1975.
Kang Sheng, "Kang Sheng tongzhi baogao jilu zhaiyao" (The Note of Comrade Kang Sheng's Speech), *Zhongyang zhengf ganxiao shehuizhuyi jiaoyu fudao zu zhengli*, Beijing, 1958, pp. 1–8.

Ke Lan, "Rechen de panwang: Bianqu nongcun fu ying weisheng wenti zhi yijiao" (Cordial Expectation: The Hygienic Problems for Women and Children in the BR), *Jiefang ribao*, March 7, 1946.

Keating, Pauline, "Review of *China in Revolution* and *New Perspectives on the Chinese Communist Revolution*," *The China Journal* 37 (January 1997): 219–23.

"The Ecological Origins of the Yan'an Way," *The Australian Journal of Chinese Affairs* 32 (July 1994): 123–53.

Two Revolutions: Village Reconstruction and the Cooperative Movement in Northern Shaanxi, 1934–1945, Stanford, CA: Stanford University Press, 1997.

Ko, Dorothy, "Pursuing Talent and Virtue: Education and Women's Culture in Seventeenth- and Eighteenth-Century China," *Late Imperial China* 13(1) (1992): 9–39.

Teachers of the Inner Chambers: Women and Culture in Seventeenth-Century China, Stanford, CA: Stanford University Press, 1994.

Kuo, Margaret, *Intolerable Cruelty: Marriage, Law, and Society in Early Twentieth-Century China*, New York: Rowman & Littlefield, 2014.

"Lan Huahua jijiang yanzou" (The Forthcoming Performance of Lan Huahua), *Jiefang ribao*, August 20, 1946.

"Lan Huahua," in Gao Wen, Gong Shifeng, and Gao Han (comp.), *Longdong geming geyao* (Revolutionary Lyrics in Longdong), Lanzhou: Gansu renmin chubanshe, 1982, pp. 26–7.

Lean, Eugenia, *Public Passions: The Trial of Shi Jianqiao and the Rise of Popular Sympathy in Republican China*, Berkeley: University of California Press, 2007.

Li Huaxing and Wang Lingyi, "Lun Mao Zedong de duli zizhu he dui wai kai fang sixiang" (On Mao Zedong's Thoughts on Independence, Self-determination, and the Open Door), *Shi lin* 23(3) (March 1991): 22–30.

Li Jin, "Wo you shiye le – Ji yi ge nü gongwuyuan de zaoyu" (I Lost My Job Again – The Life of a Female Civil Servant), *Xinhua ribao*, October 4, 1944.

Li Juan, "Geming chuantong yu xifang xiandai sifa linian de jiaofeng jiqi shenyuan yingxiang" (A Cross Fire between the Revolutionary Tradition and Western Legal Thought and its Influence), *Fazhi yu shehui fazhan* (Rule of Law and Social Development) 4 (2009): 38–47.

"Ma Xiwu shenpan fangshi chansheng de beijing fenxi" (An Analysis of the Historical Context of Ma's Way), *Falü kexue* (Legal Science) 2 (2008): 163–9.

Li Lingling, *Ge Jianhao zhuan* (Biography of Ge Jianhao), Beijing: Zhongguo funü chubanshe, 2005.

Li Pu, "Yi jian qianghun an" (A Case of Marriage by Capture), *Xinhua ribao*, April 11, 1945, cited in Liu Fengge *et al.* (comp.), *Shaan-Gan-Ning bianqu Longdong de qunzhong yundong*, Qingyang: Zhonggong Qingyang diwei dangshi ziliao zhengji bangongshi, 1992, pp. 90–3.

Li Qicheng, *Wan Qing ge ji shenpanting yanjiu* (A Study of the Court System in the Late Qing), Beijing: Beijing daxue chubanshe, 2004.

Li Qun, "Xiao gu xian" (A Good Sister-in-law), in Li Qun and Yan Han, *Jiefang qu muke lianhuanhua* (Woodprint Cartoon Series Produced in the Liberation Areas), vol. IV, Harbin: Heilongjiang meishu chubanshe, 2001.

Li Qun and Yan Han, *Jiefang qu muke lianhuanhua* (Woodprint Cartoon Series Produced in the Liberation Areas), Harbin: Heilongjiang meishu chubanshe, 2001.

Li Wei (comp.), *Wannianli* (A Calendar for Ten Thousand Years), Beijing: Zhongyi guji chubanshe, 2008.

Li Xiuqing, "Xin Zhongguo hunyin fa de chengzhang yu Sulian moshi de yingxiang" (The Evolution of the Marriage Laws in PRC and the Influence of USSR Models), *Falü kexue* (Science of Law) 119(4) (2002): 76–89.

Li Youyi, "Hongjun jiaodao shi zai Qingyang pianduan" (Some Memory Pieces on the Red Army in Qingyang), in *Gansu wenshi ziliao xuanji* (Selected Documents of Gansu History and Culture, vol. XII), Lanzhou: Gansu Provincial Committee of Political Consultative Conference [zhengxie] (print), 1982, pp. 6–10.

Liang Qichao, "Bianfa tongyi" (A General Proposal for Reform), in *Yinbingshi heji: wenji* (Collected Works from Drinking Ice Studio: Article Collections), vol. I, Shanghai: Zhonghua shuju, 1932, pp. 1–64.

"Lun nü xue" (On Women's Schooling), in *Yinbingshi heji: wenji* (Collected Works from Drinking Ice Studio: Article Collections), Shanghai: Zhonghua shuju, 1932, pp. 37–8.

Yinbingshi heji: wenji (Collected Works from Drinking Ice Studio: Article Collections), Shanghai: Zhonghua shuju, 1932.

Liang Zhiping, *Qing dai xiguan fa: Shehui yu guojia* (The Common Law of the Qing: Society and State), Beijing: Zhongguo zhengfa daxue chubanshe, 1996.

"Liangge shuoshu ren, zou de liangtiao lu" (Two Story-tellers on Two Different Paths), *Jiefang ribao*, September 2, 1946.

Lieberman, Sally Taylor, *The Mother and Narrative Politics in Modern China*, Charlottesville: University of Virginia Press, 1998.

Lin Boqu, "Guanyu gaishan sifa gongzuo" (On Improving Judicial Works), in Shaan-Gan-Ning bianqu zhengfu bangongting (comp.), *Tiaojie wei zhu shenpan weifu* (Using Mediation as the Dominant Way and Adjudication as an Assistant), Yan'an: Shaan-Gan-Ning bianqu zhengfu bangongting (print), 1944, pp. 1–4.

Lin Shan, "Gaizao shuoshu" (Reforming Story-telling), *Jiefang ribao*, August 5, 1945.

"Shuo shu xunlianban de shouhuo" (The Achievement of Training Program for Storytelling), *Jiefang ribao*, November 23, 1945.

Link, Perry, "The Crocodile Bird: Xiangsheng in the Early 1950s," in Jeremy Brown and Paul G. Pickowicz (eds.), *Dilemmas of Victory: The Early Years of the People's Republic of China*, Cambridge, MA: Harvard University Press, 2007, pp. 207–31.

Link, Perry, Richard Madsen, and Paul G. Pickowicz (eds.), *Unofficial China: Popular Culture and Thought in the People's Republic*, Boulder, CO: Westview Press, 1990.

Liu Fengge *et al.* (comp.), *Longdong de tudi geming yundong* (Land Revolution in Longdong Area), Qingyang: Zhonggong Qingyang diwei dangshi ziliao zhengji bangongshi, 1992.

Qingyang diqu Zhonggong dangshi renwu (The Historical Figures of CCP Members in Qingyang District), Qingyang: Zhonggong Qingyang diwei dangshi ziliao zhengji bangongshi, 1992.

Shaan Gan Ning Bianqu Longdong de qunzhong yundong (The Mass Movement in the Longdong Region, Shaan-Gan-Ning Border Region), Qingyang: Zhonggong Qingyang diwei dangshi ziliao zhengji bangongshi, 1994.

Liu Guoquan (director), *Li ersao gaijia* (Remarriage of Li the Second Sister-in-law), Lüju (Shandong opera) (musical film), Changchun Film Studio, 1957.

Liu, Jianmei, *Revolution Plus Love: Literary History, Women's Bodies, and Thematic Repetition in Twentieth-Century Chinese Fiction*, Honolulu: University of Hawai'i Press, 2003.

Liu Jingfan, "Guanche hunyin fa shi dang qian ge ji renmin zhengfu he quan guo renmin de zhongyao zhengzhi renwu" (Implementing the Marriage Law Is an Important Political Task for All Governments at Each Level and the People Nationwide), in *Guanche hunyin fa yundong de zhongyao wenjian* (The Important Documents of the Campaign of Implementing the Marriage Law), Beijing: Renmin chubanshe, 1953, pp. 23–34.

Liu Zhi, "Lu Yi jia de yangge" (The Yangge Performed by Lu Yi), in Yan'an Lu Yi huiyilu bianweihui (comp.), *Yan'an Lu Yi huiyilu* (A Collection of Memoirs from the Yan'an Lu Xun Academy of the Arts), Beijing: Guanming ribao chubanshe, 1992, pp. 326–31.

"Liu Qiao'er' you xinzhuan, liangxiang Beijing da wutai" (Liu Qiao'er Making a New Story and Showing on Beijing's Grand Stage), *Qianlong wang* (Qianlong website), http://culture.qianlong.com/6931/2004/05/11/1340@2047123.htm (accessed January 24, 2005).

Liu Quan'e and Li Juan, "Shaan-Gan-Ning bianqu gaodeng fayuan dang'an ji qi xueshu jiazhi" (The Documents of the SGNBR High Court and Their Academic Value), *Falü kexue* (Science of Law) 1 (2006): 156–62.

Liu Xiang (77–6 BCE), *Lienü zhuan* (Biographies of Exemplary Women), Harbin: Harbin chubanshe, 2009 reprint.

Liu Zengjie (comp.), *Zhongguo jiefang qu wenxue shi* (History of Literature in the Liberated Region), Zhengzhou: Henan daxue chubanshe, 1988.

Liu Zhengtan *et al.*, *Hanyu wailai ci cidian* (A Dictionary of Loan Words and Hybrid Words in Chinese), Shanghai: Shanghai cishu chubanshe, 1984.

Liu, Lydia, *Translingual Practice: Literature, National Culture, and Translated Modernity, 1900–1937*, Stanford, CA: Stanford University Press, 1995.

"Longdong gaodeng fenting chuli anjian duo yong tiaojie fangshi, Zhenyuan chuli anjian duo wei xiaxiang diaocha" (Longdong Dispatched-High Court Uses Mediation for Most Cases, But Zhenyuan County Failed to Do On-site Investigation in Dealing With the Majority of Cases), *Jiefang ribao*, December 19, 1944.

Lötveit, Trygve, *Chinese Communism 1931–1934: Experience in Civil Government*, Lund, Sweden: Studentlitterature, 1973.

Lou Xiyuan, "Zoufang Yuan Jing yi xi tan" (An Interview with Yuan Jing), Kaidi shequ (Kaidi net), http://club.kdnet.net/dispbbs.asp?boardid=5&id=6834049&page=1&1=1#6834049 (accessed May 13, 2012).

Lu Di, *Zhongguo xiandai banhua shi* (A History of Modern Chinese Woodcuts), Beijing: Renmin meishu chubanshe, 1987.

Lu Qiuxin, "Hunyin ziyou he de mo ke la xi" (Freedom of Marriage and Democracy), in Quanguo fulian funü yundong yanjiu lishi yanjiushi (comp.), *Wu si shiqi funü wenti wenxuan* (Collections on Women's Issues Published in the May Fourth Period), Beijing: Sanlian shudian, 1981, pp. 242–5.

Lu Xun Yishu xueyuan (Yan'an Lu Xun Artist Academy) (comp.), *Shaanbei minge xuan* (Selected Folk Songs from the North Shaanxi Region), Yan'an: Xinhua shudian, 1949.

Lu Xun, *Selected Stories of Lu Hsun*, trans. Yang Hsien-yi and Gladys Yang, Beijing: Foreign Language Press, 1972.

"Shang shi" (Regret for the Past), in *Selected Stories of Lu Hsun*, trans. Yang Hsien-yi and Gladys Yang, Beijing: Foreign Language Press, 1972, pp. 197–215.

"The New Year's Sacrifice," in *Selected Stories of Lu Hsun*, trans. Yang Hsien-yi and Gladys Yang, Beijing: Foreign Language Press, 1972, pp. 125–43.

"Wo zhi jie lie guan" (My View of Chastity), in Quanguo fulian funü yundong yanjiu lishi yanjiushi (comp.), *Wu si shiqi funü wenti wenxuan* (Collections on Women's Issues Published in the May Fourth Period), Beijing: Sanlian shudian, 1981, pp. 106–14.

Lu Zonglin and Wang Zaijue, "Kong Jue shi lue" (Short Biography of Kong Jue), *Xin wenxue shiliao* (Historical Documents on New Literature) 3 (1985): 165–8.

Lu, Weijing, *True to Her Word: The Faithful Maiden Cult in Late Imperial China*, Stanford, CA: Stanford University Press, 2008.

Lubman, Stanley, "Mao and Mediation: Politics and Dispute Resolution in Communist China," *California Law Review* 55 (1967): 1284–359.

Luo Shaozhi, "Cai mu Ge Jianhao" (Mother of the Cai Family, Ge Jianhao), in Hu Hua (comp.), *Zhonggong dangshi renwu zhuan* (Biographies of the CCP Members), vol. VI, Xi'an: Shaanxi renmin chubanshe, 1982, 47.

Lynch, Catherine, Robert B. Marks, and Paul G. Pickowicz (eds.), *Radicalism, Revolution, and Reform in Modern China: Essays in Honor of Maurice Meisner*, New York: Lexington Books, 2011.

Ma Wenrui, "Chuang ban chuqi de Longdong zhongxue" (Longdong Middle Schools in Its Early Years), in *Qingyang xian wenshi ziliao, di yi ji* (Historical and Cultural Documents of Qingyang County) series 1, publisher unknown, 1999, pp. 153–7.

Ma Xiao, "Ming dai xibei keyu yu shehui huanjing – yi Qingyang fu jinshi yu juren de shi kong fenbu, tedian yiji chengyin wei xiansuo" (The Civil Service Examinations in the Northwestern Region during the Ming Time – in the Cases of Jinshi and Juren of Qingyang Prefecture and their Historical and Geographical Distribution), *Ningxia daxue xuebao* (Ren wen shehui kexue ban) (The Journal of Ningxia University [Humanity and Social Sciences Edition]) 32(4) (July 2010): 118–30.

Ma Xiwu, "Xin minzhu zhuyi geming jieduan zhong Shaan-Gan-Ning bianqu renmin sifa gongzuo" (People's Judicial Works in the SGNBR during the Period of the New Democratic Revolution), in Zhang Xipo, *Ma Xiwu shenpan fangshi* (Ma Xiwu's Way of Judging), Beijing: Falü chubanshe, 1983, pp. 80–100.

"Ma Xiwu tongzhi chuxun shen'an jingyan" (Comrade Ma Xuwu Doing Trials in His Circuit), *Jiefang ribao*, December 20, 1944.

"Ma Xiwu tongzhi de shenpan fangshi" (Comrade Ma Xiwu's Way of Judging), *Jiefang ribao*, March 13, 1944.

Ma Yanglin, "'Ma zhuanyuan', ni zai nali?" (Prefect Ma, Where Are You?), *Renmin ribao*, July 13, 1983.

Mann, Susan, *Gender and Sexuality in Modern Chinese History*, New York: Cambridge University Press, 2011.

"Grooming a Daughter for Marriage," in Rubie Watson and Patricia Buckley Ebrey (eds.), *Marriage and Inequality in Chinese Society*, Berkeley: The University of California Press, 1991, pp. 203–30.

"Learned Women in the Eighteenth Century," in Christina K. Gilman, Gail Hershatter, Lisa Rofel, and Tyrene White (eds.), *Engendering China: Women, Culture and the State*, Cambridge, MA: Harvard University Press, 1994, pp. 27–46.

Precious Records: Women in China's Long Eighteenth Century, Stanford, CA: Stanford University Press, 1997.

"The Education of Daughters in the Mid-Ch'ing Period," in Benjamin A. Elman and Alexander Woodside (eds.), Education and Society in Late Imperial China, 1600–1900, Berkeley: University of California Press, 1994, pp. 19–49.

The Talented Women of the Zhang Family, Berkeley: University of California Press, 2007.

Mao Zedong, "Duiyu Zhao nüshi zisha de piping" (On the Criticism of the Suicide of Ms. Zhao), "Zhao nüshi de renge wenti" (The Character of Ms. Zhao), and "Shehui wan'e yu Zhao nüshi" (The Evil Society and Ms. Zhao), in Zhonggong zhongyang wenxian yanjiushi and Zhonggong Hunan shengwei *Mao Zedong zaoqi wengao* bianjizu (compl.), *Mao Zedong zaoqi wengao* (An Article Collection of Young Mao Zedong), Changsha: Hunan chubanshe, 1990, pp. 413–14; 416–17; and 424–7.

"Fan dui zi-you zhuyi" (Opposing Zi-you-ism), in *Mao Zedong xuanji* (Selected Works of Mao Zedong), vol. II, Beijing: Renmin chubanshe, 1963, pp. 330–2.

Mao Zedong xuanji (Selected Works of Mao Zedong), Beijing: Renmin chubanshe, 1963.

Mao Zedong xuanji (Selected Works of Mao Zedong), Beijing: Renmin chubanshe, 1968.

"Tongyi zhanxian zhong de du li zi zhu wenti" (The Issue of [the CCP's] Independence and Self-Determination in the United Front), in *Mao Zedong xuanji* (Selected Works of Mao Zedong), vol. II, Beijing: Renmin chubanshe, 1963, pp. 502–05.

"Zai Yan'an wenyi zuotan hui shang de jianghua" (Speeches at the Yan'an Forum on Literature and Art), in *Mao Zedong xuanji* (Selected Works of Mao Zedong), vol. II, Beijing: Renmin chubanshe, 1963, pp. 804–35.

Masini, Fedrico, *Xiandai hanyu cihui de xingcheng* (The Formation of Modern Chinese Lexicon and its Evolution toward a National Language: The Period from 1840 to 1898), trans. Huang Heqing, Shanghai: Hanyu da cidian chubanshe, 1997.

Meijer, M. J., *Marriage Law and Policy in the Chinese People's Republic*, Hong Kong: Hong Kong University Press, 1971.

Meng Yue, "Baimaonü yanbian de qishi – jianlun Yan'an wenyi de lishi duo zhi xing" (The Revelation from the Evolution of *The White-Haired Girl* – On the Multi-dimensional Nature of Yan'an Literature in Historical Context), in Meng Yue, *Ren, lishi, jiayuan: wenhua piping san diao* (Humans, History, and Homeland: Cultural Critics in Three Tones), Beijing: Renmin wenxue chubanshe, 2006, pp. 251–76.

"Female Image and National Myth," in Tani E. Barlow (ed.), *Gender Politics in Modern China, Writing and Feminism*, Durham, NC: Duke University Press, 1993, pp. 118–36.

Ren, lishi, jiayuan: wenhua piping san diao (Humans, History, and Homeland: Cultural Critics in Three Tones), Beijing: Renmin wenxue chubanshe, 2006.

Meng Yue and Dai Jinhua, *Fu chu lishi di biao* (Emerging from the Horizontal), Zhengzhou: Henan renmin chubanshe, 1989.

Michael, Franz, "The Role of Law in Traditional, Nationalist and Communist China," *China Quarterly* 9 (1962): 124–48.

Mohanty, Chandra Talpade, Ann Russo, and Laurdes Torres (eds.), *Third World Women and the Politics of Feminism*, Bloomington: Indiana University Press, 1991.

Morgen, Sandra (ed.), *Gender and Anthropology: Critical Reviews for Research and Teaching*. Washington, DC: American Anthropological Association, 1989.

Nelson, Cary and Lawrence Grossberg (eds.), *Marxism and the Interpretation of Culture* (with introduction by the editors), Urbana: University of Illinois Press, 1988.

Nü xuebao (Women's Journal) (1898).

Nüzi yuekan (Women's Monthly), nos. 1 (January 1934), 4 (April 1934), and 7 (July 1934).

Ono Kazuko, *Chinese Women in a Century of Revolution, 1850–1950*, ed. Joshua Fogel, trans. Kathryn Bernhardt, Timothy Brook, Joshua Fogel, Jonathan Lipman, Susan Mann, and Laurel Rhodes, Stanford, CA: Stanford University Press, 1978.

Pa Chin (Ba Jin), *Family*, trans. Sidney Shapiro, Prospect Heights, IL: Waveland Press, 1972.

Perry, Elizabeth J., *Anyuan: Mining China's Revolutionary Tradition*, Berkeley: University of California, 2012.

"Pingju huanghou Xin Fengxia xiju rensheng liu jiahua" (The Wonderful Life Story of Xin Fengxia as the Empress of Pingju), http://bjyouth.ynet.com/3.1/1204/18/6999091.html (accessed November 15, 2014).

Pu Songling, "Xihu zhu" (Master of the West Lake), in *Liao zai zhi yi* (Strange Tales from a Chinese Studio), Beijing: Guangming ribao chubanshe, 2009 (reprint).

Qian Feng, "Pangting lihun an" (Auditing a Divorce Case), *Jiefang ribao*, March 5, 1946.

Qian, Nanxiu, *Politics, Poetics, and Gender in Late Qing China*, Stanford, CA: Stanford University Press, 2015.

"The Mother *Nü xuebao* versus the Daughter *Nü xuebao*: Generational Differences between 1898 and 1902 Women Reformers," in Nanxiu Qian,

Grace S. Fong, and Richard J. Smith (eds.), *Different Worlds of Discourse*, Boston, MA: Brill, 2008, pp. 257–92.

Qian, Nanxiu, Grace S. Fong, and Richard J. Smith (eds.), *Different Worlds of Discourse: Transformations of Gender and Genre in Late Qing and Early Republican China*, Boston, MA: Brill, 2008.

Qiang Shigong, "Quanli de zuzhi wangluo yu falü de zhilihua" (Power in Organized Networks and Law in Administration), *Beida falü pinglun* (Peking University Law Review) 3(2) (2000): 1–61.

Qiang Xiaochu, *Yan'an zhengfeng yundong huiyilu* (My Recollection of the Yan'an Rectification Campaign), Harbin: Heilongjiang renmin chubanshe, 1958.

Qin Yan, "Cong shehui xingbie shijiao dui Yan'an shiqi xin nüxing de yanjiu" (A Study of New Women in Yan'an Period from the View of Gender), *Funü yanjiu luncong* (Collection of Women's Studies) 75(5) (September 2006): 38–42.

Qing mo Min chu de Shaanbei shehui (The Society of Northern Shaanxi in the Late Qing and Early Republic), Xi'an: Shaanxi renmin chubanshe, 2000.

Qin Yan and Hu Hong'an, *Qing dai yi lai de Shaanbei zongzu yu shehui bianqian* (Changes in Clans and Society in Northern Shaanxi since the Qing), Xi'an: Xibei gongye daxue chubanshe, 2004.

Qin Yan and Yue Long, *Zou chu fengbi: Shanbei funu de hunyin yu shengyu (1900–1949)* (Getting Out of Confinement: Women's Marriage and Childbearing in Northern Shaanxi, 1900–1949), Xi'an: Shaanxi People's Publishing House, 1997.

"Qingjian de hunsu" (Marriage Customs in Qingjian County), *Jiefang ribao* (Liberation Daily), November 3 and 4, 1942.

Qingyang diqu zhi bianzuan weiyuan hui (comp.), *Qingyang diqu zhi* (Qingyang District Records), Lanzhou: Lanzhou daxue chubanshe, 1993.

Qingyang shi zhengxie and Huachi xian zhengxie, *"Liu Qiao'er" chuanqi rensheng* (The Legendary Life of "Liu Qiao'er"), Lanzhou: Gansu renmin chubanshe, 2005.

Qingyang xian fulian, "Cai Chang tongzhi zai Qingyang" (Comrade Cai Chang in Qingyang), in Qingyang xian zhengxie, *Qingyang wenshi ziliao* (A Documentary Collection of Qingyang's History and Culture), ser. 1, Qingyang: Qingyan xian zhengxie (print), 1999, 69–79.

Qingyang xian wenshi ziliao, di yi ji (Historical and Cultural Documents of Qingyang County), series 1, publisher unknown, 1999.

Qingyang xian zhengxie, *Qingyang wenshi ziliao*, 1 (A Documentary Collection of Qingyang's History and Culture), series 1, Qingyang: Qingyan xian zhengxie (print), 1999.

Qingyang xian zhi (Qingyang County Gazetteer), Lanzhou: Gansu renmin chubanshe, 1993.

"Qiong si qiong huo bu bianxin" (Never Change My Heart Regardless), in *Longdong geming geyao* (Revolutionary Lyrics in Longdong), Lanzhou: Gansu renmin chubanshe, 1982, pp. 32–5.

Quanguo fulian funü yundong yanjiu lishi yanjiushi (comp.), *Wu si shiqi funü wenti wenxuan* (Collections on Women's Issues Published in the May Fourth Period), Beijing: Sanlian shudian, 1981.

Quanguo fulian lao ganbu ju (comp.), *Jinguo huihuang: jinian Zhonghua quanguo funü lianhehui chengli wushi zhounian* (Glorious Heroines: Celebration

of the Fiftieth Anniversary of the All-China Women's Federation), Beijing: Zhongguo funü chubanshe, 1999.
Rankin, Mary Backus, *Elite Activism and Political Transformation in China, Zhejiang Province, 1865–1911*, Stanford, CA: Stanford University Press, 1986.
Reiter, Rayna R. (ed.), *Toward an Anthropology of Women*, New York: Monthly Review Press, 1975.
Ren Zhonghe, "Shaa-Gan-Ning bianqu xingzheng quhua yanbian gaishu" (The Changes in Administrative Mapping in the SGNBR), *Lishi dang'an* (Historical Archives) 3 (1988): 116–19 and 126.
Rong Jingben, Luo Yanming, and Ye Daomeng, *Lun Yan'an de minzhu moshi* (On the Model of Yan'an Democracy), Xi'an: Xibei daxue chubanshe, 2004.
Ropp, Paul, Paola Zamperini, and Harriet Zurndorfer (eds.), *Passionate Women: Female Suicide in Late Imperial China*, Leiden: Brill Academic, 2001.
Rou Shi, *Wei nuli de muqin* (A Mother as a Slave), Shanghai: Shijie Yingyu bianyishe, 1947.
Saich, Tony and Hans van de Ven (eds.), *New Perspectives on the Chinese Communist Revolution*, London: M. E. Sharpe, 1994.
San Mu, "Beida xuesheng Zhao Meisheng de chuanqi rensheng" (The Legendary Life of a Student of Beida, Zhao Meisheng), *Dangshi bolan* (Broad View of the Party's History) 2 (February 2006): 25–7.
Jiu rizi, jiu renwu (The Old Days and the People of that Time), Guangzhou: Huacheng chubanshe, 2007.
Scott, James C., *Seeing Like a State: How Certain Schemes to Improve the Human Condition Have Failed.* New Haven, CT: Yale University Press, 1998.
Scott, Joan W. "Gender: A Useful Category of Historical Analysis," *The American Historical Review* 91(5) (December 1986): 1053–75.
Selden, Mark, *China in Revolution: The Yenan Way Revisited*, London: M. E. Sharpe, 1995.
The Yenan Way in Revolutionary China, Cambridge, MA: Harvard University Press, 1971.
"Shaan-Gan-Ning bianqu hunyin tiao li, 1939" (Marriage Regulation of the SGN Border Government, April 4, 1939), in Shaanxi sheng fulian (comp.), *Shaan-Gan-Ning bianqu funü yundong wenxian ziliao xuan bian* (A Documentary Collection on the SGN Women's Movement), Xi'an: Shaanxi Provincial Women's Federation (print), 1982, pp. 54–6.
"Shaan-Gan-Ning bianqu hunyin tiaoli, 1946" (Marriage Regulation of the SGNBR, 1946), in Shaanxi sheng fulian (comp.), *Shaan-Gan-Ning bianqu funü yundong wenxian ziliao, xuji* (A Documentary Collection on the SGN Women's Movement), Xi'an: Shaanxi Provincial Women's Federation (print), 1982, pp. 422–4.
"Shaan-Gan-Ning bianqu kangshu lihun chuli banfa" (Measures Dealing with Soldiers' Divorces), Shaanxi sheng fulian (comp.), *Shaan-Gan-Ning bianqu funü yundong wenxian ziliao xuan bian* (A Documentary Collection on the SGN Women's Movement), Xi'an: Shaanxi Provincial Women's Federation (print), 1982, pp. 155–6.
"Shaan-Gan-Ning bianqu min xing shijian tiaojie tiaoli" (The Statute of the SGNBR on the Mediation Used in Criminal and Civil Cases), in Gansu

sheng shehui kexueyuan lishi yanjiu suo (comp.), *Shaan-Gan-Ning geming genjudi shiliao xuanji* (Selected Documents on the History of the SGN Revolutionary Base), vol. I, Lanzhou: Gansu renmin chubanshe, 1981, pp. 317–20.

Shaan-Gan-Ning bianqu zhengfu bangongting (comp.), *Tiaojie wei zhu shenpan weifu* (Using Mediation as the Dominant Way and Adjudication as an Assistant), Yan'an: Shaan-Gan-Ning bianqu zhengfu bangongting (print), 1944.

Shaan-Gan-Ning xiezuo qu (comp.), *Yan'an diqu geming wenhua shiliao ji* (A Collection of the Historical Documents on Revolutionary Culture in Yan'an Region), Yan'an: Yan'an diqu wenhua wenwu ju print, 1991.

Shaanxi Qinqiang shiyan jutuan (reviser), *Liu Qiao'er* (Shaanxi Qinqiang shiyan jutuan gaiwei Qinqiang ben [Adopted Libretto for Qin Opera by Shaanxi Provincial Experimental Theater]), Xi'an: Chang'an shudian, 1958.

Shaanxi sheng difangzhi bianzuan weiyuanhui (The Compiling Committee of Shaanxi Provincial Gazetteer), *Shaanxi sheng zhi – Bao kan zhi* (Shaanxi Provincial Gazetteer – Newspapers and Magazines), Shaanxi renmin chubanshe, 2000.

Shaanxi sheng fulian (comp.), *Shaan-Gan-Ning bianqu funü yundong wenxian ziliao xuan bian* (A Documentary Collection on the SGN Women's Movement), Xi'an: Shaanxi Provincial Women's Federation (print), 1982.

Shaan-Gan-Ning bianqu funü yundong wenxian ziliao, xu ji (Historical Documents on the SGNBR Women's Movement, Sequel), Xi'an: Shaanxi sheng fulian (print), 1985.

Shi Ximin and Fan Jianya (eds.), *Xinhua ribao de huiyi, xuji* (A Recollection of the Xinhua Daily, A Continued Collection), Chengdu: Sicuan renmin chubanshe, 1983.

Shi Xiuyun, "Bianqu funü diyici daibiao dahui taolun zongjie jianghua, 1938" (Concluding Remarks at the First Conference of Women Representatives in the BR, 1938), in Shaanxi sheng fulian (comp.), *Shaan-Gan-Ning bianqu funü yundong wenxian ziliao xuan bian* (A Documentary Collection on the SGN Women's Movement), Xi'an: Shaanxi Provincial Women's Federation (print), 1982, pp. 25–28.

"Bianqu funü yundong de renwu" (The Task of Women's Movement in the Border Region), in Shaanxi sheng fulian (comp.), *Shaan-Gan-Ning bianqu funü yundong wenxian ziliao xuan bian* (A Documentary Collection on the SGN Women's Movement), Xi'an: Shaanxi Provincial Women's Federation (print), 1982, pp. 17–22.

Shu Xincheng, *Cihai* (The Ocean of Words), Shanghai: Zhonghua shuju, 1940.

Snow, Edgar, *Red Star over China*, New York: Grove Press, 1968.

Sommer, Matthew, "Making Sex Work: Polyandry as a Survival Strategy in Qing Dynasty China," in Bryna Goodman and Wendy Larson (eds.), *Gender in Motion: Divisions of Labor and Cultural Change in Late Imperial and Modern China*, New York: Rowman & Littlefield, 2005, pp. 29–54.

Sex, Law, and Society in Late Imperial China, Stanford, CA: Stanford University Press, 2000.

Song Naiqian and Wu Xiu, "Suiyue wuhen, shengming buxi – fangwen zhuming nü zuojia Yuan Jing" (No Trace of Time but Life Has Never Stopped – Interview with Famous Female Writer Yuan Jing), *Hua Xia changshou* (Longevity in China) 5 (1999): 38–9.

Spence, Jonathan, *The Death of Woman Wang*, New York: Viking Press, 1978.

Spivak, Gayatri Chakravorty, "Can the Subaltern Speak?," in *Marxism and the Interpretation of Culture*, ed. and introduction Cary Nelson and Lawrence Grossberg, Urbana: University of Illinois Press, 1988, pp. 271–313.

Stacey, Judith, *Patriarchy and Socialist Revolution in China*, Berkeley: University of California Press, 1983.

Stranahan, Patricia, "Labor Heroines of Yan'an," *Modern China* 9(2) (April 1983): 228–52.

Yan'an Women and the Communist Party, Berkeley: University of California, Institute of East Asian Studies, 1984.

Strand, David, *Rickshaw Beijing: City, People and Politics in the 1920s*, Berkeley: University of California Press, 1989.

Sun Geli, "Pei tong zhuming zuojia Yuan Jing caifang yishi" (Some Anecdotes on Accompanying Famous Writer Yuan Jing for Interviews), http://203xcd.blog.sohu.com/187599463.html (accessed May 9, 2012).

Sun Qi, "Wag Huai'an Xiansheng fangtan lu" (An Interview with Mr. Wang Huai'an), *Huanqiu falü pinglun*, xiaji kan (Global Law Review, Summer Issue) (2003): 173–9.

T'ien Ju-k'ang, *Male Anxiety and Female Chastity: A Comparative Study of Chinese Ethical Values in Ming-Ch'ing Times*, Leiden: Brill, 1988.

"Tan jia" (Visiting Home), in Lu Xun Yishu xueyuan (Yan'an Lu Xun Artist Academy) (comp.), *Shaanbei minge xuan* (Selected Folk Songs from the North Shaanxi Region), Yan'an: Xinhua shudian, 1949, p. 88.

Tan Tongxue, *Qiao cun you dao: zhuanxing xiangcun de diode, quanli yu shehui jiegou* (The Way of Qiao Village: Morality, Power and Social Structure in a Transitional Village), Beijing: Sanlian shudian, 2010.

Teng Yuhong, "San ge nüren de gushi" (The Stories of Three Women), *Zhongguo dianshi bao* (Chinese Television Weekly) 10 (March 9, 2000).

The Ministry of Justice, Republican Government (compilation), *Minshi xiguan diaocha baogao* (Surveys on the Customs of Civil Affairs), Beijing: Zhongguo zhengfa daxue chubanshe, 2005 (reprint).

The Soviet Law on Marriage: Full Text of the Code of Laws on Marriage and Divorce, the Family, and Guardianship, Moscow: Co-operative Publishing Society of Foreign Workers in the USSR, 1932.

Theiss, Janet M., *Disgraceful Matters: The Politics of Chastity in Eighteenth-Century China*, Berkeley: University of California Press, 2004.

"Managing Martyrdom: Female Suicide and Statecraft in Mid-Qing China," *Nan Nü: Men, Women and Gender in China* 3(1) (2005): 47–76.

Tianjin tushuguan (Tianjin library), "Jin men qun xing: Yuan Jing," http://dlibrary.tjl.tj.cn/jmqx/renwu/yj.htm (accessed May 12, 2012).

Unknown author, *Di Gong An* (Judge Di and the Law), Ji'nan: Qi Lu shushe, 1993 reprint.

Wang Feng, "Kang zhan shiqi 'zhishi qingnian ben fu Yan'an' xianxiang" (On the Phenomenon of 'Educated Youth Going to Yan'an' during the Anti-Japanese

War Period), *Ershi yi shiji* (Twenty-First Century) (Hong Kong) 114(8) (August 2009): 51–8.

Wang Geya, "Yu wai fa yingxiang xia de Zhongguo hunyin fa gaige" (The Reform of the Marriage Law under the Influence of Foreign Laws), *Bijiao fa yanjiu* (Journal of Comparative Law) 5 (2007): 70–81.

Wang Hengshou *et al.*, *Xinding xin mingci cidian* (A Newly Revised Dictionary of Neologisms), Shanghai: Chunming chubanshe, 1952.

Wang Hui, "Difang xingshi, fangyan tuyu yu kang Ri zhanzheng shiqi de 'minzu xingshi' de zhenglun" (Local Form, Vernacular Language, and the Debate on the National Form during the Anti-Japanese War), in *Yazhou shiye: Zhongguo lishi de xushu* (Asian Perspective: The Narration of Chinese History), Hong Kong: Oxford University Press, 2010, pp. 237–81.

Yazhou shiye: Zhongguo lishi de xushu (Asian Perspective: The Narration of Chinese History), Hong Kong: Oxford University Press, 2010.

Wang Jing (comp.), *Yan'an Jiefang ribao shi* (History of Liberation Daily in Yan'an), Beijing: Xinhua chubanshe, 1998.

Wang Peiyuan, *Yan'an Lu Yi fengyun lu* (The History of Time at Yan'an Lu Yi), Guilin: Guangxi shifan daxue chubanshe, 2004.

Wang Shirong, Liu Quan'e, Wang Jide, and Li Juan, *Xin Zhongguo sifa zhidu de jishi – Shaan-Gan-Ning bianqu gaodeng fayuan* (The Foundation of the Judicial System for New China – SGNBR High Court), Beijing: Shangwu yinshuguan, 2011.

Wang Xiaoting, Jiang Changren, and Huang Wenyi (comp.), *Beida yinglie* (The Heroic Alumni of Beijing University), ser. 3, Beijing: Beijing daxue chubanshe, 1997.

Wang Xicong (comp.), *Xin hunyin fa wenti jieda huibian* (A Collected Interpretation of the New Marriage Law), Shanghai: Lianying shudian, 1950.

Wang Yan (reviser), "Guanyu Liu Qiao'er de gaibian" (Regarding the Revision of Liu Qiao'er), in *Liu Qiao'er* (Beijing: Baowentang shudian, 1954), pp. 1–3.

Liu Qiao'er, Beijing: Baowentang shudian, 1954.

Wang Yiqun, "Preface," in Shaanxi Qinqiang shiyan jutuan (reviser), *Liu Qiao'er* (Adopted Libretto for Qin Opera by Shaanxi Provincial Experimental Theater), Xi'an: Chang'an shudian, 1958.

Wang Yuesheng, *Qingdai zhongqi hunyin chongtu toushi* (An Analysis of Marriage Conflicts during the Mid-Qing Period), Beijing: Shehui wenxian chubanshe, 2003.

Wang, Zheng, "Dilemmas of Inside Agitators: Chinese State Feminists in 1957," *The China Quarterly* 188 (December 2006): 913–32.

"'State Feminism?' Gender and Socialist Formation in Maoist China," *Feminist Studies* 31(3) (Fall 2005): 519–51.

Women in the Chinese Enlightenment: Oral and Textual Histories, Berkeley: University of California Press, 1999.

Wang Ziyi, "Shenpan yu tiaojie" (Adjudication and Mediation), *Jiefang ribao*, January 17, 1946.

Wang, Lingzhen, *Personal Matters: Women's Autobiographical Practice in Twentieth-Century China*, Stanford, CA: Stanford University Press, 2004.

Watson, Rubie and Patricia Buckley Ebrey (eds.), *Marriage and Inequality in Chinese Society*, Berkeley: The University of California Press, 1991.

Wen Xiang, *Gaoceng en yuan yu Xi Zhongxun – cong Xibei dao Beijing* (Xi Zhongxun's Grudges with Other Senior Communists), Hong Kong: Mirror Books, 2008.

Widmer, Ellen and Kang-I Sun Chang (eds.), *Writing Women in Late Imperial China*, Stanford, CA: Stanford University Press, 1997.

Wolf, Margery, *Revolution Postponed: Women in Contemporary China*, Stanford, CA: Stanford University Press, 1985.

Women and the Family in Rural Taiwan, Stanford, CA: Stanford University Press, 1972.

Wolf, Margery and Roxane Witke (eds.), *Women in Chinese Society*, Stanford, CA: Stanford University Press, 1975.

Wollstonecraft, Mary, *A Vindication of the Rights of Women: with Strictures on Political and Moral Subjects*, ed. Ulrich H. Hardt. Troy, NY: Whitston, 1982.

Wou, Odoric Y. K., *Mobilizing the Masses: Building Revolution in Henan*. Stanford, CA: Stanford University Press, 1994.

Wu Xueshan, "Cong Ma Xiwu tongzhi tiaojie susong dao Liu Qiao'er: geming hunyin de huayu jiangou" (From Comrade Ma Xiwu Mediating a Litigation to Liu Qiao'er: Constructing a Revolutionary Discourse on Marriage), in *Wu Xueshan Zhongguo meishu shi yanjiu wenji* (A Collection of Wu Xueshan's Research on Chinese Art History), Beijing: Zhongyang minzu daxue chubanshe, 2009, pp. 135–72.

"Forging Marriage," trans. Hui Xiao, *Inter-Asia Cultural Studies* 7(3) (2006): 504–12.

Wu Xueshan Zhongguo meishu shi yanjiu wenji (A Collection of Wu Xueshan's Research on Chinese Art History), Beijing: Zhongyang minzu daxue chubanshe, 2009.

Wu Yuzhang, "Zhongguo funü zai Wu Si yundong zhong zou shang le ziji jiefang de daolu" (Chinese Women on the Road of Self-liberation in the May Fourth Movement, 1939?), in Shaanxi sheng fulian (comp.), *Shaan-Gan-Ning bianqu funü yundong wenxian ziliao xuan bian* (A Documentary Collection on the SGN Women's Movement), Xi'an: Shaanxi Provincial Women's Federation (print), 1982, pp. 84–91.

"Wuge fangyang" (Shepherd Boy), in Gao Wen *et al.* (comp.), *Longdong geming geyao* (Revolutionary Lyrics in Longdong), Lanzhou: Gansu renmin chubanshe, 1982, pp. 14–16.

Xi Zhongxun zai Shaan-Gan-Ning bianqu compiling committee (comp.), *Xi Zhongxun zai Shaan-Gan-Ning bianqu* (Xi Zhongxun in Shaan-Gan-Ning Border Region), Beijing: Zhongguo wenshi chubanshe, 2009.

Xia Xiaohong, "Tianyi bao and He Zhen's Views on 'Women's Revolution,"' in Nanxiu Qian, Grace S. Fong, and Richard J. Smith (eds.), *Different Worlds of Discourse*, Boston, MA: Brill, 2008, pp. 293–314.

"Xiaojinzhuang shijian xinshi" (Ten New Customs in Xiaojinzhuang Village), *Renmin ribao*, August 4, 1974.

Xie Donghui, "Nanjing guomin zhengfu minshi tiaojie zhidu kaolun" (An Examination of Mediation in Civil Litigation by the Nanjing Government), *Nanjing shehui kexue* (Nanjing Social Sciences) 10 (2009): 86–93.

Xie Juezai, *Xie Juezai riji* (Xie Juezai's Diary), Beijing: Renmin chubanshe, 1984.

Xie Qing, "Ping Liu Qiao tuanyuan" (A Review of Liu Qiao's Reunion), *Jiefang ribao*, September 4, 1946.

Xin Fengxia, "Da xie re ai 'Qiao'er' de guanzhong men" (My Gratitude to the Audience Who Love 'Qiao'er'), *Zhongguo qingnian bao* (Chinese Youth Daily), February 16, 1957.

The Memoirs of Xin Fengxia, trans. and ed. John Chinnery, New York: Oxford University Press, 2001.

Wo jiao Xin Fengxia (I Am Xin Fengxia), Beijing: Beijing chubanshe, 1998.

Xin Fengxia de huiyi (The Recollection of Xin Fengxia), Beijing: Beijing chubanshe, 1982.

Xin Fengxia huiyi lu (Memoir of Xin Fengxia), Tianjin: Baihua wenyi chubanshe, 1980.

Yi ku wei le: Xin Fengxia yishu shenghuo (Enjoying the Bitterness: The Artistic Life of Xin Fengxia), Beijing: Zhongguo xiju chubanshe, 1983.

'Xin tian you' (Songs Wandering on the Sky), in Lu Xun wenyi xueyuan (Yan'an Lu Xun Artist Academy) (comp.), *Shaanbei minge xuan* (Selected Folk Songs from the North Shaanxi Region), Yan'an: Xinhua shudian, 1949, pp. 29–36.

Xing Moqing (comp.), *Xin mingci cidian* (A Dictionary of Neologisms), Shanghai: Xin shengming shuju, 1934.

Xiong Fu, 'Guanyu Xinhua ribao de lishi diwei jiqi tedian' (On the Historical Position of Xinhua Daily and Its Characters), in Shi Ximin and Fan Jianya (eds.), *Xinhua ribao de huiyi, xuji*, Chengdu: Sicuan renmin chubanshe, 1983, pp. 61–74.

Xiong Xianjue, 'Lue tan dangqian lihun de yuanyin wenti' (A Brief Discussion of the Cause of Divorce in the Present Days), *Zhongguo funü* (Chinese Women) 8 (1957): 16–17.

Xiong Yuezhi, 'Wan Qing ji ge zhengzhi cihui de fanyi he shiyong' (The Translation and Uses of Some Political Terms in the Late Qing), *Shi lin* (History Forest) 1 (1999): 57–62.

'Xiuzheng Shaan Gan Ning Bianqu hunyin zang xing tiaoli' (The Amended Provisional Marriage Regulation in the SGNBR), in Shaanxi sheng fulian (comp.), *Shaan-Gan-Ning bianqu funü yundong wenxian ziliao xuanbian* (A Documentary Collection on the SGN Women's Movement), Xi'an: Shaanxi Provincial Women's Federation (print), 1982, pp. 192–4.

Xu Huiqi, *"Nala" zai Zhongguo: Xin nüxing xingxiang de suzao ji qi yanbian, 1900s–1930s* ("Nala" in China: The Image of New Women and Its Evolution, the 1900–1930s), Taiwan: National Cheng-Chi University, 2003.

Xu, Xiaoqun, "The Fate of Judicial Independence in Republican China, 1912–37," *The China Quarterly* 149 (March 1997): 1–28.

Yan Fu (trans.), *Qun xue yi yan* (A Study of Sociology), Beijing: Commercial Press, 1981 (reprint).

"Yan shi beiqu weisheng jiancha, Suide ertong siwang lü jing ren" (A Public Health Investigation in the North Region of Yan'an; The Death Rate of Suide Children is Surprisingly High), *Jiefang ribao*, April 2, 1942.

"Yan xian shujiang Han Qixiang zhuanbian shuo xin shu" (Yan'an County Minstrel Han Qixiang Turned to Telling New Stories), *Jiefang ribao*, July 23, 1945.

Yan, Yunxiang, *Private Life under Socialism: Love, Intimacy, and Family Change in a Chinese Village, 1949–1999*, Stanford, CA: Stanford University Press, 2003.

The Flow of Gifts: Reciprocity and Social Networking, Stanford, CA: Stanford University Press, 1996.

Yan'an Lu Yi huiyilu bianweihui (comp.), *Yan'an Lu Yi huiyilu* (A Collection of Memoirs from the Yan'an Lu Xun Academy of the Arts), Beijing: Guanming ribao chubanshe, 1992.

Yan'an shi funü yundong zhi bianzuan weiyuanhui (comp.), *Yan'an shi funü yundong zhi* (Historical Records of the Women's Movement in Yan'an City), Xi'an: Shaanxi renmin chubanshe, 2001.

Yan'an zhengfeng yundong bianxiezu, *Yan'an zhengfeng yundong jishi* (The Chronicle of the Yan'an Rectification Campaign), Beijing: Qiushi chubanshe, 1982.

Yang Junchen, *Huiyi Yan'an zhengfeng yundong* (Recalling the Yan'an Rectification Campaign), Changsha: Hunan renmin chubanshe, 1957.

Yang, Mayfair Mei-hui, "From Gender Erasure to Gender Difference: State Feminism, Consumer Sexuality, and Women's Public Sphere in China," in Mayfair Mei-Hui Yang (ed.), *Spaces of Their Own: Women's Public Sphere in Transitional China*, Minneapolis: University of Minnesota Press, 1999, pp. 35–67.

Yang, Mayfair Mei-hui (ed.), *Spaces of Their Own: Women's Public Sphere in Transitional China*, Minneapolis: University of Minnesota Press, 1999.

Yang Zaofeng (comp.), *Qingyang fu zhi* (1660) (Qingyang Prefecture Gazetteer), Lanzhou: Gansu renmin chubanshe, 2001 (reprint).

Yang Zhengfa, *Feng Zhiqin, Liu Qiao'er* (Feng Zhiqin, Liu Qiao'er), Beijing: Zhongguo guangbo dianshi chubanshe, 2004.

Yi Lin (director), *Liu Qiao'er* (film), Changchun dianying zhipianchang (the Changchun Film Studio), 1956.

Yin Jiamin, *Guo Gong wangwshi fengyunlu: cong Huangpu dao beifa* (The Old Stories of Time between the Nationalist Party and Communist Party: From Huangpu Academy to the North Expedition), Beijing: Dangdai Zhongguo chubanshe, 2012.

Yoshiaki Nakajima, *Mingdai de xiangcun jiufen yu zhixu* (Village Disputes and Order during the Ming Era), trans. Guo Wanping and Gao Fei, Nanjing: Jiangsu renmin chubanshe, 2010.

You Lin (ed.), *Lun Yan'an jingshen* (On the Yan'an Spirit), Beijing: Gaodeng jiaoyu chubanshe, 2008.

Young, Marilyn B. (ed.), *Women in China: Studies in Social Change and Feminism*, Ann Arbor: Center for Chinese Studies, University of Michigan, 1973.

Yu Minling (ed.), *Liang an fen tu: leng zhan chu qi de zheng jing fazhan* (Divided Roads on the Two Sides of the Taiwan Strait: Political and Economic Development of [the Mainland and Taiwan] in the Early Cold War Period), Taipei: Zhongyang yanjiuyuan jindashi suo, 2006.

"Nüren fu li? – Nü tuolaji shou zai Zhongguo" (Women Ploughing? – Female Tractor Drivers in China), in Yu Minling (ed.), *Liang an fen tu: leng zhan chu qi de zheng jing fazhan*, Taipei: Zhongyang yanjiuyuan jindashi suo, 2006, pp. 1–29.

Yu, Anthony, *Rereading the Stone: Desire and the Making of Fiction in Dream of the Red Chamber*, Princeton, NJ: Princeton University Press, 1997.

Yuan Jing, *Liu Qiao'er gaozhuang* (Liu Qiao'er Goes to the Law), place of publication unknown: Dongbei Bookstore, 1947.

"Zai Longdong zhongxue de rizi li" (Life at Longdong Middle School), in *Qingyang xian wenshi ziliao, di yi ji* (Historical and Cultural Documents of Qingyang County), series 1, publisher unknown, 1999, pp. 161–2.

Yuan Jing and Kong Jue, *Xin ernü yingxiong zhuan* (The Story of New Heroic Sons and Daughters), Beijing: Renmin wenxue chubanshe, 2006 reprint.

"Yuan Jing and *Xin ernü yingxiong zhuan*" (Yuan Jing and The Story of New Heroic Sons and Daughters), http://news.enorth.com.cn/system/2005/09/06/001111863.shtml (accessed May 12, 2012).

Yuan Xiaoyuan, Wikipedia: http://zh.wikipedia.org/wiki/袁晓园 (accessed May 9, 2012).

Yuan Xingpei (chief comp.), *Zhongguo wenxue shi* (History of Chinese Literature) vol. IV, Beijing: Gaodeng jiaoyu chubanshe, 1999.

Yuan Zhaoxiu (comp.), *Longdong zhongxue xiao shi* (History of Longdong Middle School), Lanzhou: Gansu wenhua chubanshe, 2000.

Yuedan jianming liu fa (Yuedan Collection of the Concised Six Codes), Taipei: Yuanzhao chubanshe, 2007 (15th version).

Zhang Binglin, "Bo Kang Youwei lun geming shu" (Letter Opposing Kang Youwei's Views on Revolution), in *Zhang Taiyan xuan ji* (Selected Works of Zhang Taiyan [Binglin]), Shanghai: Shanghai renmin chubanshe, 1981, pp. 155–86.

Zhang Taiyan xuan ji (Selected Works of Zhang Taiyan [Binglin]), Shanghai: Shanghai renmin chubanshe, 1981.

Zhang Caiqian, *Liushou Longdong* (Stationing in Longdong), Lanzhou: Gansu renmin chubanshe, 1984.

Zhang Shibin, Feng Yingchun, and Hui Xingwen, *Shaan-Gan-Ning bianqu gaodeng fayuan shiji* (The Historical Records of the SGNBR High Court), Xi'an: Shaanxi renmin chubanshe, 2006.

Zhang Xipo, *Ma Xiwu shenpan fangshi* (Ma Xiwu's Way of Judging), Beijing: Falü chubanshe, 1983.

Zhang Xipo and Han Yanlong (comp.), *Zhongguo geming fazhi shi* (A History of the Chinese Revolutionary Legal System), Beijing: Zhongguo shehui kexue chubanshe, 2007.

Zhang Zhiyong, "1950 niandai chuqi Zhonggong ganbu hunyin wenti chu tan: Yi 1950–1956 Hebei sheng ganbu qunti wei li" (Examining the Marriage Issue of the CCP Cadres in the Early 1950s: The Cadres in 1950–1956 Hebei Province), *Ershiyi shiji* 60(3) (March 2007), www.cuhk.edu.hk/ics/21c/index.html.

"Huabei kang Ri genjudi funü yundong yu hun wai xing guanxi" (Sexual Affairs and Women's Movement in Northern China Revolutionary Base Areas), *Kang Ri zhanzheng yanjiu* (Studies on the Anti-Japanese War) 1 (January 2009): 77–86.

Zhang, Naihua, "In a World Together Yet Apart: Urban and Rural Women Coming of Age in the Seventies," in Xueping Zhong, Wang Zheng, and Bai Di (eds.), *Some of Us: Chinese Women Growing up in the Mao Era*, New Brunswick, NJ: Rutgers University Press, 2001, pp. 1–26.

Zhao Shuli, "Xiao Erhei jiehun" (Xiao Erhei's Marriage), in *Zhao Shuli zuopin xin bian* (A New Compilation of Zhao Shuli's Works), Beijing: Renmin wenxue chubanshe, 2011, pp. 6–21.

Zheng Dahua and Zou Xiaozhan (eds.), *Zhongguo jindai shi shang de ziyou zhuyi* (Liberalism in Modern China), Beijing: Shehui kexue wenxian chubanshe, 2008.

"Zhenyuan ganbu jin xing xuexi hou, chufa qunzhong xianxiang jianshao, Mengba qu quzhang renyi chufa qunzhong, bu xuxin jieshou piping bei gezhi" (After Studying [the Policies], Zhenyuan Cadres Reduced a Number of Fines for the Masses; Ward Head of Mengba Ward Arbitrarily Fined the Masses but Rejected All Criticism, Thus He Is Dismissed), *Jiefang ribao*, December 17, 1944.

Zhong, Xueping, Wang Zheng, and Bai Di (eds.), *Some of Us: Chinese Women Growing up in the Mao Era*, New Brunswick, NJ: Rutgers University Press, 2001.

Zhonggong zhongyang wenxian yanjiushi (comp.), *Mao Zedong nianpu, 1949–1976* (The Chronicle of Mao Zedong, 1949–1979), vol. IV, Beijing: Zhongyang wenxian chubanshe, 2013.

Zhonggong zhongyang wenxian yanjiushi and Zhonggong Hunan shengwei *Mao Zedong zaoqi wengao* bianjizu (compl.), *Mao Zedong zaoqi wengao* (An Article Collection of Young Mao Zedong), Changsha: Hunan chubanshe, 1990.

"Zhonghua renmin gongheguo minfa tongze" (The General Civil Law of the People's Republic of China, promulgated on April 12, 1986). For the Chinese version, see *Falü tushuguan* (Law Library website), www.law-lib.com/law/law_view.asp?id=3633 (accessed October 21, 2010).

"Zhonghua renmin gongheguo xianfa" (The Constitution of the People's Republic of China, 1978), *Renmin ribao* (People's Daily), March 8, 1978.

"Zhonghua renmin gongheguo xianfa, 1982" (The Constitution of PRC, 1982), www.gov.cn/gongbao/content/2004/content_62714.htm (accessed September 20, 2014).

Zhonggong zhongyang wenxian yanjiushi (comp.), *Mao Zedong nianpu, 1949–1976* (The Chronicle of Mao Zedong, 1949–1979), vol. IV, Beijing: Zhongyang wenxian chubanshe, 2013.

"Zhongguo gongchandang zhongyang weiyuanhui guanyu guanche hunyin fa yundong yue gongzuo de buchong zhishi" (The Supplementary Instruction from the CCP Central Committee on the Campaign Month of Promoting the Marriage Law), in *Guanche hunyin fa yundong de zhongyao wenjian* (The Important Documents of the Campaign of Implementing the Marriage Law), Beijing: Renmin chubanshe, 1953, pp. 6–11.

"Zhongguo Gongchandang zhongyang weiyuanhui guanyu kang Ri genjudi muqian funü gongzuo fangzhen de jueding" (The Central Committee of the CCP's Decision on the Recent Development of Women's Work in Various Revolutionary Base Areas), in Shaanxi sheng fulian (comp.), *Shaan-Gan-Ning bianqu funü yundong wenxian ziliao xuan* (A Documentary Collection on the SGN Women's Movement), Xi'an: Shaanxi Provincial Women's Federation (print), 1982, pp. 162–4.

Zhongguo xiqu quyi cidian (An Encyclopedia of Chinese Operas and Other Oral Performing Arts), Shanghai: Shanghai cishu chubanshe, 1981.

Zhonghua minguo xingfa, 1935 (The Penal Code of the Republic of China, 1935), 6–21, 6–36.

Zhonghua minguo xingshi susong fa, 1935 (The Criminal Law of the Republic of China, 1935), *Yuedan jianming liu fa*, 7-59-60.

Zhonghua quan guo funü lianhe hui (comp.), *Hunyin fa xuanchuan shouce* (Pamphlet for Promoting the Marriage Law), Beijing: Falü chubanshe, 1980.

"Zhonghua renmin gongheguo hunyin fa, 1950" (Marriage Law of the People's Republic of China, 1950), in Zhongyang renmin zhengfu fazhi weiyuanhui (comp.), *Hunyin fa ji qi youguan wenjian* (The Marriage Law and Related Documents), Beijing: Xinhua shudian, 1950, pp. 1–9.

"Zhonghua renmin gongheguo hunyin fa, 1980" (The Marriage Law of the People's Republic of China, 1980), in Zhonghua quan guo funü lianhe hui (comp.), *Hunyin fa xuanchuan shouce* (Pamphlet for Promoting the Marriage Law), Beijing: Falü chubanshe, 1980, p. 6.

"Zhonghua renmin gongheguo minfa tongze, 103 tiao" (The General Civil Code of the People's Republic of China, term 103), 1986 (promulgated on April 12), *Falü tushuguan* (Law Library website), www.law-lib.com/law/law_view.asp?id=3633 (accessed September 8, 2011).

"Zhonghua renmin gongheguo minfa tongze" (The General Civil Code of the People's Republic of China, promulgated on April 12, 1986), *Falü tushuguan* (Law Library website), www.law-lib.com/law/law_view.asp?id=3633 (accessed January 19, 2007).

"Zhonghua Suweiai gongheguo hunyin fa, 1934" (Marriage Law of the Chinese Soviet Republic, 1934), in Jiangxisheng fulian and Jiangxi sheng dang'an guan (comp.), *Jiangxi Su qu funü yundong shiliao xuanbian* (Selected Documents of the Women's Movement in Jiangxi Soviet Region), Nanchang: Jiangxi renmin chubanshe, 1982, pp. 176–8.

"Zhonghua Suweiai Gongheguo hunyin tiaoli" (The Marriage Regulation of the Chinese Soviet Republic, 1931), in *Jiangxi Su qu funü yundong shiliao xuanbian* (Selected Documents of the Women's Movement in Jiangxi Soviet Region), Nanchang: Jiangxi renmin chubanshe, 1982, pp. 33–7.

Zhongyang renmin zhengfu fazhi weiyuanhui (Legislature Committee of the Central Government, comp.), *Hunyin fa ji qi youguan wenjian* (The Marriage Law and Related Documents), Beijing: Xinhua shudian, 1950.

Zhou Enlai, "Zhongyang renmin zhengfu zhengwuyuan guanyu guanche hunyin fa de zhishi" (An Instruction from the State Department of the Central Government on Implementing the Marriage Law), in *Guanche hunyin fa yundong de zhongyao wenjian* (The Important Documents of the Campaign of Implementing the Marriage Law), Beijing: Renmin chubanshe, 1953, pp. 1–5.

Zhou Erfu, "Hou ji" (Epilogue), in Han Qixiang, *Liu Qiao tuanyuan* (Liu Qiao's Reunion) (recorded by Gao Minfu), Hong Kong: Haiyang shuwu, 1947, pp. 139–47.

Zhou Heng, "'Liu Qiao'er' you you dongren xinzhuan" (Liu Qiao'er Once Again Has a Touching New Story), *Renmin ribao, haiwai ban* (People's Daily, overseas version), September 27, 2004.

Zhou Huiru *et al.*, *Xin mingci xuexi cidian* (A Dictionary of Neologisms), Shanghai: Xingchao chubanshe, 1949.

Zhu Hongzhao, *Yan'an: Ri chang shenghuo zhong de lishi, 1937–1947* (Yan'an: Daily Life in History, 1937–1947), Guilin: Guangxi shifan daxue chubanshe, 2007.

Zhu, Suli, "Political Parties in China's Judiciary," *Duke Journal of International and Comparative Law* 17 (2007): 533–60.

Zito, Angela and Tani E. Barlow (eds.), *Body, Subject and Power in China*, Chicago, IL: University of Chicago, 1994.

Zui Gao Renmin Fa Yuan (People's Supreme Court), "Hunyin sifa jieshi, 2" (Judicial Explanation on Marriage Law, no. 2), *Lihun fawang* (Website on Divorce Law), www.lihunfa.org/59w9.html (accessed January 15, 2014).

"*Hunyin Fa sifa jieshi* 3" (2011-8-9) (Judicial Explanation on Marriage Law, no. 3, August 9, 2011), see *Xinhua baoye wang* (Xinhua News Web), http://news.xhby.net/system/2011/08/12/011448797.shtml (accessed December 20, 2014).

Index

Lightning Source UK Ltd.
Milton Keynes UK
UKHW020812071118
331904UK00022B/434/P

9 781316 602614